Managing Classroom Behavior Using Positive Behavior Supports

Managing Classroom Behavior Using Positive Behavior Supports

Terrance M. Scott
University of Louisville

Cynthia M. Anderson
University of Oregon

Peter Alter
University of Louisville

PEARSON

Boston   Columbus   Indianapolis   New York   San Francisco   Upper Saddle River
Amsterdam   Cape Town   Dubai   London   Madrid   Milan   Munich   Paris   Montreal   Toronto
Delhi   Mexico City   Sao Paulo   Sydney   Hong Kong   Seoul   Singapore   Taipei   Tokyo

Vice President and Editorial Director: Jeffery W. Johnston
Executive Editor: Ann Castel Davis
Editorial Assistant: Penny Burleson
Vice President, Director of Marketing: Margaret Waples
Marketing Manager: Joanna Sabella
Senior Managing Editor: Pamela D. Bennett
Senior Production Editor: Sheryl Glicker Langner
Production Manager: Susan Hannahs
Senior Art Director: Jayne Conte
Cover Designer: Suzanne Behnke
Full-service Project Manager: Sudip Sinha, Aptara, Inc.
Composition: Aptara®, Inc.
Text and Cover Printer/Bindery: Courier/Westford
Text Font: Palatino

Credits and acknowledgments for material borrowed from other sources and reproduced, with permission, in this textbook appear on the appropriate page within the text.

Every effort has been made to provide accurate and current Internet information in this book. However, the Internet and information posted on it are constantly changing, so it is inevitable that some of the Internet addresses listed in this textbook will change.

Library of Congress Cataloging-in-Publication Data

Scott, Terrance M.
  Managing classroom behavior using positive behavior supports / Terrance M. Scott, Cynthia M. Anderson, Peter Alter.
    p. cm.
  Includes bibliographical references and index.
  ISBN-13: 978-0-205-49834-5
  ISBN-10: 0-205-49834-5
  1. Classroom management.   2. Behavior modification.   I. Anderson, Cynthia M. II. Alter, Peter (Peter J.) III. Title.
  LB3013.S42 2012
  371.102'4--dc22   2010053447

10 9 8 7 6 5 4 3 2 1

PEARSON

www.pearsonhighered.com

ISBN 10:   0-205-49834-5
ISBN 13: 978-0-205-49834-5

For my parents Bill and Joyce Scott, true teachers.

PREFACE

Schoolwide positive behavior support applies the principles and technology of behavior analysis to school systems. Thanks to the efforts of a number of professionals working in universities, school districts, and classrooms around the world, the beneficial outcomes associated with schoolwide positive behavior support have been widely demonstrated and disseminated. Of course, the principles, practices, and procedures associated with these efforts are not new. Collaboration, explicit instruction, the use of contingencies to affect the occurrence of behavior, and data-based decision making have consistently been recognized as effective tools in promoting successful schools, but have not always been implemented in a manner that produces results. In many respects positive behavior support is simply a very well packaged and well described version of effective systems management and effective instruction. As has often been said, positive behavior support really is not about changing students—it is about changing adult behavior in a manner that predicts positive changes in student behavior. Approaching schools and classrooms from this perspective puts the onus for student behavior change squarely on the shoulders of the adults with whom they interact daily. There is no reason to believe that a student's inappropriate or undesired behavior will change unless we take steps to make that change.

We believe that good teachers possess all the tools necessary within their instructional repertoire to change behavior in a positive and efficient manner. We also realize, however, that there are students whose behaviors will challenge the limits of our repertoires. Our task is to find the right combination of elements that teachers control—including interactions, routines, and physical environments—to facilitate student success. When we are unsuccessful in this endeavor it is not our fault that students do not respond, but it is our responsibility to return to our strategies and continue to search for the right combination of tricks and tools to facilitate the success that students so desperately require in order to continue.

This text, which was several years in the making, is a written version of the course lectures and trainings that we have collectively repeated and perfected over time. As always happens when training monologues describing a concept or skill are repeated frequently, the delivery, wording, or examples used change. Some efforts were ad-libs that were immediately regretted and never repeated, while others were improvements that remain. We have tried to write this text using the language and examples that we have found most effective in the past. To be certain, some of the examples, voices, and inflections cannot be translated to writing. The intent here is to make reading as simple as possible while maintaining content.

This text was written for those who work directly with students in classroom settings. The principles and procedures described, however, are equally applicable to other settings including day care centers, clinics, treatment centers, correctional institutions, and homes. Our intent was to write a book that would serve both as a description of the principles associated with effective practice and as a resource for practitioners when they ask *"What should I do if...?"*. We started with the idea that the text should be readable by the average person on the street, but descriptive enough to promote effective practice. We have attempted to keep the language simple and to provide examples culled from our own experiences with children of all ages. Further, we have purposefully avoided the use of references and citations of the research behind the content we present.

The first chapter provides an overview of the key concepts and principles inherent throughout the book and cites the research on which these are founded. Thereafter, each chapter focuses on the logic and activities associated with particular practices and procedures. While each chapter builds upon the last and represents what may be conceived of as a step in a larger process described across the text, each chapter also is meant to stand alone. We hope that readers will find this book easy to navigate and that it helps them deal with managing classrooms and instruction on a daily basis. Because we three authors share a background in education and working with children and youth with challenging behavior, we have written what we ourselves would have wanted to know when we were starting out. We express our sincere appreciation for those who continue to dedicate their lives to improving the lives of our future generations—especially those who toil to facilitate success among those for whom success is not common or automatic.

ACKNOWLEDGMENTS

We are grateful to the following reviewers for their thoughtful comments and suggestions: Margaret Ackerman, Liberty University; Alice Anderson, University of Findlay; Tara Brooks, West Virginia University; Susan Claflin, Missouri Western State University; Joyce Downing, Central Missouri State University; Michele C. Gerent, St. Petersburg College; Gary Jacobs, Walsh University; Gholam Kibria, Delaware State University; Vicki McGinley, West Chester University; Carol Means, West Virginia Wesleyan College; Alec Peck, Boston College; Jacqueline Thousand, California State University, San Marcos; Jayne Vanegas, Xavier University; Deborah Watkins, York College of Pennsylvania; and Gwendolyn Williams, West Texas A & M University.

BRIEF CONTENTS

CONTENTS

1

Introduction to a Prevention-Focused Model of Behavior Support

CHAPTER OBJECTIVES

After reading this chapter, you should be able to describe the following concepts:

- The use of proactive management to prevent predictable behavior problems
- Multitiered intervention strategies
- Primary, secondary, and tertiary levels of intervention
- Systematic screening mechanism for identifying students in need
- Schoolwide implementation of support systems

It is 12:30 p.m. at Lincoln Elementary, and Ms. Hawkins is on recess duty. She wanders the blacktop surface of the playground while all around the playground area children swing, climb on bars, play four square, and move about. On the adjacent field, a group of boys and girls play soccer. In the far corner of the field, a few children play in and around a small clump of trees. An adult approaches from the parking lot and tells Ms. Hawkins that someone threw a rock at his car, and he believes that it came from the field. Ms. Hawkins apologizes to the driver and tells him the students will be dealt with. She then walks to the far corner of the field where she finds a small group of students surrounding a pile of rocks and tossing them in the air. At the same time, a young student approaches and asserts, "Ms. Hawkins, those kids were throwing rocks at cars." Ms. Hawkins tells the students to come with her, goes back to the building, writes them each an office referral slip, and sends them to the office.

The students sit in the office reception area and wait for Principal Olsen to see them. In the meantime, Ms. Hawkins arrives and enters the principal's office. She tells Ms. Olsen that several students were caught throwing rocks at cars from the field. The principal sighs and says, "Don't tell me, let me guess," whereupon she proceeds to name the children involved and describe their location behind the trees. When confirmed by Ms. Hawkins, the principal responds, "Okay, let's prepare the paperwork for after-school detention—again." Principal Olsen's reaction makes it clear that this is not the first time this has happened—she knew which students likely were involved and where they were when the rock throwing occurred. Further, she has an idea about what consequences probably are not effective, such as after-school detention. What Principal Olsen does not seem to realize is that because she can predict the perpetrators and the circumstances under which the problem occurs (students behind the trees during recess), she has the information necessary to prevent such behavior.

DISCIPLINE PROBLEMS IN THE SCHOOL

The student body in every school consists of a range of students. Some of them do well in school—earning good grades, getting along well with peers and adults—and some of them present a significant challenge. If we were to enter a typical school and randomly ask passing adults to name three students whose behaviors pose a great challenge and who are in need of intervention, the same names likely would be heard repeatedly. Schools do not need complicated screening instruments or professional in-service training to identify these most challenging students—their behavior makes them obvious (Bowen, Jenson, & Clark, 2004; Walker, Colvin, & Ramsey, 1995). Further, many of these students likely are exhibiting behaviors such as disruption and other "minor" problems at relatively high rates. Although the news media focuses primarily on very serious problem behavior, such as bringing weapons to school and assaulting peers or other students, less severe behaviors such as bullying, noncompliance to adult requests, defiance, and arguing are far more common and—because they occur so often—are more disruptive to the learning environment and school culture (Furlong, Morrison, & Dear, 1994; Stephenson, Linfoot, & Martin, 2000).

Educators, parents, other students, and communities are struggling to find solutions to these difficult problems. Many advocate the use of strategies perceived as punishing, such as detention or suspension; or moving such students to a new setting—either a separate classroom or a separate school—where they cannot negatively affect the learning of others; or a combination of these strategies. Recently, these efforts have included "zero tolerance" policies, such as suspending a student following the first offense (e.g., fighting) and "three strikes and you're out" policies. To illustrate, a survey conducted during the 1996–1997 academic year found that more than 75% of all schools reported having zero tolerance policies for various student offenses and reported an increase in the presence of law enforcement officers and metal detectors in public schools (U.S. Departments of Education and Justice, 1999). But evidence suggests that such measures are ineffective and often counterproductive; in schools implementing such strategies, the very problems these measures are intended to prevent often increase (American Psychological Association Zero Tolerance Task Force, 2008; Hyman & Perone, 1998; Mayer & Leone, 1999).

One reason such approaches are ineffective in reducing the overall number of students challenging the system is because a continuing stream of new students is entering the schools. Although the majority of disciplinary referrals generally are attributable to approximately 10%–15% of the school population (Sugai, Sprague, Horner, & Walker, 2000), there will always be a new group of difficult students "just around the corner" until the culture of the schools is changed so as to actively prevent the development of problem behaviors. As a result, focusing on responding to students with the most challenging behavior in a reactionary manner is like plugging a hole in a dam with your finger: You may temporarily slow the water flow, but the problem has not been solved.

The problem is complicated further by the effects of labeling and adult expectations. Adults will expect a student who has been identified as "a problem," rightly or wrongly, to behave in inappropriate ways. For example, several studies have shown that students known to frequently exhibit problem behavior are responded to more negatively by adults—even when they are *not* doing anything wrong (Van Acker, 2002; Van Acker, Grant, & Henry, 1996; Wehby, Symons, & Shores, 1995). Further, and as might be expected, research has shown that student behavior is shaped by teacher expectations. That is, students tend to live up, or down, to the teacher's expectations, and teacher behavior can actually set the occasion for student failures (Gable, Hendrickson, Young, Shores, & Stowitschek, 1983; Shores, Gunter, & Jack, 1993; Weinstein, 2002). Further, among students who misbehave, those who look different or whom teachers expect to have problems are more likely to receive harsh punishment and suspension (Hinojosa, 2008; McFadden, Marsh, Price, & Hwang, 1992; Shaw & Braden, 1990; Skiba, Petersen, & Williams, 1997).

The "Causes" of Misbehavior

A large body of research has focused on identifying factors associated with an increased risk for exhibiting problematic behavior in school (and in other situations). Below we briefly review findings from this literature.

DEMOGRAPHIC FACTORS LINKED TO RISK.   In the search for the causes of student problem behavior, demographic factors often are identified. In fact, characteristics of children's homes and communities constitute the earliest indicators of potential academic and social failure. Studies of factors associated with school dropout have led some to conclude that students who are at increased risk to leave school prior to graduation can be identified at the time of birth, based on their social class and family characteristics (Farrington, 1995; Hawkins et al., 2000; Patterson, Reid, & Dishion, 1992). More specifically, research has demonstrated a connection between poverty and school dropout for both regular (Harding, 2003; Rumberger, 1987; Walker & Sprague, 1999) and special education students (Gierl & Harnish, 1995; Rylance, 1997). Other characteristics correlated with a failure to successfully complete school include parents who themselves did not complete school, homes in which academic skills such as reading are neither valued nor modeled (Adams, 1988; Hammond et al., 2007; Hart & Risley, 1995), and homes characterized by multiple stressors such as alcohol or other drug abuse, divorce, and family violence (Glaser et al., 2005; Patterson et al., 1992).

Adams (1988) found that children of middle- and upper-income families often come to school with 1000 hours of exposure to print material, whereas children in poverty typically enter school with as little as 25 hours of exposure. Further, in a 6-year longitudinal study of parent–child interactions, Hart and Risley (1995) found that children in lower-income homes tended to have less verbal interaction with their parents than did children from middle- or upper-income homes, resulting in significantly lower vocabularies at the time they entered school. When these children reach school, they typically are served by teachers from middle- or upper-income backgrounds who use a vocabulary and assume a level of familiarity with print materials that are far above those of many low-income children.

Thus, through no fault of their own, these students are academically behind their age peers from the time they first enter school. Hart and Risley's work also demonstrates that simply providing a "booster shot"-type intervention at this point is not sufficient. Instead, these students require effective and intensive instructional strategies throughout the elementary years. Without intensive and prolonged academic instruction that produces substantial improvement in their school performance, these children will fall increasingly further behind their peers. Fortunately, research suggests that effective instruction and a positive school and classroom culture—developed using strategies delineated in this book—can counteract many of these societal ills.

THE LINK BETWEEN ACADEMICS AND PROBLEM BEHAVIOR.   A growing literature base documents a clear link between academic struggles and problem behavior. Children who struggle to learn basic foundation skills such as reading are significantly more likely to exhibit behavior problems in school than are students at grade level in skill acquisition. In fact, recent research has demonstrated that reading deficits measured in kindergarten are powerful predictors of student misbehavior in both third and fifth grades (McIntosh, Chard, Boland, & Horner, 2006). In fact, according to Adams (1988), a child who is not reading by fourth grade has only a 12% chance of ever learning to read, or as Lyon (2003) has indicated, children who do not develop basic reading skills by age nine are very likely to suffer a lifetime of illiteracy. This research illustrates the critical importance of ensuring that *all* students receive adequate, evidence-based instruction as a key component of ensuring student success.

Students may struggle academically and exhibit problem behavior for at least two reasons. First, as described earlier, some students begin to exhibit discipline problems as a result of experiencing school failure. For these students, academic requests have become aversive—because the students typically are not successful in fulfilling these tasks—and the students therefore exhibit problem behavior in an attempt to avoid those aversive tasks. Such students may frequently be late to class, truant from school, or engage in behaviors that result in office referrals or suspension (thus avoiding academic work). Second, students may, for reasons described earlier, enter school without the appropriate social behaviors necessary for facilitating learning. Such behaviors include following directions, listening to others, cooperating, and so on. Such students often are argumentative and do not get along well with peers or adults from the day they first enter school. In addition, this group of students may quickly fall behind, not necessarily because of poor instruction or a need for extra academic assistance to learn, but because their behavior interferes with learning. Unfortunately, these students, once they get behind, likely will continue to exhibit challenging behavior to avoid the increasingly aversive academic tasks—and will continue to fall further and further behind.

These trends start early, and the outcomes are troubling; research shows that students with chronic and pervasive behavioral problems that have been unaffected *by the end of second grade* are more likely to go to jail than to graduate from high school (Walker, Colvin, & Ramsey, 1995). Once they've failed in school, such students are far more likely later on to be involved with the social services, welfare, and corrections systems and to use drugs, be involved in automobile accidents, and become single parents (Nelson & Pearson, 1994; Walker, Colvin, & Ramsey, 1995).

Clearly, the projected life paths of students who fail early in school are tragic. We can wait for these predictable results or we can use evidence-based approaches to prevent the emergence and exacerbation of problem behavior and to enhance the likelihood of academic success, thus breaking the cycle of failure. This book focuses on approaches shown to be effective in achieving this critically important outcome. As educators, it is our responsibility to facilitate the success of all students by (a) using proactive approaches to encourage appropriate behavior of all students and (b) identifying students at risk for failure and providing them with individualized support.

Summary

Students struggle academically and with social behavior in schools for a variety of reasons, many of which (e.g., poverty) are beyond our ability to immediately address. Schools and society have tried different measures to address discipline problems in schools, but the emphasis has been on reactionary systems designed to discourage students from misbehaving again or on removing students from regular education, or on a combination of these methods. These strategies have not been effective in (a) reducing the overall occurrence of problem behavior in school, (b) teaching students to exhibit more appropriate behavior, or (c) enhancing school climate. What is needed is a proactive discipline system—one that focuses on explicitly teaching expected behavior and emphasizes evidence-based strategies to prevent the occurrence of problem behavior.

PROACTIVE MANAGEMENT

The overarching theme of this text is that the best way to reduce discipline problems is to *prevent them from occurring*. Prevention is less time-consuming in the long run and also leads to more opportunities for learning and social engagement because discipline problems are not interfering with teaching. In the example of Lincoln Elementary introduced at the beginning of this chapter, we know that because the students are being placed on detention "again," addressing the problem after the fact with detention has not been and will not be sufficient. Further, repeatedly reacting to misbehavior in this manner is time-consuming for Ms. Hawkins, Principal Olsen, and any teachers who supervise in-school detention. A much more efficient approach to this problem would be to identify the circumstances that predict rock throwing and then arrange the environment in such a way that this behavior is less likely to occur. When we look at behavior in this manner, we can be said to be engaging in **proactive management**.

Proactive Management
Using information about past behavior to teach skills and arrange the environment in a way that prevents future occurrence of the problem.

Facilitating student success is actually a combination of prevention and instruction. As educators, we are responsible for providing students with the skills necessary for success in life. This often is taken to mean academic skills because it is clear that students who cannot read adequately or perform basic math are severely limited in their life opportunities. Social behavior, however, is just as important as academic behavior and must be taught as well. For example, the student who leaves school with academic skills but who has few social interaction skills and quickly resorts to physical violence during a disagreement is as likely to fail in life as the student with academic deficits. The difference is that while skills associated with academic success are defined by fairly standard criteria and are taught systematically and explicitly, the skills associated with social success are contextually specific to different settings and cultures and often are not taught explicitly or systematically. We have learned that it is critical that appropriate social behavior be defined and taught explicitly in schools as well as in the community. To illustrate, research shows that, in schools where social expectations are clearly defined, taught, and acknowledged, approximately 90% of students will be successful, receiving only zero or one office referral in a given year (Horner et al., 2000).

Of course, even in schools using such approaches, approximately 10%–15% of students will require some intervention. This fact reveals two important points regarding behavioral support. First, the use of systemwide preventive strategies dramatically reduces the number of students requiring more intensive interventions. Second, educators require efficient, evidence-based strategies for preventing and responding to problem behaviors among the few students who will not be successful under proactive schoolwide systems. In this text we first delineate how systemwide approaches can be implemented within classrooms to prevent the occurrence of problem behavior; we then provide evidence-based approaches for responding effectively to those few students requiring further support.

Preventing Failure by Promoting Success

Preventing failure begins with identification of the events that set the occasion for problem behaviors. Whether it be a crowded noon cafeteria with a low adult-to-student ratio that predicts fights, addition problems with regrouping that predict incorrect answers, or a lack of adequate supervision on the field that predicts throwing rocks at passing cars, identifying these predictors is the first step to preventing problems. To identify the predictors we must have information about the problems that have previously occurred. We can use this information to identify predictors for problem behavior exhibited by specific students—as was the case with the rock-throwing students in the chapter-opening example—or circumstances that predict problems for many students; for example, a narrowing hallway that might induce many of the students who pass through it to push and shove. We then can alter those predictors and, at the same time, teach students in more appropriate ways to respond and acknowledge desirable behavior in such a way that it "pays off" for the student. This concept will be returned to and described in greater depth throughout the book.

Prevention and the Academic–Social Behavior Connection

Too often, prevention of failure is thought of only in the context of social behavior. In reality, social and academic behaviors are inextricably linked (Gunter, Hummel, & Conroy, 1998; Kauffman, 1997; Scott, Nelson, & Liaupsin, 2001) and both must be the focus of instruction. Conventional wisdom has held that students cannot learn academics until problematic behaviors are under control. Conversely, more recent instructional models have assumed that problem behaviors will disappear only when students are engaged in and successful with learning tasks. In fact, both positions are correct in that the relation between academic and social behavior is reciprocal. Thus, it is fruitless to focus on only one of these interrelated realms. We must strive to use success in one to facilitate success in the other. The case of Jake is an example of this relation.

> Jake, a 14-year-old boy in middle school, was placed in a self-contained room for students with emotional and behavioral disorders. He was a large and athletic student with a history of fighting in school and poor or no effort in academics. He recently had been assessed by the school psychologist and was found to have no reading skills at all—failing to demonstrate even simple letter–sound correspondence. Under an agreement with the local university, he was to receive some intensive reading instruction as part of an ongoing research project. On the first day of the study, the university researcher, Dr. Watson, arrived and approached Jake to describe the reading program. Jake immediately turned to the researcher and exclaimed, "Get the (expletive) away from me; I ain't doin' no reading with you!"

If we as educators believe that we must address Jake's challenging behavior before attempting to enhance his academic skills, what management techniques will be effective in forcing him to engage in academics? Conversely, if we take the position that academics must be addressed prior to behavior, how will Jake ever learn if he is unwilling even to try? Considering Jake's history gives us some insight into his behavior. Try, for a minute, to put yourself in Jake's position. After 14 years of being a nonreader and 8 years of failed attempts at reading in school, what incentive do you think he has to attempt reading? By considering what it must be like to have failed at the same task over and over again in life for so many years, we can see a predictable pattern in his behavior. Because failure is not a pleasant experience, we can surmise that reading instruction has become highly aversive for Jake. To the extent that he can successfully avoid reading by behaving in such a way, his reaction is extremely effective. Now our task is to determine how to blend the social and academic management strategies to facilitate success in both realms. The natural reinforcers for reading are successful reading and gaining useful and interesting information, but how can we facilitate success in reading without managing behavior? Conversely, how will we manage behavior when reading is so aversive?

> Dr. Watson understood that he had a dual problem. He needed to facilitate success in both academic and social behavior in order for either one to be affected. Thinking of the analogy of teaching as priming

the pump by setting the student up to receive natural reinforcement, Dr. Watson determined that extra incentives would be necessary to sufficiently override the aversive nature of reading to allow for appropriate social behavior. He called Jake aside and explained that if Jake would spend 10 minutes each day engaged in instruction with Dr. Watson, he could then do or have something he enjoyed. Dr. Watson asked Jake what he might like to earn and provided some possibilities including a 5-minute break with a snack before returning to class, watching a football video for a few minutes, and hanging out with the soccer coach after school. After goofing for a minute (Jake said, "No more school"), he said he "wouldn't mind" any of them. Dr. Watson then told Jake that, prior to each day of reading instruction, Jake could choose which of the three incentives he would work to attain. Jake agreed to this but requested that instruction occur in a private room in the library—away from his peers.

Imagine how aversive it must be to have repeatedly failed at a task and then be held up in front of your peers as an example of failure. Jake's every attempt to read in the classroom only demonstrated his deficiencies in front of all his peers. Jake's incentives for misbehavior during reading times in class are huge, while his incentives for compliance are nil.

Dr. Watson knew that he had a difficult task ahead of him. Now that he had gotten Jake's agreement to engage in reading instruction, he had to help him attain some success in reading immediately because Jake soon would tire of the failure and again opt out; repeated failure is almost always more aversive than any incentives we can develop. Dr. Watson decided to teach Jake some basic letter sounds. He selected five letters that are common to many simple English words. He referred to these letters, a, e, s, t, and n, as the "*Wheel of Fortune*" letters because they are the letters that typically are selected first in the popular television game show. He presented each of the letters to Jake and modeled the corresponding sounds, allowing Jake to practice each. At the end of the 10 minutes, Jake practiced each letter in isolation and was successful. He received his chosen incentive—a brief break and a snack—and then left. The next day Dr. Watson began by reviewing the letters from the previous day and then began introducing sound blends, again modeling and allowing time for practice with feedback. Jake was initially resistant to this, exclaiming "I'll do ones, but I'm not doing twos!" But Dr. Watson guided Jake to see that he already knew the sound of "a" (short a) and of "t"—he just needed to say the sounds one a time and fast enough to make a new sound. Jake continued with both sounds while Dr. Watson encouraged speed. Finally, Dr. Watson said, "Yes, that sounds like a word. What word is it?" When Jake responded "at," Dr. Watson raised his voice in celebration, "Exactly. Great job!"

At the end of the session Jake was presented with a novel blend "n – e – t" and asked to think about the sounds. Jake then was asked to read the word and successfully pronounced "net." Dr. Watson praised Jake and exclaimed, "You can read!" Jake smiled, watched a bit of a football movie, and then returned to his class. The third and fourth days of instruction were similar to the second day, with increasingly more sound blends being introduced and practiced, and with novel words being presented at the end of each lesson. Jake continued to be successful.

On the fifth day of instruction, Dr. Watson again reviewed learned words and modeled some new words—using the same labored sequence of saying them fast together. Toward the end he put several words together to form simple sentences. Jake began reluctantly but quickly read with excitement as he was able to sound out all the words, even though several were new. Dr. Watson congratulated Jake and then made his pitch. He told Jake that he really enjoyed working with him and that he was extremely impressed at how quickly he was learning to read. Dr. Watson explained, however, that, although he would continue working with Jake, he could not afford to continue buying him snacks and renting football movies. Jake quickly responded that, as long as his reading sessions took place in the library (away from his peers), he would like to continue, even without the incentives.

Dr. Watson eventually phased himself out of the teacher's role and introduced an instructional assistant. With the help of a structured reading program focused on facilitating success in every lesson, Jake gained over 2 years in his reading level during that school year.

Let's look back to what Dr. Watson accomplished with Jake. Because Jake was unwilling to even attempt reading, he was not going to experience the naturally occurring consequences that reinforce reading for most students (e.g., pleasure of learning new things, relaxation). Further, Jake's skill level was so low that, without explicit instruction, he was unlikely to simply pick up reading skills. Dr. Watson combined the use of incentives for simply engaging in the lesson with the natural reinforcement for reading to create success in both. It is unlikely that, using only the social behavior management, Jake would have attempted to read on his own. Likewise, using only the reading management was not an option because Jake could not receive reinforcement from reading attempts without instruction.

PROACTIVE MANAGEMENT SYSTEMS.　Proactive management means using strategies that prevent behavior problems. Because we are interested in prevention strategies that affect all students, management needs to be systemic, encompassing the entire school day and every area within the school (including classrooms) and involving all staff members. We want to avoid placing responsibility for prevention on one or two specialists in the school or having a few teachers take complete responsibility for all challenging students. For instance, if the counselor is responsible for all students who exhibit problem behaviors, the other staff members have little opportunity to collaborate in identifying problem behaviors, establishing expectations for student behavior, and selecting the best course of action for addressing them. Under these conditions, creating and facilitating prevention strategies across all students would be extremely difficult. Further, it is unlikely that any individual—even a very skilled one—would have the time and expertise to work effectively with all students requiring additional support in a school. Likewise, if the responsibility for a student with challenging behavior is left to the teacher who, by chance, happens to have that student for the year, there again is too little input from others to create the far-reaching management system necessary to prevent problems across the range of school settings. *A proactive management system is one that is created and implemented by all in the system (which can include the entire school or specific areas of the school, such as nonclassroom areas or a specific classroom) with equal voice and participation.* Proactive systems typically include multiple levels or tiers of intervention.

A Three-Tiered Approach to Proactive Management

The goal of a proactive management system is to prevent the occurrence and exacerbation of problem behavior and to facilitate academic success. This requires a **multitiered prevention** approach that can provide increasingly intensive and individualized interventions to students requiring more support.

Across tiers, proactive management is characterized by several common themes. *First, strategies are developed based on data-based analyses of recurring problems* (for many students across the classroom or school or for a particular student). Observations and records of problem behaviors in the past are used to predict problems in the future. For example, a teacher might study attendance records to detect overall patterns, such as days of the week when absenteeism occurs most often, or specific students who frequently are absent. *Second, all strategies are aimed primarily at prevention, with effective reactions to both desired and problem behaviors agreed on and implemented consistently by all adults across the setting.* For example, a teacher and his aides need to agree to use the same acknowledgement system and to respond to both appropriate behavior and misbehavior in a consistent manner. *Finally, multiple individuals work together as a system to identify predictors and develop and implement interventions.* For example, a group consisting of several teachers, specialists, and administrators might work together to create a schoolwide system for teaching appropriate behavior. Similarly, a teacher might meet with her teaching assistant and the school counselor to develop an intervention for a student who is disruptive. For students with the most intense needs, the system necessarily expands to also *involve* community agencies and interested parties outside the school. A graphic model of a three-tiered approach for academics and social behavior is presented in Figure 1.1.

The most basic of the three proactive levels of intervention is *universal prevention*, which is for all students in the system. At this level, the focus for social behavior is on developing and explicitly teaching rules for student behavior, acknowledging appropriate behavior, and responding consistently to inappropriate behavior. We focus on this level of prevention throughout the text but especially in Chapters 4–6, where the focus will be on creating effective classroom environments for all students. Universal prevention is important for academics as well and includes the use of evidence-based curriculum and routine screening to ensure that students are progressing. Academic interventions are beyond the

Multitiered Prevention
Prevention efforts require a comprehensive and proactive approach, beginning with universal efforts designed for all students in the system and progressing, in stages as necessary, to intensive efforts designed for students with the most significant needs.

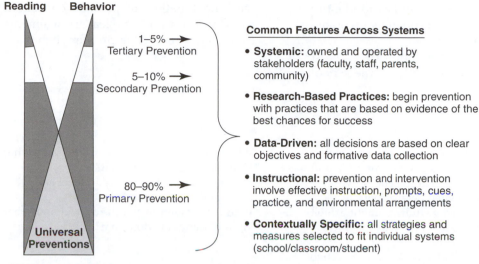

FIGURE 1.1   Combined Reading and Behavior Prevention Systems

scope of this text, but see (Fien, Kame'enui, & Good, 2009) for an extensive discussion of implementing a universal academic intervention as well as additional, more intensive academic interventions. The next level of intervention is *targeted intervention*, designed for students at risk for more serious behavior problems. Interventions at this level often are implemented across groups of students and might include social skills instruction, behavior report card programs, homework clubs, and so forth. We delineate targeted interventions later in Chapter 6. For academics, targeted interventions include focused reading groups and extra, more intensive instruction. Students at this level are monitored more frequently—at least weekly—to determine whether they are progressing. Finally, *intensive interventions* are reserved for students exhibiting significant challenges who do not respond to universal or targeted interventions. Intensive interventions are based on the results of a functional behavior assessment and are individualized to address the specific needs of the student. A process for considering and intervening with such problems is presented in Chapters 7–13.

Chapter Review

- Proactive management involves the use of information about past behavior to teach skills and arrange the environment in a way that logically prevents predictable behavior problems.
- Multitiered intervention strategies involve intervention and continuous assessment to identify increasingly smaller groups of students in need of increasingly more intense and individualized intervention.

- Primary, secondary, and tertiary levels of intervention describe schoolwide, small group, and individual student levels of intervention. Each successively smaller tier is composed of students who have not responded favorably to the larger tier(s).
- Systematic screening mechanisms for identifying students in need include office referrals data, curriculum-based assessments, and standardized test scores. Cutoff or

criterion scores are determined to identify students who are not responding favorably to intervention.

• Schoolwide implementation of support systems refers to all adults in the school working together to provide consistent rules, routines, and physical arrangements to prevent predictable problem behavior.

Application

1. Someone you know disagrees with prevention and suggests that this is a waste of time and money. What is the logical argument for working from a prevention-oriented perspective?
2. What are the reasons why students might exhibit behavior problems in schools? What should we do to assist these students?
3. Describe the three tiers of a proactive approach to supporting students.

   a. Who is involved in the first level and what kinds of things are done in it?
   b. Who is involved in the second level and what kinds of things are done in it?
   c. Who is involved in the third level and what kinds of things are done in it?

References

Adams, M. J. (1988). *Beginning to read: Thinking and learning about print*. Cambridge: MIT Press.

American Psychological Association Zero Tolerance Task Force. (2008). Are zero tolerance policies effective in the schools? An evidentiary review and recommendations. *American Psychologist, 63*(9), 852–862.

Bowen, J. M., Jenson, W. R., & Clark, E. (2004). *School-based interventions for students with behavior problems*. New York: Springer Publishing.

Fien, H., Kame'enui, E. J., & Good, R. (2009). Schools engaged in school-wide reading reform: An examination of the school and individual student predictors of kindergarten early reading outcomes. *School Effectiveness & School Improvement, 20*(1), 1–25.

Furlong, M. J., Morrison, G. M., & Dear, J. D. (1994). Addressing school violence as part of schools' educational mission. *Preventing School Failure, 38*(3), 10–17.

Gable, R. A., Hendrickson, J. M., Young, C. C., Shores, R. E., & Stowitschek, J. J. (1983). A comparison of teacher approval and disapproval statements across categories of exceptionality. *Journal of Special Education Technology, 6*, 15–21.

Gierl, M. J., & Harnish, D. L. (1995). *Estimating a model for dropping out for youth with disabilities: A latent variable analysis using data from the National Longitudinal Transition Study*. Paper presented at the annual meeting of the American Educational Research Association, San Francisco, CA.

Glaser, R. R., Horn, M. L. V., Arthur, M. W., Hawkins, J. D., & Catalano, R. F. (2005). Measurement properties of the Communities that Care Youth Survey across demographic groups. *Journal of Quantitative Criminology, 21*(1), 73–102.

Gunter, P. L., Hummel, J. H., & Conroy, M. A. (1998). Increasing correct academic responding: An effective intervention strategy to decrease behavior problems. *Effective School Practices, 17*, 36–54.

Gunter, P., Hummel, J. H., & Venn, M. L. (1998). Are effective academic instruction practices used to teach students with behavior disorders? *Beyond Behavior, 9*, 5–11.

Hammond, C., Linton, D., Smink, J., & Drew, S. (2007). *Dropout risk factors and exemplary programs: A technical report*. Clemson, SC & Alexandria, VA: National Dropout Prevention Center at Clemson University and Communities in Schools, Inc.

Harding, D. J. (2003). Counterfactual models of neighborhood effects: The effect of neighborhood poverty on dropping out and teenage pregnancy. *The American Journal of Sociology, 109*(3), 676–719.

Hart, B., & Risley, T. (1995). *Meaningful differences in the everyday experiences of young American children*. Baltimore, MD: Paul H. Brookes.

Hawkins, J. D., Herrenkohl, T. L., Farrington, D. P., Brewer, D., Catalano, R. F., Harachi, T. W., et al. (2000). Predictors of youth violence. *Juvenile Justice Bulletin*. Washington, DC: U.S. Department of

Justice, Office of Juvenile Justice and Delinquency Prevention.

Hinojosa, M. S. (2008). Black-white differences in school suspension: Effect of student beliefs about teachers. *Sociological Spectrum, 28*(2), 175–193.

Horner, R. H., Sugai, G., Dunlap, G., Hieneman, M., Lewis, T. J., Nelson, C. M., et al. (2000). Applying positive behavior support and functional behavioral assessment in schools. *Journal of Positive Behavioral Interventions, 2,* 131–143.

Hyman, I. A., & Perone, D. C. (1998). The other side of school violence: Educator policies and practices that may contribute to student misbehavior. *Journal of School Psychology, 36,* 7–27.

Kauffman, J. (1997). *Characteristics of emotional and behavioral disorders of children and youth* (6th ed.). Upper Saddle River, NJ: Merrill/Pearson.

Lyon, G. R. (2003). Reading disabilities: Why do some children have difficulty learning to read? What can be done about it? *Perspectives, 29*(2).

Mayer, M., & Leone, P. (1999). A structural analysis of school violence and disruption: Implications for creating safer schools. *Education and Treatment of Children, 22,* 333–356.

McFadden, A. C., Marsh, G. E., Price, B. J., & Hwang, Y. (1992). A study of race and gender bias in the punishment of school children. *Education and Treatment of Children, 15,* 140–146.

McIntosh, K., Chard, D., Boland, J., & Horner, R. H. (2006). A demonstration of combined efforts in school-wide academic and behavioral systems and incidence of reading and behavior challenges in early elementary grades. *Journal of Positive Behavior Interventions, 8,* 146–154.

Nelson, C. M., & Pearson, C. A. (1994). Juvenile delinquency in the context of culture and community. In R. L. Peterson & S. Ishii-Jordan (Eds.), *Cultural and community contexts for emotional or behavioral disorders* (pp. 78–90). Boston: Brookline Press.

Patterson, G. R., Reid, J. B., & Dishion, T. J. (1992). *Antisocial boys: Vol. 4. A social interactional approach.* Eugene, OR: Castalia.

Rumberger, R. W. (1987). High school dropouts: A review of issues and evidence. *Review of Educational Research, 57,* 101–121.

Rylance, B. J. (1997). Predictors of high school graduation or dropping out for youths with severe emotional disturbances. *Behavioral Disorders, 23,* 5–17.

Scott, T. M., Nelson, C. M., & Liaupsin, C. (2001). Effective instruction: The forgotten component in preventing school violence. *Education and Treatment of Children, 24,* 309–322.

Shaw, S. R., & Braden, J. P. (1990). Race and gender bias in the administration of corporal punishment. *School Psychology Review, 19,* 378–383.

Shores, R. E., Gunter, P. L., & Jack, S. L. (1993). Classroom management strategies: Are they setting events for coercion? *Behavioral Disorders, 18*(2), 92–102.

Skiba, R. J., Petersen, R. L., & Williams, T. (1997). Office referrals and suspension: Disciplinary intervention in middle schools. *Education and Treatment of Children, 20*(3), 295–316.

Stephenson, J., Linfoot, K., & Martin, A. (2000). Behaviours of concern to teachers in the early years of school. *International Journal of Disability, Development & Education, 47*(3), 225–235.

Sugai, G., Sprague, J. R., Horner, R. H., & Walker, H. M. (2000). Preventing school violence: The use of office discipline referrals to assess and monitor school-wide discipline interventions. *Journal of Emotional and Behavioral Disorders, 8,* 94–101.

Taylor-Greene, S., Brown, D., Nelson, L., Longton, J., Gassman, T., Cohen, J., et al. (1997). School-wide behavioral support: Starting the year off right. *Journal of Behavioral Education, 7,* 99–112.

U.S. Departments of Education and Justice. (1999). *Indicators of school crime and safety, 1999.* (NCES 19989-057/NCJ-178906). Washington, DC.

Van Acker, R. (2002). *Developing effective behavioral intervention plans and supports.* Paper presented at the Working Forum of the Council for Children with Behavioral Disorders. Tampa, FL.

Van Acker, R., Grant, S.H., & Henry, D. (1996). Teacher and student behavior as a function of risk for aggression. *Education and Treatment of Children, 19*(3), 316–334.

Walker, H. M., Colvin, G., & Ramsey, E. (1995). *Antisocial behavior in school: Strategies and best practices.* Pacific Grove, CA: Brooks/Cole.

Walker, H. M., & Sprague, J. R. (1999). The path to school failure, delinquency, and violence: Causal factors and some potential solutions. *Intervention in School and Clinic, 35,* 67–73.

Wehby, J. H., Symons, F. J., & Shores, R. E. (1995). A descriptive analysis of aggressive behavior in classrooms for children with emotional and behavioral disorders. *Behavioral Disorders, 20,* 87–105.

Weinstein, R. S. (2002). *Reaching higher: The power of expectations in schooling.* Cambridge, MA: Harvard University Press.

2

Understanding Behavior

CHAPTER OBJECTIVES

After reading this chapter, you should be able to describe the following concepts:

- The functional perspective of behavior change in the school environment
- The definition of "environment" as a variable in the behavior change process
- The definition of discriminative stimuli and their use in both describing and changing behavior
- The effect of setting events on behavior in classroom and schoolwide settings
- The logic and use of reinforcement in the teaching process
- Both positive and negative reinforcement as processes for increasing behavior
- The logic and use of punishment in the teaching process
- Both delivery-type and removal-type punishment as processes for decreasing behavior

As Mr. Flint turns the corner in the hallway he sees a fifth-grade student, Brandi, pushing a second grader, Malcolm, into the locker bank. A small group of students is standing nearby, laughing. Mr. Flint rushes to Malcolm's aid and separates the two students. He says, "Brandi, what is wrong with you? What are you doing?" as he marches her down the hall to the office. Brandi simply shrugs her shoulders and, looking backward, smirks at the group of students standing around. Malcolm runs to his classroom. When Brandi and Mr. Flint reach the office, he tells the secretary what he observed, the secretary writes Brandi's name down on the list of students to see the principal, and Mr. Flint leaves the office. Soon, the principal, Dr. Lux, is ready to see Brandi. She ushers Brandi into her office where the school counselor is waiting. The counselor asks Brandi, "Why were you pushing Malcolm? This is the third time this month you have been sent down here for bullying small children. Why do you keep doing this?" Brandi responds, "They are in my way!" and a long conversation between the counselor, Dr. Lux, and Brandi commences. Brandi tells the counselor that Malcolm started it and that she "always gets blamed when other kids start it." For about 10 minutes, the counselor talks to Brandi about why it is wrong to bully children and what she could do instead of bullying. Brandi then names many more appropriate responses including ignoring the child or simply asking the person in her way to move. When the conversation is over, Dr. Lux gives Brandi another slip for in-school detention—her third this month.

For those who work with children, situations like this one are frustrating. Brandi appears to know that bullying others is wrong and can even talk about how she should behave, yet her behavior does not change. We wonder, "Why does she keep bullying other children?" and, perhaps more importantly, "What can we do about it? How can we stop this behavior?" Fortunately, we have evidence-based approaches that are very useful for responding to situations like this one. Years of research and practice have taught us that we can intervene effectively if we approach behavior from a **functional perspective**—focusing on events that are related to the behavior.

Of course, the functional approach is just one of many different ways to attempt to understand human behavior. We adopt a functional perspective in this text for several reasons. First, as noted earlier, a large and robust literature demonstrates that this model is useful both for understanding behavior and for developing effective interventions. Second, this model has been successfully applied in schools both for individual students and for systems such as classrooms and entire schools. Third, a functional model of behavior allows us to create a logical framework for consistently applying practices that logically link to intended outcomes and can be communicated across school personnel. Finally, and perhaps more persuasive from our perspective as teachers, the functional approach is a teaching approach. It assumes that teachers can teach children how to behave and that effective instruction (i.e., what teachers do) is the most powerful tool they have for changing behavior. In this text we operate from a functional approach because we believe it best approximates what teachers are trained to do and because it provides us the best chance of success in our efforts to change behavior via instruction.

In this chapter, we define and explore the basic principles underlying a functional approach. We conclude by providing a framework for dealing with the behavior of individuals and entire systems from a functional approach. While a complete review of the principles and research underlying this model is beyond the scope of this text, valuable resources for the interested reader are listed in the Appendix at the end of this chapter.

Functional Perspective Determining the causes of a behavior by focusing on events outside the person that reliably precede and follow the behavior, thus making it more or less likely to occur.

A FUNCTIONAL APPROACH

A functional approach to understanding behavior begins with a seemingly straightforward assumption: Most behavior is learned via an interaction between the individual and his or her environment. Of course, this statement is simplistic because not all behavior is learned. Many basic behaviors, such as the beating of our heart, blinking, startling when we hear a loud noise, sweating, and so forth, occur automatically and are largely beyond our control. So when we say in this text that behavior is learned, we are speaking of more complex behaviors, such as what people do and say.

Understanding a student's behavior from a functional perspective requires us to identify how behavior interacts with the environment. If our focus is on a group of students—for example, Ms. Rommel's third-period class—then we are interested in features of the classroom and interaction patterns between students in the class and between Ms. Rommel and the students. If we are interested in the behavior of a specific student, we will want to learn more about the setting or settings in which that student most often exhibits the behavior of concern. Identifying these events often is referred to as functional behavior assessment. In this chapter we provide an introduction to this functional approach, which will serve as a foundation for the remainder of the text. In subsequent chapters, we apply this logic—and functional behavior assessment—to understanding and designing effective responses to student behavior. We begin by reviewing the basic assumptions underlying the functional model of behavior.

ASSUMPTIONS OF A FUNCTIONAL MODEL

The functional model of behavior is based on several assumptions about people's behavior. These assumptions are not simply fashioned for convenience, nor are they "best guesses." Instead, they were derived from decades of rigorous research (see the Appendix for more information) in the field of behavior analysis. The core assumptions of this model are that (a) behavior is learned, (b) behavior is lawful, and (c) behavior can be changed.

Behavior Is Learned

All behaviors are either innate or are learned as a result of interactions with the environment. Innate behaviors are those that we were born with. For example, if someone blows in your eye, you will reflexively blink, and when your knee is tapped, your leg will jerk. Similarly, you did not have to learn to breathe or to sleep. Other behaviors are learned and range from relatively simple behaviors (e.g., a child pointing at an object she wants) to complex behaviors such as the skills we might refer to as social competence (e.g., standing the appropriate distance from someone when talking, making eye contact but not staring, asking questions in a friendly manner). Generally speaking, innate, reflexive behaviors are not problematic. Rather, it is learned behaviors that we are probably interested in changing. People first exhibit a behavior for various reasons. For example, a child may swear for the first time because he or she is imitating someone, because a peer dared her to do it, or by accident (e.g., trying to say one word and saying something else instead). The behaviors that people continue to exhibit, however, are those that more often than not are followed by positive outcomes. We will return to this important point later in this chapter and repeatedly throughout the text.

Learning occurs in one of two ways: We learn due to the consequences of behavior, and we learn by watching others or from their instructions. These two types of learning actually are closely related. As we will discuss in more detail later in this chapter, one way we learn behavior is by observing what happens when we act in a certain way. For example, a student who swears when around peers and gets a positive reaction such as laughing may be more likely to swear again when her peers are around. But if instead her friends frown or become quiet when she swears, then she may be less likely to swear in the future. Thus, we posit a basic principle: *Behavior that results in a positive outcome is more likely to be repeated, and behavior that results in an unpleasant outcome is less likely to occur again.* The second way that learning occurs is by watching others or by instruction. When we watch others, we watch not only what they do, but also what happens afterward. For example, suppose that before jumping off the swing, Marshawn tells his friend, "You go first," and then watches to see how the teacher responds. If the teacher ignores his friend's jumping and if he doesn't get hurt, Marshawn may then jump. If, however, the teacher scolds Marshawn's friend or has him sit on the sidewalk (or if his friend gets hurt), Marshawn may be less likely to jump off the swing. We also learn a great deal from both observation and directed instruction. From a very young age, children are told by adults how to behave and how not to behave. The consequences for following and failing to follow these instructions are also provided (although they often are implicit). For example, parents tell children, "Don't touch the burner when it is hot or you will get burned." Over time, if there is a good correspondence between the instruction and the stated or implied outcome, children learn that it is a good idea to follow instructions given by adults.

Unfortunately, children who don't experience this correspondence often learn to disregard what adults tell them, which often leads to difficulty in school. For example, if Sue-Ling's mother tells her, "Clean your room, or you won't be able to go outside and play," but then lets her go play even though the room isn't clean, Sue-Ling is learning that her mother's instructions don't always matter. If this pattern continues, Sue-Ling may begin to disregard adult instructions whenever she chooses; after all, there is no logical correspondence between what she is told and what actually happens. This leads to the "Do as I say and not as I do" phenomenon in which children learn that words are reinforced, but their corresponding actions are not. When asked, these children can easily recite all the particulars of desirable behavior and are rewarded with adult praise. However, these behaviors are not displayed by the children because there is no followthrough from adults to link verbal behavior to actions.

Behavior Is Lawful

As we described earlier, people behave as they do because of an interaction between behavior and the environment. We say that behavior is lawful because the environment affects behavior in predictable ways. If a certain behavior is reliably followed by a positive outcome, then it is more likely to occur. For example, Tom probably continues to tease peers because the outcomes are pleasurable to him. Perhaps his friends laugh and perhaps other children in the school seem to respect him (for example, by backing down quickly when he challenges them). In contrast, if a behavior is not followed by a positive outcome, then it is less likely to occur again. If Tom's friends responded negatively every time he teased a peer, then he would be less likely to behave in this way. Of course, behavior occurs only in certain contexts, and so it is important to understand the antecedents to behavior as well. Perhaps Tom teases peers only when adults are not close by; for example, during recess or before class when the teacher has not yet entered the room. We say that behavior is lawful because it does not happen haphazardly; rather, it is the result of which events precede and follow it. When we understand these events—the antecedents and consequences—we are in a better position to intervene because, once we understand these events, we can alter them to affect the behavior. We will return to this point in more depth later in this chapter and in Chapter 3, as well as throughout the text.

Behavior Can Be Changed

Understanding how the environment affects behavior leads us directly to an intervention. Once we understand the *when* and *why* of behavior (predictors and outcomes), we can develop instruction to change it. For example, if we want Desiree to stop bullying other students, we need first to determine when the behavior most often occurs and what typically happens afterward. Our intervention likely will involve changing what happens before the behavior—such as perhaps increasing supervision—and what happens after the behavior. In addition, we might find that we need to teach Desiree in more appropriate ways to behave. These actions represent the key components of effective classroom management: facilitating success, instruction, and feedback.

To summarize, the functional approach adopted in this text states that the best way to understand behavior is to evaluate the environment in which the behavior occurs. We need to evaluate patterns over time, looking for the events that most often occur before and after the behavior we are interested in. Although the functional approach focuses on features of the setting, it is important to recognize that this perspective does not deny the importance of other factors such as physiological or genetic variables or events that occurred far in someone's past. Clearly both of these factors often play a role in behavior. For example, attention deficit hyperactivity disorder seems to have a physiologic component. But even when physiologic or genetic factors play a role in the onset of the problem, research has shown that a functional approach can decrease the impact of the problem. Continuing with attention deficit hyperactivity disorder, a large body of work demonstrates that environmental modifications such as structuring the setting, using clear instructions, and consistent consequences for desirable and undesirable behavior dramatically decrease problem behaviors such as inattention and increase on-task and other prosocial behavior. In addition to physiological features, events from one's past also might play a role in current behavior. To illustrate, one of the authors once worked with a little boy who was severely mentally retarded and engaged in self-injurious behavior. The little boy had been developmentally normal until, at the age of about 6 months, his father came home drunk and, in a rage, threw the boy down the stairs. In this very sad example, the boy's mental retardation and self-injury were ultimately caused by being thrown down the stairs. Unfortunately, nothing could be done to change those events. As a result, intervention efforts focused on identifying current situations that were related to self-injury. Approaching behavior from a functional perspective thus calls for changing features of the setting to affect behavior.

APPLYING THE FUNCTIONAL MODEL TO STUDENT BEHAVIOR

If we work from the assumption that most behavior is learned, lawful, and changeable, we shift our focus away from the person's internal state (e.g., low self-esteem) to what happens when the person behaves in certain ways. The reason for this shift is that focusing on nonobservable (and often nonexistent) constructs such as self-esteem does not help us identify things that we can do to improve the situation. To illustrate, consider the case of Liam.

> Liam is a third-grader in a large urban elementary school. He is a somewhat quiet student and has a reputation of being a perfectionist. He earned high grades in first and second grades, turns his work in on time, and in many ways is a model student. Liam's parents have contacted the school counselor because they are worried. His father reports that Liam spends at least three hours per night on his homework and that he looks anxious the entire time. When Liam finishes an assignment, his father goes over it with Liam and, if there are any mistakes, Liam bursts into tears and talks about how stupid he is; he often is inconsolable and does not finish the rest of his homework until the next morning, waking up early to do it. As Liam's father is talking, the teacher realizes that she has heard Liam make self-deprecating remarks on several occasions, most often when she corrects his work. When this occurs, she often talks with him a long time about what a good student he is, but his day, from his perspective, seems to be ruined. He often disengages and simply sits in his desk with his head down, no longer participating in class discussions or completing assignments.

At this point, Liam's parents, teacher, and counselor realize that there is a problem and the question then becomes what to do about it. Often this involves first identifying the cause. Imagine what would happen if Liam's counselor said something like, "Liam clearly has low self-esteem; that is what is causing him to shut down." It is easy to see how this conclusion could be reached, and it seems reasonable doesn't it? Now ask yourself how useful this "cause" is for helping the group figure out to do: What should be done about low self-esteem? Although there are many interventions for problems like this, such as counseling, skills training, and so forth, picking the correct intervention requires us to ask more questions—we need to find out why Liam has low self-esteem. It turns out that constructs such as low self-esteem are not causes at all; they are better thought of as labels for behavior. Think about this: We have just suggested that the cause of Liam's self-deprecating remarks, crying, and shutting down is his low self-esteem. But, how do we know that Liam has low self-esteem? We infer it from his behavior, right? For example, he becomes quite upset when he makes an error, he makes self-deprecating remarks, and he shuts down. What we have done is to offer a "circular explanation." The cause of the behavior—low self-esteem—is inferred from the behavior that it is supposed to cause. Imagine instead that Liam's counselor adopts a functional approach to Liam's behavior:

> Up to this point, Liam's parents and teacher have identified similar concerns: Liam becomes upset and makes self-deprecating remarks when he makes an error. He often shuts down for a prolonged period of time. Liam's counselor says, "Okay, we seem to agree that we have a problem. What we need to do now is to understand more about when it occurs so that we can figure out what to do. From what you have said, it sounds like Liam makes self-deprecating remarks, becomes upset, and disengages when an adult points out an academic error—is this correct?" Everyone nods their head in agreement. The father reminds the counselor that Liam often is tense beforehand, and seems quite anxious when he is working on assignments. Liam's teacher realizes that he often seems tense in class as well, particularly during quizzes or when working independently. The counselor says, "Okay, so he often looks tense during any academic work that he is completing alone, particularly on quizzes." Everyone agrees and so the counselor tells the group that what they need to do to develop an intervention is to determine what happens afterward that might be motivating the behavior. Although his father and teacher do spend some time talking to him, Liam does not seem particularly interested in this interaction—he often ends it quickly. His counselor points out that after errors, Liam often disengages from work for a fairly long time; he asks, "Could Liam be making self-deprecating remarks, becoming upset, and disengaging as a way to avoid making future errors?" The team considers this, and then Liam's mother pipes in, "Gosh, I never really thought about this before, but do you remember when you asked us last year if we would like to have Liam tested for placement in advanced classes? Well, we asked Liam about it, and he became very upset and begged us not to make him take the tests. He said that the work would be too hard in those classes, and that he wouldn't be able to do it! That is why we never pursued the testing with you."

The team continues discussing Liam's behavior and realizes that indeed, Liam does seem to be behaving in this way to avoid future mistakes. The story his mother relayed helped to confirm this. Focusing on what happens before and after Liam becomes upset and disengages instead of on labels and hypothetical causes helped the team identify factors in the environment that seem to evoke and possibly maintain Liam's behaviors. Now they had a clear idea about what they could change to help Liam not be so hard on himself and continue working after making an error. For example, instead of trying to convince Liam that he wasn't stupid, his teacher and parents could encourage him not to disengage by saying something like, "It is okay to make mistakes; we all do. The important thing is to get right back in there and try again."

As this example illustrates, a functional perspective helps us to focus on the interaction between behavior and what is going on in the person's environment. Specifically, a functional perspective helps clarify (a) exactly what the person is saying or doing that is a concern, and (b) key features of the environment that are relevant for a given behavior. We call these key features antecedents and consequences.

DEFINE WHAT THE PERSON SAYS OR DOES

The first step in the functional approach is to identify exactly what the person says or does; we sometimes call this an **operational definition of behavior**.

When developing operational definitions, the goal is to avoid using labels and to focus on the behavior of concern that is observed. In the example with Liam, the counselor defined the behavior of concern as making self-deprecating comments, crying, and disengaging (refusing to work) for a prolonged time. Often it is helpful to develop both examples and nonexamples. For example, self-deprecating remarks for Liam might include saying things like, "I am stupid," or "I can't do anything." Nonexamples include remarks that focus on the task such as, "This is hard," or remarks like, "I am tired." A definition is adequate when everyone agrees on it and it describes precisely what a person says or does, using observable and measurable terms. For example, "lazy" or "defiant" are not good terms because they may mean different things to different people. Also, it would be very hard to measure how lazy a person is. If lazy is defined as "failing to complete assignments," however, we have shifted to something that is observable and measurable because we can measure the amount of work a person completes or the amount of time spent working. Good definitions avoid broad personality descriptions and focus on very specific behaviors. In general, behavior can be defined along five dimensions: topography, frequency, duration, latency, and intensity. Topography is what the behavior looks like, that is, what you see. Frequency refers to how often the behavior occurs. This can be categorized based on varying lengths of time depending on the behavior. If the behavior is observed only occasionally, you might ask how often it occurs in a given week or day. If the behavior occurs quite often, you might focus on an afternoon, or within a given hour. Duration refers to how long the behavior lasts, that is, once the behavior starts, how long does it go on? Latency is useful for behaviors that often start—or do not start—after a specific signal. For example, if you are observing tantrums that occur following a request, latency would refer to the length of time that passes between a request and the onset of a tantrum. Finally, intensity is used to indicate how forceful the behavior is. Table 2.1 presents a summary of these dimensions of behavior.

Each of these dimensions provides us with specific information about a behavior. The goal is to obtain information that will guide an intervention. For example, we could say that Sally is lazy and disruptive in class, or that she lacks independent work skills—but what does this mean, and what would we measure? Defining her behavior using dimensions, we can say that, during quiet work times, Sally engages in repeated open-mouth yawns lasting about 6 seconds that are loud enough to be heard across the room—about 15 times per period. This provides us with a very concrete and measurable definition of behavior. Most behaviors will not require all dimensions in order to be well defined. However, all will require a topography so that we know what we are looking for. Notice from the examples in the table that without the topography, we really don't know what we're measuring.

Operational Definition of Behavior Specifies what a person says or does in observable terms that others agree on.

TABLE 2.1   Dimensions of Behavior

Dimension	Description	Example – James	Example – Toni	Example – Vera
Topography	*Exact description of the behavior (sight, sound, feel, etc.)*	Hits others with his fist	Yawns with her mouth wide open	Delays in following the teacher's directions for more than 30 seconds
Frequency	*How often/how many?*	During 100% of name-calling episodes	15 times per period	Always
Duration	*How long did it last?*	—	6 seconds per yawn	—
Latency	*How long between some signal and the behavior?*	Within 5 seconds of being called a name	—	30 seconds after the teacher's direction
Force or Intensity	*How hard or how much?*	Hard enough to leave a bruise	Loud enough to be heard across the room	—

IDENTIFY KEY FEATURES OF THE ENVIRONMENT

Once the problem behavior has been operationally defined, the next step is to figure out what is going on around the person that seems to affect the behavior. Recall how, with Liam, the counselor guided Liam's parents and teacher to identify what happened before Liam cried, made self-deprecating remarks, and disengaged, and then helped them figure out what went on after these behaviors occurred. His counselor was helping the team identify antecedents and consequences.

Antecedent Events

Antecedent events are things that happen before the behavior of concern occurs. All behavior occurs in a context because there is always something going on; our job is to figure out what events, out of all the events that are happening (e.g., other children talking, the teacher giving instructions, cars going by outside), actually are related to the behavior. Antecedent events can be categorized into two groups: discriminative stimuli and setting events.

DISCRIMINATIVE STIMULI.   Discriminative stimuli are events that occur before the behavior and act as a signal to engage in a particular behavior. They come to act as a signal because certain consequences have reliably occurred—or not occurred—in their presence in the past. For example, the ringing of a phone signals a specific behavior—picking up the receiver and saying "hello." The ringing can be said to be a discriminative stimulus because when the phone rings (but not otherwise) a specific consequence—a voice at the other end of the line—occurs. Most of us do not pick up the phone and say, "Hello" when it does not ring because this behavior is reinforced only when the phone rings. When a behavior is predicted under one specific stimulus condition (or class of similar conditions), but not under all other conditions, we refer to this relationship as **stimulus control**. All learning is a process of establishing stimulus control. We want the answer "4" or the statement "bike" only under certain conditions and not all

Antecedents
Antecedents are all the things that happen before the behavior. These include actions, events, and conditions that may or may not have an effect on whether the behavior is exhibited.

Stimulus Control
Refers to a situation in which a given antecedent condition evokes a specific behavior because, in the past, that behavior has been differentially reinforced in the presence—but not the absence—of that antecedent condition.

conditions. There are several conditions (a class of stimuli) under which the response "4" is appropriate (e.g., 2 + 2, 8 − 4, 1 = 3, etc.). But the response "4" should not occur under other conditions (e.g., 6 − 1, 8 + 2). The response "bike" should be under stimulus control for several conditions that we have taught (e.g., when we spell the letters out and ask "what word," or when we point to a bike). Stimulus control is developed by ensuring that reinforcing consequences occur when the correct behavior, and not the incorrect behavior, occurs (e.g., saying "4" when asked, "What is 6 + 2?").

Let's explore stimulus control a bit more by looking at examples. Suppose you ask me the answer to 2 + 2 and I respond "4" each and every time. Would you now say that this response is under stimulus control of the one particular stimulus 2 + 2? It has met at least half the conditions—predictable under a particular condition. But what about the other condition, not predictable under other conditions? Suppose you ask me 3 + 3 and I again answer "4," or suppose you ask me my name and I say "4," and then I say "4" randomly as I walk around the room. Now it seems clear that this is not stimulus control because the response is not predictable under a particular stimulus condition *and* not under all other conditions. The concept of stimulus control will be an important one for us and we continue with attempting to predict student behavior under different circumstances.

SETTING EVENTS. Discriminative stimuli usually occur just before the response and seem to trigger it. They have become important because specific consequences are more or less likely when they are present. Other antecedents are important as well. Setting events are antecedents that often (but not always) occur far in advance of the target behavior. They do not seem to trigger the behavior, but they do make it more or less likely. Some people refer to setting events as establishing operations, but this is a scientific term with a very specific meaning and so we will not use it here. For example, let us suppose that Tom sometimes teases peers during unsupervised times when his friends are around. After several observations and discussions with his teacher and parents, we learn that Tom usually teases peers after a fight with his big brother in the morning before coming to school. If we discover that Tom almost always teases peers in unsupervised situations with his friends around after he fights with his brother, but almost never when he hasn't fought with his brother, we would say that fighting with his brother seems to be a setting event for teasing peers.

Setting events make a consequence more or less reinforcing. The most basic example of this is food deprivation and satiation. If we have not eaten for some period of time, food likely will function as a reinforcer. For example, I am more willing to walk across the street in the rain for a snack if I have not eaten for several hours. If I have recently eaten, however, then I will be less likely to walk across the street. As a more complicated example, let's imagine that Tamika's talking out of turn is maintained by teacher attention. Her teacher decides to spend several minutes talking with Tamika before class begins, giving her undivided attention. When class begins, Tamika is less likely to talk out because having undivided attention early in the class period made teacher attention less attractive once class began.

Setting events help us understand why a behavior might not always occur when the discriminative stimulus is present. As we will discuss in further chapters, setting events sometimes can be altered to affect the behavior. Many events that occur before behavior can seem to be setting events. But an event is a setting event if and only if (a) it is present sometimes and not present at other times and (b) the behavior occurs when the setting event is present, but not when it is absent.

Consequences

Consequences
Consequences are all the things that happen after the behavior. These include actions, events, and conditions that may or may not have affect the future probability of the behavior.

A functional perspective requires us to focus on what happens before and after the behavior; the former are called antecedents, and the latter are referred to as consequences. Consequences have one of two effects on behavior: They either make it more likely that a response will occur again, or they make it less likely that a response will occur again. These two consequences are referred to as reinforcement and punishment, respectively.

Reinforcement
The process by which a behavior is followed by a given consequence, resulting in an increase in the probability that the behavior will occur again.

REINFORCEMENT. Reinforcement is a consequence that follows a response and makes it more likely that the behavior will occur again. Note that, in the definition of reinforcement given here, the word *probability* is used. Although consequences affect behavior, it is not a mechanical relation; important consequences do not have to occur each and every time to be effective, and sometimes the behavior doesn't immediately seem affected. The change is in the overall probability of the behavior. This is why, as we discuss in more depth in Chapter 3, it is important to observe the behavior several times, that is, to look for patterns over time rather than to rely on just one instance of the behavior.

Positive Reinforcement
Contingent on a specific response, something is received, which then results in the behavior being more likely to occur again in the future.

Reinforcement always increases a behavior, but it can do so in two different ways. One way, often called **positive reinforcement**, is when something occurs or is delivered after the behavior. For example, suppose that the expectation one day during history class is to work on a quiz. Julian pokes the child in front of him, and other students respond by laughing. If his teacher notices that Julian begins to poke the child in front of him almost every day during the morning quiz, we would consider this to be positive reinforcement. This is positive reinforcement because something was added—peer attention—after the behavior (poking), which makes the behavior more likely to occur again. Now imagine that after Julian poked that child the first time, he was sent to timeout in the back of the room. If Julian then began poking more frequently, we might say that the poking was increased by **negative reinforcement**—removal of the requirement to work on the quiz.

Negative Reinforcement
Contingent on a response, something is removed or avoided, which then results in the behavior being more likely to occur again in the future.

Look at the examples in Table 2.2. To quiz yourself, cover the middle and right columns and decide which are examples of positive or negative reinforcement, then check your answers.

As illustrated in the table, reinforcement always results in an increase in the behavior. When trying to determine whether something is a reinforcer, it is important to look at how the behavior is affected and not to focus on what we wish was happening. Consider the example of Jerome presented earlier. The administrator in the school certainly does not want Jerome to fight more; he suspended him in an effort to decrease fighting, but unfortunately the opposite happened—Jerome's fighting was reinforced by suspension.

Punishment
is the process by which a consequence decreases the future probability of a behavior occurring.

PUNISHMENT. Jerome's administrator was hoping that suspension would function as punishment, resulting in a decrease in fighting. The word "punishment" has many connotations in our society. Here, we use it in a functional perspective.

TABLE 2.2   Examples of Positive and Negative Reinforcement

Example	Type of Reinforcement	Rationale
Patrice frequently is teased by other students for wearing glasses. One day, when students tease her, she responds by pushing one of them. They all run away. Now she threatens to push whenever other students come near her.	Negative reinforcement	When Patrice pushes or threatens students, something is removed—the students move away—which increases her pushing and threatening.
Mr. Drumond had trouble getting students to class on time. He implemented a game in which, if students are in their seats when the bell rings, he puts two marbles in a jar. When the marbles reach a line on the jar, the class earns a pizza party. Now students are almost always in their seats when the bell rings.	Positive reinforcement	When delivery of marbles (which are related to a pizza party) follows in-seat behavior, the behavior increases; something was added (the marbles) to increase the behavior.
Ms. Novak's students often do not complete their homework. She institutes a new policy by which any student who brings their homework to class completes three fewer problems on the morning worksheet. Now almost all students are bringing their homework.	Negative reinforcement	If students bring their homework, something is removed (three problems on the worksheet), which results in an increase in homework completion.
Ms. Youngren sends Tyrone to the counselor for mouthing off in class. He is gone for 20 minutes, and she enjoys the peace and quiet. Now, she often sends Tyrone to the counselor as soon as he enters the classroom.	Negative reinforcement	When Ms. Youngren sends Tyrone to the office, he no longer is in her class. The removal of this student serves to negatively reinforce (increase) her behavior of sending him to the counselor.
When Jerome is suspended for fighting, he spends the day running around town with friends who have dropped out of school or have been suspended. He begins to start fights more often.	Positive reinforcement	Fighting increases because of what is added—unsupervised time with friends.

Punishment occurs when an event follows a behavior with the result that the behavior occurs less often.

If suspension had resulted in fewer fights, then we could say that Jerome's fighting was punished by the delivery of suspension. Remember, reinforcement always increases a response and punishment always decreases a response. As with reinforcement, punishment can work in two different ways: Sometimes something is added, and sometimes something is taken away. Either way, the result is a decrease in the response.

Alaqua has decided to start smoking. She has seen other kids do this, and she thinks it looks cool. One day, when hanging out with her friends after school, she lights up a cigarette. Her friends are surprised and ask her what she is doing. Alaqua says, "I smoke now," and proceeds to smoke the cigarette. Two of her friends talk about this later and realize that they hate the smell of cigarette smoke. They decide that they won't hang out with Alaqua when she is smoking. They tell her this, but Alaqua just laughs. That weekend, the girls all go to the mall together. When they are standing outside trying to decide what store to go to, Alaqua pulls out a cigarette. Immediately, Lysa and Shawn walk away. Alaqua asks them where they are going, and they tell her that they don't like cigarette smoke and won't hang around while she smokes. Alaqua puts the cigarette out and follows her friends. She never smokes when they are around again.

Think about this example: Is this reinforcement or punishment?

Consider the behavior, smoking, and the effect of the consequence, decreased smoking around her friends. This suggests that punishment occurred. Notice, however, that something was removed: Her friends no longer spend time with her if she smokes. We consider this to be **removal-type punishment** (sometimes referred to as *Type II punishment*); something is removed, which results in the behavior decreasing. If Alaqua's friends had yelled at her when she smoked, and this resulted in Alaqua being less likely to smoke around them, we would still say that punishment had occurred. This, however, would be a case of **delivery-type punishment** (sometimes referred to as *Type I punishment*); something is delivered that decreases the response.

To make this easier to understand, remember that reinforcement always increases a response and punishment always decreases a response. To determine whether punishment is positive or negative, think about them as mathematical operations; delivery-type punishment gets a "+" sign because something is added, and removal-type punishment gets a "−" sign because something is removed. Consider the examples below. To quiz yourself, cover everything but the far left column in Table 2.3. Determine first whether reinforcement or punishment has occurred and then whether it is positive or negative.

Removal-Type Punishment
Contingent on a response, something is removed or avoided, which then decreases the likelihood of the behavior.

Delivery-Type Punishment
Contingent on a specific response, something is received, which then decreases the likelihood of the behavior.

TABLE 2.3   Examples of Positive and Negative Punishment

Example	Type of Consequence	Rationale
When Jerome looks at the teacher she often calls on him, which he does not like. Jerome begins to spend most of the class looking at his desk. He rarely looks at the teacher anymore.	Delivery-type punishment	Jerome was called on often when he looked at the teacher, so he began to look at her less often. Thus, the receipt of the consequence (being called on) decreased looking at the teacher. (You also could say that looking at the desk was negatively reinforced by removal of being called on.)
When Lila is sent to the office for not having her materials, she misses the first part of class during which students solve math problems on the board. Lila begins to "forget" her materials more often.	Negative reinforcement	Not bringing materials increases because it was followed by the removal of having to participate in the first part of class.
When Marcos turns his assignment in early, his teacher praises him and puts his work on the board. Now he almost always turns work in early.	Positive reinforcement	Turning work in early was followed by praise and posting of work. These things were added, and this resulted in an increase in the behavior.

Chapter Review

- In a functional perspective, most behavior is the result of learning experiences in the environment, based on how behaviors have been associated with specific outcomes in the past.

    Behavior is learned.

    Behavior is lawful.

    Once understood, behavior can be changed.

- The word "environment" refers to all actions, events, and physical properties that are present before, during, or after a person's behavior.

- Discriminative stimuli evoke a response because certain consequences occur more often when they are present.

- Setting events set the occasion for a response because they make consequences more or less valuable.

- Reinforcement is the process by which a consequence results in an increase in the future likelihood of a response occurring.

    There are two types of reinforcement: positive and negative.

- Positive reinforcement occurs when something is delivered, resulting in the behavior being more likely to occur again in the future.

- Negative reinforcement results in an increase in the response as well. But in negative reinforcement, something is removed following the response.

- Punishment is the process by which a consequence results in a decrease in the future probability of a response. There are two types of punishment: positive and negative.

- Delivery-type punishment occurs when something is added after a response, resulting in a decrease in the future probability of the response (also referred to as type I punishment).

- Removal-type punishment occurs when something is removed after the response, resulting in the response decreasing in the future (also referred to as type II punishment).

Application

1. Fill in the blanks below:
   - Mr. Bullet gives Steve a marble every time he completes his work. Over time, Steve's work completion behavior becomes more frequent. In this case, marbles appear to be a(n) _____ stimulus to Steve.
   - Janice dislikes her friend Mary's singing, so every time she hears Mary sing, she takes one of Mary's toys and doesn't return it, ever. Over time, Mary's singing becomes less frequent when Janice is around. Janice has used

     _____ .
   - Edward regularly flips off teachers as they walk down the hall. One day, Principal Fandino decides to suspend Edward from school every time he flips someone off. Edward stops flipping people off when they walk down the hall. Suspension has functioned as a _____ for Edward.
   - Mr. Slate is annoyed that Fred often leaves work before the whistle blows at the end of the day. In response, Mr. Slate begins docking Fred 1/2 hour of pay whenever he leaves even an instant before the whistle blows. Over time, Fred's leaving early decreases. Mr. Slate has used _____ to affect Fred's departure time.

2. In the following scenario, determine (1) the problem behavior of concern, (2) the discriminative stimulus for problem behavior, and (3) the function of the behavior (access to something, or escaping/avoiding something).
   - When the fire alarm goes off, Martha holds her ears and runs out of the building. She does not wait for the other students or the teacher, but simply runs as fast as she can.
     - What is the behavior of concern?_____ _____
     - Can we predict when it might occur?_____ _____
     - Why does it occur under these conditions? _____

- During independent work at work stations, Billie Jo often wanders around to other people and plays with their things. Other students stop working and playing with her.
  - What is the behavior of concern?_____

    _____
  - Can we predict when it might occur?_____

    _____
  - Why does it occur under these conditions?

    _____

- Every day in circle time, Dakota shouts out answers to the teacher's questions. If the teacher ignores him, he begins to bounce up and down and to shout even louder. Eventually she is forced to respond to him.
  - What is the behavior of concern?_____

    _____
  - Can we predict when it might occur?_____

    _____
  - Why does it occur under these conditions?

    _____

References

Kamps, D. M., Ellis, C., Mancina, C., Wyble, J., Greene, L., & Harvey, D. (1995). Case studies using functional analysis for young children with behavior risks. *Education and Treatment of Children, 18,* 243–260.

O'Neill, R. E., Horner, R. H., Albin, R. W., Sprague, J. R., Storey, D., & Newton, J. S. (1997). Functional assessment and program development for problem behavior: A practical handbook (2nd ed.) Pacific Grove, CA: Brooks/Cole.

Scott, T. M., Liaupsin, C. J., & Nelson, C. M. (2001). Behavior intervention planning: Using the functional assessment data. [CD-ROM]. Longmont, CO: Sopris West.

Umbreit, J., Ferro, J. B., Liapsin, C. J., & Lane, K. L. (2007). Functional Behavioral Assessment and Function-Based Intervention. Upper Saddle River, NJ: Pearson Education.

3

Overview of a Functional Approach to Intervention

CHAPTER OBJECTIVES

After reading this chapter, you should be able to describe the following concepts:

- Function as a description of "why" students engage in behavior
- The definition and use of functional behavior assessment (FBA)
- The key steps of a functional behavior assessment
- Assessing predictable antecedents and consequences as clues to the function of behavior (including the use of ABC assessment)
- Testable hypotheses of function

This chapter presents a generic conceptual foundation for considering function-based support and intervention at both the group and individual levels. The concepts and guides laid out in Chapters 2 and 3 provide the groundwork for multiple examples presented across both the classroom and individual student sections of the text.

In the previous chapter we talked about understanding behavior from a functional perspective and looked at how the environment can both predict and maintain behavior. We saw that when behavior is met with desirable consequences, it tends to occur again when those consequences are available. Thus, behavior is functional in that it helps individuals meet their needs. The process of assessment to determine the function that a behavior serves is called *functional behavior assessment*. Because an FBA results in no scores, rankings, or comparative information, its only purpose is to better understand the behavior so as to develop an effective intervention. In this chapter we will look at processes for completing an FBA and how that determination of function leads to the development of effective interventions.

ASSESSMENT FROM A FUNCTIONAL PERSPECTIVE

As we have mentioned several times, developing an effective intervention requires first identifying features of the environment that affect behavior. This often is referred to as a functional behavior assessment (FBA). We will describe specific strategies for conducting a functional behavior assessment in different settings and contexts throughout the text. For example, in Chapter 4 we delineate how a functional behavior assessment might be applied to an entire classroom. In Chapter 8, we describe how to conduct a functional behavior assessment with a specific student. Shortly we will provide an overview of the key steps involved in conducting a functional behavior assessment. These steps include defining the behavior of concern, identifying maintaining consequences, and describing the events that precede the behavior.

Function of Behavior

The term "function of behavior" refers to the reason why a behavior is occurring, that is, what is reinforcing the behavior. Sometimes the function of a behavior is very easy to see: A baby cries, and the parent tries a variety of things to soothe the infant, such as changing him, providing food, and simply holding the baby. Thus, we might say that the function of the infant's crying is to gain access to any of these things. Similarly, a child may scream and cry when presented with strained beets until the parent removes the food. Thus, the child learns that crying can function to escape the hated beets. Two caveats should be mentioned here. First, the concept of function does not imply that the individual consciously decided to engage in a behavior. Although functional behaviors are learned, they often operate more habitually than consciously. Second, one occurrence of a behavior followed by a particular consequence is not sufficient to identify function because we cannot overestimate the power of coincidence. To be certain of the true predictability and function of a behavior, patterns must be identified over time. Thus, we can say that the function is identified if a certain behavior usually is evoked by specific stimuli and followed by certain consequences. While function is a rather simple concept, it often is difficult to identify the function of a given behavior because many things may be occurring at once. In a classroom, for example, a student's teasing might result in negative attention from the student that was teased, positive attention from friends, and a correction from the teacher. Discerning which consequence actually is reinforcing the teasing will take some work.

Too often we encounter difficulty when we ask what is wrong with the *student*, thereby focusing on behavior management problems and looking for a cause inside the person (e.g., he is just mean) or in a setting other than the school (e.g., his parents must not be good parents). Unfortunately, as discussed in Chapter 2, this often provides little guidance regarding what can actually be changed to improve the student's social behavior and learning. What if we change our focus and instead ask what the student might be getting or avoiding by exhibiting this behavior; that is, what is the function of the behavior? Broadly speaking, social behavior can serve one or both of two functions. First, behavior can provide a student with attention, tangible items, activities, or sensory stimulation. As

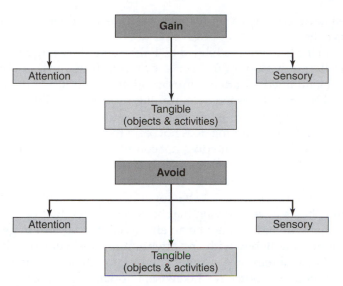

FIGURE 3.1   A Summary of Functional Outcomes

discussed in Chapter 2, these are all examples of positive reinforcement. Second, behavior can also provide a means for escaping or avoiding attention, tangible items, activities, or sensory stimulation—all types of negative reinforcement. Figure 3.1 provides a summary of functional outcomes.

Occasionally, a single behavior will serve both purposes. For instance, the behavior of a student who throws a book across the room when the teacher announces that it is time for math class may provide peer attention; at the same time, however, it allows the student to escape the activity because the teacher may respond by removing the student from the class. Although many things typically happen after a behavior, usually only one consequence is really important. In the example just presented, although both peer attention and escape may follow, generally only one of these consequences will actually reinforce the behavior. In addition, sometimes behaviors may look the same but serve very different functions. Consider the cases of Bobby and Mary. Bobby and Mary are in the same elementary school classroom and have been identified by their teacher, Ms. Smith, as students with challenging behaviors. Both students frequently yell and argue with other students and, on occasion, with adults. Bobby typically talks back and becomes argumentative when asked to complete any independent work. Ms. Smith typically tries to convince him to do his work, repeatedly providing Bobby the same rationale for the work. Other children respond in various ways: Some giggle and watch what is going on; others seem annoyed, telling Bobby to be quiet. Ms. Smith typically ends up standing close to Bobby and encouraging him to do his work; and when she is close by, he does the work very well. In contrast, Mary typically becomes argumentative when asked to work with a group on reading assignments. Because Mary disturbs others, Ms. Smith often sends her to the office. Ms. Smith has noticed that Mary, unlike Bobby, is no more likely to complete assignments when she is close by;

Mary almost never completes her reading assignment unless Ms. Smith provides the answers to her.

Although the behaviors exhibited by Bobby and Mary (arguing with others) are very similar; they may in fact serve different functions. Bobby's arguing seems to be maintained by attention from others; other students certainly pay attention, and Ms. Smith responds to arguing by talking to Bobby, staying near him, and encouraging him to work. Mary is argumentative only during group reading; however, Mary's arguing does not seem to function as an attention-getter. She is sent to the office often, and does not complete her work even when she has lots of teacher attention. We might say that her behavior functions to avoid requests to complete group reading.

Identifying the function of a behavior is critical for developing an intervention plan. In Bobby's case, knowing that he acts to gain attention tells us a great deal about what will and will not be an effective intervention. In general, interventions that provide Bobby with any attention for misbehavior will be ineffective because they will reinforce misbehavior by providing attention, which is the desired (i.e., functional) outcome. Likewise, knowing that Mary engages in the same behavior to avoid group reading leads us to question why she wants to avoid reading. We must then ask whether the reading tasks are at her ability level; if they are not, this should be addressed immediately.

Let's take some time to practice by considering the likely function involved in each of the scenarios below.

> Desmond is happy to answer teacher questions in most instances. However, he is not very skilled in math and does not like it. When the teacher asks him a math question, he often yells "Shut up, you old bag!" and the teacher sends him into the hallway to sit.

Why would Desmond answer questions happily in one instance and be so rude in another? First, we know that he struggles with math. Second, his problems tend to occur when the teacher asks him a math question. So we can surmise that the discriminative stimulus is math questions. Now we must figure out what the function of his rude responses is. Notice that when he is put on the spot in math, his behavior always results in his being excused from math. Therefore, we might say that Desmond's behavior is negatively reinforced: It functions to escape or avoid math, and it works.

> Latona is a very good student, earning A's in most of her classes. She seems to enjoy being the center of attention. She always raises her hand to volunteer information during discussions, and frequently is the leader during group work. When the teacher is not looking directly at her during independent work times, Latona often makes loud groaning noises—and the teacher moves toward her to ask what she needs. Latona then engages the teacher in a long discussion about irrelevant things—her dress is itchy, the ceiling seems to be in need of painting, and the color is bothering her, and so on. Interestingly, Latona almost always has her work done when the teacher comes to her—and it is done very well.

Why would Latona make groaning noises? First, we know that Latona often exhibits appropriate behavior that results in attention from others (e.g., raising her hand to provide answers, leading the group). Second, her problems tend to occur when the teacher is not attending to her during independent work times; independent work when the teacher's attention is diverted is the discriminative stimulus. Latona's theatrical groaning seems to be positively reinforced; that is, it functions to get the teacher's attention. Now the question is why would she do this instead of just asking the teacher to come over? All we know is that the groaning functions to get teacher attention, so as long as it works well, why would she do anything different? For Latona, an intervention might focus on first figuring out *why* she wants teacher attention in this situation. We notice that her work is almost always finished. Perhaps she gets bored sitting around and waiting for everyone else to finish, so maybe she needs something else to do that is interesting and fun for her. Next, Latona might be taught a more appropriate way to get the teacher's attention, noting that she already knows how to raise her hand and that she often does this quite appropriately. Finally, an intervention would need to be sure that Latona no longer gets attention when she moans and engages in this somewhat inappropriate conversation. Her teacher will have to avoid interacting with Latona when she behaves in this way; instead, she should talk with Latona when she requests attention by raising her hand and then talks about more relevant topics.

> Salvadore is a loner and does not seem to have many friends. Whenever the teacher asks the students to get out their books in the classroom, he makes groaning noises. The teacher ignores this, but the students all laugh. After a minute or two, Salvadore gets his book out somewhat dramatically, which again inspires laughter from his peers, and begins to work.

Like Latona, Salvadore groans—but we can't assume it is for a similar function. The first thing to do is identify the discriminative stimulus; in this case, it is any request to get out books. Next, we look at what happens after Salvadore groans: What does he get or avoid? Although Latona got the teacher's attention, for Salvadore, peers seem to be responding. This suggests that Salvadore's groaning when asked to get out books functions to get peer attention. As you can see, we will need a very different intervention for Salvadore than for Latona. Providing him with something to do won't work because he already has something to do—the assignment. In addition, teaching him another way to get teacher's attention probably would have no effect; what he is after is peer attention. For Salvadore, we need to figure out (a) why he wants peer attention in this situation (perhaps because he has few friends and gets little peer interaction at other times) and (b) what we can do about it. We might provide Salvadore with opportunities to recruit peer attention more appropriately, such as by serving as the group leader during activities. Also, Salvadore might benefit from some skills training focusing on peer interactions if he does not have good social interaction skills with peers. Rachel is a very quiet student. She often is characterized as withdrawn. She spends a lot of time with her head down and seems to disappear into the background. She is taking several special education classes, and in the hallways other students often harass her by coming up close and calling her "dummy." Now when students get near her she spits at them, and they generally run from her. Why would a quiet student spit at others? As before, the first thing to do is identify the context in which the behavior occurs and figure out what the discriminative stimulus may be. For Rachel, spitting occurs in the hallway when other students tease her, so the teasing is the discriminative stimulus. Next we must ask what Rachel gets or avoids: What is the function of the spitting? Notice that when she spits, other students move away and stop teasing her. So for Rachel, spitting serves to help her escape from aversive interactions with peers. What would you do for an intervention for Rachel? Would your focus be on Rachel's behavior, the behavior of other students' behavior, or both? How would you use the information you have learned about the function of her behavior to guide your intervention?

FUNCTIONAL BEHAVIOR ASSESSMENT

Functional behavior assessment is a process for determining how the environment predicts and maintains a response, that is, why the behavior is occurring. The FBA process can be broken into the following distinct steps: (1) defining the behavior, (2) assessing predictable patterns, (3) developing a hypothesis about the behavior's function, and (4) verifying the hypothesis in some manner. In this chapter we focus on the first three steps. More information on hypothesis verification will be presented in Chapter 8. What follows is an overview of the FBA process; we provide more detail about the process of conducting FBA in other chapters (Chapter 6 for classroom-focused FBA and Chapter 10 for FBA focused on an individual student). The goal of this chapter is to provide an overview of the logic of FBA, which should set the context for the information presented in the remainder of the text.

> Functional behavior assessment (FBA) is a process of gathering information about the relation between the environment and a behavior so as to understand what events make the behavior more likely to occur and also what events serve to reinforce the behavior. This information is used in the development of an individualized intervention plan.

Step 1: Defining Behavior

The first step of the FBA process is to define the behavior of concern. Recall from the previous chapter that behaviors can be defined by their dimensions and that each of the basic dimensions can be defined in a measurable and observable manner. A good definition of behavior for purposes of an FBA entails at least two dimensions that include the topography of the behavior (its physical properties) and some indication of the amount of behavior (i.e., duration, frequency, latency, intensity). This is true whether you are trying to do an FBA for an individual student (discussed in Chapter 4) or for a group of students (explained in Chapter 6).

Consider a teacher who says she is concerned about Andrea, who talks in class. This is not enough information to begin an FBA; we know nothing about why this behavior is a problem or the context in which it is observed. However, consider the following: *When the teacher is giving morning directions, Andrea talks loudly across the room to her friends 3 out of 5 times.* We now know that the behavior is a problem because it happens when the teacher is talking (locus), that she talks across the room to friends (topography), and that it happens on about 60% of days (frequency). This gives us a much better sense of the problem, and it will also help us decide when to schedule observations and whom to talk to when we gather more information.

When attempting to do an FBA across a group of people, the behavior is defined in much the same way. The difference here is that the definition must include all the behaviors of concern—what any student might say or do. The focus remains, however, on observable behavior. You might start with a general label such as "off task" or "loud," but then you must identify specifically what occurs and what does not occur. For example, in a classroom the teacher might define off-task behavior as including the following: "When the expectation is to be in seat working quietly, off-task behavior involves being out of seat without permission, talking to a peer, or interacting with an object that is not required for the assigned task."

Step 2: Assess Predictable Patterns

Once the target behavior(s) have been defined, the next step in the FBA process is to gather information to develop a hypothesis about the relation between antecedents (discriminative stimuli and setting events), the problem behavior, and the consequences that maintain it. The process of predicting patterns of behavior involves collecting data via direct observations, interviews, questionnaires, and a variety of other means.

To begin the process of identifying predictable patterns, identify first any problematic routines. Routines are activities that occur during the school day and involve the student or students whose behavior is of concern. O'Neill et al. (1997) called this step of the FBA a routines analysis and recommended that the **routines analysis** begin by recording the student's schedule and then continue by noting the likelihood of problem behavior during each activity. For routines in which problem behavior is highly likely, a description is given of problems that often occur.

As demonstrated by O'Neill et al. (1997), focusing an FBA on specific routines instead of the entire day has several important advantages. First, a routines analysis helps focus attention only on those routines that are problematic, which can save valuable time. Second, we can ask questions or conduct observations to determine why a problem occurs during one routine but not others; that is, what relevant features of the environment are present in the problematic situation but not in other routines? This information can be used to guide development of an intervention. Imagine, for example, that a student frequently gets in trouble for lying in social studies, but that lying never occurs in any other routine—not during other classes, not during lunch, and so on. We can then begin determining what evokes lying in social studies and what maintains it, and we know we are looking for variables that are not present in other situations. For example, a small group of students that is not present at other times of the day may sit near the

Routines Analysis
Identification of regularly occurring, functional activities and noting the likelihood of problem behavior during each routine.

student in social studies to encourage the student to lie. A third reason to conduct a routines analysis prior to identifying predictable patterns of behavior is that the same behavior can be evoked by different antecedent variables and maintained by very different consequences in different contexts.

> Mr. Black is concerned about Michael, a third-grade student who is rude to other students and often is in trouble for aggressive behavior towards peers including pushing, kicking, and shoving. You help Mr. Black complete a routines analysis and find that aggressive behavior and rude statements (e.g., "you are ugly" happen most often during recess and during group work in class. You begin to conduct an FBA (as described in Chapter 9) and find that rude comments and aggression occur most often on the playground when Michael and his friends approach equipment, such as the swing set, that is occupied by other students. He often pushes or shoves them and they run away, leaving Michael and his friends to play on the equipment. Michael's three friends spend lots of time rehashing his actions with him, which he seems to enjoy. In contrast, pushing and shoving in the classroom happens most during group activities. Michael reportedly likes to be in charge of groups, and when other students don't want to complete an activity in the way he has suggested, he often pushes them. When this occurs, other students tell Mr. Black, who responds by removing Michael from the group and having him work alone.

In this example, the same behaviors, pushing, shoving, and rude comments, seem to be triggered by different discriminative stimuli and maintained by different consequences in the two distinct routines in which they occur. On the playground, Michael's aggressive behavior seems to be evoked by occupied equipment and maintained by access to that equipment and possibly attention from his friends. In contrast, that same behavior during group work is evoked by peers not following Michael's lead and is maintained by escaping from group work situations. If the FBA had not been conducted within a routines analysis such that these two distinct routines were focused on separately, then this valuable information might not have been gathered. Without a routines analysis, FBAs usually involve simply asking what events usually seem to trigger the problem behavior (to which Mr. Black might respond, "Being around other students" because this certainly is the case in both situations). When asking about consequences, peer attention and access to preferred objects might be mentioned, as well as escape or avoidance of peers. As you can see, the result of an FBA without performing a routines analysis first can be quite confusing.

Across all methods of FBA, whether you are focused on an individual student (as detailed in Chapter 10) or a classroom system (described in Chapter 4), the results of the FBA are the same: a statement that is a "best guess" about what events seem to predict the problem (the antecedents) and what events maintain the problem (the reinforcing function). O'Neil et al. (1997) described the results of an FBA as a "hypothesis statement." Although they were applying the FBA logic only to individual students, this applies just as well to an FBA of a system, such as a classroom. When an FBA is completed you should be able to frame the

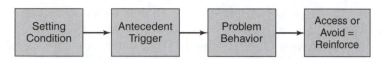

FIGURE 3.2   Behavior Pathway

results using the chart in Figure 3.2. This hypothesis statement format, first developed by O'Neil et al., allows for an easy display of the relation between problem behavior and events in the environment. Although hypothesis statements are concise, never they are derived from just one observation or recollection but instead summarize what most often occurs before and after the behavior.

Step 3: Developing a Hypothesis About the Function of Behavior

As we discussed in Chapter 2, the vast majority of behaviors fall into one of two categories: behaviors that are maintained by access to something (e.g., attention from a peer or an adult, access to an activity or object), and behaviors that are maintained by escape from or total avoidance of any of these same events. Once a hypothesis has been developed about the relation between the behavior, antecedents, and consequences, the next step is to figure out how the consequences function to reinforce the problem behavior—why does the behavior continue to occur? The following two examples show how the results of a hypothesis statement can be used to identify the function of the behavior. In the first example we focus on Kurt, an individual student. The second example details the FBA process in Mr. Lee's tenth-grade, second-period algebra class.

KURT.   Imagine you are the school counselor. Three teachers come to you with a request: They want Kurt to be removed from school so that he can access mental health services because he is "crazy." Hopefully, you would ask some questions before simply granting their request. Likely, you would at least want to know what Kurt is doing or why they think he is crazy, so we'll start there.

You:	Why do you think he's crazy? What is he doing?
Teacher #1:	He's weird! He does lots of weird things that are just plain bizarre and even scary. This kid needs to be in a hospital where some doctors can observe him and give him some help.
You:	Weird is a description, but it isn't a behavior. What exactly is he doing?
Teacher #2:	The other kids don't even want to be around him because he'll do odd things like eat stuff that's not food.
You:	Give me an example. What does weird look like for Kurt?
Teacher #3:	He has actually licked another person's spit off of the wall!
You:	C'mon, he didn't really do that.
All 3 Teachers in Unison:	Yes, he did. He even admits it.

It's going to be pretty hard to argue with that. Certainly this sounds like a pretty strange kid, and maybe a psychological assessment wouldn't be such a bad idea. But before we go to that extreme, what information are we missing? Is there anything that could make you think that his spit licking behavior isn't the result of insanity or mental illness? As we can see, a mere description of the behavior of concern (and indeed a definition of only one behavior out of possibly many odd behaviors), without a description of the antecedents and consequences, makes it very difficult to consider function. We then are quick to situate the problem within the student—as part of his personality or the result of mental illness. However, it's not too late to assess the environment. Let's pretend we were the proverbial fly on the wall during the spit licking episode and see what's going on in the environment while Kurt is around.

> During a transition break between classes, several middle school students converge in a restroom. Kurt stands near the sinks waiting for an open urinal and does not interact with any of the students. While most go about their business, two older and rather popular boys enter and stop near the sinks talking about a fight they observed the day before. Kurt moves to within a few feet of the boys. He listens to their description of the fight before speaking up and offering his opinion of the fight "Hey, that was great when John fell." The two boys ignore Kurt and continue their conversation. At the same time students continue to file in and out of the restroom hurriedly. The conversation continues between the boys, and Kurt, waiting for a natural pause, interjects, "Do you guys think they'll fight again tomorrow?" Again the boys ignore Kurt and continue to talk, albeit after a brief glance at Kurt and a subtle rolling of the eyes. At this time a smaller sixth-grade boy hurries into the restroom and walks past Kurt. Kurt grabs the boy and pushes him, saying "Who said you could use my restroom, geek?" The smaller boy is thrown off balance and bumps into one of the two popular boys, who grabs him and pushes him against the wall while the other boy says, "Here's what you get for messing with us" and spits at the boy. But the younger boy was moving quickly and eluded the spitting, causing the spittle to land harmlessly behind him and slowly ooze down the wall. Kurt steps in and says to all present, "Here's why you don't want to mess with me. I'm tough and I'm crazy!" He then licks the spit off the wall and turns to soak in the open-mouthed stares of amazement from those in attendance. Immediately the two popular boys approach Kurt and, as if in shock, stutter, "Did you really do that?" Kurt answers in the affirmative and the boys laugh in excitement at the sight they witnessed. They accompany him out of the restroom and walk down the hall at his side, laughing and telling all who pass about Kurt's spit licking. Many students approached Kurt that day and asked whether the story was true. To all, Kurt replied, "Yep; I told you, I'm crazy."

Of course, it is still possible that Kurt has some sort of mental illness, but now it seems at least equally likely that there might be a function to his behavior. We can look at how the environment and his behavior are connected by charting

Antecedents	Behaviors	Consequences
Students coming and going in restroom	Standing alone waiting—no interaction	None obvious
Two popular students enter and talk about a fight	Attempts to enter into conversation with a comment	Ignored
Two students continue conversation	Waits for opening and asks question	Ignored
Younger student approaches	Pushes younger student	Other two boys negatively interact with younger student
One boy spits at younger student	Licks the spit	Students give attention
Hallway—other students ask him about spitting	Acknowledges spitting—says he's crazy	Students give attention

FIGURE 3.3   ABC for Kurt

his behavior in terms of what was going on both before and after he behaved (see Figure 3.3). We call this type of assessment an ABC (antecedent-behavior-consequence). Notice that only Kurt's behavior goes into the Behaviors column, and that all behaviors are defined in concrete observable terms. Anything that is not Kurt's behavior may be listed in the Antecedents and Consequences columns. Once this is done, we can try to determine the discriminative stimuli and identify why Kurt's behavior continues.

Now let us look at what we have observed. We can say that Kurt has some appropriate behaviors because he approaches and attempts to enter a conversation with two popular boys in a very appropriate manner—even waiting for a pause before speaking. But we can see that these behaviors got him nowhere; he was just ignored. However, when Kurt engages in bullying or bizarre behavior, he gets engagement and then attention from the popular boys. These inappropriate behaviors tend to happen in the presence of the popular boys—they were not observed when the popular boys were not present. Of course, this is a very limited view, just one example, of Kurt's world. But if this is typical of his "weird" behavior, we might draw some preliminary conclusions about what is going on. First, it appears that the two popular boys are a discriminative stimulus for bizarre behavior. Remember, a discriminative stimulus makes it more likely that a behavior will occur because it signals that certain consequences are differentially available. For Kurt, the appearance of these popular boys signals that attention/interaction from high-status peers might be available. Second, attempting to converse in a "normal manner" tends to result in no attention, while bizarre behavior results in huge amounts of attention. Thus, the function of Kurt's behavior may be to get peer attention. If this is true, intervention will be much simpler and involve less people than if we were to assume that it is all a mental health issue. In this case, intervention must involve helping Kurt understand the social mores of the school (perhaps older students typically don't hang out with middle schoolers) and other social skills interventions. In addition, the school might supervise the bathroom more closely and could teach all students more appropriate responses to bullying (e.g., escort the bullied student away from the situation, find a teacher, etc.).

Conducting an FBA

Again, although conducting an FBA can be a very formal, intensive, and legally mandated process, here we use FBA in a simplified and realistic manner to develop effective classroom management plans. Table 3.1 summarizes the steps involved in using an FBA to consider a student's problem behavior. These steps, described only in very general terms here, will be presented in a much more detailed format later in Chapters 4 and 8.

Let us look now at the specific steps that were involved in our FBA with Kurt.

1. *What appropriate and inappropriate behaviors are observed?* First, we observed that Kurt did exhibit some appropriate behavior. Sure, the topic of the conversation may have been undesirable, but it was natural, and he did attempt to enter the conversation in an appropriate manner. We also observed Kurt pushing and threatening a student and engaging in the bizarre behavior of licking spit off the wall.

2. *What types of actions or events tend to precede instances of appropriate and inappropriate behavior?* Next, we noted that instances of both appropriate and inappropriate behavior tended to occur in the presence of two popular students. When these students were not present, Kurt simply waited quietly.

3. *What types of actions or events tend to follow instances of appropriate and inappropriate behavior?* Then we noted that Kurt was flatly ignored following appropriate behavior but was showered with much peer attention when he engaged in inappropriate behavior.

4. *What is a measurable statement of the relationship between behavior and the environment?* Finally, taking what we observed and noted in the first three steps we could say that Kurt tends to act in a bizarre manner by licking spit (among other things) when in the presence of particular peer groups because he gets lots of attention that is otherwise unavailable. Thus, the function of his problem behavior appears to be access to peer attention.

TABLE 3.1   The Basic Steps Involved in a Functional Behavior Assessment

Step	Task
Define Behaviors	Identify and define problem and appropriate behaviors in observable terms
Identify Antecedents	Determine the types of actions and events that tend to precede both appropriate and inappropriate behavior
Identify Consequences	Determine the types of actions and events that tend to follow both appropriate and inappropriate behavior
Hypothesize Function	Analyze the typical patterns of behavior and create a clear statement of what function the behavior serves for the student

Knowing that the function of Kurt's behavior is to access peer attention prescribes some particular components of an intervention. First, we know that any intervention that calls attention to Kurt in front of his peers likely will be reinforcing and thus ineffective, if not counterproductive. Second, we know that situations in which Kurt is unable to access any peer attention are likely to result in bizarre behavior on his part. Third, we can assume that peer attention in the absence of problem behavior would predict that problem behavior will not occur. Thus, intervention will need to focus on (1) creating instructional environments that provide Kurt with multiple opportunities to receive peer attention for positive behavior, (2) avoiding situations in which he will be ignored, (3) teaching him to recruit and maintain peer attention in an appropriate manner, and (4) minimizing the availability of peer attention in the case of problem behavior. Principles and procedures for each of these steps are highlighted below and will be presented in detail in later chapters.

SUMMARY: UNDERSTANDING BEHAVIOR THROUGH A FUNCTIONAL BEHAVIOR ASSESSMENT

In this chapter we provide a framework for understanding behavior by focusing on events outside the person that make it more or less likely that the behavior will occur. Identifying features of the environment that affect behavior is critical for developing effective interventions, and this is the purpose of a functional behavior assessment. A functional assessment identifies consequences that maintain behavior and events that precede behavior. Armed with this information we can develop an intervention consisting of any or all of the following strategies: (a) altering the setting to make it less likely the behavior will occur in the first place (e.g., by increasing supervision if the behavior usually occurs when few adults are around), (b) teaching new skills if the functional assessment reveals that the student or students might not know more appropriate ways to behave, (c) ensuring that the behavior we would like to see occur is reinforced, and (d) minimizing reinforcing consequences for problematic behavior. The remainder of this text focuses on how a functional behavior assessment can be used to gather this information and to develop an effective intervention. Section II focuses on the application of functional assessment to classroom systems, and Section III applies this logic to individual student behavior.

Chapter Review

- The concept of function describes the purpose that a behavior serves for an individual. In general, we assume that people behave either to obtain things they like or to escape/avoid things they do not like. We refer to this as the function of behavior and we attempt to understand how behaviors "function" to meet an individual's needs.

- Functional behavior assessment (FBA) is a process of assessing behavior in the context of the environment in which it exists to identify when it is likely to occur and what its purpose (function) is. The outcome of an FBA is information that is useful in developing an intervention plan.

- The key steps of a functional behavior assessment include clear definitions of behavior and conditions, identification of predictable antecedents and consequences that surround behavior as it occurs naturally, and development of an explanation as to how the behavior functions for the individual.
- Assessment as part of the FBA involves making naturalistic observations of behavior while recording all events that occur immediately before and after. This is referred to as an ABC (antecedent-behavior-consequence) assessment.
- Testable hypotheses of function are developed from observations and assessments. These hypotheses are stated in a testable manner and involve the hypothesized function of behavior. For example, the function of Fred's yelling is to access attention from students, or the function of Suzie's book throwing is to avoid math class.

Application

1. What would you say to someone who says that a student behaves because "that's just the way she is" or "he does it to gain control"?
2. The functional assessment can be time-consuming. How would you give a rationale for its use as an efficient strategy?

3. What are some other ways of describing the concept of function, say, if you were describing it to a novice?

Reference

O'Neill, R. E., Horner, R. H., Albin, R. W., Sprague, J. R., Storey, K., & Newton, J. S. (1997). *Functional assessment and program development for problem behavior: A practical handbook* (2nd ed.). Pacific Grove, CA: Brooks/Cole.

4

Measuring Behavior in the School

CHAPTER OBJECTIVES

After reading this chapter you should be able to describe the following concepts:

- Operational definitions of behavior
- Six dimensions by which behaviors may be defined
- A generic set of steps for developing a behavior monitoring process
- Critical differences between event-based and time-based measures
- Selection of appropriate measurement systems based on behavior
- Monitoring behavior across all students in the school

Why should we bother with collecting data—aren't success and failure generally obvious? As anyone with experience in schools will affirm, data collection is among the least favorite requirements of teaching. The reason likely is because behavioral assessment is perceived as time-consuming, laborious, and even scary in its complexity. Teachers seem to regard data collection as involving lab coats, safety goggles, and huge instruments carried around on a cart. In reality, data collection can be simple. Assessment is a part of teaching and, as such, should be seen as a regular part of the instructional process rather than an add-on. But besides the instructional value of assessment there are three other significant rationales for data collection. First, in a broad sense we use assessment information as a means of communicating about behavior. Without data on behavior, we would have no way of comparing our observations or to judge change. Second, we have discussed the premise that prediction is the first step to prevention. Collecting data on the occurrence of behaviors (who, what, when, where) allows us to develop interventions that are better tailored to prevent predictable problems. Third, assessment of behavior is the only mechanism we have for evaluating the effects of our interventions. As an analogy, consider medicine without assessment data. We would feel uncomfortable with medicine that "seems pretty good" or a treatment that a doctor "really likes." Empirical observation of student performance is the most effective manner we have for evaluating change and comparing interventions, students, or problems.

This chapter will define and describe the basics of behavioral assessment in the school and will present a range of examples. An understanding of some basic features of behavioral assessment will demonstrate that (1) there are a number of very simple and "teacher friendly" methods for collecting an array of student behavioral data and (2) the right data can actually make teaching more effective and efficient.

DEFINING BEHAVIOR

In order to be useful, data must be accurate. If we were to send a group out to count how many "tall" people were in a classroom, we probably would get a range of answers, depending on each person's definition of "tall." However, if we were to first define "tall" as "any person over six feet" then the data would be far more likely to be consistent across observers. Of course, the designation of six feet is arbitrary, but it provides us all with a definition, and we could certainly now determine whether future classes varied in the number of "tall" people (over six feet in height). The first step in any assessment endeavor is to create an operational definition of the behavior of interest. An operational definition is one that is (1) observable (perceptible by one of the senses (sight, sound, touch, feel, taste)) and (2) measurable (distinguishable in degree from other examples of the same behavior). For example, we would all say that we know what it means to be "lazy" and that we'd know it if we saw it. However, we are probably thinking only of the extreme, maybe someone lying on a couch and refusing to do any work. But unless this is the only definition of "lazy," we have no objective way of measuring how much lazier lying on a couch is than sitting in a chair. Perhaps both behaviors are considered lazy and can be observed, but without a definition that is more measurable, assessment would be difficult. However, if we were to define "lazy" as "not starting on assigned work within 5 minutes of a request," we could now judge not only whether the behavior occurred, but also the degree to which it changes over time.

Dimensions of Behavior

How we define behavior has huge implications for how we measure it. To begin, operational definitions should be developed in consideration of the most important features of the behavior, which we refer to as dimensions. In some cases we are concerned with how often a behavior occurs, while in other cases the length of time that a behavior lasts or the degree of forcefulness may be more important. Typically, we define behaviors by multiple dimensions, looking for behaviors that occur in a certain manner, at a certain time, and for a certain number of times. The following sections describe six different dimensions of behavior that can be used in creating an operational definition.

The first two dimensions of behavior, topography and locus, should be part of any definition of behavior. These dimensions define when and where we will be observing and what we are measuring.

TOPOGRAPHY (WHAT DID IT LOOK LIKE). The topography of a behavior simply refers to its observable properties and is the most important part of the definition. Defining topography involves describing in concrete terms exactly how one

TABLE 4.1   Topographical Definitions

Problem	Topographical Definition
Out of seat	Student's rear end is not touching the chair seat.
Talking out	Student makes comment without first being acknowledged by teacher.
Physically aggressive	Student strikes, pinches, or otherwise touches peer in a manner that would reasonably cause physical pain.

would know that the behavior had occurred. For adequate specificity, "hitting" might be defined as "striking another with a closed fist," and "off task" defined as "not engaged in an activity that has been verbally directed by the teacher." Each definition must be as broad or as narrow as necessary to accurately reflect the behavior of concern. Further examples of typical classroom problems and possible topographical definitions are presented in Table 4.1. Note that the last of these, physical aggressive, requires examples as part of the definition to avoid simply renaming one poorly defined term (aggressive) with another unobservable one (e.g., hurtful, thoughtless, hostile).

LOCUS (WHEN/WHERE DID IT HAPPEN).   The locus of a behavior indicates when and where it is to be observed and provides the observer with a context. For example, running is a topographical definition of a behavior that is likely to be considered inappropriate in the hallway but quite acceptable on the playground. Because it uses a locus as part of the definition, the phrase "running inside the school building" puts the behavior in context for observation. Locus might also include specific times (e.g., "during nap time") or conditions (e.g., "when in the classroom and given a direction").

The remaining three dimensions are focused on the behavior itself, and define the important aspects of the behavior. These dimensions by themselves, however, are meaningless when not attached to a topographical definition.

FREQUENCY (HOW MANY WERE THERE).   The most simple and obvious measure of a behavior is its frequency. Frequency counts reveal how often a behavior occurs or how many occurrences were observed. If the time period for observation is also recorded, a rate can be computed in the form "behavior occurred X times per (minute, hour, etc.)." Examples of frequency include the number of questions asked, the number of correct answers, and the number of sentences written per minute.

DURATION (HOW LONG DID IT LAST).   When measuring a length of time, duration needs to be a part of the definition. Duration can be considered in three different ways. First, we can measure the total amount of time engaged in a behavior (e.g., "student was out of seat for a total of 21 minutes during reading"). Second, we can measure the average duration of a behavior (e.g., "student tantrums have an average duration of 7 minutes"). Third, we can use a variation of duration recording called "latency," in which we measure the time between an antecedent event and a student behavior (e.g., "student took 4 minutes to respond to the teacher's direction to put materials away"). Duration recording requires a timepiece, and examples of techniques for duration recording are presented later in this chapter.

LATENCY (HOW LONG BEFORE IT HAPPENED).   Latency is a measure of the time it takes between some antecedent and the behavior. Latency recording is important for monitoring whether there is change in response time. For example, we may wish for a student to begin clean-up routine when we give a direction, but the student generally is very slow to follow the direction. We could record the length of time between the teacher's direction (antecedent) and the student's initiation of the clean-up routine. This length of time is referred to as the latency. Over time we could monitor to see whether an intervention was effective in decreasing the latency. Like duration recording, latency recording requires a timepiece, but the only recording required is of the antecedent and subsequent initiation of a response.

INTENSITY (HOW HARD WAS IT).   Intensity is a measure of the force with which a behavior is displayed. While intensity is probably the least common dimension used in operational definitions, it can be extremely important. For example, we may be interested in a topography such as talking in class, but only if the talking is disruptive. In such cases, we could define talking in terms of intensity by saying "student speaks loudly enough to be heard across the room." Observers then would record student talking only if it were heard from across the room. Other examples of intensity might include "hitting hard enough to leave a bruise" or "kicking shoes all the way out from under the desk."

MEASUREMENT PROCESS

Individually, the components of effective measurement are profoundly simple. As we've discussed, we simply want to know how often a behavior occurs under a certain set of conditions. But knowing what, when, and why to measure along with deciding who will measure and how become unwieldy and sometimes frustrating to school personnel when presented as a process. To simplify, the process of effective and efficient data collection can be presented as a series of step-by-step tasks.

Step 1: Determine What to Monitor

The first step in the measurement process is to determine what to monitor. Generally, a problem or question drives the need for assessment and points clearly to a behavior. For example, a teacher may determine that Jennifer is completing too little work during independent reading time because she spends too much time away from her desk. This problem leads directly to questions such as *How much time does Jennifer spend away from her desk during independent reading?* or *How much work does Jennifer complete during independent reading?* For every problem, the teacher must determine the most important question to be answered. Depending on which question is deemed most important, the teacher may choose either to measure the amount of time spent out of seat or the amount of work completed by Jennifer during independent reading. In either case, the problem provides the impetus for determining what behaviors are more relevant to measure.

Step 2: Determine the Simplest Way to Collect Data

A clear operational definition of behavior is crucial in determining the simplest method of assessment. The simpler the assessment method, the easier it will be for the teacher to use and the more accurate the data will be. But even simple methods will require teacher practice to gain fluency. In addition, data collection methods must be taught to all observers, allowing all to practice the system before it is put into place. An array of monitoring systems is presented later in this chapter.

Step 3: Monitor Behavior in a Consistent Manner

A clearly detailed locus in the operational definition provides the direction for when and where to collect data. If the locus describes independent reading time, then data collection is to occur only during independent reading time. While it is not necessary that data be collected during every time independent reading time, the more regularly and consistently a measurement system is used, the more accurate the data will be. Each episode of data collection should be completed using the same set of procedures and in the same manner—even when done across several different observers. Consistency is key to accuracy.

Step 4: Use Data to Evaluate and Make Decisions

Data should be summarized and recorded after each observation. If possible, data should be graphed or otherwise summarized in a format that allows a quick visual appraisal of trends (see Chapter 5). Goals set prior to intervention should be used as a criterion for evaluation. When data indicate that student behavior problems are not changing, a change in intervention is warranted. When data indicate that student behavior is changing in a sufficiently positive direction, intervention should be continued or gradually faded. The keys for each of these steps are presented in Table 4.2 and more information on these procedures is presented in Chapter 5.

TABLE 4.2   Steps in the Process of Measuring Behavior

Step	Task	Keys
1	Determine what to monitor	• Identify the observed problems • Identify the important questions • Determine what you want to know
2	Determine the simplest way to collect data	• Find the simplest way to collect data • Practice the data collection method • Teach the method to other observers
3	Monitor behavior in a consistent manner	• Monitor on a regular basis • Monitor in the same way each time • All observers use the same way
4	Use data to evaluate and make decisions	• Summarize and graph data • Evaluate against criteria for success • Make decisions based on outcomes

BEHAVIOR MONITORING METHODS

Because behaviors can be defined by a range of dimensions, a range of behavior monitoring methods have been developed to match. The goal is to find the simplest available method to match the behavior of concern. Generally, all monitoring methods can be divided into two broad classes. The first is known as event-based recording and includes most simple methods of counting behavior. The key feature of all event-based methods is that the observance of a behavior drives recording. That is, when a behavior does not occur, there is no need to record; but when a behavior does occur, even at very high rates, data must be recorded. The biggest advantage of event-based methods is the accuracy that accompanies such direct transfer of observations to data. However, the disadvantage is that these methods require essentially constant attention and can often be too cumbersome for teachers to use while teaching or performing other daily tasks. The second class is known as time-based recording. The key feature of all time-based methods is that the passage of time, and not behavior, drives recording. That is, when a timed interval passes, the observer records whether the behavior has occurred. Thus, although the behavior may occur repeatedly, there is no recording until a signal indicates the end of a recording interval. Obviously, time-based recording methods are not as accurate as event-based methods. However, time-based methods are much easier to use in classroom settings and under other circumstances where event-based systems are too burdensome. Still, each of the different event-based and time-based methods presents its own set of advantages and disadvantages, which will be discussed shortly. The task of the teacher is to find the best balance between accuracy and ease of use when monitoring any specific behavior.

With all monitoring methods, a clear operational definition is crucial to determine which is most appropriate and when and for how long observation should take place. In addition, the metric (unit of measure) used to summarize data varies by behavioral dimension and must be considered prior to implementation of assessment to facilitate converting raw data to a form that can be used for comparisons.

The following six methods are all event-based. Consequently, the occurrence of behavior is what drives recording. Each method results in a unique metric, the calculation of which will be described as part of the assessment process.

Event-Based Recording

FREQUENCY RECORDING.   *Staff are concerned that Jimmy is falling too much on the playground. Principal Meanie wants to know just how many falls Jimmy has when on the playground.* The problem identified here is Jimmy falling on the playground and the question is how many episodes occur in one day. Clearly, this issue calls for a count of falling episodes. Because the locus in the definition of behavior is the playground, we need to monitor behavior only when Jimmy is on the playground.

The simplest and most direct method of monitoring behavior is frequency recording. This method simply requires that the observer somehow record each instance of a behavior. The most familiar frequency count is probably the simple tally, a mark made to correspond with each observed instance of behavior (e.g., make a mark when Jimmy falls). When tallies are not feasible, a teacher may fill a pocket with paper clips and, whenever a target behavior occurs, move a paper clip to another pocket. At the end of an observation period, the student's behavior can be summarized by counting the total paper clips in the second pocket. As long as each instance of behavior is recorded in some manner, a frequency count can be obtained.

Variations.   Variation in the duration of the observation period can create problems for frequency recording because the number of occurrences is affected by the length of observation. However, the basic methodology of frequency recording can be slightly altered to account for this by adding notation of time to achieve a rate calculation for behavior. For example, if the faculty were to record the duration of playground observation of Jimmy (e.g., 20 minutes), that figure could be divided by the total number of instances of falls observed (e.g., 4) to get a rate of crying episodes per time interval (e.g., 20/4 = 5 episodes per recess; or 1 episode every 4 minutes; or 0.25 episodes per minute). Thus, if playground time were to vary between 10 and 25 minutes on a daily basis, data could still be compared as the rate creates a standardized metric.

Considerations.   Frequency recording requires both (1) a clear topographical definition of a behavior with an obvious beginning and ending and that (2) behaviors be of equal duration in order to provide accurate data. For example, suppose that a student is out of his seat one time for 2 hours total on one day and then out of his seat twice for a total of 2 minutes on the second day. A frequency count alone would produce data that would make day 1 look better than day 2 (1 out of seat versus 2 out of seat), but the reality would be that day 2 was a better day (2 minutes out of seat versus 2 hours out of seat). When behaviors are not of equal duration, duration recording or one of the time-based methods will be a more appropriate choice. A sample frequency recording instrument is presented in Figure 4.1.

PERMANENT PRODUCT.   *Jane has been doing worksheets on her own to gain accuracy with her addition skills. Ms. Blinder wants to monitor her accuracy on math worksheets but can't watch her continuously.* The identified problem is that Ms. Blinder needs to monitor Jane's performance with addition facts, and the question concerns Jane's accuracy. This issue could be approached with frequency recording, but

Frequency Recording		
Student: *Jimmy Jokes*	**Observer:** *Mr. Sanders*	**Date:** 10/12

Directions: Begin watching Jimmy when he arrives on the playground and continue observation throughout recess time. Each time that Jimmy is observed to fall to the ground (so that part of his body other than his feet is touching the ground), make a tally in the box below.

HHI

Total Frequency of Falling behavior today was ____5____

FIGURE 4.1   Frequency Recording Instrument

Ms. Blinder does not have time to watch Jane complete each problem. But Ms. Blinder can provide Jane with a worksheet each day, collect it when complete, and assess the accuracy of the problems completed. Permanent product recording is used when a behavior results in a product that can be saved and assessed at a later time. Because the locus in the definition of behavior identifies the math worksheet as the context for monitoring, we need only monitor behavior that occurs as part of the worksheet completion.

Variation.   Permanent product recording measures the effects or outcomes of a behavior with metrics such as percent correct, number completed, or (with time) rate of completion. Examples might include worksheets or problems completed, vandalism, bedwetting, or even bruises left. It is also possible to use video- or audiotape to create a permanent record of behavior from which to make observations later. This would be considered as a hybrid of permanent product and whatever other method is being used.

Considerations.   Though it does not require constant attention, permanent product is considered to be an event-based method of recording because the occurrence of behavior still drives recording (albeit after the fact). However, it does share with time-based recording the common disadvantage of lack of direct observation. That is, the behavior is inferred by a product and, in the absence of direct observation, we can't necessarily be certain of what produced the result. For example, Ms. Blinder may collect Jane's worksheet and record 100% completion. But Ms. Blinder probably did not see that Jake helped Jane during much of the lesson. Thus, not directly observing the behavior leaves us open to errors of measurement. To avoid such problems the observer must regularly observe the student being monitored, possibly even by looking over her shoulder to assess behavior more fully. Clearly, permanent product recording works only for behaviors that result in permanent and durable outcomes. Behaviors such as talk outs, out of seat, and on task have no such products and therefore are not appropriate for permanent product recording. An example of permanent product recording instrument is presented in Figure 4.2.

CONTROLLED PRESENTATION.   *Felicity has been shouting out answers to questions posed by Mr. Query during class discussions. Mr. Query has talked with Felicity and wants to monitor the number of times she raises her hand to answer his questions.* Felicity's problem has been identified as shouting out answers during class discussions. Mr. Query's question concerns the number of times that Felicity raises her hand when asked a question. The locus in this definition tells us that we must observe Felicity's behavior during class discussions, but only when the teacher asks her a question. Thus, Mr. Query must first engage in a behavior (i.e., pose a question) to provide Felicity an opportunity to be observed. The controlled presentation method is appropriate whenever a student's target behavior depends on some antecedent event. Consider Felicity's behavior under a couple of circumstances. On Monday, Mr. Query asks Felicity six questions, and she raises her hand and waits appropriately during four of those opportunities. Then, on Tuesday, Mr. Query asks Felicity 10 questions, and she raises her hand and waits appropriately during five of those opportunities. If we were to use a

---

Permanent Product Recording

Student: *Jane Hack*   **Date:** 11/2

Directions: Provide this worksheet to Jane and ask her to complete it. Set a watch for 5 minutes and come back to pick up the worksheet at the end of that interval.

10 + 8 18	9 + 5 ✓ 12	4 + 7 11	2 + 3 5	12 + 1 13
11 + 4 15	6 + 7 13	1 + 8 9	9 + 3 12	12 + 7 ✓ 12

Total problems finished correctly   *8*

Accuracy of problems completed   *8/9 = 89%*

Rate of problems completed correctly

Number of problems completed correctly/5 minutes = *1.6 problems per minute*

FIGURE 4.2   Sample Permanent Product Recording Instrument

simple frequency count we would say that Tuesday was a better day than Monday for Felicity (five hand raises versus four hand raises). However, because she had many more opportunities on Tuesday, her percentage of appropriate responses was actually better on Monday (4 of 6 = 67% versus 5 of 10 = 50%). The metric for a controlled presentation recording will always be percent of opportunities and stated as "the percent of opportunities for a behavior to occur in which that behavior was performed correctly."

Variations.   While the antecedent for student behavior has been discussed here as something that is controlled by the teacher, many other antecedents in the environment may control student behaviors. For example, we may record a student's response to being teased by a peer; in that case, we could record only when and if peer teasing first occurred. Other uses might include recording following teacher directions, appropriate line-up behavior over a week of line-up opportunities, or appropriate responses when greeted by others.

Considerations.   The advantage of a controlled presentation recording is simply that it allows the observer to account for varying opportunities. If the number of opportunities for behavior were always the same, a frequency count would provide the same data. But if the teacher controls the antecedent, such as when Felicity answers Mr. Query's questions, Mr. Query has the added advantage of choosing exactly when he wants to collect data. That is, he knows that his questioning behavior creates the opportunity for her behavior; thus, he controls when he will collect data. If the teacher does not control behavior, however, observation is continuous because the teacher watches for the antecedent first and then for the student's response. Although constant attention is required, controlled presentation is often the only method of accurately recording behaviors that occur only in response to antecedents. A sample controlled presentation instrument is presented in Figure 4.3.

Controlled Presentation Recording

Student: *Felicity Flick* **Observer:** *Mr. Query* **Date:** 1/19

Directions: During class discussions, whenever the teacher asks a question the observer should place a circle in the box below–indicating an opportunity has been presented. Each time that Felicity raises her hand, place a slash through the circle to indicate that Felicity engaged in appropriate behavior. If Felicity yells out her response or does nothing at all do nothing with the circle to indicate no appropriate behavior.

Total number of opportunities (teacher questions) *5*

Total number of appropriate responses (hand raises) *3*

Percent of opportunities in which appropriate behavior occurred *60%*

FIGURE 4.3 Sample Controlled Presentation Recording Instrument

TRIALS TO CRITERION. *Ms. Flunk is trying to get Rupert to do a better job of reciting his multiplication tables. He generally will reach his criterion of 100%, but only after several trials. Ms. Flunk wants him to require fewer trials before reaching 100%.* The identified problem is that Rupert is taking too many trials to reach 100% on his multiplication tables. The question then is what that number of trials is and whether it is changing. Trials to criterion recording is appropriate whenever we wish to record the number of attempts needed to complete a behavior to some predetermined criterion. The locus in the definition tells us that we need to observe the student only when he is engaged in trials with multiplication tables.

Variation. This is most appropriate for use with instructional interventions—both academic and social—and the metric is stated as the number of trials to reach the criterion. For example, we may wish to assess the effects of social skills instruction by recording the number of trials a student needs to demonstrate a multicomponent behavior to a 90% criterion. We would teach a student to engage in a three-step greeting procedure and then provide opportunities for practice. We could then record the number of trials the student needs to use all three steps appropriately to greet a peer in a role-play situation. In this case, our criterion is 100% of the three steps, and we may count 4 trials to meet that criterion on the first day of practice. Future observation would be compared to this number to evaluate the success of the training procedure. Other application might include the number of trials to hit ten 15-foot putts with 80% accuracy.

Considerations. Trials to criterion recording fits nicely into instructional designs as a measure of acquisition or fluency. The observer (teacher) must define an acceptable criterion for performance and then count the number of trials to criterion. Although it requires constant attention, the method is clearly tied to an instructional model in which the teacher is already providing direct attention to the student. The main disadvantage of this approach is that it is applicable only under limited circumstances. A sample trials to criterion recording instrument is presented in Table 4.3.

TABLE 4.3   Sample Trials to Criterion Recording Instrument

Trials to Criterion Recording

Student: *Rupert Rucker*   **Observer:** *Ms. Flunk*   **Starting Date:** 5/22

Directions: Each day present Rupert with a set of 10 flash cards covering multiplication facts for a number 1-10. For each trial write Ruupert's percent correct. Continue this for 10 trials or until Rupert meets the criteria correct in one trial.

Fact Number 4   Criteria = 100%

Trial	Day 1 5/22	2 5/23	3 5/24	4 5/25	5 5/26	6	7	8
1	80	80	90	90	100	100		
2	80	90	90	100				
3	90	90	100					
4	90	100						
5	90							
6	100							
7								
8								

Trials to Criteria Day 1____6____   Trials to Criteria Day 5____1____

Trials to Criteria Day 2____4____   Trials to Criteria Day 6____1____

Trials to Criteria Day 3____3____   Trials to Criteria Day 7____—____

Trials to Criteria Day 4____2____   Trials to Criteria Day 8____—____

DURATION RECORDING.   *Mr. Sedoun wants Tamara to stay in her seat, but she often wanders the room for various reasons and various amounts of time. He feels that she is missing too much instructional time and wants to assess just how much time is lost to this behavior.* The problem noted is that Tamara is often out of her seat during instructional times, and the question concerns the total amount of time that she actually spends engaged in out-of-seat behavior. We should first note that this behavior is of unequal duration—sometimes brief and at other times lengthy. Thus, frequency recording will not be appropriate. Second, because an antecedent does not seem necessary to create an opportunity for the behavior, controlled presentation recording is not appropriate. Duration recording is used when we wish to record the amount of time that a student spends engaged in a behavior. The metric for duration is always reported in intervals of time (i.e., seconds, minutes, hours, etc.) and can be reported as a total or an average per episode. Examples of duration recording include the amount of time that a student spends engaged with a task, in time-out, or working on a problem.

Variations.   The most common method of duration recording is cumulative, or summarizing the total amount of time that the student was observed to engage in the behavior. To use cumulative duration recording, the observer simply starts a stopwatch every time the behavior begins and stops the watch when the behavior ends. This process is repeated until the end of the observation period, at which point the total elapsed time on the watch is recorded. A variation of this process provides an average of the time elapsed during each episode. To use average duration recording, the observer simply starts a stopwatch every time the behavior begins and ends—the same as was with cumulative duration recording. However, average duration recording requires the observer to record the time on the watch and then reset the watch after each episode of behavior. At the end of the observation period, the observer adds the durations of all the individual episodes and divides by the total number of episodes to get an average.

Considerations.   Both cumulative and average duration methods have the same advantage: They provide a direct and accurate metric for episodic or high-rate behaviors of unequal duration. Of course, duration recording requires constant attention by the observer and the use of a stopwatch or a similar timing device. Thus, this method of recording can be rather burdensome. Duration recording should be considered only when the teacher has sufficient time to complete all the steps. When time is of the essence, time-based recording probably offers more realistic methods, albeit with less accuracy. A sample duration recording instrument is presented in Figure 4.4.

Duration Recording

Student: *Tamara Tandy*   **Observer:** *Mr. Sedoun*   **Date:** *3/16*

Directions: Each day during instructional time in the classroom, observe Tamara for times when she is not sitting at her desk (rear-end touching chair seat). When this occurs, start the stopwatch that you will keep on a string around your neck. When Tarama sits down, stop the watch and write the elapsed time on the chart below. Reset the watch and continue this process until instructional time is over.

Episode	Time out of seat		Episode	Time out of seat
1	1 : 25		11	
2	4 : 35		12	
3	6 : 05		13	
4	: 10		14	
5	2 : 50		15	
6	5 : 20		16	
7	3 : 35		17	
8			18	
9			19	
10			20	

Total number of episodes of out of seat behavior (x) _7_

Total amount of time engaged in out of seat behavior (y) _24 minutes_

Average amount of out of seat behavior per episode (y/x) _3.42 minutes_

FIGURE 4.4   Sample Duration Recording Instrument

LATENCY RECORDING.   *The entire class is aware that one paragraph in the writing journal is the first expectation of the day—and Tommy is often the last one to finish. Ms. Patton is concerned that Tommy is taking far too long to begin his morning journal writing once he sits down. She wants to know how much time he spends engaged in behaviors other than writing after he takes his seat.* The identified problem is Tommy's failure to get started on his writing, which causes him to finish late. The question presented by Ms. Patton is how long Tommy generally takes to get started on his work once he is seated. Ms. Patton wants to know about a duration of sorts—how long Tommy is not engaged in a behavior. Latency recording is used when we wish to know the length of time between an antecedent and a behavior. Like controlled presentation, the student can be monitored only after an opportunity has been presented. In this case, the locus in the definition of the problem tells us that data need only be collected in the morning, and then only after Tommy sits down. Latency recording is very similar to duration recording except that the watch is started when the antecedent occurs and is stopped when the student engages in the behavior. We are not concerned with the length of the behavior, only with how long it took to begin. This method is most appropriate for recording how quickly students respond to antecedents such as teacher directions, signals such as bells or warning buzzers, prompts from peers, or even verbal or physical reminders from the teacher.

Considerations.   Latency recording has limited application but is very well suited to stimulus-response type contexts. As long as the typical latency duration is not excessively long, the constant attention required by the observer can be minimized. When antecedent conditions are frequent or when latencies are quite long, however, time-based recording methods likely are advantageous. A sample latency recording instrument is presented in Figure 4.5.

Time-Based Recording

The following three methods are examples of time-based recording. As such, the passage of a set period of time will drive recording. Although the three methods are very similar in process, each offers distinct advantages and is most appropriate under specific circumstances. Recall that time-based measures require the constant use of a timer, provide only an approximation of behavior, and are not as accurate as event-based methods. On the positive side, time-based methods generally require less teacher time and can account for behaviors of variable duration. Researchers generally like to use time-based recording measures because they are easy to develop, teach, and use. In addition, time-based recording allows for simplified recording of multiple students or multiple behaviors at one time.

Time-based recording involves breaking an observation period into smaller time intervals. At the end of each interval the observer records whether the behavior occurred. As a general rule, longer intervals are easier to use; that is, it is easier to record whether a behavior occurs at intervals of 5 minutes than to record the same every 10 seconds. As the interval increases in size, however, the accuracy of the data decreases. Thus, observers need to find the appropriate interval size by balancing shorter intervals for accuracy and longer intervals

Latency Recording

Student: *Tommy Trapp*   Observer: *Ms. Patton*   Start Date: *9/14*

Directions: Each morning when Tommy enters the classroom watch for him to be seated at his desk. As soon as he is seated, start a stopwatch and continue it running until he begins writing in his journal. Record the total elapsed time between being seated and journal writing for each school day.

Day	Elapsed time
1	3:25
2	3:35
3	8:05
4	3:10
5	6:50
6	8:20
7	5:35
8	6:00
9	2:11
10	4:49

Average latency for Tommy's journal writing = (total duration/number of observations)
52 minutes/10 days = average latency of 5.2 minutes

FIGURE 4.5   Sample Latency Recording Instrument

for feasibility. The metric with all time-based methods relates the percentage of intervals in which the behavior was observed and is expressed as X% of intervals. This metric is important because it denotes the estimate. It does not say that a behavior happened 0, 50, or 100 percent of the *time*—it says that it occurred during a given percent of the intervals that were observed. Percent of time can be generated only from duration recording.

PARTIAL INTERVAL RECORDING.   *Ms. Blunt observes occasional and unexpected tantrum (yelling and screaming) episodes of varying duration from Toby throughout the day. She is concerned about the amount of time he spends engaged in this behavior, but doesn't have time to use duration recording.* The problem of note is Toby's tantrum behavior, and the question is how much of his day is spent engaging in tantrums. It seems clear that the behavior is a duration issue because the episodes are of unequal duration and occur at various times that are neither predictable nor expected. Ms. Blunt has said, however, that she does not have time to use a duration instrument. Partial interval recording is used when behaviors occur occasionally or at a low rate and event-based methods are inappropriate or not feasible. In partial interval recording, the observer records a positive occurrence if the behavior occurred at any time during the interval. For example, if the interval is 5 minutes in length and the behavior occurred during the first 5 seconds, the observer records a positive occurrence at the end of the interval.

Considerations.   Because the partial interval method records a positive occurrence even if the behavior occurred only once during an interval, it is likely to overestimate the occurrence of behavior. For this reason, partial interval recording is indicated with behaviors that occur at a low frequency or rate. For example, if we were to use partial interval recording to monitor a student's talk-out behavior, and the student typically talked out on a very frequent basis, we would generally see results in the 95%–100% of intervals range, which tells very little and provides very little sensitivity to change in rate. Overestimation problems are minimized as the length of the interval is decreased. Obviously, using 1-second intervals would ensure quite accurate data from a time-based system. But recording while also observing once per second is not feasible, which negates one of the largest advantages of time-based recording. A rule of thumb is to make the interval lengths shorter than the highest number of behaviors observed during an observation period divided into the total amount of time observed. Thus, if a student has been observed to engage in as many as 25 tantrums in a 5-hour (300 minutes) school day, interval lengths should be set to no longer than 12 minutes (300 minutes/25 tantrums = 12-minute interval lengths). A sample partial interval recording instrument is presented in Figure 4.6.

WHOLE INTERVAL RECORDING.   *Mr. Fripp notices frequent pouting behavior from Larry in which he sits with his head down and refuses to make eye contact or speak. These episodes vary in length and have been occurring with increasing frequency throughout the day. Mr. Fripp does not have time to constantly monitor Larry, although he often observes pouting behavior when he does look at him.* The problem here is pouting behavior from Larry, which has been topographically defined as putting his head down and refusing to communicate. The question is how much pouting behavior Larry is exhibiting. The teacher's description shows that this is a duration

---

Partial Interval Recording

Student: *Toby Tapp*   **Observer:** *Ms. Blurt*   **Date:** *10/30*

Directions: Set a vibrating timer to signal at 12 minute intervals throughout the day. Begin the timer when Toby enters the room in the morning and continue until he leaves at the end of the day. Each time the timer vibrates to signal the end of an interval, mark through a + if he engaged in tantrum behavior at any time since the last signal or a 0 if he has not.

+	0	+	0	+	0	+	0	+	0
+	0	+	0	+	0	+	0	+	0
+	0	+	0	+	0	+	0	+	0
+	0	+	0	+	0	+	0	+	0
+	0	+	0	+	0	+	0	+	0
+	0	+	0	+	0	+	0	+	0

Total number of intervals observed (x) __30__

Total number of + observations (y) __11__

Percent of intervals in which tantrumb behavior occurred (y/x) *36.6% of intervals*

FIGURE 4.6 Sample Partial Interval Recording Instrument

issue because the behavior occurs for variable durations and does not depend on any noted antecedent. Larry's behavior is frequent, however, and sometimes continues for long durations, so partial interval recording would tend to greatly overestimate its occurrence. Whole interval recording is appropriate when behaviors are of high rate and duration but event-based methods are inappropriate or not feasible. In whole interval recording, a positive occurrence is recorded only if the behavior occurred for the *entire interval*.

Considerations.   Because whole interval recording requires that a positive occurrence be noted only if observed during the entire interval, it tends to under-estimate behavior. For example, a student engages in a behavior on and off again throughout the entire interval, but the observer cannot note a positive occur-rence because the behavior did not occur consistently. But if the behavior is of long duration, whole interval recording will give the best picture with the least effort. As with all time-based methods, the smaller the interval, the more accu-rate the data is likely to be. Because of its tendency to underestimate behavior and its ease of use, whole interval sizes should be set near the length of the short-est observed occurrences of the behavior. The observer must realize that any behaviors less than that length will be considered to be nonoccurrences. If the behavior is sporadic rather than of long duration, then momentary interval recording provides a better option. A sample whole interval recording instru-ment is presented in Figure 4.7.

MOMENTARY INTERVAL RECORDING.   *Ms. Flutter is concerned with Amy's finger-snapping behavior, which has been occurring so often that it disrupts the class. She tried counting finger-snaps, but they occurred so frequently and quickly that she was unable to keep count. She would like to measure the amount of time she engages in this behavior, but using a timer also has been difficult because the behavior starts and stops constantly.*

Whole Interval Recording

Student: *Larry Lare*   **Observer:** *Ms. Fripp*   **Date:** 12/6

Directions: Set a vibrating timer to signal at 12 minute intervals throughout the day. Begin the timer when Larry enters the room in the morning and continue until he leaves at the end of the day. Each time the timer vibrates to signal the end of an interval, mark through a + if he engaged in pouting behavior throughout that entire interval or a 0 if this behavior did not occur during the entire interval.

+ 0	+ 0	+/ 0	+ 0	+ 0
+ 0	+ 0	+ 0	+ 0	+ 0
+ 0	+ 0	+ 0	+ 0	+ 0
+ 0	+ 0	+ 0	+ 0	+ 0
+ 0	+ 0	+ 0	+ 0	+ 0
+ 0	+ 0	+ 0	+ 0	+ 0

Total number of intervals observed (x) __30__

Total number of + observations (y) __15__

Percent of intervals in which tantrum behavior occurred (y/x) *50% of intervals*

FIGURE 4.7   Sample Whole Interval Recording Instrument

The problem here is finger-snapping behavior from Amy. The question is how much finger-snapping behavior Amy is engaging in. The teacher's description shows that this is a duration issue, but the high rate and sporadic nature of the behavior have made it difficult to count or time. Clearly, partial interval recording would tend to greatly overestimate its occurrence and, because it is sporadic with quick starts and stops, whole interval recording would tend to greatly underestimate. Momentary interval recording is appropriate when behaviors occur sporadically at high rates, when event-based recording methods are inappropriate or not feasible, and when the observer has precious little time to observe. In momentary interval recording, the end of an interval signals the observer to observe the student and record whether the student is engaging in the behavior *at that moment*.

Considerations.   Because momentary interval recording requires that a positive occurrence be noted only if observed at the end of each interval, it will tend to underestimate behavior. For example, suppose that a student exhibits a target behavior throughout the entire interval, which is observed by the teacher; then the interval ends and, when the teacher looks at the student at that moment, the target behavior is absent. The teacher must record a nonoccurrence of the behavior for that interval because the behavior was not occurring at that *moment*. But if the behavior is of a high rate or long duration on average over time, the momentary system will tend to capture a more accurate picture. Again, the smaller the interval is, the more accurate the data is likely to be. Because of this method's tendency to underestimate behavior and its ease of use, momentary interval sizes should be set smaller. The observer should consider the baseline rate of behavior and develop an interval size that can capture both occurrences and nonoccurrences of the behavior. A sample momentary interval recording instrument is presented in Figure 4.8.

Momentary Interval Recording

Student: *Amy Anderson*   **Observer:** *Ms. Flutter*   **Date:** 12/6

Directions: Set a vibrating timer to signal at 12 minute intervals throughout the day. Begin the timer when Amy enters the room in the morning and continue until she leaves at the end of the day. Each time the timer vibrates to signal the end of an interval, look over at Amy and mark through a + if she engaged in finger-snapping at that very moment or a 0 if this behavior is not occurring.

+	0	+	0	+	0	+	0	+	0
+	0	+	0	+	0	+	0	+	0
+	0	+	0	+	0	+	0	+	0
+	0	+	0	+	0	+	0	+	0
+	0	+	0	+	0	+	0	+	0

Total number of intervals observed (x) _30_

Total number of + observations (y) _13_

Percent of intervals in which tantrum behavior occurred (y/x) _43.3% of intervals_

FIGURE 4.8 Sample Momentary Interval Recording Instrument

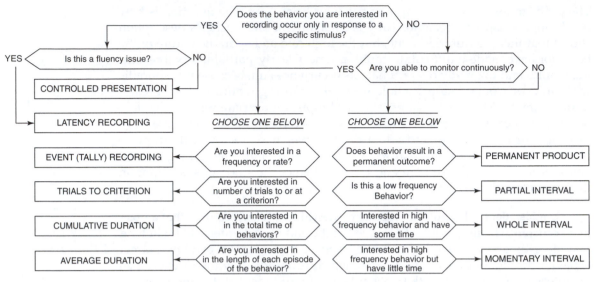

FIGURE 4.9

Decision Model

Figure 4.9 is a flow chart for determining the most appropriate recording method.

Data is as important at the schoolwide or classroom level as it is for individual students. The decisions we make for rules, routines, and arrangements are programming and intervention decisions that must be both predicated on and evaluated by data. As discussed earlier, in school, the best predictor of when, where, and under what conditions problem behavior will occur in the future is the history of when, where, and under what conditions it occurred in the past (Scott, 2004). When available, event-based data in the school or classroom provide the simplest method of evaluating the predictors of past problem behaviors. Many schools summarize data on behavior problems, collecting data on office referrals or other behavioral incidents. This information can be used as a basis for deciding where and when prevention strategies are needed. If these referrals contain detailed information regarding observances of behavior, prediction and prevention efforts can be specifically tailored.

An effective referral form includes all the information of interest, documented in as simple a manner as possible. Generally, this means using checkboxes rather than open-ended questions, detailing who, what, when, and where for every observed problem. This level of information is critical to the development of effective prevention strategies. For example, if referral data indicate that problems frequently occur in the cafeteria, a logical prevention strategy may be to reteach rules or improve supervision in the cafeteria. Continuous cafeteria monitoring will answer questions regarding the effectiveness of these responses. But if referrals supply additional information, we also can plan responses around when cafeteria behavior problems occur, what the behaviors are, and who is engaging in these behaviors. The use of event-based school or classroom data can facilitate strategic planning to create more effective and more efficiently delivered procedures.

Woodlawn Elementary School **Report/Referral Form**	**Teacher Response** __redirection __physical proximity __warning	__loss of privilege __parent contact date_____
Time_____ Date _____ Grade_____	__time-out in class __detention	__buddy room __parent conference
Student(s) Involved_____	__community service __private conference	date_____
Reporting Staff Person_____	__other_____	

Incident

__homework (repeatedly)   __offensive language/gesture
__tardy   __intimidation
__defiance   __physical aggression/fighting
__disruptive behavior   __insubordination
__other   __property damage

Administrative Response
__private conference   __alternative placement
__time-out   __detention
__loss of privilege   __parent conference
__suspension   __community service

Location

__hallway   __outside dismissal/arrival
__playground   __restroom (caf., add., 6th, 2nd)
__room #____   __cafeteria

Comments

Administrative Signature_____

FIGURE 4.10   Sample Referral Form

The content and complexity of an event-based behavior referral form depends on the types and amount of information desired. That is, a school that wishes to assess the predictability of problem behaviors by time and location must include this information on the data collection form. Similarly, a school that is interested in determining whether staff respond differently to the problem behaviors of special versus general education students must include information regarding student characteristics and outcomes on the form. Each school must develop its own data collection form to answer its own unique questions and fit its own unique needs. Typically, data forms that are small, portable, and formatted as a checklist are the easiest to use and promote the greatest level of staff consistency in use. A sample referral form is presented in Figure 4.10.

A simple method of summarizing data is to display it on a spreadsheet. To accomplish this, a school might design a procedure in which all referrals are placed into a box in the office. Each Friday, an office worker can transfer data from the forms onto the spreadsheet, generating a weekly summary of all behavior problems. Figure 4.11 is an example of a weekly referral summary. Note that the information summarized for Flanders Elementary allows school staff quickly to see who had problems, what those problems were, where they occurred, and who observed them. Additional characterizing information (e.g., educational placement, student gender, or minority status) also can be collected and summarized as necessary to answer school questions. In Flanders Elementary, the staff might determine from their analysis of weekly data summaries that behavior problems are predictable in the cafeteria during the lunch hour. Additionally, it appears that Tim Edwards is having multiple problems, and defiance seems to be a common problem. Collecting and summarizing this information is the first

Student	Date	Time	Location	Problem	Referred By
Tilly, Matt	10-1	10:15	Playground	Fight	Mr. Hanson
Edwards, Tim	10-2	12:10	Cafeteria	Defiance	Ms. Foster
Ott, Shiela	10-3	9:30	Hallway	Running	Mr. Randall
Franks, Bob	10-5	10:10	Playground	Defiance	Ms. Stone
Edwards, Tim	10-5	10:20	Playground	Defiance	Ms. Stone

FIGURE 4.11   Flanders Elementary—Office Referral Summary October 1–5

step in schoolwide decision making. The data direct staff to where more information should be gathered. For instance, the data from Flanders Elementary suggest that Mr. Hanson and Ms. Stone should be asked about the exact nature of problems on the playground and what they see as potential solutions. Furthermore, staff likely would want to look further into the defiance problem. Appropriate questions to ask about Tim include, "What seems to predict his behavior problems?" and "Which teachers are most likely to have more in-depth information?" The staff at Flanders Elementary would continue to collect data and summarize it weekly throughout the year, while at the same time they would analyze the entire database for emerging trends across months.

While data collection and analysis across the school is the most effective and efficient way to identify the predictors of behavioral failure, many schools neither collect nor routinely summarize data in a manner that provides the information necessary for designing effective prevention systems. In such cases, the next best strategy is to survey the school staff to identify the problem behaviors they see most often in the school, as well as when and where they observe them (Scott, 2004). This process is time-consuming, but it does offer the advantage of engaging all staff and encouraging their input regarding the problem behaviors to which they most often respond. This staff engagement also may encourage them to be more involved in the process of developing strategies to prevent these predictable problems. These issues will be further discussed in Chapter 6 in the context of a classwide FBA.

Chapter Review

- Behaviors are operationally defined when they are described in an observable and measureable manner.
- Six dimensions by which behaviors may be defined include topography (what it looks like), frequency (how often it occurs), duration (how long it lasts), locus (conditions under which it occurs), latency (time between event and behavior), and intensity (amount of force).

- The behavior monitoring process involves identifying a target behavior, determining the simplest way to collect the data, monitoring in a consistent manner, and using data to make evaluative decisions.
- Event-based measures record the occurrence of a specific event at the time it occurs, while time-based measures record whether a behavior occurred during a specified period of time.

- Selection of an appropriate measurement instrument depends on both the nature of the behavior and what is realistic for the data collector.

- Office discipline referrals can provide information on behaviors, times, and locations to be used in monitoring student behaviors across the entire school.

Application

1. Describe when time-based measures would be preferred over event-based measures.
2. Give a good rationale for using operational definitions rather than broad categorical labels.
3. Consider how you might develop a system for monitoring student behaviors across an elementary school. Would it be different if it were developed for a middle or high school?

5

Using Data to Make Instructional Decisions

CHAPTER OBJECTIVES
After reading this chapter, you should be able to describe the following concepts:
- Task analysis procedures to lead instructional planning
- Critical differences between temporal, response difficulty, and criterion task analyses
- Differences among goal statements and both long-term and short-term objectives
- The essential components of instructional objectives
- A process for writing instructional objectives
- The key components of graphs for visual representation of performance
- How to plot and use both aim and trend lines to analyze data
- Using data to make instructional decisions

In the previous chapter we discussed various methods for monitoring student behavior in the classroom setting. Initial monitoring gives us a measure of the student's current level of functioning, which serves as a baseline from which to evaluate change. But decisions remain as to what behaviors are of most importance, where to begin data collection, what the appropriate expectations should be, how to determine whether change is significant, and how to piece all this together in a simple way.

Appropriate behavior is dictated by what is appropriate in the natural environment (i.e., what other successful students do) and the values of significant others in the environment (e.g., parents, teachers, peers). Problem behaviors are those that inhibit or interfere with success. While some students have only one easily identified behavior problem, others may have multiple problems or an array of issues that are of concern. As a general rule, the most immediate concern is with identifying the behaviors that most inhibit student success and with teaching students appropriate alternatives as defined by the environment. But where to begin instruction, how instruction is to be delivered, and the goals of instruction are uniquely the teacher's decision. For example, all in the environment may agree that a student's mastery of algebra is a priority; but the teacher's role is to determine the priority of skills that must be taught, the most appropriate methods for teaching those skills, the scope and sequence required to meet an identified end goal, and how the student's progress will be evaluated. The development of individualized teaching plans and evaluations is the focus of this chapter.

SCOPE AND SEQUENCE: WHAT SHOULD BE TAUGHT FIRST, SECOND, AND SO ON?

Determining the goals for instruction provides the teacher with a clear picture of the required student behaviors. For example, the skill of long division necessarily requires mastery of basic math skills including place value, addition, and multiplication. If the student does not possess the component skills, instruction will not be successful. Even the simplest of skills involve prerequisites. Saying "Hello" requires an ability to understand English, to recognize a time to greet, and so on. The teacher must consider the full array of required behaviors and then break instruction into teachable components. If every skill is conceived of as existing in a continuum of component skills, instruction should begin one step above the highest mastered skill on the list. For example, if a student has mastered place value and addition but not multiplication, then instruction for long division must begin by teaching multiplication.

The process of considering the requisite component skills for a complex behavior is known as *task analysis*. The term task analysis refers to both the process of breaking down a complex behavior (verb) and the resulting product (noun). Generally, if a teacher is familiar with the behavior to be taught, task analysis is simply considering all that is involved in the behavior. Thus, effective teaching requires the teacher to have a fairly deep understanding of the skill to be taught. Task analysis is an important step in the teaching process because it provides a map of the skill being taught, making sure that each component and prerequisite skill is taught.

Performing a Task Analysis: How Is It Done?

As we'll see in this chapter, a completed task analysis outlines the individual steps for instruction and provides an objective measure for where instruction should begin and end. In short, the task analysis provides a roadmap for delivery and measurement of instruction. A task analysis can be conducted in three distinct ways, each of which provides the teacher with a focus for instruction. The first and most common type of task analysis is temporal, or breaking a behavior into a set of discrete steps (e.g., step 1, step 2, step 3, etc.) sequenced through time. To perform a temporal task analysis the teacher must have sufficient knowledge of the skill so as identify the component steps, determine their correct sequence, and then teach each in order. Obvious examples of a temporal task analysis include getting dressed (underwear must precede pants, socks must precede shoes), washing hair (wet hair, apply lather, and rinse must occur in the correct order), and classroom routines (hang up coat, sit at desk, get out language

TABLE 5.1   Temporal Task Analysis: Anger Control

Step	
1	Identify signs of anger or frustration
2	Stop
3	Select a replacement
4	Follow through with strategy
5	Self-assess

workbook). Temporal task analyses are useful in teaching students to perform a series of steps and are often paired with self-management tools that help the student keep track of their progress. Chaining procedures (see Chapter 10) are also especially useful with temporal task analysis. An example of a temporal task analysis for a behavior plan is presented in Table 5.1. Note that each step is a prerequisite for the following step in this example.

The response difficulty task analysis is the second method of deconstructing a complex skill. It involves sequencing steps in the order of their difficulty in terms of learning and mastery. The idea is that mastery of a relatively simple step will provide the necessary success to motivate the student to perform the following, more difficult step. In contrast with the temporal task analysis, which may be accomplished via a simple viewing of the behavior, response difficulty task analysis requires more in-depth knowledge of the behavior. The response difficulty task analysis is most common in academic learning examples where temporal steps do not always provide a logical manner of teaching. For example, long division may be considered temporally as including the following steps: divide, multiply, subtract, and bring down (i.e., place value). But to teach in this order would mean teaching division first and place value last, which is obviously illogical. A response difficulty task analysis would identify place value as the first component, followed by subtraction, multiplication, and then division. Clearly, this is the manner in which math is taught. Figures 5.1 and 5.2 show the

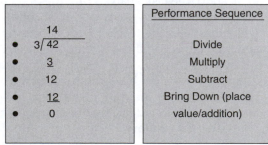

Response Difficulty Task Analysis
Teach the least difficult step, then the next least difficult, etc.
How long division is *performed*

FIGURE 5.1   How Long Division Is Performed: Temporal Sequence

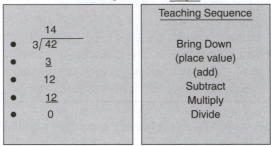

FIGURE 5.2   How Long Division Is Taught: Response Difficulty Sequence

comparison of how long division is performed (temporal sequence) and how it is taught (response difficulty).

Response difficulty task analyses help the teacher maximize success throughout the process of teaching complex tasks and are especially useful when teaching with a shaping procedure (see Chapter 10). An example of a response difficulty task analysis for a behavior plan is presented in Table 5.2. Note that each step is considered to be more difficult than the previous one.

The third method of task analysis, known as a criterion task analysis, simply breaks instruction of behavior down by using increasingly more stringent criteria for success. The criterion task analysis is very useful for breaking down fluency building goals. The teacher identifies regular intervals between baseline and the end objective and uses each as a step in the task analysis. For example, suppose that a student was to complete her multiplication flash cards with 3's in a one-minute period but we would like her to do this within 20 seconds. We could set the first step in the task analysis at 50 seconds; then, when that criterion was met, we could move to 40 seconds, continuing until we hit the final criterion of 20 seconds. Such procedures are especially appropriate for procedures such as constant time delay (see Chapter 10). An example of a criterion task

TABLE 5.2	**Response Difficulty Task Analysis: Hand Raising**
1	Demonstrate an ability to raise hand
2	Describe when and why to raise hand in the classroom
3	Raise hand in response to teacher questions when prompted first
4	Raise hand in response to teacher questions without prompts
5	Self-initiate raised hand in the classroom at appropriate times with teacher prompts
6	Self-initiate raised hand in the classroom at appropriate times without teacher prompts

TABLE 5.3 Criterion Task Analysis: Work Completion

1	Student will complete and hand in 50% of work during week
2	Student will complete and hand in 60% of work during week
3	Student will complete and hand in 70% of work during week
4	Student will complete and hand in 80% of work during week
5	Student will complete and hand in 90% of work during week

analysis for permanent product and latency recording behavior plans is shown in Tables 5.3 and 5.4.

The most efficient and effective task analysis for any particular skill will depend on the nature of the skill. For complex skills, the teacher must consider whether each teachable step is an independent skill or a prerequisite for the remainder of the task. Those that are prerequisites must be taught first, whereas those that are not prerequisites may be taught in sequence. If all the skills are within the student's repertoire, task analyses move more logically toward each criterion, moving the student toward more fluent performance.

GOALS AND OBJECTIVES: PLANS FOR TEACHING AND EVALUATION

Breaking a complex behavior into a series of discrete behaviors provides an easy-to-follow set of steps that leads instruction and sets the occasion for more individually detailed teaching plans. Consider the example presented earlier of a task analysis for the behavior of hand-raising in the classroom. Suppose an instructor is interested in beginning instruction to teach hand-raising to a student, Rupert. This instructor must consider the step in the task analysis at which instruction would begin, the amount of hand-raising required of Rupert, the conditions under which hand-raising should occur and be measured, and the criteria for successful performance. These considerations are spelled out in three levels: educational goal statements, long-term objectives, and short-term objectives.

Educational Goal Statement

An educational goal statement clearly describes the end goal of the instruction. Goal statements are general descriptions of mastery of a behavior—what we

TABLE 5.4 Criterion Task Analysis: Following Directions

Following Directions in a Timely Manner	Task Analysis by Standard
• Already knows how to listen and follow directions	with < 30 seconds latency
• No need to break skill down into component pieces	with < 25 seconds latency
• The issue is to increase response efficiency	with < 20 seconds latency
	with < 15 seconds latency
	with < 10 seconds latency
	with < 5 seconds latency

wish for the student when instruction is completed. They do not lead instruction on a daily basis but rather provide a focus point toward which daily instruction is focused. Although goal statements are individualized to the student, they are not necessarily measurable except in terms of success with the more specific component behaviors. For Rupert, the educational goal statement is simply *"Rupert will engage in appropriate classroom discussions and follow classroom rules."* Note that this statement does not specifically describe the hand-raising behavior and, thus, may involve other individual component behaviors and skills deemed necessary to meet the goal.

Instructional Objectives

More specific than the educational goal statement are long-term and short-term instructional objectives. Instructional objectives are statements of the teaching plan that reflect what is being taught, to whom, under what conditions, and the criteria for successful performance. These elements, a learner, a behavior, a condition, and a criterion, are the four essential components of a legal instructional objective. Instructional objectives are extremely precise, specifying exactly what the teacher is teaching and evaluating. Instructional objectives are legally required for students who are on an individualized education plan (IEP) but can also assist in implementing and evaluating other types of instruction regardless of the nature of the student or behavior.

LONG-TERM OBJECTIVES.   Long-term objectives (LTOs) reflect the task analysis of the educational goal statement, describing student success for each step of that analysis. For Rupert, the LTO is *"Given a teacher question to the class and a prompt to raise his hand, Rupert will raise his hand and wait quietly for teacher acknowledgement during 80% of opportunities over 2 consecutive days by the end of the month."* This is broken down in Table 5.5.

SHORT-TERM OBJECTIVES.   Short-term objectives (STOs) reflect the instruction and evaluation of teaching on a daily basis. Because several days of instruction may be needed to meet an LTO, the STO enables the teacher to prescribe and evaluate where the student should be at the end of a lesson. Successful STOs lead to successful LTOs and help successfully to meet educational goals. For Rupert, the STO would be *"Given a teacher question to the class and a prompt to raise his hand,*

TABLE 5.5   Long-Term Objective for Rupert

Objective Component	Example
Condition	Given a teacher question to the class and a prompt to raise his hand
Learner	Rupert
Behavior (step 3 from earlier task analysis)	Raise his hand and wait quietly for teacher acknowledgement before speaking
Criteria	80% of opportunities over 2 consecutive days by the end of the month

Task Analysis and Instructional Objectives

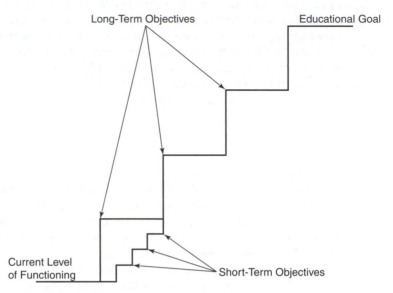

FIGURE 5.3 The Relationship Between Goals and Objectives

Rupert will raise his hand and wait quietly for teacher acknowledgement during 50% of opportunities by the end of the period." It is true that this objective prescribes a behavior at a lower criterion for success over a period of just one lesson period. But the accumulation of successful STOs leads to success with the LTO by building on daily successes, which in turn leads to success with the educational goal. Instructional objectives are simply road maps that prescribe the delivery and evaluation of instruction.

Figure 5.3 graphically represents the relationship between goals and objectives. Remember that a task analysis simply represents a stairway from where we are now to where we would like to be. As such, the ground floor represents what the student can do now (current level of functioning), and the top step represents our goal for the student when instruction is complete. Each step in the stairway represents an LTO that must be met in order for the student to move to the top. Similarly, success with each LTO springs from a series of STOs representing instructional tasks that are planned, implemented, and evaluated by the teacher each day.

Writing Instructional Objectives: Process

We can use our knowledge of task analysis to develop a set of key steps for completing a task analysis. This temporal task analysis, in turn, provides a set of steps toward the writing of a complete instructional objective.

STEP 1: IDENTIFY THE SPECIFIC BEHAVIOR BEING TAUGHT. The first step in writing an instructional objective is to identify the behavior to be taught to the student as an appropriate replacement for problem behavior. In an academic sense this is very straightforward. For example, suppose that a student does not say "4" when presented with the problem "2 + 2". The desired behavior is for the student to say "4" under those conditions, so that's what we teach and measure. Replacement behaviors in the social realm are discussed further in Chapter 10 but can be defined simply as an appropriate behavior that serves the same function as the problem behavior. For example, suppose that Rupert yells out answers to the teacher's questions in order to get teacher's attention. The hand-raising can serve as a logical replacement for the yelling because it is both appropriate in the environment and can function to obtain teacher's attention. Each individual instructional objective focuses on the skill that is to be taught and expected from the student.

STEP 2: DETERMINE THE CONDITIONS UNDER WHICH THE BEHAVIOR IS DESIRED.
In the academic example presented earlier, we only measured the student's behavior of saying "4" when queried with "2 + 2." We did not need to follow the student throughout the day and monitor the number of times that "4" was said. Defining a behavior with a clear locus allows us to determine the exact times that the behavior is required and thereby prescribes the conditions under which data will be collected. We may wish to collect data at a fixed time (during reading), in a specific place (in the hallway), or under a certain condition (when called a name). In each case, the defined locus tells us when to measure. In Rupert's case, the required behavior should occur when the teacher asks group questions; so, this represents the condition under which the behavior is to be measured.

STEP 3: DETERMINE THE BEST WAY TO MEASURE THE BEHAVIOR (SELECT A METHOD).
Once the behavior to be measured and the conditions under which measurement will be required are determined, we must select the most appropriate measure. Recall that appropriate measures are those that are logical in light of the behavior of interest and realistic enough to be implemented under the required conditions. For example, to monitor Rupert's hand-raising behavior, a controlled presentation system is the most logical because it controls the number of opportunities (i.e., questions asked by the teacher) that are presented. Similarly, to monitor out-of-seat behavior, either a duration system or a time-based system would be most logical. When selecting a recording method it is especially important to note the metric resulting from that method so that it can be used to help determine a criterion for terminal performance (step 5). For example, if the recording method is time-based, then the metric will be percent of intervals and must be used in the objective's criteria. That is, "percent of time" cannot be measured with a time-based system.

STEP 4: MEASURE THE STUDENT'S CURRENT LEVEL OF FUNCTIONING.   Initial use of the selected monitoring system provides a baseline of performance, which is the student's current level of functioning. This baseline, the ground floor on the task analysis stairway, directs what will be taught in the first lesson and provides a frame of reference for developing criteria for performance. For example, if we see that Rupert currently engages in hand-raising during 50% of the opportunities provided by teacher questions, his future performance must exceed 50% to be considered success.

STEP 5: DETERMINE CRITERIA FOR TERMINAL PERFORMANCE.   Because success or failure is determined by the student's performance, success should represent the minimal level of performance necessary to maintain sufficient progress toward the LTO or educational goal. For example, an appropriate goal for Rupert might be to respond to teacher questions with a raised hand during 80% of opportunities. Whether tomorrow is an appropriate time frame to achieve this goal as opposed to a month or year from now depends on Rupert's current level of performance and what is deemed realistic for Rupert. Although the jump from 50% to 80% might be too difficult for Rupert to achieve in only one month, expecting this criterion to be met by the end of the quarter, or in eight weeks, might be reasonable.

STEP 6: WRITE THE OBJECTIVE USING STANDARD FORMAT.   The groundwork has now been laid for putting a formal instructional objective on paper. The standard format dictates that, under a given set of conditions, the student will engage in a specific set of behaviors at a specified criterion. As we saw in step 5, a timeline for meeting that criterion is also an important part of the objective. Without the timeline, we have no way of judging progress. Knowing that a student has progressed 5% toward a goal of 50% tells us nothing without knowing how long intervention has been in place or when we had hoped that it would be finished. Progress of 5% one day into a 6-month intervention looks very promising, but the same progress 5 months into the same intervention does not. These issues will be discussed in more detail later in this chapter. The objective for Rupert, written in our standard format, is as follows: Given that the teacher asks a group question in the classroom, Rupert will raise his hand and wait quietly for teacher acknowledgement before speaking during 80% of opportunities.

HELPFUL HINTS.   Several simple considerations should be kept in mind when writing instructional objectives. These will help you write instructional objectives that inform the teaching process and standardize evaluation. First, when writing about the student's behavior, be sure that the main verb is observable and measurable. Phrases such as "will feel" or "will notice" do not provide an adequate operational definition for observation. If a behavior of concern is described in terms that include what the student "feels" or "notices," the teacher must be asked how she or he knows when this behavior occurs. This generally produces a more concrete description of the behavior ("Because he'll say or do . . ."). Second, be sure that the criterion, measure, and metric all match up. A common mistake is a mismatch between the measures and the criterion. For example, if data collection is done using controlled presentation recording, then the metric in the objective must use "percent of opportunities." Likewise, if the measure is time-based, then the objective must use "percent of intervals." An objective with a mismatched metric cannot be measured. Further helpful hints are presented in Table 5.6.

EVALUATING INSTRUCTION

Evaluation of any intervention makes sense only when judged against a criterion. How would you respond if you were told that a student yelled three times this week and then were asked whether that was good or bad? Clearly, you'd ask

---

TABLE 5.6   Helpful Hints for Writing Objectives

Be sure . . .

- the main verb is operationally defined
- the conditions for monitoring are clearly defined, relevant, and replicable
- the criterion and the measurement instrument's metric match
- the objective is stated in positive terms
- baseline rates have been used to set criteria
- to avoid filler words (e.g., will be able to, will demonstrate), just say what the student will do

---

how often the behavior had been occurring earlier and what the goal was. Without this information there is no objective way to evaluate performance. Thus, the first step in evaluation is to get a baseline or current level of functioning for the student. A clear and measurable objective for performance provides a standard criterion for judging the success of an intervention in comparison to baseline. The objective reflects the skills that we are teaching and our criteria for success, but it is not an intervention plan. That is, the objective does not provide any detailed information on how instruction will be delivered, what changes might be made in the environment, or what contingencies will be in place for positive and negative behavior. These are issues for the behavior intervention plan (BIP), which is developed based on the objective.

Generally, objectives are written for the replacement behavior that we want students to use in situations where they usually have exhibited problem behavior. Focusing the objective on the replacement behavior enables us to emphasize the use of instructional interventions (teaching the student how to do something) rather than reductive interventions (responding to instances of undesired behavior with aversive consequences). Teaching interventions are preferable because they employ strategies with which most teachers agree (using prompts, cues, direct instruction, reinforcement, and error correction) instead of strategies that must be added to normal instructional routines (punishment). Clearly, under some circumstances we may wish to monitor the negative behavior while having a goal to decrease problem behavior. An alternate approach is to write objectives for the target behavior while still emphasizing teaching interventions as the dominant strategy. But focusing on replacement behavior is advantageous in that the procedure for monitoring student progress is much more straightforward in a teaching model. For example, proposing that Rupert use his replacement behavior during 80% of opportunities forces us to intervene in ways that encourage appropriate behavior (and thus positive intervention) and to follow progress in our teaching.

Graphing Behavior: Visual Representations of Performance

DATA-BASED DECISION MAKING.   Because success or failure is determined by the student's performance, success should represent the minimal level of performance necessary to maintain sufficient progress toward the ultimate behavior goal. For example, suppose that after observing performance across a range of successful students, we determine that Rupert currently responds to teacher's questions with a raised hand during only 35% of opportunities. We may then determine that an appropriate goal would be for Rupert to respond to teacher's questions with a raised hand during 50% of opportunities by the end of the week and 80% of opportunities by the end of the month. These figures become the criteria for our short-term and long-term objectives. Recall that Rupert's current level of performance and what we feel is a realistic goal for Rupert are what determine whether we set this as a goal to be achieved by tomorrow as opposed to a month or year from now.

EVALUATING PERFORMANCE

The development of instructional objectives provides a standard by which we can evaluate progress. Because a simple line graph provides the best visual representation of progress, this discussion of evaluation begins with a review of some basic graphing protocol. A line graph represents the relationship between performance and time. As presented in Figure 5.4, the vertical or Y-axis is referred to as the ordinate, and it represents the scale on which behavior is measured; that is, the ordinate should reflect the metric associated with the measurement instrument used to monitor behavior. The horizontal or X-axis is referred to as the abscissa and represents the time. Usually, time on this axis is broken down by day, but the abscissa also may show hourly data, monthly data, or data collected at any other interval of time. When data is not collected at regular intervals, time on the abscissa may reflect observation sessions. The result of each assessment is plotted on the graph at the appropriate point for the period or episode on which the data was collected. Thus each new data point must be plotted to the right of the preceding data point. Points for data that are collected prior to intervention represent baseline data and may be referred to as the current level of performance. This level provides the standard by which the criterion for an instructional objective is determined.

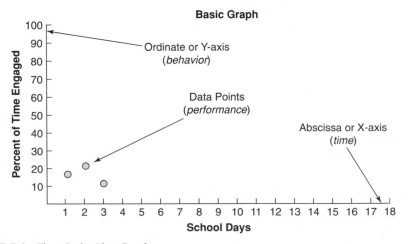

FIGURE 5.4   Time Series Line Graph

PLOTTING LINES OF PROGRESS ON A GRAPH.   Lines of progress are plotted on a graph both as a visual standard for evaluating future performance and as a summary of current performance to predict future performance. Plotting lines requires a rudimentary knowledge of the concept of median, or the middle of a consecutive group of numbers. The median is often confused with the mean, which is the average. Remember, the median is simply the middle of a string. Thus, in the series "1, 3, 8," the median is 3 because it is simply the middle of the string. Likewise, if the series is "4, 5, 7, 8, 2000," the median is 7. Two conditions warrant further discussion. First, when the string contains an even number of numbers, the median is calculated as the average of the middle two numbers. Thus, in the string "7, 8, 9, 10" we would calculate the median as 8.5 (the average of the middle two numbers). Second, when a string contains multiples of a single number, each is still counted as a separate entry. In the string "1, 3, 3, 3, 5" we would calculate 3 as the median because each number is counted in determining the middle number. The median is used to calculate where to begin plotting for lines of progress.

Lines of progress use the intersection median rate (mid-rate) and date (mid-date) of a grouping of three data points. That is, when looking at three points on the graph we first consider them as a string of numbers running up the ordinate (mid-rate) and find the median of the three values. Next, we consider them as a string of numbers running across the abscissa (mid-date) and find the median of the three values there. These two medians are marked on the graph, and lines are drawn intersecting the two. This is one point across which a line of progress will be plotted. Figure 5.5 shows the process of determining a mid-rate and a mid-date from a string of three data points.

Aim Lines

An aim line is simply a line on a graph that connects the current level of performance to a criterion level of performance at a designated point in the future. First, the mid-date/mid-rate is calculated from the last three points representing the current level of performance. Next, a point is plotted on the graph to represent the criterion from the instructional objective. For example, if the criterion stated that performance was to be at 75% by the end of the month and there were 3 weeks left in the month, a mark would be placed 3 weeks down the abscissa (5 school days per week) and then at the corresponding 75% mark on the ordinate (see Figure 5.6). This mark is called an aim star and is typically represented by a capital "A". The aim line is then drawn by connecting the mid-date/mid-rate intersection from baseline to the aim star. This line represents the minimal line of progress for the student. That is, as long as performance is at or above that line, adequate progress is being made toward meeting the objective. If, however, the data do not keep up with the line of progress, the student's progress would be considered inadequate and a change warranted. A general rule of thumb for considering adequate progress is to monitor whether data fall below the aim line for more than two consecutive days. Three consecutive days of performance below the aim line indicate inadequate progress and warrant change in programming. The student that falls well below the aim line on two days and then performs at

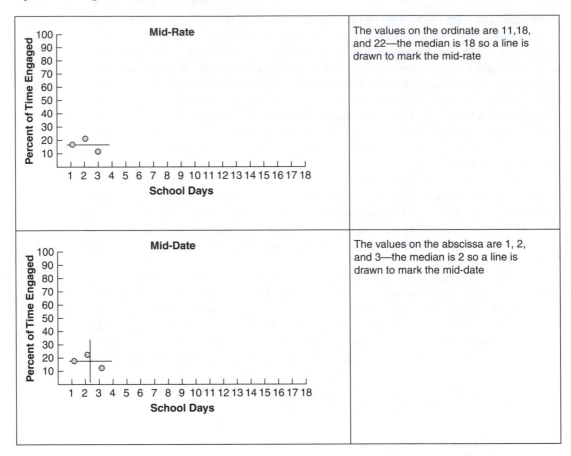

FIGURE 5.5   Steps to Determining Mid-Date and Mid-Rate from a Series of 3 Points

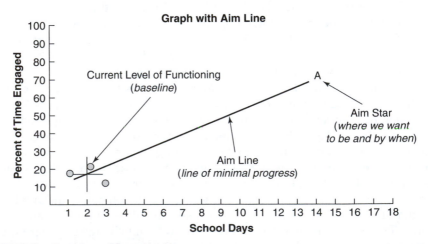

FIGURE 5.6   Graphing with an Aim Line

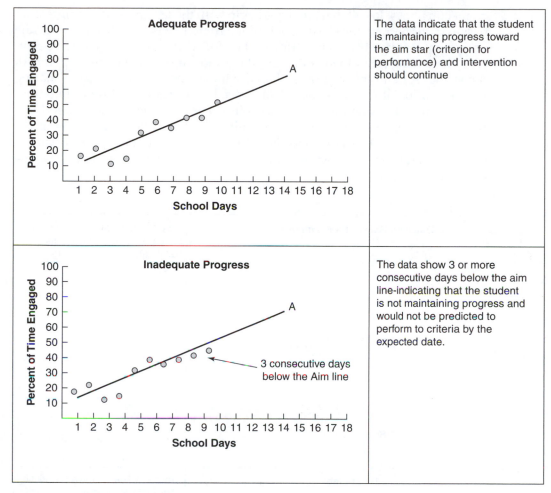

FIGURE 5.7   Sample Data Patterns and Indications

or above on the third day must still be considered capable of meeting the objective. More considerations for data-based decision making are presented later in this chapter. Figure 5.7 provides examples of data patterns that demonstrate both success and failure.

Trend Lines

Trend lines are lines of progress, plotted through a string of existing data points, that represent a trend and a prediction for the future. Trend lines may be plotted through baseline data to determine whether intervention is required, or through intervention data to predict where a student's perform-ance might be at some point in the future. Both instances require the same basic steps, including calculating mid-rate and mid-date intersections and drawing connecting lines. Recall that aim lines begin with the last three data points from baseline. In contrast, the starting point for a trend line is the mid-date/mid-rate of the first three points in any string of data for which a trend line is to be plotted. The ending point then is the mid-date/mid-rate of the last three points of the string. A trend line could be plotted with as few as five points by sharing the median point for mid-date calculations, but a meaningful trend line typically requires a minimum of six data points. For example, to plot a trend line through baseline data we would first calculate the mid-date/mid-rate of the first three points of baseline and then do the same for the last three points of baseline. Figure 5.8 demonstrates the plotting of a trend line through a baseline data set.

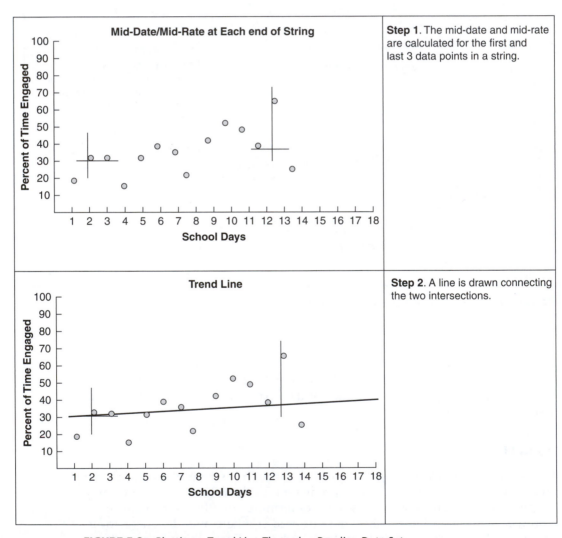

FIGURE 5.8   Plotting a Trend Line Through a Baseline Data Set

DATA-BASED DECISION MAKING

Regardless of whether problem behavior is addressed by group systems, teacher-based intervention, supported/small group interventions, or full SCP teams, the merit of intervention can be judged only by measurable changes in student behavior. That is, regardless of how well the intervention was received or implemented, if student behavior does not improve to the extent that failure for the student or disruption to the environment is less likely, the intervention cannot be considered a success. Such judgments must be made by comparing student performance to clear data-based criteria for success and making intervention decisions accordingly.

Determining the Effectiveness of the Plan

CRITERIA FOR SUCCESS.   Part of the planning process involves determination of the goal of intervention in terms of student behavior. To do this, the team first determines the level of success necessary to alleviate the problem and then measures the current level of performance to determine a reasonable timeline for success. Again, because the student's performance determines success or failure, success should represent the minimal level of performance necessary to maintain sufficient progress toward the ultimate behavior goal. For example, suppose that after observing performance across a range of successful students, the team determines that an appropriate goal would be for Jimmy to respond to teacher questions with a raised hand during 90% of opportunities. Jimmy's current level of performance and what the team feels is a realistic goal for Jimmy are what determine whether the team sets this as a goal to be achieved by tomorrow as opposed to a month or a year from now.

USING DATA TO INFORM PLANNING.   Data collected during the FBA indicate that Jimmy currently raises his hand in response to teacher questions during an average of 40% of opportunities presented. The team feels that the jump from 40% to 90% is too large to achieve in only one month; however, because Jimmy already possesses the requisite skill (i.e., he knows how to raise his hand and regularly demonstrates it), the team determines that a reasonable expectation would be that the goal will be met by the end of the quarter, which is eight weeks away. On the graph in Figure 5.8, Jimmy's current level of functioning is plotted to the left, and his goal date and criterion are plotted eight weeks out. The straight line drawn from his current performance to the date and rate of desired performance represents the minimum level of performance necessary to meet his goal and allows the team to formatively track his progress. On any given day, Jimmy's success can be judged by his daily performance compared to the line on the graph (Bender & Shores, 2007; Lewis, DiGangi, & Sugai, 1990).

Because performance is continually monitored, decision-making criteria for success and failure are continually monitored. The criterion for success is simply that the student meets the behavior goal for intervention. Under these circumstances several courses of action can be considered, depending on the data. The criterion for failure generally is considered to be three consecutive days of performance below the line of minimal performance (Johnson, Mellard, Fuchs, & McKnight, 2006; Lewis, DiGangi, & Sugai, 1990). Under these circumstances, again, several courses of action can be considered, depending on the data.

Decisions: Successful Performance

When performance is deemed successful, the team may determine that intervention is complete and may disband at that point. In other cases, the team may continue with other skills or with the same skill but in a different context or at a different phase of learning. Each of these decisions is made based on the circumstances represented by the data (see Stecker, Fuchs, & Fuchs, 2008; Wolery, Bailey, & Sugai, 1988).

STUDENT HAS FULLY MET CRITERIA FOR SUCCESS. Once the student has met the criteria for successful performance, there is no reason to continue the intervention; however, teams may decide to move to a different skill area, working from a prioritized list of identified student problems. For example, once Jimmy's behavior meets the criterion set by the team, they may increase the criterion nearer to 100% or move on to homework completion or some other skill area.

STUDENT USES SKILL FLUENTLY AND CONSISTENTLY IN LIMITED CONTEXTS. In some cases, the student may meet the behavior goal for performance but still have some difficulties under specific circumstances such as when performing in other settings or with other adults. These conditions suggest the need to create intervention plans to facilitate generalization. The team may then develop criteria for success across a range of natural circumstances and alter intervention to provide natural consequences for appropriate behavior under these generalized conditions. For example, when Jimmy meets the conditions for success in his homeroom, the team may implement intervention in the library or other settings where the problem behavior continues to occur.

STUDENT CONSISTENTLY USES SKILL WITH PROMPTS AND REINFORCEMENT. When the student has demonstrated successful performance with reliance on instructional prompts and artificial reinforcers, the team may decide to continue intervention, but with changes. To build maintenance, the team may gradually fade artificial components of intervention (i.e., prompts and consequences) while still monitoring performance and expecting the behavior to occur at the original goal level. For instance, if Jimmy were to meet his goal with lots of prompting from the classroom teacher each day, the team may set a new criterion for successful performance under conditions where smaller or more natural prompts are used. This could continue until Jimmy's performance is at the desired criterion with only naturally occurring prompts.

STUDENT HAS MET ACQUISITION OBJECTIVE FOR SKILL. In cases where the student has met a behavior goal that simply reflects acquisition of a new skill, the team may elect to continue intervention with a new goal that facilitates increased responding. Fading of artificial prompts may be appropriate under these conditions, too. The intent is to facilitate more fluency with the skill so that it occurs more readily and automatically. For example, if Jimmy were a low functioning student, the team would begin intervention by teaching him how to physically raise his hand. Then, once this skill is acquired at criterion levels, the team could set a goal for more frequent and unprompted hand-raising by providing reinforcement based on the number or fluency of responses.

STUDENT IS MAKING SATISFACTORY PROGRESS TOWARD CRITERION.   When the goal has not been met but the student is making satisfactory progress toward it (i.e., has not met the decision rule for failure), the team should ensure that the intervention plan continues without alteration. Until the student meets either the goal or the criterion for failure there is no need to change the intervention. Referring back to Figure 5.8, at week 5, Jimmy's performance is about 68% of opportunities—well below the criterion set as his goal. If we look at the line of minimal progress, however, we see that Jimmy is on track to meet his goal if he continues at this rate of progress. Under these conditions the team should continue intervention for Jimmy until he either meets his goal or fails to continue progressing.

Decisions: Failed Performance

When performance is determined to be unsuccessful, the team must make decisions on how or if intervention should continue. In some cases, performance may be close enough to success that the team decides to do nothing. In other cases, the team may decide either to change the behavior being taught or to alter the intervention itself. Each of these decisions is based on the circumstances represented in the data (see Stecker, Fuchs, & Fuchs, 2008; Wolery, Bailey, & Sugai, 1988).

STUDENT HAS FAILED TO EVER ENGAGE IN BEHAVIOR.   When a student has never demonstrated the behavior, it should be a sign to the group that basic prerequisite skills or understanding are not present. Under these conditions intervention should be adapted to preteach identified requisite skills. Should this prove too difficult or complicated, the team also may consider alternative appropriate replacement behaviors for the student. A simpler version of the original replacement behavior may provide the student with the same function while being much more easily acquired. For example, if, upon intervention, Jimmy still had never demonstrated hand-raising, the team would need to determine whether he possessed the requisite skills and knowledge (i.e., what is a hand, what does hand-raising look like, etc.) to perform the skill in the first place. If he did not, then those skills would need to be taught. If the requisite skills and knowledge were in place, then the team would need to consider other, simpler behaviors that might be more effective for Jimmy.

STUDENT WAS PROGRESSING WELL BUT HAS STOPPED.   If a student has been progressing consistently and successfully and then suddenly stops, the team should consider both the events in the environment that immediately preceded the drop in performance and the nature of the task or criterion at that point of instruction. Instruction should then continue with reteaching of critical skills required at that level or with instruction to help the student overcome any issues that have arisen in the environment. Suppose, again, that Jimmy were a low functioning student who was being taught how to physically raise his hand. Suppose also that the team was quite successful at teaching him to identify a hand, pull it up in the air, and stretch it over his head; but when it came time to hold it over his head, the progress of instruction fell off. The team may want to consider whether Jimmy possesses the motor coordination and musculature to carry out this step of the skill. If he does not, intervention may focus either on building these skills or on teaching alternative strategies to complete the step.

STUDENT ENGAGES IN BEHAVIOR BUT IS INCONSISTENT.   If a student engages in the behavior at some times and does not at others, whether it be by minute, day, or week, the student may be bored or not sufficiently reinforced for behavior. Under these conditions the team may wish to manipulate reinforcement amounts or to change reinforcers by offering a menu of items or activities. In their assessment the team also should be aware of any environmental conditions that might predict changes in performance. For example, one day Jimmy comes to class and appropriately raises his hand during 90% of opportunities, but on the next day he performs appropriately during only 20% of opportunities—and this inconsistent trend continues. The team first must determine whether any environmental actions or events tend to predict this behavior. If none are obvious, the team may decide to introduce novel reinforcers or to create a menu of possible reinforcers from which Jimmy can select when he meets his daily criterion for success.

STUDENT CAN DEMONSTRATE BEHAVIOR BUT NATURAL EVENTS COMPETE.   If a student has problems with performance under certain environmental conditions (e.g., the presence/absence of peers, time of day, particular subjects, etc.), the team may consider changing the environment to remove or overpower the identified obstacles. In addition, instruction for ignoring irrelevant stimuli and consequences to differentiate appropriate and inappropriate behavior also may be necessary. For example, suppose that Jimmy tends to be less likely to raise his hand when he sits next to Hank. Having noticed this, the team first separates Jimmy and Hank and then gives both students instruction in how to ignore students who do not raise their hands. In addition, both are again reminded of the positive consequences associated with successful performance. Gradually, the two students can be reintroduced into the same area during instructional times with clearly communicated expectations for success.

STUDENT IS JUST SHORT OF SATISFACTORY PERFORMANCE BUT MAKING PROGRESS. Sometime the student may be very close to success but meets the criterion for failure, falling just below the line of minimal progress for three consecutive days. Although the failure rule has been met, progress is being made and no substantive alterations in the intervention seem warranted. Under these conditions, the team may wish simply to institute some instructional prompts or to slightly decrease the criteria in the objective so as to change the perception of success. At week 5, Jimmy's performance level is at 68% and is just below the minimal criterion of 70% for the third consecutive day. Rather than make major changes to the intervention that all agree has been largely successful, the team decides to push the completion date back a week and to redraw the line of minimal progress. The new line of minimal progress falls just below Jimmy's most recent performance, meaning that he is on track for meeting his goal—but just a week later than originally anticipated.

Chapter Review

- Task analysis is a procedure for breaking complex tasks into teachable components.
- Task analyses can be temporal (step-by-step through time), response difficulty (do easiest first), or criterion (gain in speed or accuracy).
- Educational goal statements provide a general statement of where the student should be when instruction is completed. Instructional objectives provide specific descriptions of where the student should be at the end of a month or a quarter (long-term objective) or at the end of a lesson (short-term objective).
- Instructional objectives must include a learner (by name), the conditions under which the behavior is to be measured (e.g., "when in math" or "when called a name by peers"), the specific behavior that is desired (e.g., "stay seated and wait for the teacher" or "walk away and tell the teacher"), and a criterion for success (e.g., "4 of 5 trials" or "80% of the time").

- Writing instructional objectives involves identifying a specific behavior for instruction, determining the conditions under which the behavior should occur, determining the best measure for the behavior, measuring the current level of functioning, identifying a criterion for terminal success, and writing the objective in the standard format.
- Graphs for visual representation of performance must have specific features such as labels, phase lines, and connect lines and must follow specific graphing rules in order to ensure consistency and validity.
- Aim lines represent the minimal level of performance for any day of instruction while trend lines provide an estimate of future performance based on current performance.
- Data patterns can be analyzed to evaluate instruction and to make decisions about how instruction might be changed in the future.

Application

1. Describe two typical behaviors that you might want students to demonstrate and develop the most logical form of task analysis to lay out five lessons of instruction.
2. Mr. Jones has been having difficulty with Roberta in the classroom. Whenever Mr. Jones asks for a volunteer to clean the board, Roberta takes off her socks and runs to the board. Mr. Jones would like her to sit quietly and raise her hand under these conditions and he'd like her to exhibit this behavior by the end of the month. He believes that he can use an event-based measure to track this behavior.

   Write an instructional objective for Roberta.
3. Use the following objective to draw an aim line on the graph provided:

   Given the teacher's direction to hold his breath, Ralph will hold his breath for a period of at least 5 minutes before passing out, within 10 days.

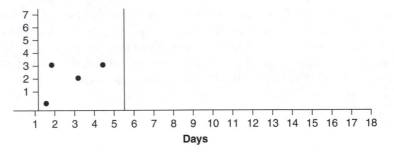

4. Draw a trend line through the following data

References

Bender, W. N., & Shores, C. (2007). *Response to Intervention: A practical guide for every teacher.* Thousand Oaks, CA: Corwin Press.

Johnson, E., Mellard, D. F., Fuchs, D., & McKnight, M. A. (2006). *Responsiveness to Intervention (RTI): How to do it.* Lawrence, KS: National Research Center on Learning Disabilities.

Lewis, T., DiGangi, S., & Sugai, G. (1990). Techniques to facilitate behavioral programming decisions. In *The Oregon Conference Monograph* (pp. 103–109), College of Education, University of Oregon.

Stecker, P. M., Fuchs, D., & Fuchs, L. S. (2008). Progress monitoring as essential practice within Response to Intervention. *Rural Special Education Quarterly, 27*(4), 10–17.

Wolery, M., Bailey, D. B., & Sugai, G. M. (1988). *Effective teaching: Principles and procedures of applied behavior analysis with exceptional students.* Boston: Allyn & Bacon.

6

A Function-Based Perspective of Classroom Management

CHAPTER OBJECTIVES

After reading this chapter, you should be able to describe the following concepts:

- Classroom behavior management
- Contextual fit
- Educative behavior management
- Classroom functional behavior assessment
- Functional routines
- Scatter plot
- Setting events and discriminative stimuli in the classroom
- Structured routines
- Consequences in the classroom
- Hypothesis statement

You also should be able to:

- Define target behaviors for a classroom
- Use a scatter plot to identify problematic routines
- Conduct a functional assessment of a classroom to develop a hypothesis statement

Mr. Lee teaches third grade at Harriet Tubman Elementary School. Although he has taught for 6 years and generally considers himself to be a good teacher, this year's third-grade class has him at wits' end. He decides to ask his school's teacher support team for assistance. During his first meeting with the team they ask him to describe his concerns. He tells the team that his students are generally disruptive and "out of line." Mr. Lee says that the students begin the day in a loud and boisterous manner "from the second they enter the room" and that this continues until the end of the day. In fact, he has had teachers in adjacent classrooms ask him to keep his students quiet because the noise is disturbing other classrooms! As if that weren't enough, Mr. Lee says that his students often are late to class in the morning. Mr. Lee tells the team that he has tried a variety of things to get his students to quiet down including sending students to the office, giving stickers for bringing homework, writing student's names on the board when they misbehave, and keeping students in for recess. None of these have been effective. Mr. Lee says that he went to a teaching workshop a couple of months ago and learned about a classroom intervention called "Three Strikes," which sounded good, so he purchased it. Unfortunately, the intervention required him to spend at least 30 minutes each day on social lessons, something that he simply couldn't fit in, given all the academic requirements he must fulfill. Further, this program required him to track behaviors that are not really problematic in his room; that is, the focus was not actually on the things he is concerned about. As a result, he gave up that intervention fairly quickly. Mr. Lee reports that he usually simply resorts to threats and yelling because these tactics produce, at least in the short term, a temporary reduction in noise and disruption.

If you were part of the school's teacher support team, what help could you offer Mr. Lee? Where would you begin? Faced with a seemingly large problem—an entire classroom that is in what appears to be a state of chaos—where would you begin? Many teachers approach situations like this by trying different interventions, sometimes several at a time—and indeed this is the approach Mr. Lee took. He has tried a variety of consequences for inappropriate behavior and for appropriate behavior, including giving stickers for bringing homework and sending students to the office, but nothing seems to work. Fortunately, if we approach classroom systems from the *functional perspective* introduced in Chapter 2 and expanded on in Chapter 3, we have a place to begin. This functional perspective provides us with the following assumptions about classrooms, including Mr. Lee's: (a) All the behavior that students exhibit in the classroom—both appropriate and inappropriate is learned; (b) Behavior is lawful: Students continue to exhibit behavior that is reinforced in some way; all we have to do is identify the antecedents and consequences to understand why students continue to behave in some ways (e.g., being disruptive) versus others (e.g., turning work in on time, paying attention in class); and (c) Behavior can be changed: Once we know why the behavior is occurring (what laws are affecting behavior), we can teach the students better ways to behave. We also can rearrange the environment in such a way that more appropriate behaviors are more likely to occur.

In this chapter, we delineate how the functional perspective can be applied to classrooms. We begin by providing a rationale for conducting a classroom assessment from this perspective—what information can be gleaned from an FBA of a classroom. Next, we describe steps for conducting a simple FBA in a classroom, describing how to (a) identify goals for the classroom, (b) turn those goals into objective and well-defined behavioral outcomes, and (c) how then to identify antecedents for both appropriate and problem behaviors as well as consequences for those behaviors. We conclude by describing how this information is used to develop a hypothesis statement that guides development of a classroom intervention. Throughout the chapter, Mr. Lee's room is used to illustrate how the FBA is conducted.

RATIONALE FOR ASSESSING A CLASSROOM

The primary job of educators is to ensure that students are learning. Usually the focus is on learning academic skills; however, students also learn a great deal about social interactions at school. Children spend a significant part of each day in school, and it is in this context that they learn such skills as turn taking, attending for extended periods, conflict resolution, compromising, and so forth. Research has shown that effective learning of academic skills and social skills is more likely to occur in a structured environment in which behavioral expectations are clearly conveyed and teacher responses to student behavior are consistent and logical (e.g., Kehle, Bray, Theodore, Jenson, & Clark, 2000; Malone & Tietjens, 2000; McGinnis, Frederick, & Edwards, 1995). **Classroom behavior management** is the term most often used for the system a teacher uses to increase appropriate student behavior and minimize disruption in the classroom.

> **Classroom Behavior Management** System a teacher uses to increase appropriate behavior and minimize disruption in the classroom.

Many teachers have informal systems of classroom behavior management. These systems use incentives and consequences that have not been planned ahead of time, or are not based on a thoughtful assessment of what is needed and why. Such systems work well for many teachers at least some of the time; however, there are several reasons to consider implementing a more proactive, formal system of classroom behavior management. This includes ensuring that interventions implemented match needs in the classroom and increasing the probability that educative strategies are used.

Matching the Intervention to the Classroom

Formal, proactive systems of classroom behavior management make it more likely that classroom management techniques match the needs of the classroom. A large number of formal classroom behavior management systems exist. Many of these can be purchased as kits that include incentives and detailed instructions for organizing a classroom [e.g., the ADHD Classroom Kit (Anhalt, McNeil, & Bahl, 1998)] or can be developed based on thorough published descriptions of the intervention [e.g., the empirically validated Good Behavior Game (Lannie & McCurdy, 2007; Tingstrom, Sterling-Turner, & Wilczynski, 2006)]. In addition, a quick Internet search reveals thousands of strategies for managing classrooms. Some of these intervention packages and strategies likely would result in little, if any improvement in a classroom; and, in fact, few of them have been subjected to rigorous research, although most of them probably would result in some improvement if implemented as designed. If teachers had limitless time and resources available, they simply could be asked to implement different interventions until they found one that is effective. But of course, this is not at all the case. Teachers increasingly are pressed to do more with less: fewer resources, less planning time, and so on. Another problem with many predesigned classroom management programs is that they may not have good **contextual fit** for any one particular classroom.

> **Contextual Fit** is the extent to which an intervention matches the skills, values, and resources of the individuals who will implement it. Successful interventions not only match the needs of the classroom but also have good contextual fit.

Conducting a classroom assessment prior to developing an intervention might seem like "just one more thing to do." This valuable step, however, can save considerable time and effort. The results can be used to identify specific intervention strategies likely to be effective for a given problem and in a specific classroom. Thus, a classroom assessment helps teachers determine when an intervention is needed and what might be most effective as well as identify their goals for the classroom. Consider Ms. Bertelson's kindergarten classroom as an example.

School has been in session for about two and a half months and Ms. Bertelson is frustrated. Her kindergartners seem incapable of moving from one activity to the next without engaging in lots of disruptive behavior. It often takes 15 minutes before most of the students are quiet and working. This troubles Ms. Bertelson, who believes that kindergartners work best in short "work stints" and that moving around frequently helps them stay focused. Indeed, this method of teaching has always worked for her before. Her schooldays are organized around what she calls "busy bee stations." After morning circle time, students move from station to station in small groups. The group organization changes each week, and every Monday morning students learn what group they are in by finding their pictures under the group name. Students stay in a station for 20 minutes. Ms. Bertelson signals the end of each busy bee station time by turning the lights off and on when 2 minutes are left. She then flicks the light off again, and all the students come into the center of the room for a short (usually about 30 seconds) game, such as red light/green light, to let off steam. The student groups then move on to the next busy bee station. Although students struggle with the busy bee station transitions, they generally succeed in performing their opening and closing circle time activities and also in transitioning to and from recess, snack, and naptime. Further, all the students get along well and work together cooperatively.

Ms. Bertelson could simply pick a classroom intervention somewhat randomly; after all, there are many classroom interventions designed for kindergarten rooms. But imagine what would happen if Ms. Bertelson conducted a brief assessment instead of choosing an intervention from a catalog or the Internet. She would begin by defining the problem. Notice that she is not concerned about student attendance or even work performance or disruptive behavior; her only concern is about transitions to busy bee stations. This suggests that Ms. Bertelson does not need a classroom intervention focused on the entire day or even on increasing students' academic skills. Instead, Ms. Bertelson wants to intervene efficiently, focusing only on transitions to new work stations. A cardinal rule of classroom behavior management is that if something is working well, don't change it. By doing an assessment, Ms. Bertelson already has shifted from a broad, general classroom behavior management intervention to something focused just on transitions between busy bee stations. As we will see in the next chapter, she will be able to use her assessment results to select strategies that likely will increase the efficiency of transitions.

Emphasizing Educative Behavior Management

Classroom behavior management strategies can be classified broadly as either reactive/punitive or educative. As their name implies, reactive/punitive strategies are implemented after an undesired behavior occurs; their goal is to stop the behavior from occurring. Commonly used approaches include reprimands, office referrals, detention, derogatory comments, and so forth. In contrast, educative approaches emphasize proactive planning to prevent problem behavior from occurring in the first place and to make it more likely that students instead will "do the right thing." A large body of research documents that educative strategies—as delineated in this book—are the most effective for increasing academic and social behavioral skills and decreasing problem behavior in the classroom (e.g., Darch, Kame'enui, & Crichlow, 2003; Lohrmann & Talerico, 2004; Schanding & Sterling-Turner, 2010; Sulzer-Azaroff, 1991; Sulzer-Azaroff & Mayer, 1991; Theodore, Bray, Kehle, & DioGuardi, 2004; Theodore et al., 2009; Witt, VanDerHeyden, & Gilbertson, 2004). Implementing educative strategies requires investing time in planning a classroom behavior management strategy before actually responding to student behavior (both appropriate and inappropriate). Planning increases the chances that the classroom behavior management system implemented will focus on active instruction and reinforcement of social behavior and will include effective consequences for problematic behavior.

Conducting a Functional Behavior Assessment of the Classroom

By now you should be convinced that conducting a pre-intervention assessment to guide classroom intervention is a good idea. In this section, we describe how to conduct a functional behavior assessment (FBA) of the classroom. Recall that in Chapter 3, key steps of an FBA were introduced: (1) defining the behavior, (2) assessing predictable patterns, and (3) developing a hypothesis statement.

STEP 1: DEFINE THE TARGET BEHAVIORS.   As described earlier, one goal of assessment is to develop a vision for the classroom. As we discussed, this can begin with very broad statements such as "All students are eager to learn," "Students are excited about class," or "Students learn to read." Once goals are identified, the next step is to transform those goals into observable outcomes. For example, instead of developing "All students will know chemistry" as the goal, the teacher would identify what "knowing chemistry" means and how this will be measured in class. A teacher might decide that "knowing chemistry" means that all students earn a "B" or better on 90% of weekly quizzes throughout the semester. Defining outcomes in this way allows teachers to determine whether any changes made to classroom management result in the desired outcomes. Although "knowing chemistry" is difficult to measure, it is easy to determine the proportion of students earning a grade of "B" or higher on quizzes.

STEP 2: ASSESS PREDICTABLE PATTERNS IN THE CLASSROOM.   Once goals have been defined operationally, the next step is to begin the actual assessment. At this point the focus shifts to understanding how the classroom intervention affects the targeted behaviors. When assessing predictable patterns, the focus can be all activities and settings in a classroom, or it might be narrower (e.g., on a specific routine). But regardless of what the focus is, assessing predictable patterns begins with getting the big picture and then narrowing the focus. First, antecedents, or general features of the environment that might set the occasion for problems, are identified (e.g., how the classroom is arranged, how instruction is delivered), narrowing to a focus on specific events that evoke problem behavior (discriminative stimuli). Next, the consequences that might reinforce the behavior are identified.

Focus on Functional Routines

Classroom activities can be broken down into multiple functional routines. Recall from Chapter 3 that functional routines are regularly occurring activities and that a routines analysis is conducted to identify those routines and to note the likelihood of problem behavior during those routines. Within a classroom, a functional routine is the activity within which a problem behavior most often occurs. For example, a fourth-grade teacher might note that her students are most disruptive during math instruction, creative writing, and science. But unless disruptive behavior occurs almost continuously throughout these classes, these are not functional routines; a **functional routine** is the specific activity within which problem behavior often occurs.

Functional Routine
Regular and predictable activities that occur in a classroom.

The teacher must now determine whether specific recurring activities within those instructional periods often precede problems. Perhaps disruptive behavior occurs most often during group work across instructional activities. In that case, group work is the functional routine that the teacher would focus on, *irrespective of the specific type of instruction*. Sometimes clearly only a specific routine needs attention. Ms. Bertelson's difficulty with transitions to busy-bee work stations is a good example of this; the functional routine is transitions to new work stations. At other times, which routine or routines are to be focused on is less clear. Remember Mr. Lee's students who reportedly are disruptive throughout the day? Although the students may be engaging in similar sorts of disruptive behavior across the day, this does not guarantee that disruptive behavior is evoked by the same antecedents and maintained by the same consequences all the time. For example, disruptive behavior that occurs upon entering the room might be maintained by attention from others—perhaps students are simply continuing conversations that began in the hallway. In contrast, talking out of turn and other disruptive behavior during reading instruction might actually be occurring to avoid the assigned activity. The only way to be sure is to focus the assessment on different routines.

Using a Scatter Plot to Identify Problematic Routines

When attempting to define which routines to focus on during the classroom FBA, a useful tool is a scatter plot (Touchette, MacDonald, & Langer, 1985). A scatter plot is used to determine the times of the day in which problems occur most often. To be useful in a classroom, the scatter plot grid is divided such that the left-hand column lists times of day or scheduled activities and the top or the bottom lists days of the week. A blank scatter plot form is shown in Figure 6.1. When determining how to break up each day, whether times of day are used or the day is broken up by activity, the teacher should focus on logical breaks between activities rather than hours of the clock. For example, if a school day begins at 8:15, homeroom is

Dates: From ___/___-___/____/ ___ Classroom/Class Period Observed: _____

Observer: _____

Target Behaviors:

_____

Instructions: Define the time interval to be used and record those intervals in the left-hand column (time). Next, develop the legend based on how often the behavior typically occurs. To use the scatter plot, at the end of each interval fill in the square that corresponds to the time and date using the legend you developed.

Legend: ☐ _____   ☐ _____   ⬛ _____

⬜ _____   ⬛ _____   ◩ _____

Time	Monday	Tuesday	Wednesday	Thursday	Friday

Adapted from Touchette, P. E., MacDonald, R. F., & Langer, S. N. (1985). A scatter plot for identifying stimulus control of problem behavior. *Journal of Applied Behavior Analysis, 18,* 343–351.

FIGURE 6.1   Classroom Scatter Plot

from 8:15 through 8:45, and first period runs from 8:50 to 9:45, it would not make sense to break the day into hour-long segments running from the top of each hour. Instead the day could be broken down into time intervals for each activity (e.g., 8:15–8:45, 8:50–9:45, etc.) or the actual activities could be listed. Although listing the actual activities is simplest, this works only if the schedule does not change from day to day. But if the schedule changes (e.g., 4th period on Mondays and Wednesdays is gym, but is art on Tuesdays and Thursdays and music on Fridays), then it might be easier just to list "4th period" or the actual times associated with 4th period. Samples of each type of scatter plot are shown in Figure 6.2.

Once the scatter plot is set up, teachers indicate when problem behavior occurs by filling in the boxes associated with the times of day and the occurrence of problem behavior. This also can be accomplished in a variety of ways. A teacher interested only in whether or not a behavior occurs could complete the scatter plot simply by putting a mark in the box when the behavior occurs. Two ways this might occur are illustrated in Figure 6.2. The top panel shows different ways of shading used to indicate the level of disruption. In the bottom panel, the teacher simply indicated whether the behavior occurred or not.

Dates: 3/13–3/17   Classroom/Class Period Observed: Morning kindergarten

Observer: Ms. Halley

Target Behaviors: Disruption—touching other's materials, voices above "indoor level," out of seat when expected to be seated

Legend: ☐ No disruptions   ☒ 1–3 disruptions   ▨ 4–6 disruptions   ■ 7+ disruptions

Time/Activity	Monday	Tuesday	Wednesday	Thursday	Friday
Opening	■				
Alphabet					
Art					
Snack	☒		☒	☒	
Nap					
Recess					
Closing	■	■	■	■	■

Dates: 10/3–10/7   Classroom/Class Period Observed: 3rd grade

Observer: Ms. Jones

Target Behaviors: students not in place when activity starts

Time/Activity	Monday	Tuesday	Wednesday	Thursday	Friday
Start of day—bell	XXXXXXXX	XXXXXXXX	XXXXXXXX	XXXXXXXX	XXXXXXXX
Change to math					
Change to science					
Out to recess					
Back from recess	XXXXXXXX	XXXXXXXX	XXXXXXXX	XXXXXXXX	XXXXXXXX
Start of spelling					
Out to lunch					
Back from lunch	XXXXXXXX	XXXXXXXX	XXXXXXXX	XXXXXXXX	XXXXXXXX
Change to reading					
Dismissal					

Adapted from Touchette, P. E., MacDonald, R. F., & Langer, S. N. (1985). A scatter plot for identifying stimulus control of problem behavior. *Journal of Applied Behavior Analysis, 18,* 343–351.

FIGURE 6.2   Sample Classroom Scatter Plots

ANTECEDENTS AND CONSEQUENCES

After identifying the routine or routines to be focused on in a classroom FBA, the next step is figuring out how student behavior is affected by what comes before the behavior (antecedents) and what occurs after the behavior (consequences). A tool useful for identifying antecedents and consequences is the Functional Assessment of Classroom Environments [FACE (Anderson & Scott, 2007)], which can be found in Appendix A. FACE can be used to assess the antecedent and consequent variables described and guides the user in developing a hypothesis statement about how student behavior is affected by what is going on in the classroom. In the following sections we first describe which antecedents and consequences might be assessed and conclude by providing an in-depth discussion of using the FACE to assess a classroom.

Antecedent Variables

Recall from Chapters 2 and 3 that antecedents are events that make it more or less likely that a problem behavior will occur. Antecedent variables fall into two groups: setting events and discriminative stimuli. After goals are defined and functional routines are identified, the focus shifts to identifying antecedents. This search begins with identification of possible setting events that affect behavior and then moves to identifying discriminative stimuli.

Setting Events and Contextual Variables
Affecting Behavior in the Classroom

As discussed in Chapters 2 and 3, setting events are contextual variables that regularly are present during problematic routines and that affect progress toward achieving goals. If these setting events are not present, the problem behavior is less likely to occur. Setting events that might be assessed include (a) the physical layout of the room, (b) the structure of routines, (c) the level of supervision, and (d) activities that occur just before or after the problem behavior. Teaching style, although it is another potential setting event, is given its own chapter because it is such an important and broad topic; thus, it is discussed in great depth in Chapter 8. In the following sections we describe how these variables might affect student behavior in the classroom.

PHYSICAL LAYOUT OF THE ROOM.   One important factor that affects the behavior of both students and adults is how the classroom is arranged. Room arrangement includes such factors as use of wall space, how student desks are situated, the location of the teacher's desk, how work stations (if any) are situated, and whether traffic has a logical flow.

The organization and use of classroom wall space is largely up to the individual teacher's preference. Most schools require certain documents (e.g., a safety plan, school rules, etc.) to be posted in each room. Beyond these documents, however, teachers generally are free to use wall space in any way they desire. In most cases, documents posted on classroom walls will have little effect on student behavior. If the walls are cluttered, however, student learning may be adversely affected. One reason for this may be that instructional prompts (e.g., a poster of vowel sounds) are difficult to locate among all the other wall hangings. For some students, and for some adults as well, cluttered environments (e.g., lots of wall hangings, classroom materials scattered about) reduce the ability to focus attention on the task at hand. If students are having difficulty paying attention in class, it may be worthwhile to assess whether the classroom environment is perhaps too stimulating.

The second consideration regarding room layout is the placement of student desks. Several classic studies have documented the effects of desk layout on student participation in class activities and task engagement (Axelrod, Hall, & Tams, 1979; Marx, Fuhrer, & Hartig, 1999; Rosenfield, Lambert, & Black, 1985; Wheldall & Lam, 1987). For example, Marx et al. compared the frequency with which fourth-grade students asked questions (as a measure of participation) when desks were arranged in rows versus in a semicircle and found that rates of question asking were higher with the semicircle arrangement. Wheldall and Lam evaluated disruptive behavior exhibited by middle-school students (ages 12–15 years) when desks were placed in rows versus when students worked together at a table. They found that across the three classes that participated, disruptive behavior occurred more often when students were seated at tables. Of particular interest is that Wheldall and Lam measured teacher behavior as well and found that when students were situated in rows, teachers emitted more positive and fewer negative comments than when students were grouped at tables—possibly as a function of student disruptive behavior.

In addition to the arrangement of the desks, patterns of traffic flow should be considered. This is especially relevant if a teacher's concerns involve such events as lengthy transitions between activities or disruptive behavior such as students bumping one another when moving about the room or getting into things that are not theirs. To evaluate the flow of traffic, observations could be conducted at the times of concern during the day. For example, a teacher concerned about students taking excessive time to enter the room when class begins would conduct the assessment during the few minutes before and immediately after the beginning of class. In contrast, if problems occur most often when a student needs to move about the room (e.g., to sharpen a pencil) while others are seated, observations might begin when the student asks to move about the room and would continue until the student is seated again. The focus in these observations is on whether there is a clear and predictable pattern through which students are expected to move. For example, is there a large open space between the door of the classroom and student desks? Is the space between desks sufficient for students to move to and from their desks with minimal disruption to others? Page 2 of the FACE interview completed with Mr. Lee, which is in Appendix B, shows how he rated his room arrangement. Mr. Lee states that his classroom arrangement allowed him to view students throughout the room and also let students observe instructional activities easily.

Structured Routines
Activities with clear behavioral expectations and prompts for appropriate behavior.

STRUCTURE OF ROUTINES.   A second variable that greatly affects student behavior is the degree to which activities are structured. **Structured routines** are those in which expectations for acceptable behavior are clear and students know what they are supposed to be doing. In other words, structured routines have established prompts that let students know what they are expected to do and when they are expected to do it.

Activities in structured classrooms follow a consistent schedule such that everyone knows what will be coming next. It often is useful to post the schedule on the wall or board. In addition, students in well-structured classrooms are aware of behavioral expectations because they have been clearly defined and taught. We focus more on how behavioral expectations can be developed and taught in Chapter 7.

SUPERVISION.   The behavior of students in a classroom is affected greatly by the extent to which the teacher provides supervision. Supervision is not a passive process. It is not accomplished by "playing lifeguard," relaxing in a chair, and observing the goings-on in the room. Rather, supervision entails moving about the room almost constantly. Effective teachers use their position in the room to encourage appropriate behavior and discourage inappropriate behavior. For example, suppose that a student struggles with staying in her seat when the bell rings. The teacher might stand next to the student when the bell is about to ring, thus discouraging the student from jumping up.

An assessment of whether the degree and quality of supervision is affecting student behavior could focus on several factors. First, the assessment might evaluate whether the teacher can observe the entire room from all locations in which he or she spends time. If the teacher at a specific time stands in a part of the room from which students cannot be observed working, you can almost guarantee that the students occasionally will engage in behaviors other than what is expected of them during that time. Second, an assessment might focus on the quality and quantity of supervision. This assessment could be conducted by the teacher or by an observer. During a predetermined time, typically in the context that the teacher has identified as problematic, observations could focus on important features of supervision. Mr. Lee, for example, believed the physical arrangement of his room was conducive to learning, but he was less sure that student behavior had been clearly delineated. He realized that his classroom rules were mostly negatively worded (e.g., no running) and that he had not taught the rules to his students. To see the actual results of the interview go to the second page of Appendix B at the end of the chapter.

Activities as Possible Setting Events

Sometimes problematic behavior during a certain part of the day is related to what was going on just beforehand or what activity is coming up. For example, if students are at recess just before math class, they may be quite loud and disruptive during the first few minutes of math. In contrast, if assemblies are held each Friday afternoon just after science class, escalating disruption during science may be related to excitement about the upcoming assembly. If the target problem behavior is occurring (or if desired behaviors are not occurring) at certain times of day, it may be worthwhile to investigate whether the problem is due to what went on before the activity or what is coming up next. To figure this out, begin by determining whether the target behavior occurs (or does not occur) at similar times each day regardless of the specifics of the activity immediately at hand (e.g., group work versus independent work). If, for example, disruptive behavior gradually increases across math regardless of whether the students are working on addition and subtraction, are doing independent work, are working in groups, or are at the board, it might be reasonable to look for a more distal event, or a setting event (e.g., what is happening after the class ends). In this case the focus shifts to what is occurring *after* the class because the disruption increases as the class progresses and problems occur regardless of what is going on in the class.

The FACE interview conducted with Mr. Lee contains questions designed to ascertain the effects of other activities on problem behavior. The following is a transcript of the FACE interview to identify potential setting events. (See Appendix B.)

[INTERVIEWER]:   Okay, we are focusing on less structured routines that occur at the beginning of class and also at the end. Let's think about those times; at the beginning of the day, at the end of the day, and also at the beginning and end of art, math, and English.

[MR. LEE]:   Right, but I think maybe something different is going on in art—it occurs just before lunch and I bet those kids are just plain hungry!

[INTERVIEWER]:   That makes sense; let's see if we can figure it out. So, does disruptive behavior reliably happen just after other activities end?

[MR. LEE]:   No, not really. First thing in the morning they have been talking to their friends in the hallway but that isn't the case at other times.

[INTERVIEWER]:   Okay, does disruption happen a lot when there is a specific activity that is coming up?

[MR. LEE]:   Yes, in art. I think that they are disruptive because lunch is coming up.

[INTERVIEWER]:   Let's talk more about that. They are disruptive in art at what times?

[MR. LEE]:   The beginning and end of class—it must be lunch.

[INTERVIEWER]:   Okay, let's review what we know. Disruptive behavior occurs at the beginning and end of the class in art. Art class is followed by lunch pretty reliably. But, doesn't the same behavior occur at the beginning and end of math and English and also at the start and conclusion of the school day? It seems like a similar behavior is happening at those times too, and lunch is not always the next activity.

[MR. LEE]:   Yes, you are right. I guess that the whether or not they are hungry isn't the key factor here.

Discriminative Stimuli

Once the routine has been defined and effects of broad contextual variables have been assessed, the focus shifts to identifying specific events that trigger problem behavior. Recall that a discriminative stimulus is an event that signals that a particular consequence will—or will not—be forthcoming. A classic example is the teacher stepping out of the room for a moment. The teacher's leaving signals that corrections and other consequences will not follow disruptive behavior; thus, the noise level often rises when the teacher steps out of the room.

When conducting an FBA of a classroom and searching for discriminative stimuli, the focus might be simply to identify discriminative stimuli for problem behavior—what events seem to trigger the identified problem behavior? It often is useful, however, to identify cues for appropriate behavior as well. Each of these options is explored next.

IDENTIFYING DISCRIMINATIVE STIMULI FOR PROBLEM BEHAVIOR.   Often a classroom FBA focuses on problem behavior that occurs in the classroom. When an FBA of a classroom is conducted, the focus is on behavior exhibited by multiple students. But if only one or two students are struggling, then an individual FBA (as delineated in Chapter 10) is most appropriate. If a teacher's goals include decreasing a problem behavior, which by now has been operationally defined, then part of the search for discriminative stimuli might focus on identifying what in the classroom seems to trigger the problems.

When conducting an FBA of a classroom, do not simply record the most logical antecedent or what first comes to mind; instead, ask follow-up questions to determine whether you have identified a relevant factor. Below is a transcript of the FACE interview conducted with Mr. Lee when the focus was on specific antecedents. The FACE interview is in Appendix B and his answers are recorded beginning on the third page.

[INTERVIEWER]:	Mr. Lee, can you think of anything that seems to reliably trigger problem behavior during those less structured times of day?
[MR. LEE]:	Well, maybe it is the presence of my teaching assistant, Ms. Jameson. Could that be it?
[INTERVIEWER]:	Let's find out. What happens most often before students get disruptive?
[MR. LEE]:	It varies a lot—depending on the activity that was going on before.
[INTERVIEWER]:	Okay. So, let's think about these less structured times then. If Ms. Jameson was present in the next 10 times when class began or ended, would disruption happen?
[MR. LEE]:	Yes, absolutely.
[INTERVIEWER]:	Okay . . . have there ever been times when she hasn't been there?

[MR. LEE]: Yes, she sometimes is working with a specific student.

[INTERVIEWER]: Does the disruption still happen?

[MR. LEE]: Yes. Oh, I guess this means she probably isn't a determining factor, huh?

[INTERVIEWER]: It sure sounds that way. Okay, let me ask you this. Has there ever been a time when you have had something really specific for the students to do when an activity begins?

[MR. LEE]: Well, sometimes at the beginning of math I have had a quiz right off. I always tell the students it will happen the day before and because it is a timed quiz they all come in and get right to work.

[INTERVIEWER]: Wow, that is interesting. So when you have had a really clear activity for students to do, they weren't so loud and disruptive. Okay, it sounds like our focus really is those less structured times and there isn't something more specific that is triggering the problem.

[MR. LEE]: Yes, I think you are right.

[INTERVIEWER]: Let's talk a bit more about those unstructured times. Can you tell me who is around at the beginning and end of math, art, and reading? What is going on?

[MR. LEE]: Okay. When math begins it usually is just me teaching. I am at my desk until students are all seated and then I begin whatever the day's first activity is—or I try to begin it anyway. Five minutes before the bell rings I have students put materials away and get ready to leave. In fact, this is the same in art and reading.

[INTERVIEWER]: Okay, so there doesn't seem to be a more specific trigger there. How about the beginning and end of the day?

[MR. LEE]: You know, as I think about it I see a pattern in my behavior. I wait for the students to be seated and ready to learn in the morning too—the trouble is it takes them awhile. At the end of the day I try to give them time to get ready to go and this is when they start to get loud.

[INTERVIEWER]: I think you've got it, Mr. Lee.

Identifying Cues for Appropriate Behavior

A second type of antecedent identified in an FBA might be cues that should signal students to engage in appropriate behavior. Signals for appropriate behavior can be permanent products such as posters of classroom rules or they might be specific teacher behaviors.

Efficient and well-managed classrooms have clearly stated classroom rules. Rules typically are few in number and are posted in an observable place in the room. In Chapter 7 we provide extensive guidelines for developing and using classroom rules. Our focus here is on assessing the extent to which classroom rules exist and are serving as cues for appropriate behavior.

To assess whether other cues are used within a given routine, ask yourself what the expected behavior is, or what the students should be doing. Once expected behaviors are identified, ask how students know what to do: Is there an explicit classroom rule related to this behavior? Next, determine whether the teacher uses any methods to "catch" students when their behavior is moving away from what is expected. For example, some teachers hold up three fingers if the room is getting too loud. If the teacher does not have any such cues, would a cue be helpful? If the teacher does use cues, the assessment should focus on (a) whether all students in the room understand the cue, and (b) whether the cue is effective; that is, when used, does the cue result in most students doing what is expected?

CONSEQUENCES

After target behaviors are determined and the routines in which the target behaviors occur (or should occur) are identified, the classroom functional behavior assessment turns to identifying antecedents and discriminative stimuli and also to determining whether setting events were affecting behavior. The search for both setting events and discriminative stimuli is related directly to correct identification of maintaining consequences. Recall the definitions of setting events and discriminative stimuli. A setting event temporarily alters the value of the consequence. In other words, it increases or decreases the likelihood that a given consequence will affect (e.g., reinforce) behavior. In contrast, discriminative stimuli signal that a consequence is more likely to be (or not be) forthcoming following a target behavior. Because consequences determine whether a behavior will continue to occur, the next step is to determine what consequences follow the behavior so that a hypothesis statement can be developed. The assessment of consequences always is conducted within the identified routine with the goal of identifying consequences for both inappropriate behavior and appropriate behavior.

Consequences for Inappropriate Behavior

Identifying consequences for inappropriate behavior involves determining what reliably occurs after the problem behavior and also how this consequence might function as a reinforcer. Recall that in Chapter 2, we described how all behavior that continues to occur is being reinforced. By using an FBA we attempt to determine what is functioning as a reinforcer. Also in Chapter 2 we learned that reinforcement can be categorized as either positive or negative. Both types of reinforcement serve to increase a response. Positive reinforcement, however, involves adding some event or activity after a behavior; whereas negative reinforcement entails removal of something after the behavior. Reinforcing consequences for problem behavior are identified by making two determinations:

(1) which consequences most often follow the problem behavior in this routine and (2) which of the consequences that occur most often most likely is reinforcing the behavior and how? For a classroom FBA, the focus is on the behavior of all students in the class.

What Consequences Follow Problem Behavior?

After setting events and discriminative stimuli are identified, the FBA shifts to identifying consequences that follow problem behavior. As was the case with antecedents, when we are trying to identify consequences, we begin broadly and then narrow our focus to specific consequences. As a first step, information often can be obtained by asking, "When problem behavior occurs during _____, what happens afterward?" Recall that for Mr. Lee the general routine was the beginning and end of class activities, times when there was not a lot of structure. For Mr. Lee, the first question asked to identify consequences was, "When students are disruptive upon entering the classroom, what happens?" Follow-up questions then can be asked as needed to ensure that the specifics of the consequence are identified. If, for example, Mr. Lee says that he redirects the students, we might ask how he redirects students: What does he say and do, and how do other students respond? The goal of these questions is to define consequences in objective, observable terms, just as we did with target behaviors and antecedents. By asking them we might find out that Mr. Lee repeatedly and loudly tells students to get to work. He also approaches individual students who continue to talk disruptively and tells them to get to work, reminding them that he will have to send them to the office if they don't begin working. Similar questions would be asked to identify consequences that follow disruptive behavior at the end of class.

As with identification of antecedents, follow-up questions should be asked to increase the likelihood that we have identified the most relevant consequences. This will, of course, require some familiarity with the structure and functioning of classrooms—a general knowledge of who else is around and what activities are occurring. Clearly, a teacher doing a functional assessment of his or her own classroom will have the most intimate knowledge of the room. But if you are conducting the assessment for another teacher's room, you will need to ask questions to determine how the room functions. Mr. Lee, for example, has told us that he repeatedly reminds students of what they should be doing (adult attention). What else might be going on after disruptive behavior? What questions would you ask? The additional questions that should be asked are determined by considering who else is around and what is going on. If other adults are around, ask what they typically do when the problem occurs; whether other students are around, and how those students respond; or, if there is a specific activity going on, whether this activity continues when the behavior occurs or it is temporarily halted.

Which Consequences Are Reinforcing the Behavior?

Once the consequences that often follow problem behavior are identified, the next step is figuring out which of those consequences is most important, that is, which consequence seems to actually reinforce the behavior. In classrooms, many events are occurring simultaneously, and it can be difficult to determine which of them is actually reinforcing students' inappropriate behavior. In Mr. Lee's room, for example, when students are disruptive, other students are talking to them, a few students are looking annoyed, Mr. Lee is talking to them, *and* they are avoiding working on assignments: Which of these is reinforcing the disruption?

Identifying reinforcing consequences involves asking follow-up questions about each consequence identified. Questions to ask include how often the consequence occurs, whether the consequence ever occurs when students are doing what is expected, and whether the behavior likely would continue even if that consequence did not happen. In the FACE interview we have found that Mr. Lee has several students who enter the room in a boisterous manner, talking loudly to one another. Although a few students are annoyed by this, the loud students don't seem to notice or care. They do not begin assignments right away, and Mr. Lee has to prompt them repeatedly to get to work. Sometimes he has to send a student to the office. To determine which of these consequences seems to be reinforcing, the interviewer asked Mr. Lee, "If the students entered the room one at a time and all the other students were working quietly would they still be loud?" Mr. Lee responded negatively but said that if one student was loud when entering the room, and other students interacted with that student, then the behavior likely would continue. This suggests that the students likely are talkative when they enter because they enjoy the interaction.

Consequences for Appropriate Behavior

Equally important as identifying consequences for problem behavior is determining what consequences follow appropriate behavior: What happens when students do the right thing? This information is used to further guide development of a hypothesis statement and also to provide useful information for creating a classroom behavior management intervention. When identifying consequences for appropriate behavior, the goal is to determine what reliably occurs when students behave as desired as well as whether this consequence is reinforcing desired behavior.

To identify consequences for appropriate behavior, ask what happens when students exhibit this behavior. Continuing with Mr. Lee, the desired behavior is that students walk in quietly and immediately begin their seatwork. The interviewer might ask Mr. Lee, "What happens when students do come in quietly and get to work?" Mr. Lee tells the interviewer, "Nothing really happens. They complete the review assignment or whatever else we are working on, and I walk around and answer questions. After 15 minutes, we go over the answers and then move on to the next activity." When asked what happens if students clean up quietly, Mr. Lee gives a similar answer: "Well, they get cleaned up quickly and we move on to the next activity; that is about it." We can surmise that this consequence is not reinforcing for many students because, on a daily basis, the majority of students do not quickly take their seats and begin the assignment. In fact, they delay getting to work for as long as possible. Further, most students do not clean up quickly; instead, they joke around with one another. After identifying consequences for appropriate behavior, consider whether those consequences are similar to the consequences that seem to be reinforcing problem behavior. If they are very different, this could help explain why problem behavior is occurring instead of more appropriate behavior. In Mr. Lee's room, students get a lot of attention from one another when they are disruptive. But what happens when they work quietly? Nothing! They simply work; they don't get a lot of attention from Mr. Lee and certainly not from one another. This is not to suggest that what Mr. Lee is doing is wrong; independent seat work and review time are part of most classrooms and can be a valuable learning tool. But we do have an idea now about why students are being disruptive instead of working quietly. One consequence pays off or is reinforcing for them, while the other consequence does not.

STEP 3: DEVELOP A HYPOTHESIS STATEMENT.   Information gleaned from the classroom FBA is used to develop a hypothesis statement. Completing the FACE leads directly to a hypothesis statement; however, the hypothesis statement can be generated from other methods of FBA as well because it simply is a summary of what was learned via the FBA. In the final section of this chapter we review other methods that might be used for a classroom FBA. As discussed in Chapter 3, a hypothesis statement summarizes the relation between the behavior and the events that precede (antecedents) and follow (consequences) the behavior. It often is useful to develop a summary statement for both problem behavior *and* desired behavior. For classrooms, hypothesis statements might take the format depicted in Figure 6.3. This format is similar to the one used for individual student FBAs (as depicted in O'Neill et al., 1997), but here problem behavior is exhibited by a group of students, not just one specific student. In addition, the hypothesis statement identifies antecedents and consequences for expected

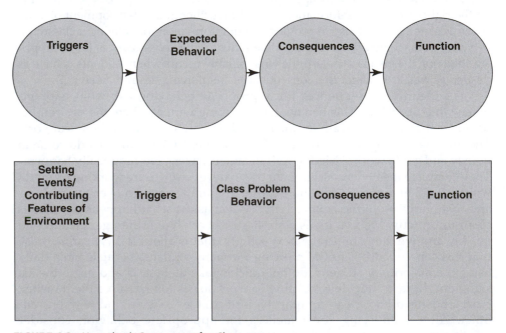

FIGURE 6.3 Hypothesis Statements for Classrooms

behaviors as well as for problem behaviors. To use the hypothesis statement, simply record the results of the FBA, beginning either with appropriate behavior or problem behavior. Note whether setting events or other environmental features (e.g., rules that are not worded clearly) are hypothesized to affect the behavior and then record triggers, or events that set the occasion for the behavior to occur. Next, record what happens after the behavior and, for problem behavior, note the perceived function (what students are getting or avoiding). The hypothesis statement developed for Mr. Lee is in Figure 6.4. This hypothesis statement focused on the routine "less structured times at the beginning and end of academic activities." During this routine, problem behavior seems to be affected by what was going on just before—students in the hall talking to one another. There did not seem to be a specific discriminative stimulus in this case because disruption reportedly occurred when structured academic activities began and ended. The absence of classroom rules and rules for transitions, however, probably plays a role in the occurrence of disruptive behavior. Although Mr. Lee said that disruptive behavior occasionally resulted in delaying of activities, he was confident that students were disruptive primarily because they enjoyed talking and joking with one another. Thus, the hypothesized reinforcing consequence for disruptive behavior is peer attention. Of course, Mr. Lee would like students to enter the room quietly and get to work. Unfortunately, when these behaviors happen they don't result in any particular consequence except that the next activity begins.

Once a hypothesis statement has been developed, it often is useful for the classroom teacher to conduct a brief observation to confirm the hypothesis. The observation should take place during the identified problematic routines and at a

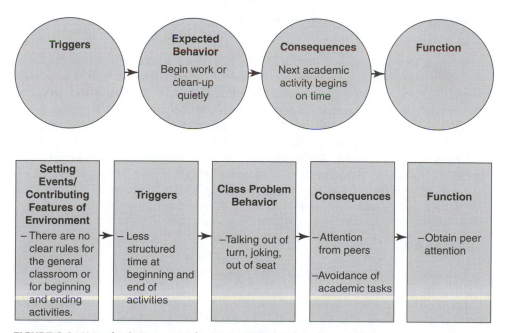

FIGURE 6.4 Hypothesis Statement for Mr. Lee's Classroom

Classroom Functional Behavior Assessment Observation

Date: ____/____/____   Time of observation; from _____ to _____.

Location of observation: _____   Observer: _____

Instructions: Circle the problem and appropriate behavior(s) you are observing and then record your definition of them below. To use the data collection form, record instances of the behavior you are recording and then write down what happened before and after the behavior. Use a new row for each occurrence of the behavior.

Problem behavior (circle one):

| Out of seat | Talking out of turn | Into other's things | Disruptive | |

Appropriate behavior (circle one):

| In seat | Raise hand | Hands to self | | |

Definition of problem behavior:

Definition of appropriate behavior

Antecedent	Behavior	Consequence	Notes

FIGURE 6.5 Classroom Observation Form—Sample

time when the hypothesized discriminative stimuli are to occur. In these situations, the teacher simply records whether problem behavior occurred as well as what happened afterward with the goal of seeing whether the results of this quick observation match with the hypothesis statement. A sample observation form is in Figure 6.5. Usually, the observation confirms the hypothesis statement. Occasionally no problem behavior occurs; in such a circumstance more observations can be conducted or, if the teacher is confident in the hypothesis statement, intervention development can begin. If, however, the observation suggests that the hypothesis statement is incorrect, then more information should be gathered. The classroom FBA should be continued until everyone involved is confident in the hypothesis statement.

SUMMARY

In this chapter, a systematic method for assessing strengths and needs in a classroom was presented. Comprehensive assessment of a classroom should be linked to the reasons why problematic behavior is occurring and desired behavior is not occurring; thus, it consists of a classroom functional behavior assessment. In this chapter we delineated common antecedents and consequences for classroom behavior, including both structural features of the classroom and interactions between different people. In addition, we provided a tool useful for conducting classroom functional behavior assessments, the FACE. In subsequent chapters we delineate how the information gleaned from a classroom functional behavior assessment can be used to alter the environment of the room.

Chapter Review

- Contextual fit, the extent to which an intervention matches with the skills, values, and resources of the individuals who will implement it, is a key consideration in developing an approach to classroom management.
- A functional behavior assessment in a classroom consists of several steps: defining the problem, assessing predictable patterns, and developing a hypothesis statement.
- Possible setting events for problem behavior in the classroom include (a) the physical layout of the room, (b) the structure of routines, (c) the level of supervision, and (d) the activities that occur just before or after the problem behavior.
- When considering discriminative stimuli in a classroom FBA, it is important to identify cues for problem behavior and cues for appropriate behavior.
- Consequences identified in a classroom FBA are events that affect the future probability of behavior of most students in the classroom.

Application

1. Provide a rationale for conducting a classroom FBA instead of using a pre-packaged classroom management intervention.
2. Identify at least two setting events and two discriminative stimuli that might evoke problem behavior in a classroom.
3. Identify consequences that could be used to increase desired behavior in a classroom.

References

Anderson, C. M., & Scott, T. (2007). Functional assessment of classroom environments. Eugene, OR: Educational and Community Supports.

Anhalt, K., McNeil, C. B., & Bahl, A. B. (1998). The ADHD Classroom Kit: A whole-classroom approach for managing disruptive behavior. *Psychology in the Schools, 35*, 67–79.

Axelrod, S., Hall, R., & Tams, A. (1979). Comparison of two common classroom seating arrangements. *Academic Therapy, 15*, 29–36.

Darch, C. B., Kame'enui, E. J., & Crichlow, J. M. (2003). *Instructional classroom management: A proactive approach to behavior management* (2nd ed.). Upper Saddle River, NJ: Pearson.

Kehle, T. J., Bray, M. A., Theodore, L. A., Jenson, W. R., & Clark, E. (2000). A multi-component intervention designed to reduce disruptive classroom behavior. *Psychology in the Schools, 37*, 475–481.

Lannie, A. L., & McCurdy, B. L. (2007). Preventing disruptive behavior in the urban classroom: Effects of the Good Behavior Game on student and teacher behavior. *Education & Treatment of Children, 30*, 85–98.

Lohrmann, S., & Talerico, J. (2004). Anchor the boat: A classwide intervention to reduce problem behavior. *Journal of Positive Behavior Interventions, 6*, 113–120.

Malone, B. G., & Tietjens, C. L. (2000). Re-examination of classroom rules: The need for clarity and specified behavior. *Special Services in the Schools, 16*, 159–170.

Marx, A., Fuhrer, U., & Hartig, T. (1999). Effects of classroom seating arrangements on children's question-asking. *Learning Environments Research, 2,* 249–263.

McGinnis, J., Frederick, B. P., & Edwards, R. (1995). Enhancing classroom management through proactive rules and procedures. *Psychology in the Schools, 32,* 220–224.

O'Neill, R. E., Horner, R. H., Albin, R. W., Sprague, J. R., Storey, K., & Newton, J. S. (1997). *Functional assessment and program development for problem behavior: A practical handbook* (2nd ed.). Pacific Grove, CA: Brooks/Cole Publishing.

Rosenfield, P., Lambert, N., & Black, A. (1985). Desk arrangement effects of pupil classroom behavior. *Journal of Educational Psychology, 77,* 101–108.

Schanding, G. T., & Sterling-Turner, H. E. (2010). Use of the mystery motivator for a high school class. *Journal of Applied School Psychology, 26,* 38–53.

Sulzer-Azaroff, B. (1991). Accepting the challenge: A behavioral perspective on improving educational performance. *Behavior and Social Issues, 1,* 27–41.

Sulzer-Azaroff, B., & Mayer, G. R. (1991). *Behavior analysis for lasting change.* Florence, KY: Wadsworth Publishing.

Theodore, L. A., Bray, M. A., Kehle, T. J., & DioGuardi, R. J. (2004). Contemporary review of group-oriented contingencies for disruptive behavior. *Journal of Applied School Psychology, 20,* 79–101.

Theodore, L. A., DioGuardi, R. J., Hughes, T. L., Aloiso, D., Carlo, M., & Eccles, D. (2009). A class-wide intervention for improving homework performance. *Journal of Educational and Psychological Consultation, 19,* 275–299.

Tingstrom, D. H., Sterling-Turner, H. E., & Wilczynski, S. M. (2006). The good behavior game: 1969–2002. *Behavior Modification, 30,* 225–253.

Touchette, P. E., MacDonald, R. F., & Langer, S. N. (1985). A scatter plot for identifying stimulus control of problem behavior. *Journal of Applied Behavior Analysis, 18,* 343–351.

Wheldall, K., & Lam, Y. Y. (1987). Rows versus tables: II. The effects of two classroom seating arrangements on classroom disruption rate, on-task behaviour and teacher behaviour in three special school classes. *Educational Psychology, 7,* 303–312.

Witt, J. C., VanDerHeyden, A. M., & Gilbertson, D. (2004). Instruction and classroom management: Prevention and intervention research. In R. B. Rutherford, M. M. Quinn, & S. R. Mathur (Eds.), *Handbook of research in emotional and behavioral disorders.* New York: Guilford.

Functional Assessment for Classroom Environments (FACE)

Teacher: _____   Class/period/grade: _____   Date: _____

PART I: BACKGROUND INFORMATION FOR FACE

STEP 1: IDENTIFY TARGET BEHAVIORS ....

TARGET BEHAVIORS *(circle or write in all that apply)*

to increase:		to decrease:	
attendance	_____	disruption	_____
transition efficiency	_____	out of seat	_____
on task	_____	_____	_____
on time	_____	_____	_____
participation	_____	_____	_____

STEP 2: DEFINE TARGET BEHAVIORS ....

Target 1: _____   Goal: increase   decrease
What do students say or do? What does the behavior look like when it occurs?

Target 2: _____   Goal: increase   decrease
What do students say or do? What does the behavior look like when it occurs?

STEP 3: IDENTIFY ROUTINES ....

Identify routines to focus on, by completing a routines analysis or scatter plot (attached).

• During which activity does the targeted **problem** behavior most often occur?
• During which activity would you like to increase a **desired** targeted behavior?

Routine 1: _____

Routine 2: _____

Routine 3: _____

Complete a separate FACE for each routine identified.

PART II: SETTING EVENTS AND TRIGGERS IN THE CLASSROOM

STEP 4: IDENTIFY SETTING EVENTS ....

Routine: _____

Rating Scale: 1 = *not at all* / 2 = *somewhat* / 3 = *all the time/absolutely*	Rating	Affecting the target behavior?	More information
Classroom Arrangement & Supervision			
1. Can you easily supervise students in all areas of the room?	1 2 3	yes somewhat no	
2. Can students easily see you and see all teaching materials from their seats?	1 2 3	yes somewhat no	
3. Is wall space used functionally but free from clutter?	1 2 3	yes somewhat no	
4. Does the seating arrangement maximize your style of teaching?	1 2 3	yes somewhat no	
5. Are traffic patterns clearly marked, functional, and used regularly?	1 2 3	yes somewhat no	
Scheduling			
6. Is the daily schedule in the classroom (or routine) consistent?	1 2 3	yes somewhat no	
7. (For an entire day or class period) Is the daily schedule posted or reviewed prior to class each day?	1 2 3	yes somewhat no	
Rules and Expectations			
8. Are general classroom expectations developed, positively worded, and no more than four in number?	1 2 3	yes somewhat no	
9. Are three to five classroom rules developed, explicitly stating what students should do in observable terms?	1 2 3	yes somewhat no	
10. Are rules posted in an accessible and easily observed location?	1 2 3	yes somewhat no	

11. Are expectations and rules taught at the beginning of the year and re-taught at least three additional times throughout the year?	1 2 3	yes somewhat no	
12. Are rules developed for functional classroom routines, (the routine of concern) and are there no more than five positively-stated rules that define expected behavior in observable terms?	1 2 3	yes somewhat no	
Other Activities			
13. Does the problem behavior occur shortly after another activity ends?	1 2 3	yes somewhat no	
14. If 2 or 3 on item 13; does the problem behavior reliably occur only if that prior activity has happened?	1 2 3	yes somewhat no	
15. If 2 or 3 on item 14; does the problem behavior occur following the prior activity regardless of what students are expected to be doing next?	1 2 3	yes somewhat no	
16. If there is an upcoming planned activity, does problem behavior often occur prior, regardless of what students are doing now?	1 2 3	yes somewhat no	
17. If 2 or 3 on item 16; does problem behavior reliably occur only if that activity is planned?	1 2 3	yes somewhat no	
18. If 2 or 3 on item 17; does problem behavior occur when there is an upcoming activity, regardless of what students are expected to be doing at the time?	1 2 3	yes somewhat no	

STEP 5: IDENTIFY IMMEDIATE TRIGGERS ....

Guiding Question:

What events precipitate targeted behaviors in the routine you are focused on?

5a. Identify the trigger generally—get an idea about what it might be

In the identified routine, what happens most often just before problem behavior?

If you put this trigger in place 10 times, how often would it result in problem behavior?

Does problem behavior ever happen when (opposite of trigger or trigger absent)?

Based on your answers, check the appropriate trigger(s) below:

| _____ tasks | _____ reprimands | _____ structured, non-academic activities |
| _____ transitions | _____ unstructured time | _____ isolated, no-one around |

5b. Identify specific features of the trigger by answering relevant questions below.
If tasks (e.g., group work, independent work, small-group instruction, lecture) are the trigger:

Describe the task in detail (e.g., duration, ease of task), what features of it likely are aversive to students and why is this hypothesized?

If unstructured time is the trigger:

Describe the setting, activities, and who is around.

If reprimands are the trigger:

Describe who delivers the reprimand, what is said, and what the purpose is.

If structured, nonacademic activities are the trigger:

Describe the context, who is around, what activities are going on, and what is expected.

If transitions are the trigger:

Describe the activity that is being terminated and the one that is being transitioned to. Identify whether any of the activities are highly preferred or non-preferred, which are structured versus non-structured.

5c. Identify cues for appropriate behavior.

What should students do?

> What cues are there to tell students what to do?

PART III: CONSEQUENCES IN THE CLASSROOM

STEP 6: IDENTIFY CONSEQUENCES MAINTAINING BEHAVIORS..

Guiding Question:

    What consequences appear most likely to maintain problems in the routine you are focused on?

6a. Identify the consequence generally.
(In the routine identified) When the trigger and problem behavior occur, what happens next?

- What do you do?
- What do other students do?
- What activities happen or stop happening?

CONSEQUENCES *(circle or write in all that apply)*

things that are obtained:		*things avoided or escaped from:*	
adult attention	_____	hard tasks	adult attention
peer attention	_____	reprimands	_____
activity	_____	peer negatives	_____
money/things	_____	physical effort	_____

6b. Identify specific features of the consequence.
Narrow it down. Take each consequence identified above:

- Would the behavior still happen if that consequence couldn't occur (e.g., if peer attention and no other students were around; or if your attention, and you were not around? If escape, would the behavior still occur if the task was easier?)
- Of the last 10 times you saw the behavior, how often did this consequence occur?

If adult or peer attention is obtained or avoided:

> Define who delivers attention, what they say, and how long the attention typically lasts. What does the student do following this attention—is there a back-and-forth that occurs? Does behavioral escalation occur?

If an activity or request follows or is removed:

> Describe the specific activity, including who else is present, what the activity consists of, and how long it lasts.

If tangible items are obtained or removed:

> Describe the specific item(s) obtained, who else is present, and how long the student has access to the item.

If sensory stimulation possibly occurs or is removed:

> Describe the context. Who is around, what activities are going on, what behaviors are expected?

6c. Identify consequences for appropriate behavior.

What happens when students do engage in the expected behavior?

*What happens following **appropriate behavior?***

• Is this response the same or different from what occurs **following problem behavior?**

How do adults respond?

	Same Response
	Similar Response
	Very Different

How do peers respond?

	Same Response
	Similar Response
	Very Different

Do students get or avoid/delay anything?

	Same Response
	Similar Response
	Very Different

PART IV: SUMMARY STATEMENT

Routine: _____

Functional Assessment for Classroom Environments (FACE)

Teacher: __Mr. Lee__   Class/period/grade: ___4th grade___   Date: __11/17/07__

PART I: BACKGROUND INFORMATION FOR FACE

STEP 1: IDENTIFY TARGET BEHAVIORS ....

TARGET BEHAVIORS *(circle or write in all that apply)*

to increase:		to decrease:	
attendance	_____	disruption	_____
(transition efficiency)	_____	(out of seat)	_____
(on task)	_____		_____
on time	_____		_____
participation	_____		_____

STEP 2: IDENTIFY TARGET BEHAVIORS

Target 1: __transition efficiency__   Goal: (increase) decrease

What do students say or do? What does the behavior look like when it occurs?
Students are engaged with one another instead of getting materials ready or cleaning up. Transitions take up to 15 minutes.

Target 2: __Disruptive behavior and out of seat.__   Goal: increase (decrease)

What do students say or do? What does the behavior look like when it occurs?
Students talk to one another when the expectation is to be quiet, they are out of seat and moving around the room, joking with one another.

STEP 3: IDENTIFY ROUTINES ....

Identify routines to focus on, by completing a routines analysis or scatter plot (attached).

• During which activity does the targeted **problem** behavior most often occur?
• During which activity would you like to increase a **desired** targeted behavior?

Routine 1: **Less structured times at the beginning and end of academic activities.**

Routine 2:

Routine 3:

Complete a separate FACE for each routine identified.

PART II: SETTING EVENTS AND TRIGGERS IN THE CLASSROOM

STEP 4: IDENTIFY SETTING EVENTS ....

Routine: **Less structured times at the beginning and end of academic activities.**

Rating Scale: 1 = *not at all*
            2 = *somewhat*
            3 = *all the time/absolutely*
	Rating	Affecting the target behavior?	More information

Classroom Arrangement & Supervision			
1. Can you easily supervise students in all areas of the room?	1 2 ③	yes somewhat (no)	
2. Can students easily see you and see all teaching materials from their seats?	1 2 ③	yes somewhat (no)	
3. Is wall space used functionally but free from clutter?	1 2 ③	yes somewhat (no)	
4. Does the seating arrangement maximize your style of teaching?	1 2 ③	yes somewhat (no)	
5. Are traffic patterns clearly marked, functional, and used regularly?	1 ② 3	yes somewhat (no)	
Scheduling			
6. Is the daily schedule in the classroom (or routine) consistent?	1 2 ③	yes somewhat (no)	
7. (For an entire day or class period) Is the daily schedule posted or reviewed prior to class each day?	1 2 ③	yes (somewhat) no	
Rules and Expectations			
8. Are general classroom expectations developed, positively worded, and no more than four in number?	① 2 3	(yes) somewhat no	
9. Are three to five classroom rules developed, explicitly stating what students should do in observable terms?	① 2 3	(yes) somewhat no	
10. Are rules posted in an accessible and easily observed location?	① 2 3	(yes) somewhat no	

11. Are expectations and rules taught at the beginning of the year and re-taught at least three additional times throughout the year?	(1) 2 3	(yes) somewhat no	
12. Are rules developed for functional classroom routines, (the routine of concern) and are there no more than five positively-stated rules that define expected behavior in observable terms?	(1) 2 3	(yes) somewhat no	
Other Activities			
13. Does the problem behavior occur shortly after another activity ends?	1 2 (3)	(yes) somewhat no	**no matter the activity, disruption occurs at the beginning and end of academic tasks**
14. If 2 or 3 on item 13; does the problem behavior reliably occur only if that prior activity has happened?	1 2 (3)	(yes) somewhat no	**when academics are not going on**
15. If 2 or 3 on item 14; does the problem behavior occur following the prior activity regardless of what students are expected to be doing next?	1 2 (3)	yes somewhat (no)	
16. If there is an upcoming planned activity, does problem behavior often occur prior, regardless of what students are doing now?	(1) 2 3	yes (somewhat) no	
17. If 2 or 3 on item 16; does problem behavior reliably occur only if that activity is planned?	1 2 3	yes somewhat no	
18. If 2 or 3 on item 17; does problem behavior occur when there is an upcoming activity, regardless of what students are expected to be doing at the time?	1 2 3	yes somewhat no	

STEP 5: IDENTIFY IMMEDIATE TRIGGERS ....

Guiding Question:

What events precipitate targeted behaviors in the routine you are focused on?

5a. Identify the trigger generally—get an idea about what it might be

In the identified routine, what happens most often just before problem behavior?

> **There is not a specific activity; instead it is the transition from the previous activity to something new or ending one activity and getting ready for something else. For example, students often are disruptive at the beginning of a class and the end of the class.**

If you put this trigger in place 10 times, how often would it result in problem behavior?

> **10**

Does problem behavior ever happen when (opposite of trigger or trigger absent)?

> **There really is not an opposite, but students do work quietly once they get settled down.**

Based on your answers, check the appropriate trigger(s) below:

____ tasks	____ reprimands	____ structured, non-academic activities
_x_ transitions	____ unstructured time	____ isolated, no-one around

5b. Identify specific features of the trigger by answering relevant questions below.

If tasks (e.g., group work, independent work, small-group instruction, lecture) are the trigger:

> Describe the task in detail (e.g., duration, ease of task), what features of it likely are aversive to students and why is this hypothesized?

If unstructured time is the trigger:

> Describe the setting, activities, and who is around.

If reprimands are the trigger:

> Describe who delivers the reprimand, what is said, and what the purpose is.

If structured, nonacademic activities are the trigger:

> Describe the context, who is around, what activities are going on, and what is expected.

If transitions are the trigger:

> Describe the activity that is being terminated and the one that is being transitioned to. Identify whether any of the activities are highly preferred or non-preferred, which are structured versus non-structured.
>
> **Disruptive behavior happens at the beginning and end of class—when active instruction has not yet begun or has ended regardless of what the prior activity was or what the upcoming activity is. Further, Mr. Lee behaves in pretty similar ways across classes that are difficult. When the class begins he waits for students to become quiet before beginning and just before class ends (about 5 minutes) he has students put whatever they were working with away and get ready for the next activity.**

5c. Identify cues for appropriate behavior.

What should students do?

> What cues are there to tell students what to do?
>
> **There are not specific cues however when Mr. Lee has a very specific activity, like a quiz at the beginning of class, students usually begin to work almost immediately.**

PART III: CONSEQUENCES IN THE CLASSROOM

STEP 6: IDENTIFY CONSEQUENCES MAINTAINING BEHAVIORS ....
Guiding Question:

What consequences appear most likely to maintain problems in the routine you are focused on?

6a. Identify the consequence generally.
(In the routine identified) When the trigger and problem behavior occur, what happens next?

- What do you do?
- What do other students do?
- What activities happen or stop happening?

CONSEQUENCES (*circle or write in all that apply*)

things that are obtained:		things avoided or escaped from:	
adult attention	_____	hard tasks	adult attention
(peer attention)	_____	reprimands	_____
activity	_____	peer negatives	_____
money/things	_____	physical effort	_____

6b. Identify specific features of the consequence.
Narrow it down. Take each consequence identified above:

- Would the behavior still happen if that consequence couldn't occur (e.g., if peer attention and no other students were around; or if your attention, and you were not around? If escape, would the behavior still occur if the task was easier?)
- Of the last 10 times you saw the behavior, how often did this consequence occur?

If adult or peer attention is obtained or avoided:

> Define who delivers attention, what they say, and how long the attention typically lasts. What does the student do following this attention—is there a back-and-forth that occurs? Does behavioral escalation occur?
>
> **A group of students is pretty consistently talking and joking around with one another. There is not a lot of escalation—they stay at about the same level of disruptiveness. Also, they don't get into a negative pattern with Mr. Lee; they usually quiet down when he reprimands them, but only briefly.**

If an activity or request follows or is removed:

> Describe the specific activity, including who else is present, what the activity consists of, and how long it lasts.

If tangible items are obtained or removed:

> Describe the specific item(s) obtained, who else is present, and how long the student has access to the item.

If sensory stimulation possibly occurs or is removed:

> Describe the context. Who is around, what activities are going on, what behaviors are expected?

6c. Identify consequences for appropriate behavior.

What happens when students do engage in the expected behavior?

> **When students begin working right away there is no specific consequence except that they get to work. When students clean up after an activity, they simply are expected to move on to the next activity.**

*What happens following **appropriate behavior?***

• Is this response the same or different from what occurs **following problem behavior?**

How do adults respond?

I begin teaching.	Same Response
	Similar Response
	Very Different

How do peers respond?

There is no real response.	Same Response
	Similar Response
	Very Different

Do students get or avoid/delay anything?

No.	Same Response
	Similar Response
	Very Different

PART IV: SUMMARY STATEMENT

Routine: _____

7

Effective Instruction for Behavior

CHAPTER OBJECTIVES

After reading this chapter, you should be able to describe the following concepts:

- The importance of instruction
- The link between social behavior and academic success
- Key features of effective instruction
- The learning curve
- Curriculum-based assessment
- Anchors for teaching rules

You also should be able to:

- State the goal of effective instruction
- Define acquisition
- Define fluency
- Define maintenance
- Define generalization
- Explain the importance of modeling and providing examples
- Define feedback and state why feedback is important for instruction
- State the role of the teacher and the classroom environment in facilitating instruction

This chapter and the last are perhaps the most important chapters in the book because they provide the foundation for all effective intervention: understanding function and effective instruction of alternatives. First, understanding function provides us with the information necessary to select the most appropriately functional replacement behaviors. Then, effective instruction gives us the tools to increase the likelihood of the student using those behaviors. Recall that teaching a child to "be quiet," regardless of the fidelity of the instruction itself, probably will be ineffective if the student desires attention and has no other way of getting it than to make noises. Instead, we teach the student to raise his or her hand to gain attention. Function tells us about hand-raising behavior as a replacement; instruction will help the student do it.

THE IMPORTANCE OF INSTRUCTION

Why should instruction play such a large role in classroom management—or in the student's life, for that matter? Aren't humans naturally curious? Won't we learn simply when given an opportunity? Obviously, in many cases the answer is yes; we do discover and learn. But the circumstances and timing of such learning are random and will not suffice for teaching complex or important skills. For example, everyone would agree that teaching a child to look both ways before crossing the street is an important skill. Further, most people would not argue with holding a child back on the sidewalk while demonstrating how to look both ways. We also could allow a child to discover on his or her own why this is an important skill. (Certainly a close shave with a car would bring this point home.) But will the child now have the skills to cross successfully or will he or she simply avoid streets? In short, the consequences of failure to master street crossing are dire. Similarly, the consequences of failure to master the ability to read, write, or treat others with respect are similarly dire in the life of a child. And so we teach children to brush their teeth, raise their hands, or to demonstrate phonemic awareness and reading fluency because we have the ability to create success and avoid failure.

In light of the human being's capacity for developing his or her own potential, it is obvious that creative individuals with the requisite skills can direct their own learning. Equally obvious, however, is the fact that without the requisite skills, individuals will not serendipitously attain new skills and behaviors. The child who cannot read will *not* read one day simply because they decide they want to. There is certainly ample evidence of this fact in the world today. Assuming that students will learn in the absence of instruction is illogical and unproductive.

Put another way, suppose that we wish to teach survival skills. We could easily take a group of children and simply drop them into the wilderness, telling them to find their way out. If the group can perform this task, some of them probably will eventually make their way to safety while others surely will immediately give up, walk in circles, or otherwise fail. We could then say that we have "taught" survival skills to some or that some now have "discovered" survival skills on their own. But while it is true that some were successful, do they really now possess the key skills and would they be able to repeat their performance in a novel wilderness? More importantly, what of those who didn't make it out? Will we find them and will the memory of such an aversive experience adversely affect their future desire to be involved with nature?

The parallel with instructing children who exhibit learning and behavioral skill deficits should be clear. When we drop all children without basic skills or direction into school (regardless of how fun the school may be), some will certainly successfully survive school. But will they be fluent readers, will they have respect for others, and will they understand why these skills are important? More importantly, will we see other who simply give up, repeat ineffective strategies, or otherwise fail, and will initial failure with reading taint the child's future desire to read or their belief in their ability to read?

Whether any child has or will demonstrate achievement or failure is an empirical question, and its relevance is peculiar to each individual case. But as with any endeavor we undertake in life, success breeds success, while failure breeds aversion, avoidance, and rejection. With many of our children already facing the lowered probability of success, we cannot afford to subject them to educational situations that do anything less than maximize the chances of success. Continued success in the future depends on success now—success that we have the ability, and responsibility, to facilitate through instruction.

Instruction = Maximizing Success Rates

The purpose of instruction is to increase the likelihood of success in a given instructional environment. If we define every school context as an instructional environment, then our mission is to provide instruction for appropriate behavior in the hallway, restroom, reading class, math class, playground, and so on. Our minimum goal should be to use our instruction to create environments in which students are successful during 80% of their opportunities (i.e., four successes for every failure). If we achieve this goal, we can conclude that instruction has indeed facilitated student success in the environment. And because every success in a given environment increases the future probability of another success in that environment, 80% success sets the occasion for continued success, or effective learning. Still, function must inform how we facilitate success. For example, if a student is failing with reading, then all instances of reading activity will result in an aversive situation for the student; and so, any intervention that does not affect success in reading will be unlikely to affect the student's behavior. Consequently, we must strive for an average of 80% success across not just the whole school day, but within each instructional environment encountered in the school day; that is to say, 80% in nine of 10 environments is great, but failure in that tenth setting may create problems that either spill over into other areas or result in exclusionary disciplinary responses.

When considering students with challenging behaviors, the role of instruction is critical. Research indicates that the most powerful interventions with this population of students include explicit instruction of behavior, consistent application of antecedent and consequence strategies to prevent problem behavior and promote prosocial skills, and effective academic instruction (Kratochwill, Albers, & Shernoff, 2004; Kratochwill & Shernoff, 2003). In essence, all three of these interventions may be considered instructional in that each involves teaching: explaining, modeling, and providing an opportunity to practice; immediate and consistent feedback for both appropriate and inappropriate behavior; and creating success in all required student tasks in a given instructional environment. As a result, we have no for teachers trained to act as counselors, social workers, therapists, or specialists in any other vocation: Instruction is already our field of expertise, and we have others available in the school with these other skills. Still, we must learn to apply instruction in the most effective manner possible, ensuring the greatest probability of success.

KEY FEATURES OF EFFECTIVE INSTRUCTION

Although effective instruction involves telling, showing, and providing feedback, it is greater than the sum of its parts. Effective instruction also involves consideration of scope and sequence: how much to teach and when, provision of a rationale for learning by making real-world connections, generation of effective positive and negative examples, thoughtful sequencing of examples to facilitate rule acquisition, facilitation of naturally reinforcing success, and effective error analysis and correction. These concepts are identical for both social and academic behavior—but our focus here will remain on the social side.

Effective Instruction for Behavior

Effective instruction is thoughtful, planned, and efficient. This means that the teacher must possess a keen understanding what is being taught. Just because we all know how to read does not mean that we are all reading teachers. Effective instruction involves an understanding of the key skills, how to use them appropriately and at the right time, and when to change the way in which those skills are used. All of this is accomplished by designing instruction in a purposeful manner.

PROVIDE A RATIONALE FOR THE LESSON.   There is perhaps no more significant association in education than that of time engaged with instruction and achievement. The more we engage students, the more learning we can expect. Thus, our first concern with instruction must be to create relevant and meaningful lessons that engage students with the content. From a teacher's perspective, this involves providing a rationale for instruction by answering the questions "Why are we doing this and how will it help us in our lives?" If the teacher's responses to such questions are fraught with apathy (e.g., "Because I said so," "Because that's what's next in the book," "Because that's what your parents want," etc.), the student has little encouragement to maintain interest. An appropriate rationale should provide a link to the student's life, other curricular content, and an example of how the lesson will be applied in the real world. Examples of effective rationale for different instructional areas are presented in Table 7.1. Note that in each case the rationale immediately precedes an explicit model or demonstration of the skill.

IDENTIFY THE OBJECTIVES FOR INSTRUCTION: THE LEARNING CURVE.   Assuming that we have already determined the content area for instruction (i.e., math, reading, line-up, making friends, saying "no", etc.), effective instruction requires that we also identify the goals and objectives for the lesson. That is, do we want to simply have the student demonstrate awareness, memorize steps, perform a task with speed, exhibit skills under novel circumstances, or do something else? Generally, the objectives for instruction fall into categories that are aligned with

TABLE 7.1 Lesson Rationale Examples

Subject	Possible Rationale
Long division	Sometimes you need to know how many things you can afford. Let's say you have $100 and you want to buy as many $10 DVDs as you can. You can use division to figure out how many you can afford, like this . . .
Raise hand before speaking	Have you ever wanted to say something, but everyone else was yelling it out, so you couldn't? Raising our hands will make sure that everyone gets a chance to say what they want to say. So it might look like this . . .
Writing a letter	Letters are an important way for us to tell other people what we are thinking. Suppose you wanted to apply for a job as a race-car driver—you'd have to write a letter. This is what you'd have to think about when writing a letter . . .
Quiet line-up	When it's noisy during line-up, it takes longer for people to hear my directions. If you are quiet during line-up, then you'll hear me sooner and we can get out more quickly and you'll end up with more recess time. A quiet line-up means . . .

a learning curve (see Figure 7.1). The learning curve is a visual representation of achievement across time—beginning with introduction to a skill and ending with mastery.

The earliest stage of learning is known as acquisition, when the student is first becoming aware of a new skill and is practicing to acquire an initial ability to perform. At this stage progress appears slow because performance does not accelerate quickly. But if the student's achievement level is 2 on one day and 4 the next, however, this is a doubling of performance. Goals at the acquisition level focus on the student's demonstrating basic skills. Table 7.2 provides some basic instructional objectives at the acquisition level.

Once acquisition of the skill has been successfully achieved, the focus of instruction turns to fluency. This stage involves working with the student to

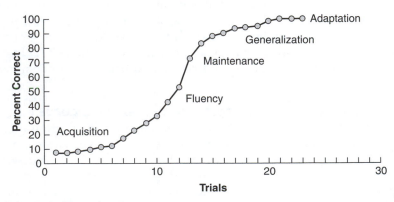

FIGURE 7.1 Typical Learning Curve

TABLE 7.2   Sample Acquisition Objectives

Subject	Acquisition Objectives
Long division	Student will state and describe the four steps of long division in sequence
Raise hand before speaking	Student will state when and why hand-raising is important in a classroom setting and will raise hand upon request
Writing a letter	Student will state the five essential components of a letter upon request
Quiet line-up	Student will state why a quiet line-up is important in the classroom and identify the three key line-up behaviors

demonstrate skills more efficiently, with speed and accuracy paired as equally important outcomes. Note on the learning curve that fluency is the stage at which performance is increasing at the highest rate. An obvious example of fluency is using flash cards to memorize multiplication facts. Although the focus of this exercise is on memorization and speed, this is necessarily preceded by an acquisition-level understanding of the concepts and skills involved in multiplication. Table 7.3 shows some basic instructional objectives at the fluency level.

Once a student demonstrates fluency, the teacher must shift the focus to maintenance by fading instructional supports and expecting the student to remember more on his or her own. This stage involves removing prompts and presenting material with less structure. Note that maintenance learning is associated with a flattening of the curve. That is, the student continues to respond at a high rate, but achievement growth levels off as the focus shifts to performance without prompts. Table 7.4 presents some basic instructional objectives at the maintenance level.

Once a student demonstrates an ability to maintain a behavior over time and in the absence of teacher prompts and structure, the focus of instruction moves to facilitating successful demonstration of skills under an array of real-world conditions. Obviously, the teacher cannot teach every potential situation in which the skill is to be used, so the teaching presents a sufficiently broad range

TABLE 7.3   Sample Fluency Objectives

Subject	Fluency Objectives
Long division	Student will correctly solve 10-problem worksheet of 2-by-3-digit long division problems within a 2-minute period
Raise hand before speaking	Given a prompt, student will raise hand within 5 seconds
Writing a letter	Student will demonstrate ability to write the 5 essential letter components for contrived letter examples within 15 minutes of a prompt
Quiet line-up	Student will line up quietly with prompts

TABLE 7.4   Sample Maintenance Objectives

Subject	Maintenance Objectives
Long division	Student will correctly solve 10-problem worksheet of 2-by-3-digit long division problems when presented on quarterly exam
Raise hand before speaking	Student will raise hand in class without prompt from teacher
Writing a letter	Given a prompt to write a letter at the end of the quarter, student will successfully complete all five essential components
Quiet line-up	Student will line up quietly without prompts from teacher

of scenarios that the student can use to generalize performance to novel circumstances. For example, reading in the text must generalize to reading a newspaper; math on a test must generalize to math in the store; and respecting other people in the classroom must generalize to the playground and elsewhere. Generalization may well be the most difficult and most important of the stages. The student who can perform only in the rather sterile environment of the classroom but nowhere outside is unlikely to be successful in life. As will be discussed, thoughtful instruction at each of the preceding stages sets the occasion for effective generalization. That is, most of the teacher's work for generalization occurs as part of effective instruction rather than as an afterthought. Note that generalization does not involve further achievement; thus, the learning curve is flat and occasionally even decreases slightly as skills are practiced under novel conditions. Table 7.5 shows some basic generalization objectives.

Generalization is the last stage of learning in which teachers have a direct influence. The final stage on the curve is adaptation, or creativity. The idea is that persons who can fluently generalize skills across a range of conditions are more able to actually change the skill in subtle ways and broaden the effect of its performance. For example, good writers often develop a style and voice that was not taught but is an extension of the skills that were the focus of instruction. While we teachers cannot directly teach creativity, we certainly can encourage it and reinforce originality. Clearly, however, adaptation or creativity can occur only

TABLE 7.5   Sample Generalization Objectives

Subject	Generalization Objectives
Long division	Student will use long division to solve the relevant problems in the science experiment
Raise hand before speaking	Student will raise hand before speaking in all classroom settings
Writing a letter	Student will write a letter in response to a real prompt in a newspaper ad
Quiet line-up	Student will line up quietly in all areas of the school

with skills that are within the repertoire of the learner. That is, we cannot expect that a person with no math skills will somehow invent new ways to use math. In fact, learning occurs in the same temporal manner as represented on the learning curve: One must have acquisition before fluency, fluency before maintenance, maintenance before generalization, and so on. The best thing that we can do to stimulate and encourage creativity is to facilitate high rates of success at every other stage of learning. Creativity will come when students are confident enough in their abilities to venture out and attempt new things. Consequently, attempting to teach creativity as an isolated objective is both illogical and futile.

SELECT AND SEQUENCE APPROPRIATE EXAMPLES.   Effective teachers make frequent use of modeling and demonstration with their students. The purpose of modeling is to show students explicit examples of the skills they are to perform. If you think about it, it always helps to see an example. Can you imagine learning to ski, swing a golf club, or play a musical instrument without having seen someone else do it first? Many of our students either have not seen the appropriate behaviors that we are teaching or were not aware of them when they did occur. Our job, then, is to clarify which of those behaviors are and are not important, what should and should not be done, and what does and does not work. The teacher's main task during this component of instruction is to select the appropriate examples and then to sequence each example with the students.

The following are key considerations for example selection. First, the teacher must adequately consider the full range of behaviors that are deemed appropriate and the range of circumstances under which they would be required. For example, when teaching handshake behavior, it will be important to know all the circumstances under which handshaking will be appropriate for the student and then all the variations of handshaking that will be important across these various circumstances. We cannot teach all the possible examples, but only a set of examples that demonstrates this range. Second, each example should show the student something with a variation from the previous example, focusing attention on the key feature of the rule and avoiding examples that are too dissimilar in juxtaposition. In this vein, good examples allow the teacher to point out things that are irrelevant (e.g., "It doesn't matter whether we write the letters in all capitals or all lower case; the sounds of the letters stay the same."). Key to understanding that certain rules govern how a skill is to be performed is perceiving that when certain components are not present, it is not correct. Carefully selected nonexamples show students the relevance of the key rule components. Of course, most rules have exceptions, and these must be taught separately as exceptions. Thus we first teach the rule and then the exceptions. But across all examples, we are bound by what is realistic in the scope of the average classroom. Some examples will simply be too complex or inappropriate for class discussion and should be saved for field trips or other teaching venues.

Remember that all examples are demonstrations of a key rule (e.g., the "+" sign means to add; running at school is OK only on the playground or in PE). When presenting examples during instruction, there are specific considerations for enhancing the effect of instruction. First, multiple examples should be presented during each lesson. The strength of multiple examples is that they are

TABLE 7.6 Teaching Example Sequence

Skill Area: Remain seated during class time
Range of Examples: All chairs that students could sit on in the classroom
Key Rule: Being seated means having your rear end touching the middle of your chair seat

Teacher Examples	Description
Example 1 in student desk: "Look at me now—I have my rear end on the seat"	*Positive example. Always state rule*
Example 2 in student desk: (turns 90 degrees in chair) "Look at me now—I still have my rear end on the seat"	*Positive example—key rule is still there, but other features change. Always reiterate key rule*
Example 3 in teacher chair: (sits sideways in the chair) "Am I still sitting the right way? How do you know? Yes, because my rear end is still in the seat—it doesn't matter what kind of chair it is."	*Positive example—change irrelevant components (chair type) and make clear to students that this is irrelevant. Always reiterate key rule*
Example 4 in roller chair: (sits in chair with legs out front) "Does it matter what kind of chair? That's right, it doesn't matter. Am I sitting the right way? Yes, because I have my rear end in the seat."	Positive example—again demonstrate an irrelevant change that shows the range of examples in the real world, state it in explicit terms, and reiterate the key rule
Example 4 in a roller chair: (sits on knees on chair) "How about now? Is this right? No, because my rear end is not on the seat. I need to put my rear end back . . ." (changes) "on the seat to do it right."	Nonexample—only one thing changed from the previous example and that was the key rule. Then it was put back and the key rule again reiterated.

juxtapositioned in such a way that students can recognize the key relevant and irrelevant components. The teacher's presentation calls attention to the differences (e.g., "Notice that this also is an example, even though this part is different, because the key part is still here."). The best sequence is to show a full range of positive examples that demonstrate the key rule and vary the irrelevant information, followed by an example that maintains the irrelevant features but changes the relevant feature. The example in Table 7.6 demonstrates these principles (e.g., "Notice that this one is the same as the last one, but it is not an example because the key part is not the same.").

ASSESS AND PROVIDE FEEDBACK. Instruction cannot be considered to be complete until the student has mastered the content. While teachers may be used to giving tests, quizzes, and projects as assessment of student mastery, social behaviors generally do not lend themselves to such summative assessments. Rather, mastery of social behaviors is assessed formatively, with observations of behavior on a very regular basis as part of the instruction. When the teacher assesses the student's progress daily, based on the goals for each lesson, it is called curriculum-based assessment (CBA). As students are successful, the teacher moves on to further objectives, moving along the learning curve toward generalization. When students are not successful, the teacher must determine the nature of the error and reteach or otherwise change instruction. The value of CBA is that it allows the teacher to identify failures immediately, creating instructional routines and strategies to facilitate success before students give up.

Feedback is an absolutely essential component of instruction. Learning without feedback is simply not logical. Suppose that you were teaching a student to play a song on a piano and told him or her to try it. They do it correctly and you only stare blankly, refusing to say whether the song was performed correctly or incorrectly. Conversely, imagine that the student plays the song incorrectly and you again stare blankly. In both cases the student will have no idea whether the performance was correct. Thus, incorrect responses very well may continue under the mistaken impression that they were correct, and correct responses may be abandoned under the mistaken impression that they were incorrect. During acquisition learning, teacher's feedback must occur immediately with every student response. The consistency of feedback at this stage is critical because students must discriminate correct responses from incorrect ones in an unambiguous manner. This requires no candy, stickers, or other tangible goodies, and it requires no yelling, slaps, or time out. Feedback during instruction should simply provide the student with information as to their performance.

Consider an academic example involving math. When the student gets the answer correct during acquisition learning, the teacher responds, "Yes, great," and when incorrect the teacher may say, "Not quite, look again." Each of these examples is typical of academic feedback. There is no reason to think that teaching social behaviors should include any different forms of feedback for general instruction. When students are asked to walk in the hall and they do so correctly, the teacher should respond with acknowledgement, "Thanks for walking." When students line up quietly, the teacher can acknowledge the group all at once: "Wow, great job of quiet line-up; you guys are awesome." On the other hand, when students are unsuccessful with a math question, we don't berate them or ask them to leave the room. Rather, we let them know that the answer was incorrect, reteach, and facilitate the student's successful performance, followed by acknowledgement of that success: "Oops, 2 + 2 is not 5. Look at my fingers. Count 2 and another 2, and that equals . . .? Yes, 2 + 2 equals 4; good job." Thus, effective correction procedures provide immediate feedback that a response is incorrect, facilitates success via reteaching, and ends with acknowledgement of success. In the hallway we may say, "Whoa, is that how we move down the hall? No, that's right, we should walk. Would you please show me how to do it the right way? Great, thanks for walking." Despite the logic of this approach, people often continue to see academic and social behaviors as requiring different instructional strategies and different forms of feedback. In reality, effective instruction is the same no matter what the context, condition, or content.

Facilitating Instruction

THE TEACHER. The teacher's role in effective instruction cannot be understated. Simply being proficient with a skill does not mean that a person will be a good teacher any more than will simply understanding task analysis, principles of behavior, or assessment. Teaching is a dynamic profession that requires content skills, pedagogical knowledge, and an ability to communicate in a genuine manner. Effective teachers (a) understand the content being taught; (b) are able to identify goals, provide effective examples, and assess with appropriate feedback and remediation; and (c) establish a relationship with the student in which there is mutual respect and trust. This third component is the most difficult to define, describe, and teach. We know that teacher-student relationships are a component of effective instruction, but it is a difficult concept to convey. Perhaps the easiest way to describe the nature of the relationship is to define a set of teacher behaviors that are strongly associated with high rates of student success.

A large and growing body of research has identified specific teacher behaviors associated with student success rates. These behaviors are separate but important additions to the previously described components of effective instruction. More specifically, teachers use these area behaviors to make the instructional components even more engaging and effective. As a general rule, these behaviors could include anything the teacher can do to make instruction more engaging. For example, good teachers usually ask frequent questions of their students, but not in a purely academic manner. That is, students may be asked what they did the night before, where they got a particular pencil, or how they decided what to have for lunch; or they may be asked questions that simply require a response that sets the occasion for the teacher to make a positive comment. The value of such questioning techniques is manifest in many ways. First, the teacher is creating positive engagement that puts the student at ease and creates the impression that interaction with the teacher can be very positive. Second, the teacher is reinforcing students to be less fearful of volunteering answers in the future. Third, the teacher is engaging the student, capturing attention that can be used in a teachable moment. Once we have the student's attention in a positive manner, we have the opportunity to insert a rationale for that day's lesson.

Proximity is another simple teacher tool to accentuate the effect of instruction. Good teachers move about the room on a very frequent basis throughout the day. This movement creates more opportunities for teachers to assess and provide feedback to individual students. Correction of misbehavior often requires individualized attention that is best delivered directly to the student without the added embarrassment of being corrected in front of the class. Further, research shows that students are more likely to remain engaged with the lesson content when the teacher is frequently nearby. The teacher who simply sits at the desk and asks students to work alone is missing a golden opportunity to engage and excite students.

THE ENVIRONMENT. We can talk about the environment as the routines and physical arrangements that are in place to facilitate student success. In reality, however, the setup of the environment is completely controlled by behavior and thus can be seen as an extension of teacher practice. Research has demonstrated that certain features of an instructional environment are more strongly associated with student success. Every teacher is familiar with basic routines and arrangements; for example, students line up at a certain place, lunch is at a certain time, and students may even have been assigned to certain seats. In fact, it would be unusual to find a classroom that did not have at least some structure in terms of routines and arrangements. For our purposes, however, it is not the simple existence of structures but their purposeful nature, the consistency with which they are applied, and the instruction that is used to teach them. Teachers must predict the contexts under which students are likely to fail during the day and design structures to prevent that failure. For example, if the teacher can predict problems for the class during line-up, then the routine may be changed to line up by row, to have a designated line leader, or to line up only when acknowledged by the teacher. For an individual student (e.g., Billy), the teacher may predict problems for Billy during line-up and thus establish a routine that may allow for Billy to be called first, called last, or called only when he is seated quietly. Routines are most effective when they are developed to maximize student success, are explicitly taught to students, are implemented with great consistency to make them habitual for students, and create successes that can be acknowledged by the teacher.

Certain areas or situations, which seem always to predict trouble for students in general, are even more likely to do so for the students who are most prone to trouble. For example, the sink, a classroom area that is more predictive of student problem behavior than most areas, is an even greater predictor of problems for Johnny, a student with frequent behavior problems. The teacher must develop routines to avoid such predictable failures in areas where students are sometimes expected to work. Examples of these are having one student at the sink at a time for the general population and asking Johnny to always request teacher permission before using the sink. For other areas that are not necessary parts of the instructional environment, teachers may simply teach that those areas are off limits or create barriers to their use. Teachers often will put especially distracting games or toys in a secure location during instructional time to prevent distraction or will even dictate that certain items are not to be brought to school. All of this is done under the notion that preventing problems is the most effective way of ensuring student success.

Placement of the teacher and students in the classroom is another component of the environment that can be manipulated. Most teachers have experienced groupings of students that are particularly predictive of problems. In such circumstances these groupings are minimized by assigning seats, keeping particularly challenging students close to the teacher, or organizing activities that separate particularly problematic groupings. Other arrangements that warrant teacher's consideration include removing furniture or other items that are barriers to observing students, maintaining separate work and play spaces, and posting obvious rule prompts (e.g., stop signs in the hall, line-up markers on the floor) in the locations where students are likely to make errors.

In sum, effective instruction involves not only instructional content development and delivery but also management of the environment. Effective instruction is thoughtfully planned in accordance with the lesson content, natural example selection and sequencing, student preferences, and an array of teacher behaviors that facilitate student success.

Considerations

Effective instruction is a science-based set of practices and procedures that maximize the probability of student success in mastering content and skills. We have discussed several applications of the key features of effective instruction, including teacher, instructional, and environmental variables. Still, difficult situations often pressure teachers to abandon effective instructional procedures. Whether out of desperation or habit, abandoning instructional principles in the face of challenging circumstances is illogical and largely ineffective.

For teachers in classrooms with multiple students with challenging behaviors, or even teachers who work exclusively with students with identified behavioral disabilities, the principles of effective instruction presented in this chapter are not just best practice; they are an absolute necessity. For these types of students, every rule must be explicitly taught; that is, the full sequence of rationale, discussion, modeling, example sequences, and practice with feedback must be presented. This means that line-up rules, rules for hand-raising, when and how to use the sink, how to be seated, how to handle frustration, and so on must be taught. Obviously the vast array of rules governing student movement throughout the classroom, peer interaction, teacher routines, and instructional expectations represents a full agenda for instruction. Recall that effective example selection dictates that examples sample the range of what is expected; that is, the teacher must provide examples that cover the range of student expectations. This is best done by establishing anchors to which all expectations can be tied. For example, the teacher may establish and define the following three anchors:

- *Respect self*—keep yourself safe and learning
- *Respect others*—treat other people as you would have them treat you
- *Respect property*—treat other people's property as you would have them treat yours

As defined, these three anchors provide rules for every time, place, and context of the day. Once students understand the anchors, all the more minor rules and expectations simply become examples of one of the anchors. The grid in Figure 7.2 provides an example of how the anchors can be used to develop classwide or schoolwide rules.

In a sense, this grid represents a curriculum for behavior. For each box in the matrix there is a behavior or set of behaviors that must be taught. The anchors provide the rationale for each individual rule, but the teacher will have to

	Respect Self	Respect Others	Respect Property
Upon arrival in AM	Turn in homework Find desk and sit	Take only one book Inside voice	Hang up coat
During lesson time	Finish work Pay attention	Raise hand to speak	4 chair legs on floor pencil on paper only
At lunch	Eat your own food	Inside voice Chew with mouth closed	Clean it up when done
On the playground	Run on field only	Line leaders referee	Use ball for games Rocks stay on ground
At the bus stop	Be on time	Stay in line	Hold your own coat

FIGURE 7.2 Anchors for Teaching Rules

determine the level of instruction necessary for each. For instance, "line leader referee" means that the first person in line in any game acts as referee should any disagreements arise. This behavior will require more than a simple mention and likely will involve actually talking to the students about the rules of each game. Other rules such as "Be on time" are fairly straightforward and will require more teacher routines and arrangements than instruction to facilitate success.

Instruction for all expected behavior should take place prior to the time or context in which it is expected to occur. To be sure, we would not decide to teach math for the first time during the first test, and so we should not wait until students are already playing on the playground to begin our discussions. Instruction begins with the rationale and discussion that can take place in the classroom. Modeling and practice then can be moved to the natural setting, whether it be the hallway, playground, bus stop, or the next activity in the classroom. In addition, all rules and expectations are taught repeatedly throughout the year as teachers continue to provide feedback on performance in the natural context. Learning takes place each time a teacher exclaims observations like "Wow, you guys are really respectful of each other out here by using the line leaders as referees" or "Johnny, you are really good at cleaning up your area."

Chapter Review

- Explicit instruction is key for ensuring that students exhibit desired academic and social behavior.
- When developing a lesson plan, objectives should be developed for initial skill acquisition, developing fluency, maintenance of the newly learned skill, and generalization.
- Feedback is a key part of instruction, both for academic and social behavior.
- Effective instruction depends on excellence in teaching and an environment that is conducive to learning.

Application

1. Provide an example of an acquisition objective for a math problem, a classroom rule, and a reading task.
2. For each acquisition objective you developed, create a fluency objective.
3. Create maintenance and generalization objectives for each task that you developed acquisition and fluency objectives for.
4. Develop a table of rules with anchors developed from common schoolwide expectations for desired behavior.

References

Kratochwill, T. R., Albers, C. A., & Shernoff, E. S. (2004). School-based interventions. *Child and Adolescent Psychiatric Clinics of North America, 13*(4), 885–903.

Kratochwill, T. R., & Shernoff, E. S. (2003). Evidence-based practice: Promoting evidence-based interventions in school psychology. *School Psychology Quarterly, 18*(4), 389–408.

8

Antecedent Interventions in the Classroom

CHAPTER OBJECTIVES

After reading this chapter, you should be able to describe the following concepts:

- Classroom expectations
- The link between classroom layout and student behavior
- Classroom rules
- Active supervision
- Neutralizing routines

You also should be able to:

- Differentiate between expectations and rules
- List strategies for developing classroom rules
- Define the steps involved in teaching classroom rules to students
- Identify setting events that occur outside the classroom and ways to minimize them

So far we have described how to conduct an FBA of the classroom. After completing the assessment and developing hypotheses about the reason(s) why problematic behavior is occurring, the results of the FBA are used to develop a classroom management plan. A key component of all classroom management plans is altering antecedents to facilitate appropriate behavior and make it less likely that problem behavior will occur. This is the focus of the present chapter. Research suggests that a key difference between effective and ineffective teachers is their use—or lack of use—of antecedent interventions; in other words, their use of instructional and environmental techniques to prevent problem behavior and facilitate appropriate behavior (e.g., Marzano, Pickering, & Pollock, 2003; Watson, Gable, & Greenwood, 2010). Preventing problem behavior requires planning taken ahead of time. Thus, in this chapter we provide guidelines for setting up a classroom so as to encourage appropriate behavior and discourage problem behavior. We first focus on altering setting events to affect student behavior;

then we discuss how discriminative stimuli can be manipulated. Of course, instructional design and teaching style are critical antecedents for appropriate (and inappropriate behavior).

CHANGING SETTING EVENTS TO IMPROVE STUDENT BEHAVIOR

As reviewed in Chapter 6, student behavior in the classroom can be affected by a variety of broad, contextual variables. Preventing problem behavior often requires altering the context by (a) changing the physical layout of the room, (b) defining and teaching expected behavior, (c) structuring routines overtly, (d) changing supervision style, and (e) altering or controlling for activities that occur before or after class.

Changing the Physical Layout of the Room

If results of the classroom FBA indicate that room arrangement might be contributing to problem behavior, then any intervention initially should focus on altering room layout. Room layout can include use of wall space is used, location of the teacher's desk and materials, arrangement of student desks, and traffic patterns.

USING WALL SPACE.   Wall space and bulletin boards are useful areas not only for displaying important information (such as classroom rules, discussed later) but also for individualizing a classroom. Some instructors spend a lot of time making their classroom uniquely theirs via intricate artwork and other displays. In our view, however, making bulletin board displays may not be the best use of teacher time. Even if you begin the year with empty bulletin boards, this space surely will become filled with student work as the year progresses. When considering the use of walls and bulletin boards in a classroom, be sure that you have identified a consistent and easily viewed space for (a) classroom rules, (b) a daily schedule, and (c) a monthly or yearly academic calendar of important upcoming events. In addition, be sure that everything on your walls is relevant to what you are teaching. When you have completed a lesson, remove any wall or board items relevant to that lesson; this will help you keep your room from becoming cluttered.

LOCATING THE TEACHER'S DESK.   Location of the teacher's desk is almost as important as how student desks are situated. Many teachers locate their desk front and center in the classroom, believing that this will best allow them to survey the classroom. Unfortunately, positioning the desk in this way may actually have a deleterious effect on classroom behavior. First, effective teachers spend little time actually seated at their desk when students are in the room (Colvin, Sugai, Good, & Lee, 1997; DePry & Sugai, 2002). Instead, they constantly move about the room, supervising their class, and provide feedback and assistance to students when needed. (Behaviors of effective teachers are discussed in more depth in Chapter 10). Second, the front of the room often is a high-traffic area. The desk therefore might hamper traffic flow, and because it is situated in the flow of traffic might actually "invite" students to investigate items on and in the desk. Because effective teachers use their desks primarily when students are not in the room, a better location for the desk is out of the main flow of traffic.

MATERIALS IN THE CLASSROOM.   When we consider what is in a classroom, the items mentioned first typically are the teacher's desk, a chalkboard, and student desks. Usually, however, there are many more objects in a classroom. Classrooms typically include at least one file cabinet, bookshelves, one or more computers, audiovisual equipment [overhead projectors or Liquid Crystal Display (LCD) projectors], and maybe other teaching tools such as an aquarium or plants. Your job as a teacher is to organize your room so that all these items facilitate rather than hinder student learning.

File cabinets and other storage furniture should be kept in a functional place that will not impede student movement about the room. Consider separate storage areas for items that you frequently use and for items that you use less often. Frequently used items are best located close to where they will be used. For example, headphones might be kept in small bins below computer work stations.

Many teachers bring personalizing items into their classroom such as plants or an aquarium. Such items add visual appeal to the classroom and also can be used as learning tools. If you introduce such items into your room, be sure students know ahead of time and are taught specific rules about how to interact with what you bring. For example, students might be taught to keep their hands off the glass if you place a fish aquarium in the room. Establish rules about when students can interact with the items you bring and locate these items in an area where they will not be distracting.

STUDENT DESK ARRANGEMENTS.   As noted in the previous chapter, research has shown that the physical layout of a room can have significantly affect student learning and inappropriate behavior (e.g., Axelrod, Hall, & Tams, 1979; Baines, Kutnick, & Blatchford, 2008; Reinke, Lewis-Palmer, & Merrell, 2008; Simonsen et al., 2008). There is no one correct way that desks should be located, however. Instead, teachers should use the assessment to determine whether the current arrangement facilitates their class goals, and why or why not. For example, if a teacher's goal is to increase collaborative problem solving (as measured by students, working together), then a grouped arrangement of desks (or students at tables) might be most effective. In contrast, a teacher concerned about students' whispering during instruction might consider placing desks in rows to decrease student-to-student interaction. Common desk arrangements are depicted in Figure 8.1.

There are pros and cons to each arrangement. It is up to the teacher, or the person conducting the assessment, to determine whether the seating arrangement might be contributing to classroom difficulties. Arranging desks in rows, as is illustrated in the top left panel of Figure 8.1, might be best for class activities involving independent work and/or teacher-led instruction. The top right panel depicts a semicircle seating arrangement. This seating arrangement, like using rows, enables teacher-led instruction and independent work to occur easily. Marx et al. (1999) showed that a semicircular seating arrangement resulted in students asking the teacher questions more frequently, which suggests that student's participation might be facilitated by such an arrangement. The bottom two panels of Figure 8.1 depict desk arrangements that might facilitate more student interaction. These are useful for classrooms or activities in which students often work collaboratively.

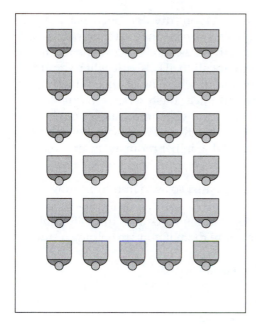
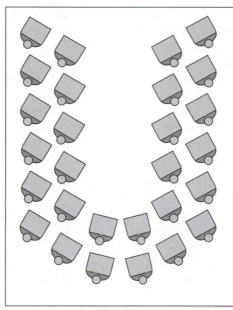
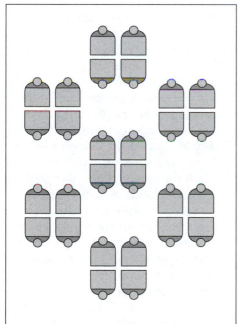
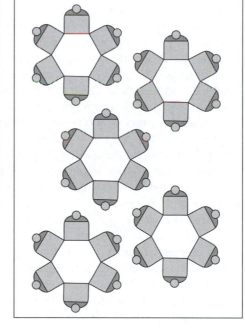

FIGURE 8.1

TRAFFIC PATTERNS IN THE CLASSROOM.   Closely related to desk arrangements is the flow of traffic about the room. There should be sufficient space between desks to allow students to move to and from their desks easily and without disrupting other students. In addition, students should be able to move to and from work stations situated around the room. Third, any room dividers should be considered carefully. Room dividers include obvious dividers such as large panels and walls (movable and permanent) but can also be objects that block the line of sight both of teachers and students. Effective classrooms allow the teacher to observe all students in the room from any location. Thus, a teacher should be able to see what students are doing regardless of where he or she is standing. In addition, all students should be able to see and hear the teacher's instruction.

Many teachers use work areas (or work centers) in a classroom. A work area is a specific part of the room where a given activity is to occur. For example, a first grade teacher may designate the back table in her room as the art area. For all work areas, use the following guidelines:

1. Place needed materials close to the work area so as to minimize movement around the room.
2. Be sure that you can supervise students in the work area from all locations in the room and that you can see the entire room if you are helping a student in the work area.
3. Establish rules specific to the work area as needed.
4. Designate when students are and are not permitted to be in the work area.

Defining and Teaching Expected Behavior

When we want students to exhibit a new academic skill—two-digit multiplication for example—we begin the process before the students enter the room. We first identify learning objectives and then define how we will measure progress. Further, we articulate precise strategies for how we will *teach* students the new skill, usually through a process of didactic instruction, frequent opportunities to practice, and feedback. Once this preparation has occurred, we implement those specific teaching strategies to guide skill development and to build fluency. Although this process is obvious to most educators in academics, it is less often applied to the teaching of social behavior. Many teachers do not identify beforehand the prosocial behaviors they would like to see students exhibit in their classrooms nor do they explicitly teach students those behaviors—either initially or in a repeated manner so as to build fluency. This is unfortunate because a substantive body of research shows that effective teachers both establish clear behavioral rules and explicitly teach those rules to their students (Kern & Clemens, 2007; Lohrmann & Talerico, 2004; Reinke et al., 2008). Therefore, a second way to enhance predictability is the development and explicit teaching of classroom rules. Rules should be developed for the classroom in general and as well for any specific routines that the classroom assessment reveals as problematic. We first focus on general rules for the classroom and then on rules for specific routines. We then provide strategies for developing, teaching, and enforcing rules.

Think back to Mr. Lee's classroom, which was discussed at the beginning of Chapter 6. Recall that his students were very disruptive when activities began and ended, and that it took Mr. Lee a long time to get students engaged in the next lesson. When you read this example (p. 88), did you think, "He needs to crack down. Those students need discipline?" Maybe you thought, "All Mr. Lee needs to do is reward students who do the right thing." Implementing consequences to decrease undesired behavior or increase desired behavior is a common response to problems. The problem is, if students have not been taught expected behavior, then simply trying to teach via consequences will result in students needing a long time to learn what to do. Students in this situation will engage in trial and error to figure out what to do, and this will occur only if the consequence is so unpleasant to the students that it overrides any reinforcement in place for the undesired behavior. So even if Mr. Lee attempted to use a reward system, he probably would not change the behavior of a lot of students.

> It is the start of the school day and all the students are in the room, a couple of students are in their seats, but most are standing in small groups talking. A couple of students are looking out the window, and in the back of the room two students are bent over something that Mr. Lee cannot see. Mr. Lee has decided to try to reward students for being in their seat when an activity is to begin, so he says loudly, "Jane and Bill, I am glad you are in your seats; you each earn a point. Destiny, thanks for being in your seat; you get a point as well." The three students look at him, and Destiny asks what the points are for. Mr. Lee tells them that students who earn 15 points will be able to use the last 5 minutes of class for a break. Destiny, Jane, and Bill seem pleased by this; however, Mr. Lee notices that no one else seems to care. He tries this same system for the rest of the week, and each day the same three students earn a point. Occasionally other students are in their seats as well, but overall Mr. Lee finds that the problem continues: Most students are not in their seats when the bell rings.

You could argue that most of the students simply don't know about the new reward system or that the reward is not powerful enough to function as a reinforcer. Both of these arguments may be true. If Mr. Lee explained the system to everyone *and* if he picked a reward that was very valuable to the students, he might see results within a few days or a week. He probably would have success much more quickly, however, if in addition to reinforcing appropriate behavior, he first taught students what to do. In other words, Mr. Lee needs to establish and teach classroom rules that focus on what to do when an activity begins. When students know exactly what is expected of them and why it is expected, they are more likely to engage in the desired behavior.

In the next section we provide guidelines for developing rules for the classroom. We begin by discussing the use of general expectations for prosocial behavior and how these are best aligned with a schoolwide discipline system. Next, we describe how to turn expectations for prosocial behavior into rules that specify precisely what students should say and do.

BEHAVIORAL EXPECTATIONS AS A FOUNDATION FOR CLASSROOM RULES.   A useful way to begin identifying rules for a classroom is to consider broadly what behavior is expected. At this point, the focus is on general statements of appropriate behavior (e.g., "Be respectful" or "Be cooperative"). Behavioral expectations are general statements of prosocial behavior; that is, they establish behavioral norms for a classroom. Expectations are a useful shorthand way of stating more specific rules. We next describe how rules are formulated from expectations. Because specific rules are tied to expectations, having three to five simple prosocial behavioral expectations makes it easier for students and teachers to remember multiple rules. For example, the expectation "Be prepared" could be defined as having homework out when class begins, having a pencil and paper at hand, and following directions the first time. All of these behaviors can be quickly summarized as "Be prepared." Thus, if a student exhibits all these behaviors, the teacher could thank the student by saying, "Thanks for being prepared today." Similarly, if a student needs to be reminded how to complete an assignment, the teacher might say, "Juan, you need to work on being prepared. Tell me how you could do a better job being prepared for oral reading next time." You could use schoolwide expectations to develop expectations for your classroom if your school has an intervention focused on enhancing school climate [e.g., schoolwide positive behavior support (Horner, Sugai, & Anderson, in press)]. Alternatively, you could simply identify the general social behaviors of which you would like to see more. Use the following questions to guide you as you imagine your perfect classroom:

1. What are students doing and saying during all the types of instruction (e.g., independent work, group work, and lecture) that go on in your room?
2. What are the students doing and saying during transitions between activities?
3. How do students come and go from the room?
4. How do students interact with one another? How do they interact with you?
5. What do students do when they need help?
6. How do students let you know that they need to leave the room?
7. If visitors came to the room, how would they describe your room? What would you like them to say?

From your answers to these questions, develop a list of expected behaviors. For example, are all students in their seats when the bell rings? Do they raise their hands when they have questions? Would visitors describe your room as active or as quiet? Once you have a list of behaviors, group them into categories and think of broad descriptors for these behaviors. For example, if many of your expected behaviors are activities such as "Have materials out when class begins," "Bring your homework to class," and "Follow directions the first time," you might have "*Be prepared*" as a label. You also can develop expectations by observing your room or your colleagues' rooms. Observe how students behave and interact with one another and with teachers. You could focus your observations around the questions presented earlier. The goal again is to develop a list of behaviors that can be summarized under broad expectations of social behavior.

DEVELOPING OVERALL CLASSROOM RULES.   As noted earlier, classroom rules provide guidelines for appropriate student behavior. Rules are specific statements of expected behavior; they delineate what a person should say or do in the classroom. Whereas expectations are global constructs, rules focus on precisely what should occur. Consider the following (summarized in Table 8.1) when developing classroom rules:

TABLE 8.1   Guidelines for Developing Classroom Rules

1. Align rules with school-wide expectations and school rules
2. Describe what people will say or do focusing on observable behavior
3. Develop only three to five rules for each expectation
4. Rules are applicable in all areas of the classroom and for all activities
5. Rules are developmentally appropriate
6. Rules are publicly posted

Align Rules with School Rules.   To develop rules for your classroom, begin by examining your school's expectations (if they exist) and rules. You will want your classroom rules to align with those of the school. For example, if a school rule is "Leave cell phones at home," then cell phones obviously will not be allowed in your classroom either. Using your school's expectations helps maintain a consistent and positive school culture, but it does not force you to have specific rules for your classroom. Instead, think creatively about how the behaviors you desire fit into your school's rules. A matrix of possible expectations and rules is depicted in Table 8.2. The examples in this table are meant as just that—examples. Teachers should not feel obligated to use these rules or expectations in their rooms; they simply are guides. Further, the table contains far more expectations and rules than you could have in any one classroom.

Describe what people will do or say in observable terms.   Rules are designed to articulate what people will do or say. Whereas expectations are global statements, rules tell someone how they should behave. In addition, rules state what students should do, not what they should not do; they are positively worded. Think about this from an instructional perspective. When teaching a student an academic skill, we typically provide instructions relating to how to accomplish the skill—what students should do. A negatively stated rule tells students one thing that they should not do. This leaves the door open for multiple other behaviors, only one of which is the behavior you wish to see. For example, imagine what might happen if Mr. Lee's rule were "No standing after the bell rings." Students might still be out of their seats, although they could be seated on the floor or on desktops or countertops. In addition, they might simply kneel in their chairs. They perhaps would sit in each other's chairs in order to talk to their friends. But if Mr. Lee's rule instead were "Be in your seats and ready to learn when the bell rings," many of these problems would be avoided. Of course, Mr. Lee would still have to teach students what "ready to learn" means. This highlights a second problem with negatively stated rules: Students might not know what they are actually supposed to do. If your rules are positively stated and taught to the students, this problem is solved. Third, rules that tell students what not to do result in a more negative climate because you constantly will be looking for negative behavior instead of focusing on what students are doing well.

Develop just a few rules for each behavioral expectation.   Each behavioral expectation can be defined by about three rules. If there are more than three rules per

TABLE 8.2 Sample Expectations and Rules for Classrooms

Elementary School

Expectation	Possible Rules
Be Responsible (Respect Property, be a good learner)	• Be prepared • Be in your seat when the bell rings • Raise your hand before speaking • When the teacher claps her hands, seal your lips and look forward—clap back. • Keep hands and feet to yourself • Clean up after yourself
Be Safe (Respect Ourselves)	• When seated, back to back, seat to seat, feet to floor • Keep all 4 legs of your chair on the floor • Take turns • Quiet body when walking
Be Respectful (Respect Others)	• Lips sealed when others are talking • Take only what is yours • Use your indoor voice

High School

Expectation	Possible Rules
Be Responsible (Respect Property)	• Be prepared • Be in your seat when the bell rings • Complete assignments neatly and on time • Bring your planner to class and keep it in your desk
Be Safe (Respect Ourselves, take care of yourself)	• Sit in your chair facing forward with your feet on the floor
Be Respectful (Respect Others, take care of others)	• Listen when others talk • Use an appropriate voice and tone • Get a hall-pass before you leave; only one person leaves at a time • Use the pencil sharpener only when the teacher isn't speaking to the class • Treat classroom materials and other's property with care • Respect the space and property of others

expectation, students will have difficulty remembering all the rules, and you will too. Thus, focus on key behaviors that will increase student participation and success in your classroom.

Rules are applicable in all areas of the classroom.   General classroom rules need to apply during all routines in the classroom as well as in different areas of the room. You will develop rules for specific settings later. Now, however, the focus is on general classroom rules. So, think about the general behaviors you'd like to see all the time. Look again at the examples of general classroom rules in Table 8.2. As this table illustrates, general rules focus on social behavioral norms that you wish to see in the classroom at all times.

Rules are developmentally appropriate.   Consider the age and developmental level of your students when identifying rules. Both the behavior specified and the wording of the rule should match the students' developmental level. What is expected in a high school often is very different from what is acceptable in elementary schools. For example, kindergartners generally are not allowed to leave the room without asking permission. In many high school classrooms, however, students are considered to be young adults who can manage themselves. Teachers thus simply leave a hall pass by the door to the room. Students pick the pass up if they need to leave the room to get a drink of water, for example, and return the pass when they come back to the room. Thus, the expectation "Be responsible" in elementary school might consist of asking permission before leaving, whereas this would not be the case in many high-school classrooms. Beyond the actual rule, the wording of the rule should match the students' developmental level. For very young students, teachers might find it easier to use pictures depicting the rules rather than writing rules out.

Rules are posted publically.   Once you have developed your rules, post them in places in the classroom where they will be easily seen. Observable rules serve as a prompt for appropriate behavior; students will see the rules frequently, which will help them to follow the rules. In addition, publicly posted rules serves as a prompt for you to refer to them and reteach them frequently. As noted above, pictures can be used rather than words for students who do not read; the goal of posting rules is to prompt prosocial behavior, which will occur only if all students are able to understand the posting. Some high school teachers may elect to give students printed copies of the rules rather than posting them. If you choose this option, keep a copy of the rules close to your desk so you can refer to them easily. We encourage all teachers, even high school teachers, to post the rules in at least one spot, however. Some teachers worry that posting rules in a classroom is too "elementary school." Think for a moment, however, about places of employment. Many employers post rules for specific settings in the site. Many restaurants have signs that prompt patrons to clean up after themselves and to refrain from smoking, for example.

RULES FOR SPECIFIC ROUTINES.   Overall classroom rules are important for establishing a consistent and positive classroom culture; they tell students how to behave while in your room. In all classrooms, there are a variety of activities that go on; these are functional routines. As defined in Chapter 3, functional routines are regularly occurring activities, such as entering and leaving the room, group work, and computer time. Rules for these routines let students know what specific behaviors should occur in each routine.

To develop rules for specific routines, first consider which routines the students will engage in while with you. Some common classroom routines are listed in Table 8.3. But don't just rely on this list; some of these routines likely

---

TABLE 8.3   Examples of Classroom Routines

- Entering and leaving the room when class begins and ends
- Leaving during class (e.g., to get a drink)
- Behavior during over-head speaker announcements
- Independent work
- Group work
- Computer time and other special areas (e.g., reading nook)
- Lining up
- What to do when you finish before an activity is over
- Getting help from the teacher or getting the teacher's attention
- Transitions from one activity to the next
- Lining up
- Walking in the hallway
- Free time
- Turning in homework or other assignments

---

will not apply in your class, and there may be other routines that are not listed here. Once you have a list of common classroom routines, consider each routine one at a time. For each routine, what behaviors do you want your students to exhibit? For example, how should students enter the room? Where should they be when the bell rings? What should they be doing? List all the behaviors students should engage in to complete the activity. When you are done, ask yourself, "What mistakes could a student make?" For example, if students are to line up when the bell rings, they might jump out of their seats and run to the door to line up; so you would specifically teach them to remain seated until called on and to walk to the door.

TEACH EXPECTED BEHAVIOR.   Once expectations and rules are developed, the next step is to teach them. It is easy to assume that students "know how to behave"; however, this often is not the case. Further, students are unlikely to know what you expect as compared to what other teachers expect. Many teachers attempt to address this by providing students a handout covering all the rules on the first day of class or by simply reviewing the rules during the first week. This approach is akin to teaching students how to conjugate a verb by giving them a sample on paper or by reading the steps to them once and expecting them to be able to conjugate all verbs successfully. In fact, we should teach expectations and rules in the same way that we teach academic skills. Rules are taught by (a) stating the rule, (b) providing a brief rationale for the rule, (c) giving examples and nonexamples, and (d) allowing opportunities for practice and providing feedback. In most cases, it is best to teach the rules in the setting where the behavior will occur. For example, if your rule is "Be prepared when the bell rings," you might teach this in the hallway outside your room or when students are seated at their desks. Providing a rationale helps students understand why a rule is valuable. Focus your rationale on how following the rule will improve the classroom and learning environment for everyone. You might even ask students to provide reasons why they believe it is important to follow the rule. The third step in teaching rules, providing examples and nonexamples, can be done orally, and often it is useful to model the behaviors as well. Many times, students will volunteer to show examples of what it means to follow and not follow the rule, and this provides an opportunity to practice. After you have taught the rule, students will need an opportunity to practice it. You can do this after instruction, for example, by saying, "Okay everyone, show me how you will come into the room tomorrow." When students engage in the correct behavior, provide explicit positive feedback; that is, tell them what they did that was correct. For example, you could say, "That was great! Everyone came into the room and used their indoor voice and we all were in our seats when the bell rang." If students make errors, correct them the same way you would an academic error: by pointing out the mistake and asking, telling, or showing students the right way to follow the rule. If Laura doesn't sit down when the bell rings, you could say, "Laura, you weren't prepared this morning. Please show me where you should be when the bell rings."

Planning how to teach a rule is facilitated by use of a rule-teaching matrix. A completed matrix is shown in Figure 8.2. In this example, the rule is "Stay seated when the bell rings."

To use the matrix, first determine what you will teach; what does following the rule look like? To figure this out, ask how you will "know it when you see it"; what will students say and do? Second, record how you will teach the rule. You could provide a rationale as the teacher in this example did. Alternatively, you might ask students why the rule is important. Third, figure out how you can ensure that students will do the right thing; what can you do to facilitate success? To make it more likely that students remain seated when the bell rings, the teacher in this example decided that she could periodically restate the rule and could ask students what they should do when the bell rings. Also, she seated the students who frequently jumped up when the bell rang near the front of the room and closer to her. Finally, she decided to move around the room, keeping close to students who struggle to follow the rule when the bell is about to ring. Tips for facilitating rule following are given in Table 8.4. The bottom half of the matrix deals with consequences for rule following. These will be discussed shortly.

Teaching should occur not only when the school year begins but also periodically throughout the year. You can preplan when to reteach rules by thinking about difficult times of the year, such as just before and after a holiday or before a schoolwide event. In addition, rules may be retaught when students are struggling to follow them. If you notice, over several days or a week, that many students are not following a classwide rule, you could spend several minutes in the next few days reviewing the rule with the students.

Finally, an important way to teach classroom rules is to follow the rules ourselves. One way that people learn is by watching what others do, and so students look to their teachers to show them what is and is not acceptable. Thus, be sure that you follow your own classroom rules. For example, if a rule is "Listen when others are talking," you should avoid interrupting your students or talking to one student when another is speaking.

Rule: *Stay in your seat when the bell rings*	
What will be taught *When the bell rings, stay in your seat, "back to back, seat to seat, feet to floor."*	**Ways to teach the rule** *1. Explain rule and rationale (staying organized makes sure no one forgets anything or gets hurt)* *2. Ask students to role play following and not following the rule* *3. Provide Bronco bucks to all students who follow the rule after teaching it the first day*
Ways to facilitate success *1. When class begins and/or near the end of class, state the rule or have students state it* *2. Seat students who struggle with the rule near the front of the room* *3. Move about the room when the bell is about to ring—stand near students who struggle with this*	
Outcomes Success: Remains seated	**Responses** *1. Verbal praise, "thanks for staying in your seat."* *2. Classroom game—weekly* *3. Students who are seated may leave first*
Failure: Out of seat	*1. First time: "Show me were you are supposed to be."* *2. Second time in a week: You are out of your seat, you will have to miss 5 minutes of recess tomorrow so we can practice what you need to do."* *3. Third time in a week: "Wow, you need more help remembering the rule. Tomorrow during recess you will go sit in the office and write a 2-page paper about why it is important to follow rules in the classroom."*

Rule:	
What will be taught	**Ways to teach the rule**
Ways to facilitate success	
Outcomes Success:	**Responses**
Failure:	

FIGURES 8.2(a) and (b)   Sample Teaching Matrix

TABLE 8.4	**Tips to Facilitate Rule Following**

Things Students See in the Room

- Signs listing the rules
  - Pictures when needed
  - Students draw signs of the rules
  - Post questions near a routine that ask students what they should have and be doing
- Areas marked on the floor where behavior should or shouldn't occur
  - Dots where students should sit during circle time
  - A line for students to line up on
- Pictures of students following rules

Behaviors You Can Exhibit

- Set a timer for an activity (e.g., free time)
- Signal to get attention
  - Clap your hands
  - Turn the lights on and off
  - Ring a wind-chime
  - Make a statement that students respond to (e.g., "One to three, eyes on me," and the students say, "One two, eyes on you")
- Position students who struggle near yourself or near a signal for appropriate behavior
- Ask students to tell you a rule before it is time to follow the rule

CONSEQUENCES ARE LINKED TO CLASSROOM RULES.   Once you have established your classroom rules and have taught them to your students, you will need to provide consequences for following and not following the rules. This is discussed in far more depth in Chapter 9, where comprehensive systems for acknowledging expected behavior and responding to behavioral challenges are delineated. But the time to consider how you will respond to student behavior with regard to specific rules is when you are developing them. The teaching matrix, depicted in Figure 8.2, is useful for determining consequences. It is worth the time to plan your responses to student behavior before it happens because this will help you to be more consistent in your responses. You should first consider how you will respond when students follow the rule. The goal here is to ensure that rule following will continue, so you will want to provide consequences that students will enjoy. Of course, it also is important to consider how you will respond when a student fails to follow the rule. This also is discussed in more depth in Chapter 10. To do this, think about what would be a logical consequence; logical consequences usually provide an opportunity for reteaching. In addition, consider how you will respond if the problem occurs a second or a third time in rapid succession. For example, consider the rule "Raise your hand before speaking." A logical consequence that provides an opportunity for teaching is to tell the student that they need to raise their hand and then to call on someone else. This makes sense the first time the behavior occurs. But if the student speaks out of turn seven times within one class period, this consequence obviously is having little effect; and in addition, this behavior probably is disruptive to other students. So instead of repeating the rule each time the behavior occurs, perhaps the second time the teacher could tell the student, "You are having trouble raising your hand. We will need to use 5 minutes of recess to practice this together." When developing consequences, be sure that you will be willing and able to implement them consistently. This means that any time the behavior occurs, you will respond to it. In addition, you will respond similarly regardless of who violates the rule. Consistency is critical for decreasing rule violations. Continuing with our example, if the teacher sometimes but not always tolerates talking without raising hands, students would never know when to raise their hands and probably would do so only rarely.

Structure of Routines

In any class, student behavior is affected more by how predictable a routine is and whether expectations for learning and social behavior are clearly stated. Predictability is enhanced by following a daily schedule.

A classroom schedule indicates the order of activities. Classroom schedules need to be flexible enough to incorporate the many instructional activities that can occur in a given day. Thus, schedules do not specify specific activities (e.g., review algebra worksheets from 10:00–10:20); instead, they provide general topics to be covered. As a result, a schedule for an algebra class might allot the first 10 minutes of each day in reviewing homework, the next 30 minutes in teaching new skills or administering a quiz, and the final 10 minutes in checking for understanding. Such a schedule allows for a variety of specific activities. For example, on some days reviewing homework might involve trading assignments with other students and grading; on others it might involve choral responding of correct answers; and on yet other days it might involve a game show format.

When building a schedule, begin by considering how much time is available for instruction. You determine this by factoring out other activities that are programmed to occur during the time students are with you. For example, a third-grade teacher might begin with a 7-hour school day, and then subtract 45 minutes for lunch and recess and an additional 50 minutes for art, music, or physical education. This leaves the teacher with 325 minutes or just over 5.5 hours. This aligns with research on instruction time allocation in school that suggests that less than 80% of available time is actually devoted to instruction in core academic areas (Hoffmeister & Lubke, 1990; Metzker, 2003). Of course, not all of the remaining 5.5 hours will necessarily be devoted to instruction because time will need to be allotted for breaks and transitions between activities. Although breaks and transition time should be included, large amounts of downtime should be avoided for at least two reasons. First and most obviously, no instruction occurs during these times, so extra minutes here represent lost opportunities for instruction. Second, lengthy periods of downtime and extended transition times mean that students are left to their own devices to find something to do. This usually results in disruptive activity such as talking to one another. Once loud or disruptive behavior has begun, quieting the class to prepare for instruction takes much longer than would otherwise be required. Tips for building a schedule follow, and sample schedules are presented in Figure 8.3. In

Times accounted for by out of class activities
- Art, music, physical education—daily from noon to 12:30
- Lunch and recess: 12:30–1:30

Activities to include in the schedule and amount of time to devote to activities
- Reading and writing: 100 minutes including small group instruction for students in Tier II reading
- Math: 60 minutes
- Science: 60 minutes
- Social studies: 60 minutes

Time	Activity	Instructor
7:45–7:55	Morning welcome/review	Me
7:55–8:00	Transition to reading	
8:00–9:00	Reading/Writing	Me
9:00–9:05	Transition to Math	Me
9:05–10:05	Math	Me and student teacher
10:05–10:10	Transition	Me
10:10–10:50	Independent reading/small group instruction	Student teacher, reading teacher
10:50–10:55	Transition to Science	
10:55–11:55	Science	Me and student teacher
11:55–12:00	Transition to Specials	
12:00–12:30	Specials	
12:30–1:30	Lunch and recess	
1:30–2:30	History/Social Studies	Me
2:30–2:45	Review, cleanup	
2:45	Dismissal	

FIGURE 8.3   Scheduling Time in the Classroom

this figure, a hypothetical schedule for a third-grade room is on the left, and a schedule for a biology class in high school is on the right.

Record all the instructional activities your students will engage in when they are with you and write down how much time you would like to devote to each activity. Make a table on paper or in a word processing program. Put in many more rows than you think you will need and use three columns labeled "Time," "Activity," and "Teacher."

1. Record when the class period or school day begins and ends in the first and last rows, respectively.
2. Begin filling in the remaining blocks with activities from your list. Consider putting core areas (e.g., reading, math) in the morning as most students are more focused in the morning. Also, this allows Tier II (small group instruction) interventions in those areas to occur in the afternoon, building on the material covered in your classroom.
3. Record who will be primarily responsible for each activity. (This is needed only if someone else, such as a teacher's aide, periodically provides instruction.)
4. If you have a teaching assistant, consider when he or she will have breaks and be sure that you can cover the activities scheduled for those times by yourself.

The final consideration with regard to schedules is whether they should be posted. In general, elementary school classes usually require that a schedule be posted on the wall. Students can thus check where they are in the day and what is coming next. In addition, teachers in kindergarten and first grade can use the schedule as part of instruction, helping students learn valuable skills in planning. Middle and high school teachers generally do not need to post the schedule; it is important, however, that the schedule be reviewed frequently. Regardless of whether a schedule is posted, teachers should inform students at the beginning of the day about any disruptions to the schedule, such as an assembly or a quiz.

Supervision Style

A great way to prevent problems from occurring is by using active supervision (Colvin et al., 1997; DePry & Sugai, 2002; Lewis, Sugai, & Colvin, 2000; Oswald, Safran, & Johanson, 2005). One part of supervision, discussed earlier in this chapter, is ensuring that you can observe the room from all areas. Equally important, however, is the way in which you supervise. To begin, let's define *active supervision*. DePry and Sugai (2002) noted that active supervision has three features: movement around the area, interactions with students, and the use of acknowledgements for prosocial behavior. In a classroom, an additional component is needed: frequently checking on student learning.

Key to successful supervision is moving around the room frequently to prevent problems and encourage appropriate behavior. Successful teachers rarely stay in the same place for long; rather, they are constantly moving around the room. Moving around the room enables teachers to observe all students and monitor their behavior. Teachers can frequently position themselves near students who require more supervision. Beyond being useful for supervision, however, moving around the room while instructing helps maintain student attention. Think about experiences you have had listening to a speaker; the most engaging speakers do not stand in one place but move around.

Active supervision also involves frequently interacting with students and checking their learning. During instruction, this could take the form of providing frequent opportunities to respond, using both choral responding and individual responses. When students are working on activities, stop beside students frequently as you move about the room to check in with them. Be sure that they understand the assignment and are completing it successfully.

Finally, active supervision includes the use of frequent reinforcement for rule following. As discussed earlier, providing incentives for rule following helps ensure that students will engage in expected behaviors.

Activities That Occur Before or After Class

Setting events that may affect student behavior in your room include activities that occur before students come to class or upcoming activities of which students are aware. Suppose that you receive a phone call from a dear friend that you have not seen in years. Your friend tells you that she will be coming through your town this evening and would love to see you. As the day goes by, you probably would grow increasingly excited and even find it difficult to concentrate on tasks at hand; your friend's anticipated visit is a setting event for your difficulties in focusing. For students, events occurring before class that may affect their behavior in the classroom include recess or another period in which there was little structure and lots of activity, or an unexpected event such as a fire drill. Anticipated events also may increase disruptive behavior and excitement. In this case, the events usually are things that students are excited about, such as a school concert given by a popular musical group or the last day of class before a holiday.

The functional behavior assessment process delineated in Chapter 6 will enable you to determine whether events occurring before or after your class are affecting student behavior. If you identify such events, you will need to take steps to minimize their impact. This can be accomplished by reviewing rules, modifying the activities in your room, or using neutralizing routines (Horner, Day, & Day, 1997) as antecedent interventions. In addition, you could increase reinforcement for appropriate behavior (a consequence intervention).

One way to minimize the effects of setting events is to review the rules. This strategy is most effective if the setting event is an anticipated event occurring after your class. To use this approach, review the rules with the students when they enter your room. (Use a manner of your choosing: You could tell the students the rules, or you could ask them to tell you the rules.) This approach is most effective if used along with other approaches such as modifying instruction or increasing reinforcement.

Modifying instruction also can prevent disruptive behavior. This approach changes some feature of the task at hand. For example, you could allow students to work in groups rather than individually, or you might shorten the task. This approach can be applied fairly easily for setting events that occur only occasionally;

for example, an upcoming holiday break. If a setting event routinely occurs before or after your class, however, this approach obviously would not be logical. After all, you would not want to shorten math instruction by 10 minutes every day merely because students go to lunch just after your class.

A third approach to setting events is to use neutralizing routines. Horner et al. (1997) demonstrated that problem behavior evoked by specific setting events (e.g., unexpected cancellation of an upcoming visit by a parent) could be reduced by implementing specific, enjoyable activities after the setting event occurs. Suppose that your students are in gym just before your class on Mondays and Fridays, and so on those days they enter your room noisily, taking up to 10 minutes to get settled down. In this case a neutralizing routine would be designed to eliminate the effects of the gym class. What activities could students engage in for a few minutes to produce this effect? One idea might be to ask the gym teacher to use the last 5 minutes of gym class as "quiet, focused time." Alternatively, you could engage your students in a quiet mindfulness exercise for the first five minutes of your class. You also could use the first 10 minutes of your class to review, teaching your students to enter the room and immediately get to work on a worksheet. All students who independently finish the worksheet in the allotted time could earn an acknowledgement.

As illustrated in this example, providing reinforcement for expected behavior is an important component of decreasing the negative effects of setting events. On days that a setting event is in place, consider increasing reinforcement for your students. For example, you could offer two points instead of one for students who meet expectations.

So far, we have discussed several different setting events for problem behavior, providing guidelines for preventing problems and encouraging prosocial behavior. We turn our attention now to discriminative stimuli or triggers.

Manipulating the Effects of Discriminative Stimuli

Discriminative stimuli are events that occur before a problem behavior and, because they signal that a consequence is differentially more likely to occur, trigger the problem behavior. Using a functional behavior assessment you identified discriminative stimuli triggering problem behavior for your students. As described in Chapter 6, classes of possible discriminative stimuli include changes in teaching style, in the social structure, or in the activity including its duration or other specific features. Review Table 6.5 for more information on these classes of discriminative stimuli.

When considering an intervention to manipulate the effects of discriminative stimuli for a group of students, answer the following questions:

1. Can the discriminative stimulus be removed?
2. Can the consequences that reinforce problem behavior be minimized or removed?
3. Can you add or increase reinforcement for appropriate behavior?

Changing features of your room or instruction to eliminate the trigger, provided that instruction is not impaired, may be the easiest way to prevent problems from occurring. For example, if your students talk among themselves when you sit at your desk in the back grading papers, can you simply move around more when students are present? Or perhaps you could sit in a more central location or grade papers only when the students are not present, instead circulating throughout the room when students are working independently.

If the discriminative stimulus cannot be removed, you will need to change the consequences that follow the behavior. This will involve minimizing the payoff for problem behavior or increasing reinforcement for appropriate behavior. Mr. Witmer's introductory algebra class illustrates this approach.

During the fall semester, Mr. Witmer knew he would miss class approximately once in every week in order to help the principal with a special project during that time. He had arranged for a substitute teacher, and they had met to review the lesson plans and materials. Further, Mr. Witmer had observed the substitute's teaching on several occasions and was confident in her skills. Unfortunately, after teaching twice for Mr. Witmer, the substitute told him that she found the students to be very disruptive. In addition, students often whispered behind her back and delayed completing assignments. She clearly was not enjoying teaching this group and, in addition, the students' learning was suffering. *In this example, the presence of the substitute is a discriminative stimulus for disruptive and off-task behavior. This behavior is more likely to be reinforced when she is present than when Mr. Witmer is there.* Mr. Witmer was in a quandary; he was invested in his class, but he also was greatly enjoying the project he was involved with. Further, he believed strongly that his students should behave appropriately whether he was there or not. Thus, simply returning to teaching and removing the discriminative stimulus was not an option. After thinking about it a bit more, Mr. Witmer decided to change the consequences for behavior when the substitute was present. He gave the substitute teacher a data sheet to fill out after each class. Using the sheet (which is shown in Figure 8.4), the substitute

	1 Very poor—very few students met this expectation	2 Poor—only a few students met this expectation	3 Acceptable—Most students met this expectation at least some of the time	4 Excellent—Most students met this expectation throughout class today
Be a good learner				
Be responsible				
Respect yourself, property, and others				

FIGURE 8.4   Rating Scale Used by Mr. Witmer's Substitute Teacher

rated the extent to which students' behavior aligned with the school's expectations: Be a good learner; be responsible; and respect yourself, property, and others. Mr. Witmer reviewed the data sheet with his students and told them that if they earned a 4 or higher on all expectations for two consecutive substitute days, then they would have no homework assigned on the following Friday afternoon. If, however, students earned a 2 or lower on any expectation on any given day, then they would have double homework assigned the next evening. The intervention worked well beyond even Mr. Witmer's expectations. Students never earned a 2 or lower, and after the first week they earned free time on almost every occasion it was available. Further, at the end of the semester the substitute told him that the class was the best behaved of any middle school class she'd ever worked with.

When attempting to change consequences, remember that it may not be possible to simply remove a reinforcing consequence. This is especially true if, as in the case of Mr. Witmer's class, the reinforcer is attention from peers. Thus, a more realistic goal often is to minimize the reinforcement, or to increase the reinforcement for appropriate behavior. In addition, you can add a negative consequence (punishment) to decrease the undesired behavior. Mr. Witmer took this approach, doubling homework for students reported as being highly disruptive on days when the substitute was present.

SUMMARY

This chapter focused on antecedent interventions for classroom settings. Antecedent interventions are implemented after conducting a classroom FBA and consist of altering events that seem to predict the occurrence of problem behavior. The goal of antecedent interventions is to diminish the occurrence of problem behavior while increasing the probability that students will behave appropriately. Our focus was on how to arrange the classroom so as to facilitate instruction and appropriate behavior. We began by reviewing ways in which setting events might be altered, and we concluded by discussing how discriminative stimuli might be modified. The topic of instruction—a crucial antecedent variable—is presented next in Chapter 10.

Chapter Review

- Student behavior is affected by several noninstructional variables that teachers can control including effective use of wall space, the location of the teacher's desk, and student desk arrangement.
- Desired behavior can be facilitated by developing and teaching relevant classroom

expectations and rules. Expectations are shorthand ways of stating desired behavior, while rules tell students precisely what to say and do.
- Classroom expectations and rules should be taught using the principles of good instruction. Students also should be taught

consequences for following rules and for rule violations, and these consequences should be implemented consistently.
- Things that happen outside of the classroom—such as what activity students are engaged in before or after your class—can

impact student behavior. There are various effective strategies to manage these events including reviewing the rules, modifying expectations, and using neutralizing routines.

Application

1. Think about a classroom you have been in where students are not as engaged as they could be. What classroom expectations and rules could you develop that might improve the learning environment?
2. There is an assembly after your class to which students have been looking forward for several weeks. About halfway through class the students are very excited and hardly able to focus on instruction.

Identify at least two strategies you could use to respond to this setting event that is after your class.
3. Identify discriminative stimuli that might affect student behavior. For each discriminative stimulus identified, determine whether you can remove the stimulus, change the consequences for the problem behavior, or alter the consequences for the desired behavior.

References

Axelrod, S., Hall, R., & Tams, A. (1979). Comparison of two common classroom seating arrangements. *Academic Therapy, 15*, 29–36.

Baines, E., Kutnick, P., & Blatchford, P. (2008). *Promoting effective group work in the primary classroom: A handbook for teachers and practitioners.* London: Taylor & Francis.

Colvin, G., Sugai, G., Good, R. H., & Lee, Y. (1997). Effect of active supervision and precorrection on transition behaviors of elementary students. *School Psychology Quarterly, 12*(4), 344–363.

DePry, R. L., & Sugai, G. (2002). The effect of active supervision and pre-correction on minor behavioral incidents in a sixth grade general education classroom. *Journal of Behavioral Education, 11*(4), 255–267.

Hoffmeister, A., & Lubke, M. (1990). *Research into practice: Implementing effective teaching strategies.* Boston: Allyn & Bacon.

Horner, R. H., Day, H. M., & Day, J. R. (1997). Using neutralizing routines to reduce problem behaviors. *Journal of Applied Behavior Analysis, 30*(4), 601.

Horner, R. H., Sugai, G., & Anderson, C. M. (2010). Examining the evidence base for school-wide positive behavior support. *Focus on Exceptional Children, 42*(8), 1–16.

Kern, L., & Clemens, N. H. (2007). Antecedent strategies to promote appropriate classroom behavior. *Psychology in the Schools, 44*(1), 65–75.

Lewis, T. J., Sugai, G., & Colvin, G. (2000). The effect of pre-correction and active supervision on the recess behavior of elementary school students. *Education and Treatment of Children, 23*, 109–121.

Lohrmann, S., & Talerico, J. (2004). Anchor the boat: A classwide intervention to reduce problem behavior. *Journal of Positive Behavior Interventions, 6*(2), 113–120.

Marx, A., Fuhrer, U., & Hartig, T. (1999). Effects of classroom seating arrangements on children's question-asking. *Learning Environments Research, 2*(3), 249–263.

Marzano, R. J., Pickering, D. J., & Pollock, J. E. (2003). *Classroom instruction that works.* Alexandria, VA: Association for Supervision and Curriculum Development.

Metzker, B. (2003). Time and learning, *ERIC Digest ED 474260.* Eugene, OR: ERIC Clearinghouse on Educational Management.

Oswald, K., Safran, S., & Johanson, G. (2005). Preventing trouble: Making schools safer places using positive behavior supports. *Education & Treatment of Children, 28*(3), 265–278.

Reinke, W. M., Lewis-Palmer, T., & Merrell, K. (2008). The classroom check-up: A classwide teacher consultation model for increasing praise and decreasing disruptive behavior. *School Psychology Review*, 37(3), 315.

Simonsen, B., Fairbanks, S., Briesch, A., Myers, D., & Sugai, G. (2008). Evidence-based practices in classroom management: Considerations for research to practice. *Education and Treatment of Children*, 31(3), 351–380.

Watson, S. M., Gable, R. A., & Greenwood, C. R. (2010). Combining ecobehavioral assessment, functional assessment, and response to intervention to promote more effective classroom instruction. *Remedial and Special Education* (March 1, 2010).

9

Using Consequences to Encourage Student Behavior in the Classroom

CHAPTER OBJECTIVES

After reading this chapter, you should be able to describe the following concepts:

- Reinforcement
- Fading
- Post-reinforcement pause
- Ratio strain
- Whole-class acknowledgement system
- Token economy

You also should be able to:

- Provide a rationale for using a classroom reinforcement system
- Explain the two "rules" for using reinforcement in the classroom
- Differentiate between positive and negative reinforcement
- Identify the three main types of reinforcers
- List potential problems with using activity reinforcers and suggest strategies to avoid these problems
- Explain when a whole-class system is and is not appropriate and when an individualized intervention should be considered instead

It's August and Ms. Earhart is setting up her fifth-grade classroom for the school year. She is just coming off the worst school year she has ever had in terms of classroom behavior. It wasn't the "high magnitude" behaviors (the ones that resulted in immediate office discipline referrals) that seemed to occur constantly, but rather the minor misbehaviors. In the previous year, she had problems with students talking out, not complying with her directions, and being off-task. Students never seemed do what she wanted them to be doing, and at particular times, especially at the end of a school day or the week, students became aggressive and the ensuing disruption was loud enough to be heard in the hallways. The behavior problems had even prevented students from completing the course units in Reading and in Math. Ms. Earhart was baffled about what to do. The school had implemented a system in which students received "Gotcha Bucks" for displaying prosocial behavior in common areas. The Gotcha Bucks enabled students to purchase various incentives from the school store; in addition, all purchased tickets were entered into daily, weekly, monthly, and semester-long drawings for larger incentives. But this schoolwide system was not designed for classroom behavior, so it did not make sense for Ms. Earhart to translate it for use in her classroom. Further, she had exhausted all of her in-class punishment procedures and had sent so many students to the office that the principal ultimately had to address the situation with her in her classroom. Ms. Earhart had no idea what to do differently this year, so she decided to consult her mentor teacher, Mrs. Parish.

In the above example, Ms. Earhart has created a classroom procedure that focuses specifically on students' problem behavior, but has no means to recognize students' doing what she wants them to do. By giving attention only to what she did *not* want to happen, Mrs. Earhart was losing valuable opportunities to teach and reinforce students. The lack of any focus on what she *did* want to happen set Ms. Earhart and her students up to fail. By relying only on punishment consequences in her classroom, Ms. Earhart is setting herself up for more challenging behavior.

In this chapter we describe two types of acknowledgement systems for multiple students (whole class and small groups): informal strategies to acknowledge desired behavior, and formal whole-class systems of reinforcement. In Chapter 12 we will present more intensive individual-student systems of reinforcement. First, to describe classwide reinforcers, this chapter begins by reviewing the definition of reinforcement and outlining the objections that many teachers (including Ms. Earhart) raise when the use of reinforcement in classroom procedures is discussed. Next, the three main categories of reinforcers (attention, activities, and tangibles) are discussed in terms of using informal systems of reinforcement. Third, formal systems of reinforcement within a classroom are reviewed and discussed together with the main categories of reinforcers; here we introduce a formal system of reinforcement supported by more than 30 years of research, the Good Behavior Game. Finally, the need to provide reinforcement to both teachers and students is discussed.

TEACHERS' OBJECTIONS TO REINFORCEMENT

When considering the use of reinforcement in the classroom, teachers often raise several concerns:

- "Reinforcement is bribery, and bribery is just wrong."
- "We should not have to reinforce students for doing the right thing; they should just do it."

- "If we reinforce students, then we will take away their intrinsic motivation."
- "Consequences should be delivered at home by parents, not by teachers."
- "Children who misbehave at school come from bad home lives, and we can't do anything to change that."
- "I don't have time to implement a fancy classroom system. I spend the entire day teaching and dealing with behavior problems."

For some teachers, the mention of reinforcement procedures evokes images of teachers running around schools and doling out enormous bags of M & Ms indiscriminately to every student in sight; or else, it is considered to be bribery and something that only persons of questionable moral character would use. This misunderstanding may be attributed to two factors. First, the concerns about reinforcement in the classroom have been fomented by an intentional campaign that suggests that students are deleteriously impacted by teachers who use reinforcement systems (see Noddings, 2005; Kohn, 1993). Second, the terminology used by different individuals, both in research and in practice, seems to be confused. For example, when people refer to reinforcement as bribery, they seem unaware that bribery is defined as an inducement or incentive to behave illegally or dishonestly. Bribery occurs when a person dishonestly persuades another to do something by paying or providing some other incentive before the behavior occurs (McKean, 2005). In contrast, reinforcement is defined as a consequence (a) delivered *after* a response that (b) results in an increase in the *future* probability of the response. Thus, whereas bribery induces a person to do something once, reinforcement follows a response and makes it more likely that the response will occur again. This chapter will focus first on clarifying the terminology, and then on relating how classroom success can be effectively reinforced without dispensing a single M & M or committing bribery.

As previously defined, *reinforcement* is the process by which a behavior is followed by a given consequence that increases the probability that the behavior will occur again. In other words, we reinforce a behavior when we give or take away things in the environment that make someone *more* likely to do that behavior in the future. For example, if a teacher insults students every time they ask a question and the students actually ask more questions in the future, these insults would be considered to be reinforcers. Recall that, even though we would *expect* or *believe* that the insults should decrease the questions, the insults actually are reinforcers because they increase future occurrences of the questioning behavior. This is what makes reinforcement different from a reward. Rewards are objects given to or actions done for an individual after a certain behavior is demonstrated; they do not have to determine future occurrences of behavior. Kaplan (1996) uses the example of Olympic gold medals to describe a reward. Imagine a swimmer who receives a gold medal and decides that they have had enough of swimming and never swim again. In this example, the gold medal is certainly a reward but it is definitely not a reinforcer. In the vignette that opens this chapter, Ms. Earhart used what she believed to be were punishment procedures to decrease challenging behaviors, but in fact the behaviors were getting worse. This indicates that her responses to the challenging behaviors were actually reinforcing them.

Teachers often feel strongly that students should behave appropriately simply because it is the right thing to do. This is true! Wouldn't it be great if everyone followed this rule? Unfortunately, this simply is not the case. Although some children in schools will follow the rules regardless of whether we implement reinforcing consequences, many children will not. At this point, we have a choice. We can either say, "Well, they should do the right thing, and if they don't, it is not my problem"; or we can implement an intervention to help these children learn to do the right thing, which will require the use of reinforcement. If you are not yet convinced, think about all the things you do throughout a typical day or week: You get up in the morning, you go to work, you spend time with your family and friends, and so on. Regardless of how much you love your job, you probably would not continue to work if you stopped receiving a paycheck; the paycheck reinforces your behavior of going to work. Of course, working is reinforced by many other consequences that occur each day including more covert ones such as the happiness we feel when we have helped a child. Similarly, why do we spend time with some people but not others? We spend time with those whose company we enjoy—that is, whose company we find reinforcing. We spend less time with people whose company is not reinforcing. Consequently, people continue to engage in behavior that is reinforced and cease to engage in behavior that is not reinforced.

The reinforcement for many of the behaviors we engage in every day does not occur all the time or even very frequently. We continue to engage in these behaviors, however, because doing so makes us feel better about ourselves. This idea will be discussed further in the final section of this chapter, "Teachers Need Reinforcement Too." With the students that we work with, our goal is to help them become better citizens of their school, community, and world by "doing the right thing" just because it is the right thing to do. Instilling this motivation, however, often requires the use of external consequences or reinforcers. We reinforce behavior with valued consequences to teach students that doing certain behaviors—doing the right thing—can pay off for them. Over time we often decrease the use of these external consequences when private feelings, such as a feeling of accomplishment, start to become more powerful.

A related concern expressed by many is that using external reinforcers will decrease intrinsic motivation; that is, students will cease to do things they once enjoyed because they now expect a reinforcer. This perspective is widely distributed in the field of education (e.g., Burton et al., 2006; Deci, Koestner, & Ryan, 1999a, b; Kohn, 1993; Vansteenkiste et al., 2004). In brief, proponents of this perspective argue that children provided with response-contingent reinforcers lose their internal motivation to act in a certain way and thus, as soon as the reinforcers are withdrawn, will cease to do the desired behavior. Although passionately argued, this perspective has been debunked by decades of research that shows that reinforcement is effective not just for increasing behavior but for maintaining it over time and by recent meta-analytic reviews of this research (Cameron & Pierce, 1996; Eisenberger, Pierce, & Cameron, 1999; Lepper, Henderlong, & Gingras, 1999). Research on the supposed detrimental effects of reinforcers on intrinsic motivation has demonstrated that reinforcement used to increase desired behavior (a) is effective and (b) does not reduce the likelihood of children's continuing to engage in desired behavior should reinforcement be removed (relative to what would occur with no reinforcement at all).

Some teachers are hesitant or unwilling to respond to behavior in school because they believe that parents should manage children's behavior at home. To some extent this is true—parents certainly should help their children learn how to get along with others. We know, however, that consequences tend to be most effective when delivered immediately after the behavior, not hours later. Imagine trying to teach a child math at school by relying on the parents for feedback on whether the child's responses were right or wrong. The feedback would be given hours after the child completed a math assignment. In this arrangement the child probably would take a very long time to learn math. This same logic applies when teaching children social behavior. If we wait to let children know that they behaved well or to correct behavioral errors, the delay between the behavior and the consequence is so long that it probably will not be effective. This is not to suggest that parents should not be involved in a student's education. In fact, teachers should develop multiple strategies to communicate with parents and involve them in the classroom. These would include newsletters and e-mails home, phone calls (not just when students misbehave but also when they do something well), and parent-teacher meetings. In addition, parents could be encouraged to volunteer in the classroom. Teachers should inform parents of classroom rules and expectations at the beginning of the school year and could, throughout the year, ask parents to focus on specific expectations or rules at home. For example, a teacher might send the following message to parents: "This week we are focusing on being respectful. You can help us by talking to your children about what it means to respect yourself, respect others, and respect property. When you see your children being respectful, be sure to thank them and point out what they did."

Many educators believe that children who misbehave at school have difficult home lives and are not prepared to be in school. Unfortunately, this is all too true in many cases. Often, children live in dire situations including extreme poverty, a drug-abusing or alcoholic parent, or abuse or neglect; such children usually focus on simply surviving and may not have learned the social skills that are crucial for success in school and society. When children come to school lacking key skills, our responsibility as educators is to help them learn these key behaviors.

Finally, some teachers say they are unable to implement a classwide behavior management system because they simply are too busy teaching and responding to problem behavior—they have no time to do anything else. These teachers seem not to realize that classroom systems can be conducted in a very time-efficient manner and that well-run classrooms enable teachers to spend less time managing behavior and more time teaching (e.g., Alric et al., 2007; Little, Akin-Little, & Newman-Eig, 2010; Poduska et al., 2008; Reinke, Lewis-Palmer, & Merrell, 2008; Schanding & Sterling-Turner, 2010; Simonsen et al., 2008; Watson, Gable, & Greenwood, 2010). This may explain why reinforcement procedures continue to be one of the most misunderstood and often underutilized elements in the classroom for effective behavior management and academic instruction. For reinforcement in the classroom, the pattern with students who continue to engage in behavioral challenges apparently is that schools wait for them to do the wrong thing and then we react to it. And not only do they wait for students to do the wrong behavior, but they wait for them to do it multiple times; this makes intervening effectively that much harder because intervention is most effective when it occurs early—soon after a problem appears (Albers, Glover, & Kratochwill, 2007; George, Kincaid, & Pollard-Sage, 2009; Severson, Walker, Hope-Doolittle, Kratochwill, & Gresham, 2007; Sprague & Walker, 2005; Sugai & Horner, 2009).

But what if schools changed this perspective and started reinforcing what they want students to do rather than what they don't want students to do? In other words, while some teachers may state that they do not believe in reinforcement, they are really saying that they do not believe in deliberately reinforcing desired academic and social behaviors. This leads to the first rule of the use of reinforcement:

> **Reinforcement rule #1:** Students will find ways to access reinforcement, and it is up to the teacher to modify the environment so as to provide reinforcement for desired behaviors rather than undesired behaviors.

Teachers who avoid using specific, deliberate reinforcement tactics for identified behaviors are simply allowing the environment to reinforce any and all types of behaviors—often students' challenging behavior. Students who pay attention to and laugh at each others' misbehaviors or engage in high-magnitude disruption to get out of class are simply using strategies to access reinforcement such as attention and escape. But reinforcement that is powerful enough and is provided systematically at a dense reinforcement schedule makes the classroom a place where students can access attention for desired behaviors and a place where they want to stay instead of leave. Throughout this chapter, we use the terms *dense schedule of reinforcement* and *thin schedule of reinforcement* to refer to how frequently or infrequently reinforcement is provided in the environment.

Positive Reinforcement

Selecting positive reinforcers for a classroom is a critical yet complex decision for the teacher. Students' tastes and interests change regardless of age, and the novelty (and therefore the reinforcing strength) of almost any reinforcer can wear thin. Because student preferences are constantly changing and different reinforcers gain or lose reinforcing strength, teachers may feel like they are trying to hit a moving target. Further, while research shows that typical reinforcers like effective praise are often underused, teachers can also fall into the opposite trap, namely, implementing reinforcers that are far too powerful, extensive, or complex for the behavior (e.g., 60 minutes of recess for completing a worksheet) because the student has become very difficult and teachers are anxious to get the student to perform the desired behavior. Because these situations are just as problematic as classrooms that provide too little reinforcement, we introduce reinforcement rule #2.

> **Reinforcement rule #2:** We should use as little reinforcement, in terms of time, energy or money, as necessary to increase the probability that the behavior will occur again.

The ultimate objective is to have the environment naturally reinforce appropriate behaviors, without artificial or teacher-distributed reinforcers. Using as little reinforcement as possible is important because our goal is to create independent, autonomous individuals who are internally motivated to complete work, observe social norms, and behave appropriately rather than dependent on external, teacher-supplied reinforcers. The reluctance to use reinforcement in the classroom setting may be partially due to teachers and other adults not observing this rule. This rule is also related to two other considerations. First, all reinforcers should be gradually removed to allow the response to occur independent of the presentation of reinforcers. This process is referred to as *fading*—the systematic removal of stimuli, including prompts, reinforcers, and so on, to foster the occurrence of the target behavior without these stimuli. In other words, reinforcers put into the environment must eventually be removed, so the less you put in, the less you have to take out. Second, the more naturalistic and authentic a reinforcer is across various settings, the better. In other words, teachers should rely on reinforcers that are closely approximated in other settings (e.g., other classrooms, work environments, etc.). Again, the end goal of this rule and its caveats is to have students become reinforced intrinsically for displaying prosocial behaviors.

Negative Reinforcement

Classroom systems that use negative reinforcement involve the removal of some desired item or privilege. For example, students might begin class with 15 points each, with points being deducted for rule violations such as talking out of turn. At the end of class, all students with 10 or more points are allowed 10 minutes of free time. Such systems have been shown to be effective, and in many cases as effective as positive reinforcement systems (Poduska et al., 2008; Theodore, Bray, & Kehle, 2004). One potential problem with negative reinforcement systems is that, because teachers are required to focus on problematic behavior, they may be less likely to notice and reinforce desired behavior. Generally speaking, teachers who use a negative reinforcement system should combine it with a system of positive reinforcement.

> When Ms. Earhart and Mrs. Parish meet, Mrs. Parish politely probes her about her existing classroom procedures. "So tell me what you do when students get a problem right in Math or when they answer a question correctly during Social Studies."
>
> "Well, I tell them 'That's right,' or 'Good job.'"
>
> "Ok, but what do you do when everyone is doing working hard on an assignment, staying on task, or following your directions?"
>
> "Well, nothing; I have always thought that if I say something I might end up disrupting the class or getting them off task."
>
> "Yes, but if you don't tell them when they are 'getting it right' with behavior, that would be just like not telling them when they correctly solve a math problem. That means you are giving all of your attention to them when they make a behavioral mistake, which sets a tone for your classroom. I want you to try something for the first

couple of weeks. Put a handful of paperclips in your right-hand pocket. Every time you say something encouraging to a student about their behavior or you let them take part in a fun activity because of good behavior, move one paperclip to your left-hand pocket," instructed Mrs. Parish.

"Ok, that sounds easy enough."

"Sure, but here is the other part: Every time you say or do something to discourage or punish a behavior, you have to move one of the paperclips back to your right-hand pocket."

"Ooh, this is going to be hard. How do I find different things to say or do to encourage behavior? I know I can't just say 'Good job, good job, good job' all day," asked Ms. Earhart.

"Well, I think it will help if you think about encouraging behavior with three main types of reinforcers . . ."

ACKNOWLEDGING APPROPRIATE BEHAVIOR

There are three broad categories of direct reinforcers that teachers can use in their classrooms to acknowledge appropriate behavior: (1) attention as a reinforcer, (2) activity reinforcers, (3) and tangible reinforcers. These can be combined in numerous ways to powerfully affect behavior. A foundation of any classroom management system is an informal system for acknowledging appropriate behavior at high rates. Effective teachers typically use more than one acknowledgement system (e.g., an individualized system and a whole-class system) and vary the use of the three types of reinforcers that can be provided. The reason we need an informal system of reinforcement is because teachers do not "remember" to acknowledge students as often as required to facilitate consistent occurrences of desired behavior; in fact, research has shown that the vast majority of teachers' noninstructional comments are corrections or negative statements (Brophy, 1981; Kalis, Vannest, & Parker, 2007). Systems of acknowledgement help teachers to provide positive feedback more often. We will present these three types of reinforcers and some basic guidelines for providing reinforcement. Then we will discuss specific strategies for whole class and small group reinforcers.

Attention as a Reinforcer

The use of teacher and peer attention is a valuable tool for classroom teachers in increasing or maintaining specific behaviors. Getting noticed, receiving praise, or having a sticky note saying "Great job..." placed on the edge of students' desks are all examples of the first category of reinforcers that students can receive from teachers. Verbal reinforcement, social recognition, and physical gestures (e.g., pats on the back) can be provided easily and frequently. These more natural reinforcers usually occur across settings, and they take much less effort to provide. However, teachers must ensure that they give these reinforcers frequently and contingently when desired replacement behaviors do occur. For example, Ms. Smith can reinforce Bobby for raising his hand with immediate descriptive verbal praise ("Good hand raising, Bobby"), being especially vigilant initially to catch every occasion on which he raises his hand. She also will need to provide some precorrective prompts ("Bobby, remember to raise your hand when you want to get my attention"). Although all individuals desire to be left alone at times, students of all ages universally have the need to be noticed, recognized, praised, and accepted (even though older students deny craving that reinforcement); and while we may deliver attention in different ways to high school students than to preschool students, attention from adults and peers will act as a powerful reinforcer up and down the age continuum. Teachers' use of their attention to reinforce desired behavior can take many different forms. One teacher recounts how the boys in his fifth-grade class loved professional wrestling, and while he didn't share this interest, he knew that learning about professional wrestling and then discussing it with students after they had engaged in desirable behaviors (like work completion) was highly reinforcing and increased all types of task completion from his students.

Within this discussion we will address effective praise as the main reinforcer that teachers can use to increase desired behaviors. But it should be noted that attention is also provided inadvertently throughout a school day, and so in many situations attention acts as a reinforcer for both desired and undesired behaviors. For example, a teacher may redirect a student who is making poor behavior choices or may send the student to the office to talk to someone about the disruptive behavior. In both of these instances the student is accessing attention for undesired behavior, and so the teacher may unwittingly be reinforcing that behavior. Using attention strategically and deliberately is a vital tool for highly effective teachers who elicit high rates of prosocial behavior from their students.

Effective praise can be defined as praise delivered together with the reason for the acknowledgement, contingent on appropriate behavior. Effective praise is typically more than just saying "Good job." Effective praise can be a verbal or written statement that both reinforces a given behavior and teaches the conditions under which the behavior is to be emitted (Sutherland, Conroy, Abrams, & Vo, 2010). There are several advantages of using effective praise as a reinforcer for desired behaviors. First, effective praise is highly efficient in terms of teacher time and energy. In other words, very little effort is needed to make statements that will increase future occurrences of that behavior. Second, attention is a reinforcer that occurs naturally in the environment. Praise is something that (we hope) occurs in all types of work environments. Third, effective praise builds a positive relationship and establishes rapport between teacher and students. This is imperative, particularly for students with long-standing patterns of challenging behavior. Often these students have experienced only coercive relationships with teachers and other adults. Effective praise is a tool for breaking these patterns of interaction. Finally, effective praise acts as a signal (or discriminative stimulus) to other students that praise is available if they engage in the same prosocial behaviors. The use of effective praise can be easily implemented, and research suggests that praise statements should outweigh redirection and punitive statements by a ratio of 4:1 (Stichter, Stormont, & Lewis, 2009).

The steps for using effective praise are straightforward. They include stating the student's names, the behavior, and acknowledgement in close proximity to the student when the response occurs. Be sincere and credible by matching

facial expressions, tone of voice, and body language to the statement. Start by selecting one behavior to acknowledge and utilize a variety of verbal and written
praise statements for multiple students. Revise the type, delivery, and frequency
of praise as needed based on individual student responses. For new skills, praise
immediately after each behavior. Gradually reduce praise as the skill is mastered. Teachers sometimes think that providing attention to students who are
doing what they are supposed to be doing will interrupt them and stop the desired behaviors; and, in fact, if a teacher were to rush over to a student engaging
in the desired behavior and loudly gush over her or him, that likely would happen. However, there are a number of ways to provide praise and attention effectively. A quick thumbs-up, eye contact, or a whispered statement all may be
effective ways to provide attention for desired behaviors without breaking a
student's momentum.

The saying "Any attention is better than no attention" is commonly offered
to explain why students engage in challenging behavior. This scenario often
plays itself out in classrooms, where students are deprived of teacher attention
for desired behaviors. This is especially true in classrooms with students with
challenging behaviors. Research indicates that students with emotional and behavioral disorders actually receive far less praise than their peers and far below
the recommended ratios of praise statements for academic success. Other obstacles to provide recommended amounts of praise include the feeling among
many teachers that praise statements are unnatural, patronizing, or insincere.
There is no "magic bullet" to overcome these perceptions of providing attention
other than practice and trying to find statements and/or strategies that work for
the individual teacher. Stating factual observations (e.g., "I see everyone is
almost done with their worksheets") may be a good place to start.

Finally, attention is also useful as a reinforcer that can be combined with
other categories of reinforcers. For example, a teacher might join a board game or
a game of kickball, thus combining an activity reinforcer with attention as a reinforcer. In an early childhood classroom a teacher could award a hand stamp to
each student who is following directions. In this instance the teacher is combining attention with a tangible reinforcer.

Activity Reinforcers

Computer games, extra recess time, and free time at the end of a class period to
talk with friends are all examples of the second category, activity reinforcers.
Activity reinforcers cover a wide gamut of individual and group reinforcers that
are available to teachers to reinforce future occurrences of desired behavior. Even
classroom jobs can be a reinforcer for many students. One teacher noted that his
fourth-grade students had difficulty with calm transitions from one activity to
the next. In order to reinforce calm transitions, he held a contest to provide
the opportunity to every student who transitioned appropriately to become the
"Emergency Helper." The "Emergency Helper" was responsible for going to
the front office in case of an emergency. The irony here, however, was that
although no emergencies ever occurred necessitating the services of the "Emergency
Helper," this did not diminish the reinforcing strength of this classroom job.

Activities have multiple advantages when used to reinforce desired prosocial behaviors. They are:

- relatively inexpensive (e.g., the cost of a board game or a deck of cards)
- helpful in developing rapport and establishing a positive environment in the classroom
- useful for teaching social skills
- easy to manipulate

Activities are as effective as reinforcers in the classroom because they do not require lots of money and they allow the teacher to interact with students in ways that are not related simply to academic instruction. Many activities also require interaction between peers, or between peers and adults, setting up "teachable moments" or opportunities to provide social skills instruction in context, which is the most appropriate way to deliver this type of instruction. Finally, although teachers should not go into their classrooms with this mindset, activity reinforcers provide the teacher something to take away when challenging behaviors occur. This will be discussed at greater length in Chapter 13 on punishment. As valuable as activity reinforcers may be, however, some limitations and drawbacks should be acknowledged.

Activity reinforcers have three main perceived disadvantages. The first is that they are time intrusive. Because instructional time is at a premium and teachers are hard-pressed to cover the required content, teachers may find it difficult to allow students to participate in noninstructive activities. But 10 minutes of free time that makes students more likely to work for 40 minutes is certainly better than 50 minutes of off-task behavior. In addition to this time limitation issue, many teachers may view fun activities as antecedents to challenging behavior. In other words, students get to take part in a preferred activity such as 15 minutes of free gym time, but when the 15 minutes are up, the students remain overly excited and are unable to transition back to academic activities. This phenomenon sometimes is described in behavioral terms as a *post-reinforcement pause*, the tendency to reduce the behavior that earned reinforcement immediately after reinforcement is given. This is a well-researched phenomenon but it can be prevented through strategies such as precorrection (e.g., "When you walk back to your desks, what am I looking for you to do?"), a gradual return from the activity back to academics (e.g., "In 8 minutes, I will look for everyone to go back to their desks calmly and quietly . . .", "In 4 minutes, I will look for everyone...", etc.), and using smaller, more frequent activity reinforcers rather than one big reinforcer (e.g., three 10-minute breaks versus one 30-minute break).

This leads to the second disadvantage for activity reinforcers, which is that they require teacher energy and attention. Teaching certainly is not for the faint of heart, and supervising as well as participating in activities (effectively combining attention with activities) is far more difficult and exhausting than assigning a worksheet and sitting at a desk. But taking on these challenges and making activities fun enable teachers to dramatically increase the behaviors that they want and decrease the behaviors that they do not want.

The final problem with activity reinforcers is that they cannot always be used immediately after the student demonstrates the behavior, which decreases their efficacy in conditioning future occurrences of the behavior. To combat this limitation the teacher should verbally connect the behavior with the earned activity, even if this reinforcer does not immediately follow the behavior, and continually should remind students why they are getting to participate in the activity (e.g.,"Don't forget that because everyone turned in their math homework, you will have 5 minutes at the end of class to visit with your friends.").

Tangible Reinforcers

The third category of reinforcers is tangible reinforcers. A tangible reinforcer is defined as the presentation of an object (as opposed to an activity or just attention), contingent on a specific behavior, that increases future occurrences of that behavior. The overuse of this category is probably responsible for the erroneous belief that a behaviorist approach to teaching consists mainly of awarding M&Ms to every student. This myth notwithstanding, there are many reasons why tangible reinforcers should be the teacher's last resort for providing direct reinforcers to students. However, there are certain instances in which this type of reinforcer is the only one that will get the job done.

Tangible reinforcers demand more time, energy, and resources than either attention or activity reinforcers, which means that they should be used carefully, especially in the light of reinforcement rule #2, which dictates that teachers should use as little reinforcement as necessary. However, tangible reinforcers are also the most powerful ones and may be necessary to elicit desired behaviors from some students. This power is what makes choosing appropriate tangibles as reinforcers particularly difficult.

Social acceptability often adversely affects what teachers should choose and avoid as tangible reinforcers. For example, the use of candy not only promotes bad dietary habits but also earns the wrath of parents, bus drivers, and other adults who contend that sugar hypes up students. Although this is a myth, pairing sugar with desired behavior can create a deleterious association between food and reinforcement. Further, food is a reinforcer that is easily satiated; as soon as the student feels full he or she no longer wants a treat, and the food may even become aversive. Similarly, cheap plastic toys that can be ordered in bulk from catalog companies also should be avoided to maintain good relationships with parents and other school personnel. These items tend to break or get lost and generally contribute to clutter at school and in the home. Some examples of good tangible reinforcers that do not have this type of social stigma are school supplies (pencils, pens, notebooks, paper, etc.), art materials (crayons, sketch paper), and even toys that promote active or imaginative play (small magic tricks, balsa wood gliders). A brand-new freshly sharpened pencil makes schoolwork a little more tolerable to many students, and for students from lower socioeconomic backgrounds these items may be as much a necessity as a treat. Finally, some schools have given away new bicycles and other "big ticket" items at the end of the school year as tangible reinforcers. The difficulty with this approach is that sheer economics demand that reinforcers such as these be few and far between, and this creates ratio strain for many students. *Ratio strain* occurs when too little reinforcement is provided for demonstration of desired behaviors and those desired behaviors occur less often or are extinguished completely.

A couple of weeks into the semester, Ms. Earhart and Mrs. Parish sit down to discuss how things are going. Ms. Earhart begins: "Well, so far things are going a lot better than last year. I am trying to use different types of reinforcers throughout the day, but I am running into a couple of issues."

"Such as?"

"Well, first, even with your paperclip system, I sometimes still forget to acknowledge when students are doing a good job. I think I am so amazed that everyone is following directions that it just catches me off guard. And then, I think I just need more of a 'system' to make sure no one is getting left out when I provide reinforcers. The only other problem is that it is always me who is determining who gets what type of reinforcer and what activity they get to do or who gets a sharpened pencil or whatever. It seems like this would work even better if students could have some choices in terms of reinforcers that they would like."

Mrs. Parish thought about this and said, "Well, you know we all use 'Gotcha Bucks' when students are doing a good job all around school . . ."

"Of course, but if I start giving Gotcha Bucks to my students during classroom time, it will throw off the whole system," Ms. Earhart interjected.

"Yes, but what about a different type of system that systematically reinforces students for certain behaviors and ultimately leads to different activity and tangible rewards? This could be a system like 'Gotcha Bucks' but it would just be specific to your classroom."

"That sounds like it might work. It would remind me to provide reinforcement. I could have students try to earn points every time they are doing what I ask them to do and I could monitor to make sure that everyone was receiving points throughout the day. I'll try it."

WHOLE-CLASS FORMAL ACKNOWLEDGMENT SYSTEMS

One of the simplest types of acknowledgment systems involves providing a reinforcer when the entire class engages in a behavior. An example of a whole-class acknowledgment system is presented in Table 9.1.

The Good Behavior Game (e.g., Barrish, Saunders, & Wolfe, 1969; McCurdy, Lannie, & Barnabas, 2009; Poduska et al., 2008; Tingstrom, Sterling-Turner, & Wilczynski, 2006) is a well researched and frequently used system for reinforcing desired behavior in the classroom. This system has more than 30 years of research showing how it increases desired prosocial behaviors and decreases challenging behaviors. There are several considerations to make before using any formal acknowledgement system like the Good Behavior Game. First, determine exactly what you want students to do and make sure that the correct behavior is easily recognized. Next, make sure you are willing and able to

---

TABLE 9.1   Examples of Whole-Class Incentives

1. The students in Mr. Brown's second-period algebra class routinely arrive to class right when the bell rings or even a little late. They are rarely seated and ready to work when he wants to begin class. Mr. Brown decides to motivate his students to arrive on time. He puts a large jar in the front of the room and marks a line on the jar about one quarter of the way up, another at half the way up, and a final line at three quarters of the way up. He tells his students that he will put a marble in the jar for every day on which the entire class is seated when the bell rings. When the marbles reach each line, students will earn a "no new algebra Friday." On the Friday of that week they instead will be able to play a review game during class. He tells the students that it will take about 2 weeks to reach each line if they are on time every day. Mr. Brown tells them that if they can fill the entire jar, they will earn a "free Friday" on which they watch a movie in class. In addition there will be no homework that weekend. Mr. Brown's students are enthusiastic about the plan and earn their first "no new algebra Friday" within about 2.5 weeks. They earn a "free Friday" just before the end of the year. Mr. Brown is very happy with the system; it takes little additional time on his part, and now the students are seated and ready to learn when the bell rings each day.

2. Ms. Crackle is unhappy with her students' loud and disruptive behavior when they line up to return to class after recess. There is a lot of talking and pushing, and several students dawdle on their way to line-up. It often takes her 5–10 minutes just to get them organized enough to enter the building. This has occurred no matter how often she reminds them of the rules, corrects misbehavior, and even sends them to the office. Ms. Crackle tells her students that from now on, they will be given an extra 2 minutes of recess if they can line up immediately when the recess whistle blows, respect others (keeping hands to self and lips sealed when in line), and respect property (put items away before lining up). Ms. Crackle thinks that 2 minutes of recess is a small price to pay for well-behaved students because she currently is losing 5–10 minutes of instruction every day. When Ms. Crackle implements this plan, her students begin lining up quickly and quietly. She now needs no more than about a minute to get her students organized and ready to go inside when the recess whistle blows.

---

deliver an incentive every time the behavior occurs. If you are, think about what you could use as an incentive: Do you want to provide students a preferred activity or item every time the desired behavior occurs or do you instead want to use a *token economy* in which students gradually work towards earning a larger reinforcer? In a token economy, students earn tokens or symbols that are later traded for reinforcers. For example, suppose that you have a ruler on the board and each time all of your students turn in their homework you mark off an inch; then, when you reach one foot, there is a "no homework" day. In this scenario, marking off the inch is the "token," which later is redeemed for a "no home-work" day. As you can see, in a whole-class system in which students work toward a larger reinforcer, it helps to have tokens or markers that students earn along the way to chart their progress.

The next step in developing a whole-class reinforcer system is to determine what you will use as a reinforcer: What will students earn? One way to identify potential reinforcers is to ask students what they would like to earn. In our experience, students are very good at suggesting feasible activities that they would like to engage in. Alternatively, you might reflect on what your students enjoy: What activities do they like to do, and how can you fit them into your day? Once you have determined potential reinforcers, consider how often they should be delivered. As described in Chapter 2, the reinforcement needs to be delivered in the least amount necessary to change behavior. Further, reinforcers may be selected for either very frequent or only occasional use. For example, if you have selected a pizza party as your reinforcer, you probably don't want to use this every time the desired behavior of coming to class on time occurs. First, this will require a significant investment of time (and money!). In addition, if there is a pizza party every day, students probably will quickly tire of it. To use a large incentive such as a pizza party, you probably will want to use a token economy in which students earn markers on their way to the pizza party. When using a token economy, it is important to schedule reinforcement often enough that students buy into the system. For example, a pizza party for all students after they have been on time for 90 days is unlikely to actually increase student timeliness because it is too far removed. If you use an incentive system like this, you will need to build in smaller incentives that students earn on their way to the pizza party. For example, you could allow 10 minutes of free time on the Friday afternoon after every 5 days on which all students are on time.

Whole-class reinforcer systems are most useful when students can work together to help others do the right thing. But when one or two students out of the entire group struggle with a rule, such systems are not advisable because they may cause the rest of the group to blame those students for preventing the class from attaining the desired incentives. In such a situation, consider more individualized systems such as those described in Chapter 12.

The Good Behavior Game

THE GOOD BEHAVIOR GAME

Ms. Earhart decides to try out the Good Behavior Game as it was described to her by Mrs. Parish. One of the major problems in her class is students' talking out during large group instruction. She first identifies the replacement behavior that she would like, which is that students would raise their hands and wait to be acknowledged before talking. Her classroom is currently arranged with clusters of four desks around the room. She lets each cluster be a team, and although each team is encouraged to try to have the most hand raises and the fewest talk-outs, she also emphasizes that the entire group will earn an extra recess period on Friday if they have three times more hand raises than talk-outs.

Whole-class acknowledgement systems like the Good Behavior Game are particularly useful for discrete instances of behavior (i.e., when it is easy to tell if something did or did not occur). Examples include being in seat when the bell rings, being prepared (e.g., having books out and on desks), walking quietly, and so on. Such a system would be more difficult to implement for behaviors that occur multiple times during class, such as raising a hand before speaking, because you probably could not actually provide the reinforcer every time the behavior occurred, which defeats the purpose of this system. Also, it is imperative to determine whether new behaviors are occurring because of a skill deficit (students do not have the skill) or a performance deficit (students have the skill but choose not to use it); the group contingency intervention is not designed to teach new skills. Therefore, before implementing this intervention, instruction and practice of the desired classroom behaviors and social skills is imperative. Additionally, using a prompt, such as precorrection, may remind students of the expected behaviors before the problematic context. Also, remember that the behaviors of a small number of students can impact the entire group. If students turn on each other or if this intervention breeds dissension or ill-feelings between students, then it needs to be modified. The focus of this intervention is not to alienate students, but to help shape positive behaviors in entire groups of students. It may be a good idea to couple students who are having more difficulty with positive role models who will encourage desired behaviors.

When using a whole-class system, there are several specific troubleshooting considerations. These are delineated in Table 9.2.

TABLE 9.2   Troubleshooting Problems and Possible Solutions

Problem	Solutions
Students don't seem to care about the system or they complain about it.	If all students complain about the system, then it should be re-evaluated. Are expectations too high? Are reinforcers not powerful enough? It will be critical to make sure that the students experience success and access the reinforcers early on in the implementation. If this has been addressed, then the system should be removed and presented again in another way. If only a small minority of the students complain, then their complaints can be acknowledged and the matter presented to the class as a whole with the caveat that the majority will rule in terms of continuing the system or discontinuing it.
It isn't having an impact.	This issue may be related to how long the system has been in place and how many times students have been able to access some type of group reinforcer. If it has been in place for 15 school days or less, or reinforcement has been accessed only five times or fewer, then it is necessary to persevere and give the system a chance to work. If it has been in place longer, then it should be reformulated with more powerful reinforcers or criteria that are easier to meet to access reinforcement.
Students find all the loopholes.	If students are able to exploit the system and are not actually demonstrating the desired behavior then we are essentially teaching the wrong message. Teachers must think their reinforcement systems out carefully and often will have to fine tune the system in light of its effectiveness.
Students are getting reinforcers all the time.	The question that must be answered is, "Are the students doing what I want to them to do?" If the answer is "Yes," then the fact that students are receiving reinforcers all the time means that the system is working. If students are receiving reinforcers but not demonstrating the behaviors that the system is designed to elicit, then it is necessary to increase or raise the criteria required to earn the reinforcement.

TEACHERS NEED REINFORCEMENT TOO

Dr. Valdez is the principal at a large urban middle school. His school has been implementing schoolwide positive behavior support for over 3 years and over all, things are going very well. Over the past year, however, the school's positive behavior support team, of which Dr. Valdez is a member, has noticed that teachers are not handing out as many "Gotcha Bucks" as they used to. This concerns the team because the school's incentive system is built upon Gotcha Bucks. When the team examines schoolwide data, they notice that the number of office discipline referrals generated in hallways is starting to increase. The team meets to consider ways to address the situation. One team member suggests that teachers who write less than 10 Gotcha Bucks in a week be required to meet with Dr. Valdez to discuss why they have not bought in to the system. After considering this option, the team decides that this might make teachers feel singled out and that, if they feel "forced" to hand out Gotcha Bucks, they might do so in a haphazard manner instead of using them to acknowledge prosocial behavior. The team decides to offer incentives for teachers who hand out Gotcha Bucks. They brainstorm ideas and Dr. Valdez suggests that she cover a class for one teacher each week. The team agrees that this would be a great incentive and they decide to implement the "Gold Brick" program. Teachers who hand out more than 20 tickets in a week are entered into a drawing. One name is drawn at the end of the week, and that teacher is eligible to have a class period covered by Dr. Valdez during the following week. This program proves to be very popular, and within 2 months students are earning as many Gotcha Bucks as ever. More importantly, office referrals in all areas of the school—including hallways—are at their lowest levels ever.

In the above vignette, the school's positive behavior support team had a problem: Teachers' acknowledgement of students' appropriate behavior was decreasing and, perhaps as a consequence, student disruptive behavior was increasing. The team considered various options to increase teacher participation and decided to use the principle of reinforcement to help solve their problem. As defined in Chapter 2, reinforcement has occurred any time the delivery of a consequence for a behavior results in an increase in the behavior. In this example, teachers began to hand out more Gotcha Bucks when they became eligible for the Gold Brick award for doing so. In this chapter we considered how consequences can be used to increase desired behavior and decrease problematic behavior in the classroom for students. But teachers also need additional reinforcers, especially when these additional measures are being put in place. Positive behavior support is grounded in a team-based approach, and so it is vital for staff and administrators to acknowledge each other's hard work using the same categories of reinforcers that are identified for students: attention, activities, and even tangibles. For example, the team might ask local restaurants to donate gift certificates that could be used to acknowledge teacher and staff behavior.

Chapter Review

- Reinforcement systems are key to a successful classroom. Although there are many arguments against the use of such systems, research has shown, time and time again, that reinforcement is not bad for students and that well managed classrooms rely on effective systems for reinforcing desired behavior.
- Reinforcement systems in a classroom can consist of positive reinforcement or negative reinforcement. Although both may be effective, positive systems generally result in a classroom that feels like a better place to be.
- There are three types of reinforcers: attention, activity, and tangible. Each type of reinforcer has advantages and limitations. Effective teachers combine the use of various types of reinforcers.
- Whole-class reinforcement systems are designed to enhance the behavior of all students in the class. Such systems are an efficient way to improve the environment of the classroom.

Application

1. Provide examples of the three main types of reinforcers and explain how they can increase desired behavior in the classroom. Consider the schedule of reinforcement and how the system can be used efficiently within the classroom context.

2. Explain how a classwide system of reinforcement such as the Good Behavior Game could be implemented within a classroom you are familiar with.

References

Albers, C. A., Glover, T. A., & Kratochwill, T. R. (2007). Where are we, and where do we go now? Universal screening for enhanced educational and mental health outcomes. *Journal of School Psychology, 45*(2), 257–263.

Alric, J. M., Bray, M. A., Kehle, T. J., Chafouleas, S. M., & Theodore, L. A. (2007). A comparison of independent, interdependent, and dependent group contingencies with randomized reinforcers to increase reading fluency. *Canadian Journal of School Psychology, 22*(1), 81–93.

Barrish, H., Saunders, M., & Wolfe, M. (1969). Good behavior game: Effects of individual contingencies for group consequences on disruptive behavior in a classroom. *Journal of Applied Behavior Analysis, 2,* 119–124.

Brophy, J. (1981). Teacher praise: A functional analysis. *Review of Educational Research, 51,* 5–32.

Burton, K. D., Lydon, J. E., D'Alessandro, D. U., & Koestner, R. (2006). The differential effects of intrinsic and identified motivation on well-being and performance: Prospective, experimental, and implicit approaches to self-determination theory. *Journal of Personality and Social Psychology, 91*(4), 750–762.

Cameron, J., & Pierce, W. (1996). The debate about rewards and intrinsic motivation: Protests and accusations do not alter the results. *Review of Educational Research, 66*(1), 39–51.

Deci, E. L., Koestner, R., & Ryan, R. M. (1999a). A meta-analytic review of experiments examining the effects of extrinsic rewards on intrinsic motivation. *Psychological Bulletin, 125*(6), 627–668.

Deci, E. L., Koestner, R., & Ryan, R. M. (1999b). The undermining effect is a reality after all—Extrinsic rewards, task interest, and self-determination: Reply to Eisenberger, Pierce, and Cameron (1999) and Lepper, Henderlong, and Gingras (1999). *Psychological Bulletin, 125*(6), 692–700.

Eisenberger, R., Pierce, W., & Cameron, J. (1999). Effects of reward on intrinsic motivation—Negative, neutral, and positive: Comment on Deci, Koestner, and Ryan (1999). *Psychological Bulletin, 125*(6), 677–691.

George, H. P., Kincaid, D., & Pollard-Sage, J. (2009). Primary-tier interventions and supports. In *Handbook of positive behavior support* (pp. 375–394). Retrieved from http://dx.doi.org/10.1007/978-0-387-09632-2_16.

Kalis, T. M., Vannest, K., & Parker, R. (2007). Praise counts: Using self-monitoring to increase effective teaching practices. *Preventing School Failure, 51,* 20–27.

Kaplan, J. S. (1996). Beyond Behavior modification. Austin, TX: Pro-Ed.

Kohn, A. (1993). *Punished by rewards: The trouble with gold stars, incentive plans, A's, praise, and other bribes.* Boston: Houghton Mifflen.

Lepper, M. R., Henderlong, J., & Gingras, I. (1999). Understanding the effects of extrinsic rewards on intrinsic motivation—Uses and abuses of meta-analysis: Comment on Deci, Koestner, and Ryan (1999). *Psychological Bulletin, 125*(6), 669–676.

Little, S. G., Akin-Little, A., & Newman-Eig, L. M. (2010). Effects on homework completion and accuracy of varied and constant reinforcement within an interdependent group contingency system. *Journal of Applied School Psychology, 26*(2), 115.

McCurdy, B. L., Lannie, A. L., & Barnabas, E. (2009). Reducing disruptive behavior in an urban school cafeteria: An extension of the Good Behavior Game. *Journal of School Psychology, 47*(1), 39–54.

McKean, E. (Ed.). (2005). *New Oxford American Dictionary* (2nd ed.). Oxford, England: Oxford University Press.

Noddings, N. (2005). Identifying and responding to needs in education. *Cambridge Journal of Education, 35,* 147–159.

Poduska, J. M., Kellam, S. G., Wang, W., Brown, C. H., Ialongo, N. S., & Toyinbo, P. (2008). Impact of the Good Behavior Game, a universal classroom-based behavior intervention, on young adult service use for problems with emotions, behavior, or drugs or alcohol. *Drug and Alcohol Dependence, 95,* 29–44.

Reinke, W. M., Lewis-Palmer, T., & Merrell, K. (2008). The classroom check-up: A classwide teacher consultation model for increasing praise and decreasing disruptive behavior. *School Psychology Review, 37*(3), 315.

Schanding, G. T., & Sterling-Turner, H. E. (2010). Use of the mystery motivator for a high school class. *Journal of Applied School Psychology, 26,* 3853.

Severson, H. H., Walker, H. M., Hope-Doolittle, J., Kratochwill, T. R., & Gresham, F. M. (2007). Proactive, early screening to detect behaviorally at-risk students: Issues, approaches, emerging innovations, and professional practices. *Journal of School Psychology, 45*(2), 193–223.

Simonsen, B., Fairbanks, S., Briesch, A., Myers, D., & Sugai, G. (2008). Evidence-based practices in classroom management: Considerations for research to practice. *Education and Treatment of Children, 31*(3), 351–380.

Sprague, J. R., & Walker, H. M. (2005). *Safe and healthy schools: Practical prevention strategies.* The Guilford practical intervention in the schools series. New York: Guilford Press.

Stichter, J. P., Stormont, M., & Lewis, T. J. (2009). Instructional practices and behavior during reading: A descriptive summary and comparison of practices in title one and non-title elementary schools. *Psychology in the Schools, 46,* 172–183.

Sugai, G., & Horner, R. H. (2009). Defining and describing schoolwide positive behavior support. In *Handbook of positive behavior support* (pp. 307–326). Retrieved from http://dx.doi.org/10.1007/978-0-387-09632-2_13.

Sutherland, K. S., Conroy, M., Abrams, L., & Vo, A. (2010). Improving interactions between teachers and young children with problem behavior: a strengths-based approach. *Exceptionality, 18,* 70–81.

Theodore, L. A., Bray, M. A., & Kehle, T. J. (2004). A comparative study of group contingencies and randomized reinforcers to reduce disruptive classroom behavior. *School Psychology Quarterly, 19*(3), 253–271.

Tingstrom, D. H., Sterling-Turner, H. E., & Wilczynski, S. M. (2006). The Good Behavior Game: 1969–2002. *Behavior Modification, 30*(2), 225–253.

Vansteenkiste, M., Simons, J., Lens, W., Sheldon, K. M., & Deci, E. L. (2004). Motivating learning, performance, and persistence: The synergistic effects of intrinsic goal contents and autonomy-supportive contexts. *Journal of Personality and Social Psychology, 87*(2), 246–260.

Watson, S. M., Gable, R. A., & Greenwood, C. R. (2010). Combining ecobehavioral assessment, functional assessment, and response to intervention to promote more effective classroom instruction. *Remedial and Special Education* (March 1, 2010).

10

Designing Individualized Instructional Strategies

CHAPTER OBJECTIVES

After reading this chapter, you should be able to describe the following concepts:

- Three critical intervention components to address skill or performance deficits
- Key attributes of replacement behaviors
- Designing instruction to facilitate success through errorless learning, shaping, and chaining
- Manipulating instruction using modeling, providing opportunities to respond, modifying task difficulty, constant time delay, and guided practice

This chapter is dedicated to the design of individualized instruction for students identified as nonresponsive to school and classwide systems. We shift the focus here to specific methods and strategies for the delivery of individualized instruction. So far in this text we have focused on prevention and strategies that maximize the probability of student success. Inherent in this model is the continual assessment of interventions at the schoolwide level, in the classroom, and across smaller groups of students to identify failures as early as possible. The students on whom we now focus are those identified as having repeated failures despite effective prevention efforts. The need for intervention with these students is immediate and dire. To use an academic example, suppose that a student, Max, continues to fall behind in reading despite a strong schoolwide reading program. We would immediately see the need for more intensive instruction, possibly manipulating what was taught, how it was taught, and the conditions under which it is taught. Specialists likely would talk about smaller groups or individualized instruction, peer tutoring, fluency, authentic literature, additional instruction, and a variety of other potentially important issues related to reading. For a student who continues to fail in relation to behavioral expectations, we must approach the problem just as we do with academic expectations.

Whenever we identify a deficit, our first question should be "Why is this a problem for the student?" The first level of inquiry focuses on whether the deficit is one of skill (i.e., the student has not mastered the skill) or of performance (i.e., the student knows how but chooses not to). Both types of deficit require three critical intervention components: instruction, facilitation of success via the natural environment, and effective consequences; however, the nature of the intervention for skill and performance deficits will necessarily be different. For example, suppose that a student, Bobby, screams for teacher attention and help when he is frustrated with work. We must determine whether Bobby has an inability to raise his hand (he has not acquired or is not fluent with the skill) or he screams simply because it works faster than hand raising. Both skill and performance deficits require instruction, but the focus of the instruction will vary.

If the problem is a skill deficit and we intervene by simply providing larger consequences for positive and negative behavior, we probably would not see a change—and Bobby would be set up for an increased level of punishment. Under these conditions, we first need to determine whether Bobby knows what hand-raising is and how to do it. If he is unable to demonstrate it correctly when asked, then he definitely needs instruction in how to raise his hand (the skill itself). But part of appropriate hand-raising also involves raising a hand during times when it will be successful. The success is the final component and represents instruction as to why he should raise his hand (what will happen if he does and doesn't). Just because the student *can* do it does not mean that he or she has mastered the skill. Knowing when and when not to use a skill is a large part of the ability to use the skill effectively, and this must be assessed and taught.

In contrast, if the problem is a performance deficit, then Bobby knows how and when to raise his hand, but the reinforcement for doing it is not as powerful as it is for other behaviors. Screaming may get attention from teacher and others, get more of it, or get it faster. In this case, focusing solely on teaching how and when is not only unnecessary but also will likely be boring for Bobby, potentially prompting escape-motivated behaviors. Under these conditions, Bobby needs instruction to focus mainly on why to raise his hand, and our task is to arrange consequences that reinforce hand-raising more than screaming. Still, part of this intervention would require us to continually remind Bobby and create an instructional environment in which his probability of success is maximized. Thus, although skill and performance deficits require different ways of approaching the problem, both require instruction, facilitation, and consequences.

Recall that effective instruction involves not just the presentation itself but the actual examples that are selected and the manner in which they are sequenced. As part of this process we must ask whether the student can perform the desired skill fluently. Sometimes it will be necessary to teach alternative behaviors to students who have extreme difficulty. For example, if Bobby were disabled so that he could not comfortably raise his hands, we might devise a system in which he could ring a small bell, clear his throat, or place a sign on his desk. In any case, we must continue to consider the effort required and effectiveness in obtaining the desired outcome. Bobby will not adopt alternative behaviors that don't work better than screaming.

REPLACEMENT BEHAVIORS

When we teach, we should have in mind some behavior that we want the student to learn and to use in natural settings and situations. This behavior is reflected in our instructional objective and is the focus of our measurement efforts. In sum, behavior is the focus of all our efforts. But what behavior should we teach? Could we say that we would like every student that yells to engage in the same alternative behavior? The answer depends upon the student, the situation, and the function of the behavior. In general, when we identify a problem behavior, we also need to identify a behavior to teach in its place; that is, we cannot successfully replace a problem behavior with nothing. This would be akin to expecting a hyperactive child to sit still for hours simply because we told them to do so—extremely unlikely. A basic premise of behavior is that problems cannot be stamped out; they can only be replaced.

A replacement behavior is one that is relevant in the environment (is typical among those who are successful), acceptable (is within the teacher's expectations), and functional for the student (provides the same reward as the problem behavior). A behavior that serves the same function as the problem behavior is known as a "fair pair." Of course, most teachers would like a screaming student to simply be quiet. But sitting quietly is not a fair pair for the student who screams to get attention or escape teasing, so the student will not do it. Likewise, replacements must be active behaviors because those that include no real behavior will not be functional. You can determine whether a behavior is active by using the dead man's test. Ask yourself, "Could a dead man do this behavior?" If so, it is not a good replacement. Using this logic makes it clear that behaviors such as "remain quiet" and "stay still" do not pass the test and are not good replacements. The hard part is finding a behavior that will both work for the student and be acceptable to the teacher. A good replacement behavior is one that looks normal in the environment, is easily taught to the student, and involves active student behavior that results in reinforcement.

Ideally, then, undesirable behaviors are replaced with desirable behaviors that will serve the same function (i.e., purpose) for the student. For example, because Bobby screams to get the teacher's attention, we should teach him more appropriate behaviors for accessing the same outcome (e.g., raising a hand, stating the teacher's name, etc.). Likewise, if we determine that Mary screams to escape unpleasant interactions with peers, we must teach her more appropriate ways of escaping such situations as well as behaviors for initiating and sustaining positive interactions. Clearly, although Bobby and Mary's behaviors look identical, the functions of their actions are quite different, and thus the appropriate replacements will be different. This illustrates the need for individualized replacement behaviors that perform the function of the identified undesired behaviors.

Replacement behaviors will be used only when they are more effective and efficient in meeting the student's needs. For example, if we teach Mary to sit quietly with her hands over her mouth when annoyed by her peers, but this does not stop the harassment, she has no incentive to engage in this replacement behavior and so there is little hope that it will persist. Conversely, if we teach Bobby to raise his hand to receive attention from the teacher, he can access his desired

TABLE 10.1   Functional Replacement Behaviors and Their Benefit

Predictor	Undesirable Behavior	Replacement Behavior and Contingency	Function of Both Behaviors	Benefit of Replacement Behavior
Additional problems with regrouping	Scream until thrown out of class	Raise hand to get assistance	Escape frustration	More math completed and less screaming
Line-up	Pushes peers and ends up at the front of the line	Don't touch anyone and is allowed to be the first one in line	Access first spot in line	No physical aggression in line
Reading groups	Refuses directions to read and ends up sitting alone at desk	Is allowed to sit and play at desk after reading a predetermined number of pages	Escape from reading/access to playing at desk	Student now gets some reading instruction
Sam	When Robert is near, Sam will engage in off-task behavior to get Robert's attention	Complete all assigned tasks and earn time to play alone with Robert	Access to Robert's attention	Student remains on task and completes assigned tasks

attention and will be more likely to use that behavior in the future as long as it continues to be effective (i.e., accesses attention).

Ms. Smith has determined that an appropriate replacement behavior for Bobby is to raise his hand and wait for the teacher to attend to him. This is an appropriate behavior for this setting and will provide Bobby with the same desired attention that the undesired behavior did. For Mary, Ms. Smith has determined that an appropriate replacement behavior is for her to walk away from peers that harass her and/or quietly inform a teacher of the problem. This is an appropriate behavior for this context and will provide Mary with the same desired escape that her undesired behavior did.

An effective replacement behavior will be performed under circumstances where it will be reinforced (see Table 10.1). No behavior, no matter however appropriate, will be effective if it is used at the wrong time, and it may even evoke a punishing response. For example, we certainly consider leaving the building when the fire alarm rings to be an appropriate response. However, a student who engages in this same behavior at the wrong time (i.e., when the fire alarm is not ringing) will not be considered successful and will be subject to punitive consequences. Once this has happened, the student may not engage in that behavior in the future, even under the appropriate circumstances (i.e., fire alarm rings).

Let's look once again at Bobby and Mary. Ms. Smith has determined that Bobby's replacement behavior will be raising his hand to access teacher attention. She now needs to determine the specific conditions under which he should raise his hand. If Bobby raises his hand when he's on the playground, there likely will be no immediate response, if any at all. Because this may affect the future probability that Bobby will raise his hand in any setting, Ms. Smith must teach Bobby that hand-raising is appropriate and reinforced *only* when he is in the classroom. Ms. Smith has determined that Mary's replacement behavior should be walking away or quietly telling a teacher. The timing of Mary's replacement behavior is much simpler: She should use this behavior whenever peers are bothering her and she wishes to escape. If the teacher begins a set of directions that Mary finds annoying and, in response, she turns and walks away, she probably will meet with greater aversives. Thus, Mary must understand that this behavior is to be used only when peers are the source of harassment.

Instruction

After we have determined an appropriate replacement behavior, we are ready to begin teaching. Teaching social behaviors should be undertaken in precisely the same manner as academic instruction. That is, instruction must be planned to facilitate student success via effective instructional practices including explanations, modeling, prompting, and guidance to ensure that students can demonstrate skills on their own.

The teacher directs instruction by creating example sets and providing students with models and examples calculated to ensure the probability of success. Naturally occurring examples from the students' environment are selected to demonstrate the range of situations under which the replacement behavior should and should not occur. After the students have demonstrated fluency with guided examples, the teacher provides them with a set of untrained probes to assess for mastery before moving on to the next skill. As with teaching examples, testing examples should be selected from the natural environment.

Ms. Smith has told Bobby that he can receive teacher attention by raising his hand, but he has not demonstrated this behavior. Ms. Smith now sits down with Bobby to describe and model hand-raising. After carefully detailing the conditions under which the behavior should occur and what it looks like, Ms. Smith selects examples from times when Bobby did need assistance and provides prompts and guidance as Bobby practices raising his hand. Bobby's responses are met with immediate teacher feedback in the form of correction or reinforcement. Finally, Bobby is presented with a role play example in which he must raise his hand to ask the teacher for assistance. Ms. Smith carefully monitors his behavior on this untrained example and immediately corrects any errors. If successful, Bobby is provided with an immediate response and verbal reinforcement.

Like Bobby, Mary has been told what to do and can perform her replacement behavior (walking away), but has not demonstrated this skill. Ms. Smith must provide models of walking away from situations involving peer harassment. To do this she enlists the help of her assistant, Mr. Jones. In the role-play, Mr. Jones, in the role of the harasser, approaches and calls Ms. Smith some names (a common problem for Mary in the natural environment). Ms. Smith says, "Please stop," and then turns and walks away. After telling Mary about the advantages and simplicity of this behavior, Mr. Jones again plays the part of the harasser while Ms. Smith coaches Mary about what to do when Mr. Jones bothers her. Mr. Jones begins the role-play by telling Mary that he's taller than her and calls her "Shorty." As the role-play unfolds, Ms. Smith precorrects Mary and provides her with verbal cues to help her succeed (e.g., "Remember what you do now."). In later role-plays, Ms. Smith fades out these prompts, allowing Mary to succeed on her own. Finally, Mary is given the opportunity to demonstrate the skill in an untrained example. In this case, Ms. Smith has a peer pretend to cut in line in front of Mary. Again, incorrect responses are met with immediate correction and reteaching while correct responses are reinforced by the teacher.

Despite effective instruction, appropriate behaviors do not automatically replace undesirable behaviors that serve a function for the student. Whether the replacement behavior is initially demonstrated and eventually maintained will depend on how effective the replacement behavior is in meeting the student's needs. Because of this, replacement behaviors initially will require prompting and guidance after instruction to ensure that they are being used at the appropriate time and in the appropriate manner. The teacher also will probably have to insure that adequate reinforcers are in place whenever the student does demonstrate the replacement behavior.

Of course, whether the student perceives the replacement behavior as successful will depend on its consequences. A replacement behavior that does not meet the student's needs (i.e., it fails to result in an effective outcome) will not persist. Instead, the undesirable behavior, which historically has very reliably met those needs, will continue to occur. For this reason, initial replacement behaviors should be simple, guided with prompts, and immediately reinforced when observed. Over time, replacement behaviors can be shaped toward more sophisticated responses or longer durations. Initially, however, we must focus on facilitating and immediately reinforcing any successful demonstration of replacement behavior, using reinforcers that are functionally equivalent to those that have been maintaining the challenging behavior.

Even as we identify functional replacement behaviors and facilitate their success through instruction, events in the environment may cause undesirable behaviors to return because those responses are easier or more efficient in meeting the student's needs. Facilitating the student's use of desired responses under conditions that are highly predictive of undesired behaviors probably will require changing the environment to mask or minimize those conditions. Often, arranging the classroom and/or positioning students to avoid disruption is the simplest method of manipulating the environment. Careful functional assessment of student behavior may indicate specific times, circumstances, or placements that predict problem behavior.

For example, if name-calling is highly predictive of Mary's aggressive behaviors, then preventing name-calling can facilitate her success. Ms. Smith might place Mary in an area of the classroom where she is less likely to encounter students who have called her names in the past; or she might speak with the other students and offer group reinforcement contingent upon appropriate conversations (without name-calling and insults) for all students in the class. In each case, Ms. Smith designs an environment that facilitates Mary's success. Of course, at some point Ms. Smith will need gradually to fade out the artificial environmental conditions while continuing to prompt and reinforce desired behavior. A history of success, facilitated by Ms. Smith's environmental arrangements, will heighten Mary's confidence in her ability to succeed with each new challenge.

Bobby's success will depend on his ability to access attention in an appropriate manner. Simply teaching Bobby a functional replacement behavior likely will be insufficient. Rather, Ms. Smith must set an environment that fosters desired behavior while precluding undesired behavior. Besides simple antecedent manipulations, consequence manipulations will be necessary to make the replacement behavior more effective and efficient than the problem behavior. Ms. Smith needs to plan how to provide reinforcement, contingent upon desired behavior, and to put consequences in place that make undesired behavior a less effective alternative. Otherwise, if Ms. Smith teaches Bobby to access attention by raising his hand, he may continue to scream because historically it has been effective and is easier. Picturing the process as a see-saw with desired behaviors on one end and undesired behaviors on the other end may be helpful: As we reduce the challenging behaviors, we increase the desired behaviors, and vice versa. So if Ms. Smith now provides immediate attention to Bobby for the desired hand-raising behavior while alternately providing time out or cutting off access to attention in response to problem behaviors, the replacement behavior will become a more effective and efficient alternative and will be more likely to continue over time and across settings.

ERRORLESS LEARNING

The term "errorless learning" refers to the development of instructional strategies and procedures that maximize the probability of student success, thereby minimizing the probability of failure. Students learn little from repeated errors, but truly errorless instruction is not likely. Rather, the goal is simply to maximize the ratio of success to failure, allowing the student to receive reinforcement and a natural incentive to continue. Errorless learning is facilitated through the use of effective instructional design (rationale, modeling, examples, practice), prompts and environmental cues, and specific strategies for instructional delivery. Errorless learning strategies increase student success rates and decrease problem behaviors while creating opportunities for increased positive teacher and student interaction (because success is more fun for both the teacher and the student). The remainder of this section describes various procedures that enhance student success during instruction.

Shaping

Shaping and chaining are methods of breaking complex behaviors into smaller components to facilitate student success and gradually build capacity with larger and more complex behaviors. Shaping can be technically defined as the systematic reinforcement of successive approximations toward a target behavior. In layman's terms, shaping involves teaching and reinforcing behaviors that are not really what we want in the end, but that approach it as we go. For example, human babies learn to speak through unintentional shaping by adults. For example, at some point a baby says something with two syllables containing a vague, short sound, "aya." The adults scream "Dada" and provide a surge of attention. Over time this behavior is reinforced enough that it is under stimulus control and is predictable in the presence of adults. Later, as adults continue to say "Dada" as a model, the baby says something that is much more clearly related, perhaps a clear hard "D" sound with "aya." This still is not the expected end result "Dada," but it results in a fresh stream of attention. At this point little attention is provided for the former sound "aya," and only "Dada" is reinforced. Over time, this process leads the child to say "Dada" perfectly, and all the simpler variations are ignored. This process is referred to as shaping because neither the desired behavior nor any component skills existed prior to instruction. Modeling reinforced an approximation for a time, but then a closer approximation was required. Thus, shaping is the systematic reinforcement of successive approximations toward a target behavior. Most of us learned basic language, writing, and athletic skills in this manner.

Shaping is the most effective strategy when a behavior is present, but is not fluent in the presence of a naturally occurring discriminative stimulus. The baby, for example, could make noises, but those noises were not in response to anything predictable; once an approximation was sufficient, reinforcement was delivered. The shaping procedure focuses on consequences and requires powerful reinforcers as a response to appropriate approximations, ignoring inappropriate or nonexistent behavior. The advantage of teaching children after infancy is their ability to verbally communicate about expected approximations. Teachers provide students with very clear models and guided practice and then monitor student behavioral progress. For students who are successful, there is reinforcement and movement toward the next successive approximation. For students who are not successful, there is reteaching and potential facilitation with prompts and other arrangements.

The shaping process generally is implemented over an extended period of time. Although some behaviors could be shaped in a shorter period of time, truly complex behaviors require a series of approximations, each of which requires days or weeks to achieve the mastery that indicates the need to model the next approximation. One concern with shaping is that students are actually reinforced for practicing errors. Thus, while reinforcing the approximation, the teacher should continue modeling the terminal behavior and inform the student that, although he or she is doing well, the ultimate goal has not yet been attained (see Table 10.2).

TABLE 10.2   General Considerations for Shaping

1. Behavior is present, but not fluent in the presence of the "signal."
2. Focus on consequences:
   –requires powerful reinforcers
   –uses differential reinforcement
3. Systematic reinforcement of successive approximations toward the target behavior:
   –specifies dimensions of the target/goal behavior
   –reinforces slight improvements/changes
   –takes time
   –avoids practicing errors

Chaining

Like shaping, chaining is used to build complex behaviors by teaching smaller and less complex components with a view toward an eventual terminal behavior. Chaining is defined as reinforcement of combinations of simple behaviors that are already in the repertoire of the individual to form more complex behaviors (Jerome, Frantino, & Sturmey, 2007; Smith, 1999). While in shaping neither the desired behavior nor any component skills exist prior to instruction, chaining links together several smaller behaviors that are already fluent in order to create a more complex behavior. Chaining is used to teach complex behaviors composed of smaller discrete steps consisting of behaviors that the student has already mastered. Long division is perhaps the most obvious example of a chain because it is taught as a series of steps: divide, multiply, subtract, and bring down. A student can perform long division only after he or she has mastered these four subskills. Conversely, it would be impossible to teach long division via shaping; there would be too many opportunities for error, and approximations would not clearly discriminate between what was right and what was wrong.

Many of the classroom expectations for students involve a series of steps that the student can perform as discrete activities but cannot string together. For example, Ms. Lundy would like Alex first to hang his coat up on the door, then place his homework in the basket on her desk, sit down at his desk, get out his journal, and fill in the goals on his daily point sheet. Although Alex can in fact do each of these tasks, he has never been able to perform all of them in one morning routine. Using a chaining technique, Ms. Lundy begins by meeting Alex at the door each morning and asking him if he knows what to do first. Alex has been prompted to go hang up his coat. When he does this, Ms. Lundy provides verbal praise and a pat on the back, then guides him through performing each of the remaining steps in order. After a couple of days in which Alex directly hangs his coat without prompting, Ms. Lundy adds the second step: placing his homework in the basket. She catches him at the door and reminds him of the second step. After Alex has completed the first two steps on his own, Ms. Lundy provides verbal praise and a thumbs-up, then guides him through the remaining steps. As Alex continues to have unprompted success, Ms. Lundy adds steps until every step in the chain is in place and Alex does each on his own every morning. Note that Alex could perform each of these behaviors before beginning the chaining procedure. Any step that he was unable to complete required instruction to mastery before beginning the chaining procedure. The process just described is known as forward chaining because Alex was asked to do the first step and the teacher guided him through the others, moving forward with what he was required to do. This also could be implemented as backward chaining. In this case the teacher would lead the student through all but the last step, and then gradually add steps backward until the student completed all of them. Although forward chaining seems more logical, backward chaining is sometimes appealing because the reinforcer is delivered at the most natural point—when the task is complete.

Chaining is generally a simple procedure to implement. First, the teacher must identify a behavior with a logical sequence of discrete skills that will increase the student's independence or functioning level in the classroom,

---

TABLE 10.3 General Considerations for Chaining

---

1. Perform a detailed task analysis
2. Form chain from behaviors that are already part of the student's repertoire
3. Use supplementary discriminative stimuli for facilitation of link formation [prompts]
4. Fade prompts
5. Differentially reinforce

---

conducting a task analysis to determine the step-by-step sequence needed to complete the task. Next, the student's mastery of the skills identified in the task analysis must be assessed and any nonmastered skill steps taught. A criterion level is then set for student performance with each component and instruction is begun by providing a prompt for the first step (forward chaining) or by initiating guidance through all but the final step (backward chaining). The teacher records student performance and teaches successive steps when the student reaches criteria. With success, the teacher fades prompts like verbal reminders or hand signals for each step by extending wait time before providing the least amount of prompts necessary. Table 10.3 presents some general considerations for the development of an instructional chaining procedure.

INSTRUCTIONAL MANIPULATIONS

While shaping and chaining represent techniques for developing errorless learning, several other teaching strategies can be used to facilitate higher student success rates.

Modeling

Modeling is simply the act of demonstrating or modeling a key skill or behavior in order to prompt an imitative response. Modeling is an effective part of any instruction because students benefit from watching how to engage in appropriate behaviors and discriminate the contexts and situations in which to use them (Werts, Caldwell, & Wolery, 1996; Whitehurst & Merkur, 1977; Jahr & Eldevik, 2002). Effective teachers show students what the desired behavior looks like, using verbal descriptions to help the students note the most salient points of the modeling. Whether demonstrated by teachers or students, modeling is an effective procedure for both simple and complex behavior.

Modeling is used explicitly as part of instruction when the teacher tells the student the behavior being modeled and its key components during the demonstration. Demonstrations typically are repeated while verbally engaging the student to evaluate understanding (e.g., "Watch what I am doing. Do you understand what I am doing? Does this make sense?"). After the student has understood the skill and its key components, the teacher asks for student demonstration. But modeling also plays another, less explicit role in teaching. Students observe the teacher and learn from how the teacher behaves. Modeling takes place not only in a planned manner as a part of direct instruction, but also throughout the day as teachable moments occur. For example, a student, Randall, has problems yelling at other students. In response, Mr. Newton develops and teaches a lesson on how to tell people politely to stop doing something. The lesson includes modeling of appropriate volume and tone of voice, eye contact, and direct statements that end with please. Mr. Newton models and discusses each component with Randall and has him practice each one. In this case, Mr. Newton is using modeling in a very direct manner. Later, a student's misbehavior bothers Mr. Newton. He looks directly at the student and says in a calm and quiet voice, "Larry, that noise is interrupting us right now, and I'd like you to stop, please." Mr. Newton then turns to Randall and says, "Did you notice how I told him exactly what I wanted in a quiet way?" Here Mr. Newton is using modeling in an impromptu manner, seizing an opportunity to provide additional instruction as part of the normal daily routine.

Modeling works best when it begins with a single behavior during a specific classroom activity and later moves on to more complex behaviors in multiple settings. Activities should be planned around specific skills and demonstrated naturally for all students. The teacher should verbally orient students' attention to the model (e.g., "Do this, follow me, watch this person, copy what he does," etc.) and teach them to imitate the modeled behavior, with additional verbal instructions if needed. As with teaching any behavior or skill, prompts and other arrangements should be used to facilitate student success, and the teacher must watch for opportunities to reinforce other students who are modeling appropriate behaviors.

When using modeling techniques to prompt behavior, choosing an appropriate model is important, especially for teaching social skills. Students are more likely to imitate a behavior demonstrated by peers, particularly friends, than one demonstrated by adults. Appropriate models include same-age peers who share characteristics with the student and are perceived as leaders or are held in high esteem; older peers who are competent in demonstrating desired behavior; classroom teachers, specialists, assistants, or other adults in the school; and video recordings of the student performing the behavior correctly. Further, just as models can reinforce the desired behavior by prompting others to imitate it, so they can reinforce unwanted behavior as well. When using peer models, it is a good idea to select students who are very likely to model the correct behavior even when the teacher or other adults are absent. Table 10.4 presents a set of general guidelines for using modeling as part of an instructional process.

Provide Opportunities to Respond

It is well established that engagement with instruction is highly correlated with achievement. During instruction, the teacher is solely responsible for the degree to which students are engaged. Certainly, students can choose not to be engaged regardless of the nature or content of the instruction, but teachers can affect the probability of engagement through their instructional strategies. One of these strategies, providing students with opportunities to respond, has been demonstrated to increase engagement of students with EBD (Sutherland, Alder, & Gunter, 2003). Providing opportunities to respond is simply presenting opportunities for students

---

TABLE 10.4   General Guidelines for Modeling

---

1. Identify the context and problem behaviors with which students are having the most difficulty. (Student expectations may differ depending on the context. Appropriate behaviors for one context may be problem behaviors in another; for example, talking without raising one's hand is appropriate during class discussions but is a problem behavior during independent work time.)

2. Determine the appropriate behaviors for the identified context. (During test time, students are to sit at their desks, keep their eyes on their own work, raise their hand for help, and work quietly.)

3. Make a verbal statement to orient student attention to the peer or teacher model. (For example, "Do this, follow me, watch this person, copy what he does," etc.)

4. Model the appropriate behavior for the students to imitate. (The teacher may model the behavior personally or allow another student to be a model.)

5. Teach students to imitate the modeled behavior with additional verbal instructions, if needed. (If the behavior has multiple components, students may need to practice each component separately before attempting the entire sequence.)

6. Watch for opportunities to reinforce other students who are modeling appropriate behaviors. (Walk around the classroom to observe all students and give praise to acknowledge appropriate behavior.)

7. Combine with other prompting and reinforcement strategies for students who choose not to imitate the behavior. (Present verbal instructions together with guided physical prompts until appropriate responses occur after instructions alone.)

8. Consider the function of students' behavior when they do not imitate the modeled demonstration. (If the function for not imitating the teacher was to get peer attention, a peer model may be used to obtain the same function as the problem behavior.)

9. Monitor student behaviors to record an increase or decrease in desired behaviors. (After reinforcing one peer model for pushing their chair in, all classmates increased the same behavior.)

10. Fade modeling prompts to natural cues in the environment to encourage appropriate behaviors. (Depending on the problem context, teachers may use rules as visual reminders, verbal precorrects, or eye contact to signal appropriate response.)

---

to actively respond to academic and behavioral instruction through interactions and requests (Sutherland, Alder, & Gunter, 2003) and can be implemented as a questioning procedure, a prompt, or a cueing technique.

Good teachers create an environment that produces many opportunities for students to be engaged. By allowing students opportunities to respond to academic and behavioral instruction through requests, open-ended questions, and engaging materials, teachers may decrease student deficits in academics and promote appropriate classroom behaviors such as staying on task. In addition, providing sufficient opportunities to respond allows the teacher to adjust lessons based on student feedback (Christel & Schuster, 2003). Student responses can be choral (group) or individual and verbal or gestural (e.g., raised hand) responses.

In addition, opportunities can be fact questions that require students to simply recall information that was previously presented or is higher cognitive in nature. Higher cognitive questions require students to analyze, evaluate, manipulate information, and use independent thinking skills (Gall, 1984; Guihua, 2006). "What do you think will happen next?" is an example of a higher cognitive question. Because fact questions typically require one- to three-word answers, students who have skill deficits are more likely to respond correctly to fact questions than to higher order questions (Sitko & Slemon, 1982). In contrast, because fact questions have very specific answers, they can sometimes inhibit responses from students who are uncertain. In such cases higher cognitive questions may be more appropriate. Teachers often are most successful when they move up and down a continuum of easy to hard questions; this gives students at all levels the opportunity to respond.

Providing students with frequent opportunities to respond is important because it is linked to on-task behavior and engagement during instruction. Elementary-age students who are slow learners, when presented with increased opportunities to respond to fact questions, are more likely to answer the questions correctly than when they are asked higher cognitive type questions and, as a result, are able to stay on-task and remain engaged during instruction (Gall, 1984; Gunter et al., 1994; Rosenshine, 1983). In addition, fact questions allow teachers to quickly assess student understanding, as well as cue students and help them focus their attention on the required task. Finally, the call-and-response format used with fact questions closely resembles the short answer and multiple choice question formats of conventional tests used to determine the amount of learning at the end of a curriculum unit (Gall, 1984).

Implementing increased opportunities for student response fits nicely into almost any instructional activity. However, opportunities to respond will be effective only when students can successfully respond to at least 80% of the opportunities. Students who often fail when given an opportunity to respond will quickly learn to avoid responding. Thus, the teacher must assess student abilities and ensure that the opportunities provided are appropriately matched. Teachers also must teach students when and how to respond correctly. For example, if the students' response is to be a thumbs-up signal, then the teacher must model and practice that response with the students to be certain that they understand how to respond correctly. Similarly, in choral responding the teacher may use a precise rhythm or signal to keep the students responding in chorus. Student responses given at different times are difficult for the teacher to assess and allow students to simply copy what others are doing rather than remain engaged in the lesson content.

A good rule of thumb for instruction is to aim for 4–6 student responses per minute. During independent practice, students should be given the opportunity to respond 8–10 times per minute. To ensure that this intervention is applied consistently, teachers should remain on topic, ask open-ended questions, and use higher cognitive solicit questions if fact-based questions prohibit responses. Hand-raising may be the least effective means to increase these opportunities, so it is important for teachers to conduct self-evaluations concerning the rate of opportunities to respond each day. Teachers may keep track of the opportunities

TABLE 10.5 **General Guidelines for Providing Opportunities to Respond**

1. Identify the context and environment in which students need increased opportunities to respond. (During math lessons, students are off-task and only a few students answer the teacher's questions correctly.)

2. Evaluate specific amounts of teacher instructional talk and number of student opportunities to respond. (Teachers monitor the amount of time they talk during the math lesson and the number of opportunities provided to respond.)

3. Teach students to respond to academic requests. (Talk to students about ways and times to respond. Allow for rehearsals and time for feedback.)

4. Teachers then prompt the classroom and/or specific student for an academic response. ("When I multiply 4 × 4, what is the answer?")

5. Teachers provide students with a sufficient amount of wait time to process the request and deliver a response. (Teacher waits 3 or more seconds following the prompt for students to reply.)

6. After a correct or appropriate student response, contingent praise or other reinforcing events should be given to maintain or increase the student's learning. (Teacher offers specific praise such as "Good job, the correct answer is 16.")

7. Monitor student responses to determine accuracy. If students are not providing accurate answers 80–90% of the time, the lesson can be altered to increase student understanding. (Teacher states, "Actually the correct answer is 4 × 4 = 16. Let's look at how to solve this problem a different way." Teacher then uses alternative methods to teach multiplication with continued opportunities to respond until student responses demonstrate an understanding of the concept.)

8. Continue to increase student opportunities to respond to academic requests and/or materials until students are responding at above-mentioned desired rates per minute. (Teachers continue to ask questions that are open-ended or require a specific response throughout the lesson.)

they provided on a graph in an effort to evaluate consistency and effective implementation. In addition, it may be best to start small with this intervention, concentrating on those children who participate least in the classroom. The intervention may also be started on a large-scale basis such as using response cards for the whole classroom. The important thing is to steadily increase the students' number of opportunities to respond until all students have the chance to respond 8–10 times per minute with a 90% accuracy rate. Table 10.5 presents general guidelines for developing and presenting opportunities for student response in instructional settings.

Manipulate Task Difficulty

The concept of manipulating task difficulty takes us back to our earlier discussions of function. Recall that we can reasonably assume that a student will not engage in a behavior for which there is no reinforcer, and almost certainly will not engage in a behavior for which there is a net punishment. If you had to choose between working hard on a task that you know you will fail at and simply ignoring the task, you probably would ignore it. If an acquaintance started pestering you to work on the task and you knew that a rude comment would make them go away, you probably would make a rude comment. But if you were provided with a modified and simplified version of the task such that you succeeded and received verbal praise from your acquaintance, you might actually start liking that task and want to do it more often. In fact, your success might provide the confidence you need to work toward completing the original, more difficult version of the task. From a functional perspective, success is reinforcing, and reinforcement increases the probability of future effort and success. This process could be referred to as taking one small step backward to take a bigger step forward.

Students' problem behaviors often result from frustration with academic work. In the face of challenging academic tasks, students with low success rates may engage in negative behavior as a means of avoiding failure. In these cases, making the student's curriculum less challenging may increase the level of success, resulting in more engagement and fewer problem behaviors. Teachers are often reluctant, for various reasons, to assign easier work. Logic would dictate, however, that creating tasks in which students work and maintain some success is preferable to assigning tasks in which students refuse to participate and have no success. The idea here is not simply to provide a student with easy work; it is to provide the student with work that provides an opportunity for higher levels of success. This strategy is particularly useful with students who need to increase the amount of time that they are on-task or the amount of work that they are completing, as well as with students who engage in other problem behaviors out of frustration with academic work (Kern et al., 2006).

Task difficulty can be reduced by developing more basic tasks within the same content, reviewing concepts that have already been mastered, or providing additional assistance or arrangements to simplify the task. Of course, the key is to determine whether the student has the necessary skills to complete the more difficult academic problems with *sufficient effort*. If he or she does, this intervention is not appropriate. In addition, the teacher must assess the amount of work the student is currently completing and determine the amount of manipulation of difficulty most appropriate. If the student is completing some work, then a dramatic shift back to previous content is not advised. However, if the student is completing very little work and appears to have some genuine skill or fluency deficits, a more substantial manipulation may be warranted. Clearly, if the student understands the basic concepts required to complete the task and simply chooses not to, this is more of a compliance issue than one of ability. But if the student has not acquired key skills necessary to complete the task, the teacher must identify and reteach the key skills until they are mastered.

Manipulation of task difficulty is a strategy that, while very effective, cannot stand alone. Again, the idea is to make the student more successful, and manipulation of difficulty should always be combined with prompts and environmental arrangements, increased teacher attention, direct instruction of academic strategies necessary to complete assigned tasks, and describing what alternative behaviors the students can use when they get frustrated with the work. To be consistent and to minimize the singling out of individual students, the teacher should make sure that the strategies for accessing help are the same for all students and that attention is fairly distributed to all students. The rule of thumb is to determine the work required to facilitate 80% or greater success and begin by assigning work at that level. These curricular changes (i.e., assigning easier work) should be for as brief a period as possible (e.g., 2–3 days) and then gradually return to the new material with which they were originally struggling. The old material should be related to the new material as a means of reviewing important concepts and the students gradually returned to the new material to help them keep up.

Another way of implementing manipulation of task difficulty is to present easier problems together with more academically difficult problems. In this case, the student is eased into the more difficult content by maintaining a high success rate. Students are reinforced by their ability to complete these problems. Students are also able to review important skills and concepts and to recognize their past successes and current abilities, which makes them more likely to stay on task. In addition, teachers not only review older material that is salient for learning new material, they also re-expose students to academic problems that they have successfully mastered. This reinforces students in their ability to solve these problems and makes them more apt to persevere through newer, more challenging material. Table 10.6 presents general guidelines for using manipulation of task difficulty as a strategy during instruction.

Constant Time Delay

The use of wait time, giving students an opportunity to respond to academic questions, is often discussed in teaching textbooks. Constant time delay is an instructional strategy that provides students time to respond to an initial direction or signal (e.g., a bell ringing) that involves few teachers' verbal prompts (i.e., extra instructions, hints, or rule reminders) while continuing to obtain compliant behaviors from the student. Constant time delay is effective for students who require extra time to respond to an initial signal, especially students who are often off-task, noncompliant, or unprepared for class (Stevens & Lingo, 2005).

Teachers often are tempted to constantly barrage students with excessive directions, not allowing them to make appropriate decisions for themselves. Constant time delay is a strategy that decreases students' reliance on teachers' excessive directions for compliance. Consistently giving students an adequate amount of time to follow initial directions allows them to learn independent behavior in response to a more natural system of directions and decreases their need for excessive teacher guidance. Because verbal prompts can be used with multiple students (e.g., "Morning announcements are starting, so sit at your desk, be quiet, and listen."), constant time delay can be used with as many or as few students as necessary. This process can be especially effective with students with processing deficits who take longer to process the initial signal and translate it into the appropriate action. For students with processing deficits, it is a good idea to reduce the number of expectations following the initial signal. For example, some kids (typically developing young ones and kids with LD) can't remember more than one or two directions or steps at a time. Finally, another variation of constant time delay is increasing time delay, which refers to

---

TABLE 10.6 General Guidelines for Manipulating Task Difficulty

1. Determine when new academic concepts might be particularly challenging and cause off-task and/or disruptive behavior for a student. Identify the severity of the behaviors caused by frustration and whether or not the student is completing any of the work. For example, Tommy is struggling with long division with remainders; as a result, he has crumpled up his math paper and refused to complete any of his work for the past three days.

2. Determine what academic concepts are related to this new concept and have been mastered by this student. For example, Tommy can multiply and do long division problems without remainders with 80%+ accuracy.

3. Formulate assignments that review the mastered material, provide a brief review, and assign review problems. Because division with remainders was introduced only a week ago and Tommy has refused to complete any assignments, the teacher will reteach and assign worksheets with multiplication and division without remainders.

4. Teach and conduct role-plays on behaviors that will enable the student to access help when stuck. Teach the academic material by modeling, providing guided practice, and offering continuous reinforcement and feedback. Continue to review and re-review. For example, verbal prompts and role-plays have been conducted with Tommy about raising his hand or putting up a "*Help, please,*" sign on his desk. Extra time has been set aside to review what a remainder is and how to write the answer correctly when there is a question.

5. Provide set opportunities for students to complete academic assignments. For example, the class has independent work time for math assignments every day from 10:00 AM to 11:00 PM.

6. If the student continues to struggle, emphasize and praise him or her for the problems that were completed. "Tommy, great job completing all of your math assignment today. I can tell you really worked hard on it."

7. Be sure that the students' reward for completing assignments matches the function of off-task and other challenging behaviors. "If you can complete all of your work today, you can buy a 'no homework pass' for tonight."

8. Monitor the plan by recording whether problem behavior occurs less and/or appropriate behavior occurs more. For example, Tommy completed 70% of his independent math assignments and had no outbursts during independent work time.

9. Fade the review material as mastery of the new material increases. The number of easy problems was decreased from every other problem to every third problem to every fifth problem over the course of the next two weeks.

---

systematically increasing the delay between the first and second sets of directions, making fading a more systematic process.

Implementation of constant time delay requires an initial analysis of the nature of the problem. The teacher must first determine whether the student has the necessary skills to engage in the appropriate behavior and to respond to initial signals regarding that behavior. If not, the appropriate intervention is to reteach the skills until they are mastered. If the student is unable to engage in the appropriate behavior, then time delay procedures are not appropriate. Time delay begins with teaching the student the correct response to the various signals for behavior (e.g., *"When I remind you of what to do when you hear the bell, what will you do?"*). Make sure that all students know what the first signal means in regard to their specific directions, so that they do not simply spend the time delay waiting to be told what to do. Consistency will be key, especially on the time that the teacher waits for a student to respond before giving a verbal prompt. Make sure that the student, upon hearing the verbal prompt, will immediately understand what is expected because it has become part of the normal routine.

Observing the student also is necessary to determine how much time should elapse before offering another direction. Be aware of contexts in which the desired behavior is least likely to occur or immediate extra directions might be necessary (e.g., a fire drill). At the beginning of the teaching phase, it is best to provide the prompt immediately after an initial signal for a specific behavior (e.g., the bell ringing, the classroom door closing, a timer going off) and then gradually increase the amount of time to a constant time delay. As the student becomes more fluent in demonstrating the behavior, the teacher will use fewer prompts and will increase the amount of time delay between the signal and the extra directions. During the initial instructional session, the teacher sets the time delay at 0, providing the correct response immediately after the prompts. This serves as both an instructional session and modeling of the correct procedures. The teacher then progressively and gradually increases the delay by specific increments—probably one to two seconds—depending on student success. Table 10.7 presents a set of general considerations for constant time delay.

Guided Practice

Guided practice is simply a component of effective instruction in which teachers provide direct practice following initial teaching of new skills. Students at the acquisition level of learning benefit most from teacher-directed practice activities and guidance to perform new tasks to mastery (Swanson & Hoskyn, 2001). As part of instruction delivery, good teachers incorporate guided practice through active application of information. When students use information, they are more likely to acquire and recall it. Teachers also benefit because it provides feedback on instruction presentation. If students are meeting learning objectives, new skills are taught. If students are having difficulty, relevant features are retaught and additional practice opportunities are provided. Whereas other instructional components prepare for competence (e.g., review, description, model), guided practice produces proficiency through active application of the information taught. Good teachers maximize guided practice during instructional time to make sure that students successfully learn a desired skill. Guided practice is central to effective instruction to prepare students for fluency and maintenance of independent performance.

After explicitly explaining and/or demonstrating the skill, the teacher must determine whether the student can demonstrate that particular skill. If not, the appropriate intervention is to provide further teaching examples of the skill. If the student is unwilling to participate, a reinforcement program may be used to motivate him or her. The teacher must teach the student to respond in ways

TABLE 10.7   General Considerations for Constant Time Delay

1. Identify the context and environment that predict problems in responding to an initial signal. (When the bell rings, the student continues to wander around the classroom.)

2. Determine the most appropriate replacement behavior for the identified context. (The student sits down at his or her desk and gets his or her books out instead of wandering around the classroom.)

3. Modify the context so that the student is less likely to make errors. (Have books set out on the student's desk before the bell rings.)

4. Teach and conduct rehearsals. (Talk to the student about how to sit down and get prepared for the day. Allow for role-plays and practice with feedback.)

5. At the appropriate time, after an initial signal has been given, wait for a brief period of time (10 to 20 seconds), then restate the instruction and remind the student of the rule or give a hint that identifies specific components of the appropriate behavior. ("The bell has rung, so it is time to sit down and get your books out.")

6. Observe the student's response and assess accuracy. If correct, provide specific praise. ("Exactly—good for you!") If incorrect, reteach the lesson. ("Think again. What would be a better way?")

7. Be sure that the student's incentive for engaging in the correct behavior is met with an outcome that is similar to the function of the problem behavior. (If the function is to avoid or escape doing school work, a similar outcome would be that a good start of the day allows the student to take a 5-minute break after working for 30 minutes, and a poor start of the day does not allow the student to take a break. Similarly, if the function is to access peer attention, then an appropriate reinforcer might be access to preferred peers.)

8. Monitor the plan by recording whether problem behavior occurs less and/or appropriate behavior occurs more. (Students are more compliant after the first signal or direction is given and less dependent on the second set of instructions.)

9. Fade verbal prompts by increasing the time between the first and second sets of directions and make the second set less frequent and more subtle. (Move from overt verbal directions or commands to gestures or less directive statements (e.g., "Think about what you should do.").)

that will lead to success in the final performance or assessment. As with most interventions, consistency is important, especially on the main instructional points during reviews of previously learned skills. Information should be presented in a clear and organized manner together with guided practice activities, independent practice, and finally assessment of student performance. Instruction should start with a guided practice that will contribute to a learning objective and result in immediate student success. Fine-tune activities by varying style and content of practice from basic to advanced to produce fluency, automaticity, or extended experience to keep students interested. Individual guided practice can be provided during small or large active practice activities. Good teachers are creative in incorporating individual interests to motivate students to practice information learned. Teachers can move beyond worksheets or reading and answering questions by employing variations of activities including peer tutoring to allow pairs

TABLE 10.8   General Guidelines for Guided Practice

1. Identify the instructional objective for the lesson and what students will be able to accomplish after the lesson. Align it with district and state standards of learning. ("To develop skill in asking permission to leave seat.")

2. Provide explicit instruction on the new skill or behavior. State what the appropriate behavior is and model how to perform the skill. (Explain that the key rule is always to get the teacher's attention with your raised hand. Show how to raise the hand in an appropriate manner that does not disturb others and will get the teacher's attention.)

3. Teach guided practice activities that are relevant to instruction. If testing facts, concepts, or principles, make sure that practice activities match the test. (To test the student's ability, ask for a demonstration under different circumstances such as a need to use the restroom or to sharpen a pencil.)

4. Give brief and precise instructions for practice, including the performance qualities desired. ("In the next 10 minutes I want you to sharpen your pencil. What will you do before you leave your seat?")

5. Provide feedback and correction as students work through an activity. Praise students when they are correct, provide prompts to encourage responses, and give correction for errors. (When the student raises a hand, immediately respond by granting the request and providing praise for correct demonstration.)

6. Practice must be motivating, and if problem behaviors occur, be sure that the student's incentive for engaging in the correct behavior accesses an outcome similar to the function of the problem behavior. (If the function of leaving the seat is to get the teacher's attention or to perform a task, hand-raising should be able to access those same outcomes.)

7. Monitor guided practice activities to adjust for student needs and varying performance levels. (Practice skills that go beyond simple acquisition of hand-raising teach how to know when the teacher will be looking and how to be patient in waiting for attention.)

8. Gradually turn over control to students so that they may learn to plan and carry out their own practice and rehearsal of information. (Student continues to raise hand without continual praise from teacher, but gets to perform desired tasks.)

of students to work together, taking turns as the tutor and tutee; asking students to formulate questions, collect and analyze data, and draw conclusions individually or in small groups; using simulation activities for students to role-play situations with peers; and creating checklists and teaching students to check their own work or a partner's work. Table 10.8 presents general considerations for using guided practice.

Chapter Review

- Students may demonstrate two types of deficits. These are skill deficits (i.e., the student has not mastered the skill) or performance deficits (i.e., the student knows how but chooses not to).

- The three critical intervention components to address both types of deficits are instruction, facilitation of success via the natural environment, and effective consequences.

- To eliminate maladaptive behaviors students need replacement behaviors. The key attributes of replacement behaviors are that they are active, are functionally equivalent to the maladaptive behavior, and are reinforced in the environment.
- In order to design instruction to facilitate success, students may need to have tasks broken into smaller steps. They then can be taught through explanations, modeling, prompting, and guidance. Errorless learning, shaping, and chaining are other strategies to promote effective instruction.
- Instructional environments can be manipulated using increased opportunities to respond. We can also modify task difficulty to promote success and use constant time delay and guided practice to make instructional environments more effective.

Application

1. A new teacher is struggling with constant calling out and other disruptive noises in her classroom. What are some ways in which she can address this behavior through effective instruction?
2. In what ways can instruction for improving behavior be adapted to teach academic topics more effectively?
3. What is a replacement behavior for a student who engages in chronic aggression to escape and avoid peers? How could you teach this new behavior and facilitate its use?

References

Christel, C. A., & Schuster, J. W. (2003). The effects of using response cards on student participation, academic achievement, and on-task behavior during whole-class math instruction. *Journal of Behavioral Education, 12*(3), 147–165.

Gall, M. (1984). Synthesis of research on teachers' questioning. *Educational Leadership, 42*, 40–47.

Guihua, C. (2006). To question or not to question, that is the question. *Canadian Social Science, 2*(3), 100–103.

Gunter, P. L., Shores, R. E., Jack, S. L., Denny, R. K., & DePaepe, P. (1994). A case study of the effects of altering instructional interactions on the disruptive behavior of a child with severe behavior disorders. *Education and Treatment of Children, 17*, 435–444.

Jahr, E., & Eldevik, S. (2002). Teaching cooperative play to typical children utilizing a behavior modeling approach: A systematic replication. *Behavioral Interventions, 17*, 145–157.

Jerome, J., Frantino, E. P., & Sturmey, P. (2007). The effects of errorless learning and backward chaining on the acquisition of Internet skills in adults with developmental disabilities. *Journal of Applied Behavior Analysis, 40*, 185–189.

Kern, L., Gallagher, P., Starosta, K., Hickman, W., & George, M. (2006). Longitudinal outcomes of functional behavioral assessment-based intervention. *Journal of Positive Behavioral Interventions, 6*, 113–120.

Rosenshine, B. (1983). Teaching Functions in Instructional Programs. *Elementary School Journal 83*(4), 335–351.

Sitko, M. C., & Slemon, A. L. (1982). Developing teachers' questioning skills: The efficacy of delayed feedback. *Canadian Journal of Education, 7*, 109–121.

Smith, G. J. (1999). Teaching a long sequence of behavior using whole task training, forward chaining, and backward chaining. *Perceptual and Motor Skills, 89*, 951–965.

Stevens, K. B., & Lingo, A. S. (2005). Constant time delay: One way to provide positive behavioral support for students with emotional and behavioral disorders. *Beyond Behavior, 14*(3), 10–15.

Sutherland, K. S., Alder, N., & Gunter, P. L. (2003). The effect of varying rates of opportunities to respond to academic requests on the classroom behavior of students with EBD. *Journal of Emotional and Behavioral Disorders, 11*(4), 239–248.

Swanson, H. L., & Hoskyn, M. (2001). Instructing adolescents with learning disabilities: A component and composite analysis. *Learning Disabilities Research & Practice, 16,* 109–119.

Werts, M. G., Caldwell, N. K., & Wolery, M. (1996). Peer modeling of response chains: Observational learning by students with disabilities. *Journal of Applied Behavior Analysis, 29,* 53–66.

Whitehurst, G. J., & Merkur, A. E. (1977). The development of communication: Modeling and contrast failure. *Child Development, 48,* 993–1001.

11

Creating Environments That Predict Individual Student Success

CHAPTER OBJECTIVES

After reading this chapter, you should be able to describe the following concepts:

- General guidelines for group antecedent strategies
- Guidelines for impactful teacher-student relationships
- Effective use of routines and physical arrangements
- Application of verbal prompts including group attention getters and visual prompts
- Strategies to increase the probability of student compliance

All of us know students who just don't seem to respond to the strategies and arrangements that facilitate success across the rest of the classroom. While such students require more individualized strategies, not all of these strategies need to be applied individually. That is, there are many strategies that provide an additional bit of assistance to the typical student and are absolutely necessary for specific individuals. As teachers, we have the ability to arrange an environment to create student success. Ask yourself, "If it were worth $10,000 to me for that student to be successful with that behavior tomorrow, what would I do extra?" This is not to suggest that we can always change student behavior simply by changing what we do—some students' problems too large and complex for us to ever influence alone. Two points are worth considering here, however. First, the only way we ever know which students will and will not respond to a given set of strategies is to try. Second, our task is to find the strategy, arrangement, instruction, or delivery that creates the highest probability of student success. Failure with any given strategy or strategies never indicates any fault on our part, but it does identify our responsibility to try something different.

The specific strategies that we use in a given situation should be based on the student, the nature of the problem behavior, the context in which it occurs, and what is realistic for the teacher. Our mindset should not be "What will we do if he/she fails again?" but rather,

"What can we do to make the student succeed?". The fundamental change in perspective between these two statements contrasts a reactive versus a proactive frame of reference. Too often, student management plans focus solely on what will happen if the student is successful or unsuccessful, and little, if any, attention is paid to creating an environment that increases the likelihood of success. Let's take an academic example to illuminate this concept. Suppose that a student has been having difficulty with a critical set of skills in math or reading. We would not spend our time devising bigger and more powerful responses to correct and incorrect answers (e.g., making larger red Xs on their papers). Rather, we would use mnemonics, practice, cues, and other antecedent or instructional strategies to increase the likelihood of success. We refer to this effort to create an environment that heightens the probability of success as "trapping success." Our job is to set the trap in such a way that the student in question walks right into the success. How big or complex that trap is depends on how successful we have been with lesser traps and the reinforcement history of the problem behavior. Problem behaviors that are well established may require complex and intensive traps that are slowly faded over an extended period of time, while less challenging behaviors may require only very small and brief traps to sustain success.

This chapter presents strategies that can be useful traps for appropriate behavior. In short, these strategies represent potential answers to the question, "What can I do to make that student successful?" There will never be a $10,000 prize contingent upon our success, however; thus, we must also be mindful of our time and effort. The strategies presented here represent a thoughtful mix of the probability of success and the reality of the teacher's time (see Table 11.1).

ANTECEDENT INTERVENTIONS

Our focus will remain on strategies to prevent problem behavior. When we focus on consequences in other chapters we are assuming that behavior has already occurred. Once a behavior is undertaken, we no longer can have an effect on that behavior. Consequences are things that we do to affect the future probability, but only after a specific instance of the behavior has occurred. If we ask the question "2 + 2 equals . . .?" and the student says "5" we provide correction to decrease the future probability of that response. But the failure has occurred and we cannot undo that. This is precisely why we must think ahead and devise methods to facilitate student success. If our traps work, we increase student success to the point where they receive far more positive consequences that sustain the behavior and allow us to fade our instruction. Much of our discussion here will seem like a review of primary intervention at the schoolwide level (see Chapter 1). The best behavior change strategies aim at antecedents and instruction (e.g., how we teach and what we put into the environment to make teaching more effective). In fact, much of what we present in this chapter may be thought of as effective instructional practices. We distinguish antecedent strategies from instructional strategies by defining the former as those that manipulate the environment surrounding instruction, while the latter are more directly related to the delivery of content.

TABLE 11.1   General Guidelines for All Antecedent Strategies

---

1. Create an operational definition of the problem behavior that includes what the behavior is (topography) and the conditions under which it is likely (locus).

2. Determine whether the problem behavior has an obvious function. Even without performing a formal FBA, the teacher can look for obvious functions.

3. Be certain that the selected antecedent strategy is functional for the student. The functional reinforcer should be present when the student engages in desired behavior and absent when the student does not engage in desired behavior.

4. Teach the student the desired behavior—when, how, and why to perform it—and assess for mastery. Do not institute an antecedent strategy for a behavior that the student cannot perform or does not know how to complete.

5. Verbal prompts can and should be used with all strategies to facilitate success. The value of any antecedent strategy is in the facilitation of success. Always use the least amount necessary to maximize the probability of success.

6. Be ready to restate, remind, and correct quickly to facilitate success. Teacher proximity, voice volume, and physical cues may help facilitate success even as other strategies are in place.

7. Always acknowledge success and reinforce as naturally as possible. Verbal praise is a good standard as it is easily and quickly available, but naturally occurring, and functional consequences must be included.

8. Monitor, record, and graph student performance. Compare to criteria from the instructional objective as represented by the aim line on the graph and make decisions about the success of the strategies employed.

9. Student success should result in fading of prompts, increasing contingencies for reinforcement, and movement toward less intrusive antecedent strategies. Student failure should result in a more formal assessment of function and consideration of other strategies.

Teacher-Student Relationships

A major concern for any teacher is how to implement a given strategy for one student in a classroom. But an even larger concern may be how to implement a strategy for multiple students with slightly different problems in the same classroom. The relationships that teachers develop with students can affect the success of the student (Hamre & Pianta, 2001). Because necessary communication and basic social interactions are part of the everyday classroom environment, the teacher has repeated opportunities to establish a rapport with each student. The key here is the concept of "opportunity." Every time an interaction (necessary or not) takes place between the teacher and a student, the teacher can use it to increase the probability of student success. As Pianta (1996) has so eloquently stated, "The asymmetry in child-adult relationship systems places a disproportionate amount of responsibility on the adult for the quality of the relationship" (p. 73). Due to this asymmetry, Pianta suggests that the teacher's responsibility should be to initiate positive interactions with students in order to encourage positive relationship development.

Here again we return to the teacher's responsibility. When pondering what to do to facilitate student success, consider some very simple strategies that can be used to create a more positive relationship. Of course, when we view these problems with a particularly behavioral lens, we need to obtain an operational definition of "positive relationship." The most basic and direct way of doing this is to define the particulars of teacher and student interaction that are demonstrated correlates of student compliance, achievement, and success rates. The following strategies are relevant to teacher and student interaction.

GREETING AT THE DOOR.   It seems (and actually is) simplistic, but a student's entry into the classroom is an opportunity for the teacher to set the tone for that day's interactions and to establish a pattern of positive interaction (Allday & Pakurar, 2007). Simply saying a student's name when he or she arrives provides an individualized acknowledgement ("Hey Johnnie, how are you?"). Although the teacher at this point can talk with the student about nonacademic things ("Did you see the game last night?"), an opportunity also exists to reinforce any notable desirable behavior ("Thanks for bringing your book!"), to provide an advance organizer ("We're gonna do computers today after a short reading—It'll be fun."), or to make environmental arrangements ("Have a seat over here today—this is a great spot to see what we're doing."). Obviously, a simple greeting at the door in the morning is unlikely to be the hallmark strategy for any plan; however, it is an easy way to increase the probability of student success throughout the day.

EYE CONTACT.   Eye contact is another simple strategy that teachers may use with individuals, targeted groups, or all students. For many students, eye contact communicates awareness and personalized attention (Everett et al., 2005). But as with any social interaction, this is best used in a reciprocal manner with both teacher and student maintaining eye contact during interaction. Maintaining eye contact requires directing the gaze at the face of the person with whom one is interacting. Interaction occurs whenever one is directing communication to another. Thus, directions, modeling, conversation, feedback, and listening all require eye contact by all who are involved in the interaction. As a compliance strategy, the student is taught to look at the person giving instruction. Although eye contact is quick and easy to implement, teachers must be sensitive to sociocultural factors and individual characteristics when using it. This also allows teachers to confirm that students are paying attention when communication is occurring. Societies have various social norms regarding how long one should look at a person during conversation. For example, eye contact may be judged positively among North Americans because it shows that one is listening; in other cultures, however, looking down is a sign of respect. In addition, for individuals who have autism, eye contact is a subtle form of nonverbal communication requiring social interpretations that often are difficult. Table 11.2 presents general guidelines for fostering positive and effective teacher and student relationships.

Consistent Routines and Physical Arrangements

SCHEDULING AND ADVANCE ORGANIZERS.   Scheduling time is not just a characteristic of an organized and purposeful teacher. It also is a way to manage student behavior. A posted schedule provides the student with information about the day so that she or he can predict what will occur. For many students who come from chaotic home environments, the classroom may be the only consistent thing in their lives. Thus, the more consistent and predictable the schedule is, the

---

TABLE 11.2   General Guidelines for Teacher-Student Relationships

1. Be mindful of how you speak to and interact with students. Instructionally, always show them the same respect that you expect in return.
2. Take an interest in the students' lives and show them that you care about them as individuals in your classroom.
3. Teach students how to communicate in a positive manner, and model, practice, and provide feedback at each opportunity.
4. Be sensitive to cultural, intellectual, and physical diversity. Some students simply will not be able to interact in the way that you expect and compromise will be needed.
5. Be genuine with students. Don't be afraid to admit your mistakes or to talk to students as equals. Always consider students' feelings in all interactions.

---

more comfortable the environment. Schedules should include arrival/start times, ending times, and times for transition and cleanup. It may also be helpful to schedule the most important activities earlier in the day, when concentration may be higher, and to schedule breaks at appropriate intervals.

Consistency is important in scheduling; each subject area or daily task (e.g., restroom, recess, break, etc.) should occur at approximately the same time and in the same order each day. Such predictability creates a chained behavior of sorts (see Chapter 10) wherein the completion of each discrete activity is a reinforcer for completing the schedule to that point. A consistent schedule creates a sort of checklist for the day. In addition, completion of each discreet activity signals to the student what is to come next and also provides a prompt. Schedules should be publicly posted, if possible, perhaps written on the board or detailed on some sort of poster board. Public posting allows the teacher to use the schedule as a visual prompt (e.g., pointing and stating "Only 5 more minutes left of math and then we will be moving on to spelling."). This is preferable to having individual students call out, "When are we done with this?" or "Do we have recess next?". The goal is for the student to use the schedule to become more independent.

Of course, no schedule is exactly the same every day. Conferences, holidays, assemblies, and various other events occasionally will alter the typical schedule. On such occasions the teacher must gain student attention and specifically describe the schedule change in a clear, concrete, and direct manner. The change should be noted on the schedule in some manner and the teacher should continue to call attention to the change throughout the day (e.g., "Remember, only 30 minutes of math this morning because of the assembly before lunch."). Some students may be more anxious in the face of schedule changes and may require additional instruction, coaching, and prompting to navigate the day successfully. Table 11.3 presents general guidelines for developing effective schedules and advance organizers as part of instruction.

TEACHER PROXIMITY.   Teacher proximity refers to where a teacher is positioned within the classroom, or how near the teacher is to a student or area at a given time or on average during a day. Certainly, all teachers employ the strategy of standing over a particularly off-task student to ensure that he or she stays on

TABLE 11.3   General Guidelines for Scheduling and Advance Organizers

1. Create a schedule that can be consistently followed on a very regular basis.
2. Teach the schedule to students and publicly post it for all to see.
3. Refer to the schedule frequently throughout the day to remind students what is next.
4. Announce and discuss any aberrations in the schedule. Allow students to ask questions and be comfortable with the impending change.
5. Schedule purposefully to avoid transitions, movements, and situations that are predictive of problems.

task and completes an assignment. But proximity can be used much more subtly to prevent problem behavior, addressing both minor misbehaviors and the very early stages of escalating behaviors that lead to a blowup (Gunter & Shores, 1995; Grossman, 2004, p. 297). Increasing proximity to misbehaving students should be one of the teacher's very first strategies; however, rather than running from student to student based on misbehavior, teachers should continue moving around the room throughout the day, wandering purposefully to maintain proximity to as many students as often as possible. Close proximity to a student provides the teacher with an opportunity to provide reinforcement ("Nice work!") or prompts ("Remember to check your answers.") and to assess student work. Students who know that the teacher is moving about and may be behind them at any moment will feel a greater urgency to stay on task.

For students who are already exhibiting problem behavior, proximity enables the teacher to more accurately monitor exactly what is occurring and to provide redirection or other strategies to regain student success. Maintaining closer proximity to a disruptive student should be done purposefully and assertively, but not aggressively. If the distance between you and the student is great, move quickly enough to stem the behavior but not so quickly that your movement seems hurried or unnatural. A reasonable distance for providing directions or feedback is somewhere between 18 inches and 2 feet, but a larger buffer zone of 2–6 feet also may be effective. Of course, exact distances depend on the overall setting, context, and students. Crowds, noise, activity, and the nature of the problem all will determine the best proximity, and often the ideal distance is something that teachers have acquired a feel for after working with particular students or in particular contexts. While maintaining close proximity to one student, the teacher must continue to attend to others by scanning visually and occasionally even moving about briefly before returning to the student exhibiting problems.

Teacher proximity may not be appropriate for students with autism, who are hypersensitive to environmental events and often do not want people near them. Proximity will also be ineffective for students whose developmental disabilities make them unaware of the teacher's close presence (Conroy et al., 2004). Additionally, students who have been physically abused may become more disruptive when an adult approaches them to correct challenging behaviors. Table 11.4 presents general guidelines for considering teacher proximity to students.

TABLE 11.4   General Guidelines for Teacher Proximity

1. Maintain proximity in a proactive manner to prevent predictable problems.
2. Move purposefully and assertively toward students who are misbehaving but avoid being seen as angry or aggressive.
3. When providing prompts, move to within 2 feet of the student to deliver the prompt, then remain until positive behavior is exhibited.
4. When monitoring as a form of teacher proximity, stay within 2–6 feet of the student. Let them know that you are there, but continue to teach the entire group.
5. When not engaging in proximity to a particular student, continue to move about the room, passing near all students frequently.
6. Whenever you are near to a student who is performing appropriately, provide reinforcement, even if very subtle (e.g., touch on shoulder, group praise—"Everyone is doing so well!")

SEATING ARRANGEMENT.   While there are those who extol the virtues of a specific seating arrangement (e.g., rows, circles, groupings, pairs, etc.), seating arrangement decisions clearly are best made in the context of the required student behaviors and outcomes. Consequently, if the goal is to have students collaborate and share work on a project, then seating them in groups makes a lot of sense, but having them sit in rows makes less sense. Similarly, if the goal is to have students quietly complete independent work, then the groupings and pairings would seem to offer less probability of student success than rows would. Seating arrangements can impact classroom discipline, student and teacher interactions, and the effectiveness of instruction (Hastings, 1995; Wheldall & Lam, 1987; Wannarka & Ruhl, 2008). Teachers can anticipate and prevent disruptive behaviors by planning the instructional environment to maximize large group discussions, cooperative group work, or independent tasks. The point is that there is no ideal seating arrangement—only decisions regarding the arrangement that increases the likelihood of student success in a given context. Good teachers plan for better classroom management by simply arranging student desks to enhance instructional objectives and maximize time on task.

Planning seating arrangement should consider ease of movement for both teacher and students. A room that does not allow ease of movement sets the stage for congestion, pushing, and bumping, which can create larger problems. In addition, seating arrangements should allow the teacher to move easily within a critical proximity of any students without disrupting other students. Second, the arrangement should allow students to choose the location that best suits their learning style or preference. For example, some students will be too distracted if seated by a window while others will learn best when seated close to the teacher. Third, seating arrangements should provide a range of alternatives, perhaps involving a mix of tables, desks, and study carrels. Of course, the shape and size of the classroom may dictate how it must be arranged.

Seating arrangements should also take individual students into consideration. Remember the question with which we began this chapter, "What can we do

---

TABLE 11.5   General Guidelines for Seating Arrangements

1. Create a seating arrangement that allows for easy flow of traffic at all times.
2. Consider seating arrangements as part of lesson planning; the arrangement should facilitate success.
3. Consider the placement of individuals as part of planning. Separate students who feed negatively off one another and avoid seating students where teacher proximity is difficult to maintain.
4. Teach clear rules for changing seating arrangement and build those expectations into a consistent daily schedule so that they become part of the routine.

---

to make the student succeed?". Suppose that a teacher knows that Sandy, if seated next to Alice, will talk and get little work done. It then makes sense for the teacher to create an arrangement in which Alice and Sandy are not seated together during independent work times. If Sally and Alice work well together, however, they should be seated together for group work or even be granted opportunities to sit together as a reinforcer for finishing work. Because we are dealing with antecedent interventions and the prevention of problems, our focus with seating is mostly on changes made before class. Moving students to isolated areas or away from reinforcing activities as a consequence for misbehavior does not apply here, but will be covered in Chapter 13 on punishment. Seating arrangements should not be punitive. Rather, they are meant to create environments in which students have increased levels of success, thereby accessing positive teacher attention and natural reinforcement. This intervention should be considered in light of the discussion at the beginning of the chapter: Try different arrangements as an intervention and see what works; if an arrangement does not work, then try a different one. It is not a failure if a new seating arrangement does not work; the only failure is not trying anything different. Table 11.5 presents general guidelines for considering and implementing classroom seating arrangements.

Prompts and Cues

Prompts and cues may take the form of gestures, sounds, signals, notes, signs, modeling, or any other physical display that increases the probability of success. Prompts and cues can be used to remind students to use appropriate behaviors before a condition predictive of high failure rates occurs. The general rule of thumb for prompts and cues is to use the least amount of them or the least intrusive prompt necessary to facilitate a successful response. Because prompts typically do not occur naturally, be sure they do not become the only stimulus for appropriate behavior. Prompts should be used only to draw a student's attention to the natural discriminative stimuli that should control behavior. They then should be systematically faded so that the desired behavior occurs reliably in the presence of the naturally occurring discriminative stimuli. For example, the dismissal bell, rather than the teacher's verbal reminder, should be the discriminative stimulus for students to put away materials, straighten their desks, and leave the classroom in an orderly manner.

TABLE 11.6 General Guidelines for Prompts and Cues

1. Always use the least intrusive and most naturally occurring prompt necessary to facilitate student success.
2. Teach prompts and practice with students to build fluency.
3. Be proactive with prompts and use them immediately before situations that are predictive of student failure.
4. When using prompts as a corrective procedure, remember that these are a form of reteaching and should not become punitive.
5. Pair prompts with naturally occurring environmental events and work to transfer stimulus control from yourself to the natural environment.
6. Continue to fade prompts with student success, moving to less and less intrusive prompts with the eventual goal of complete removal.
7. Reinforce successful performance.

Once students begin the behavior or routine, you can provide hints, suggestions, reminders, and questions designed to facilitate success (e.g., "Remember to wait for the student who is at my desk to return to his seat before coming up."). Finally, prompts and cues can be used to lead students who have failed to demonstrate the appropriate behavior back through the situation and show them the stimuli that should have signaled the appropriate behavior (e.g., "When you approached me, Johnny was at my desk, so I didn't have time to help you. If I'm working with someone else when you need me, what should you do?"). Even when applying a negative consequence for misbehavior under these conditions, corrective prompts and cues should be used to decrease the likelihood of repeated failure in the future. When misbehaviors are regarded as errors rather than intentions to be "bad," applying a correction procedure is a more logical intervention than is punishment. Table 11.6 presents general guidelines for considering and implementing instructional prompts and cues.

VERBAL PROMPTS. Verbal prompts are perhaps the most frequently used response to misbehavior. But as we have discussed, after a misbehavior has occurred, we no longer have an opportunity to prevent that behavior. Thus, we will focus here on the use of verbal prompts as an antecedent strategy. Verbal prompts in the form of hints, rule reminders, or instructions increase the probability that the student will demonstrate the behavior more quickly and accurately (Hodges, 2001; Werts, Caldwell, & Wolery, 2003). Verbal prompts can be used across the school day for both individuals and groups of students.

Several considerations must be made before using verbal prompts as a prevention strategy. First, the teacher must determine whether the student has the necessary skills to engage in the appropriate behavior and to respond to verbal prompts. If not, the appropriate intervention is to reteach the skill until it is mastered or to include some more-intensive prompts that may include physical guidance. For a student who is aggressively resistant or unwilling to engage in appropriate behavior this strategy is the first step, although it may not be intensive enough to be appropriate. Second, the student must be taught the correct response to the various signals for behavior (e.g., *"When you hear my reminder, you need to start cleaning up right then."*). The prompt is a strategy to promote success with another behavior, so the teacher needs to be certain that the prompt is understood. Third, if prompts are to become a predictor of success, they must be delivered consistently so that the student learns that a specific prompt is always a signal to engage in a particular behavior. That is, creating an effective prompt is, in essence, creating a mediator for stimulus control (see Chapter 2). Observe the student to determine the best time to deliver the verbal prompt. The prompt is best provided immediately after an initial signal for a specific behavior (e.g., the bell ringing, the classroom door closing, a timer going off). Be aware of contexts in which the desired behavior is least likely to occur. In addition, consider whether the verbal prompt should be delivered privately to the student or as part of the group routine. Fourth, prompts at first should be large and obvious ("Sam, it's time to clean up, so get started now!") and, as they are successful, should gradually be faded out to less obvious ("Clean-up time is right now.") and then to the most natural prompt that would typically occur for all students ("Clean-up, everyone.").

To use verbal prompts the teacher should first identify the contexts in which prompts are necessary to facilitate student success, then develop a prompt and teach the meaning of that prompt to the student. The prompt is simply a reminder for the student to engage in an appropriate behavior, so the appropriate behavior also must be taught to and mastered by the student. That is, the verbal prompt does not teach the student how to perform the appropriate behavior; it only signals when to engage in the behavior. Thus, verbal prompts are not useful with behaviors that the student has not yet mastered. For example, for a student who does not know how to swim, simply yelling "Remember to swim" after he or she falls into a pool would have little effect. Teaching involves modeling and practice to ensure that the student knows what to do, when to do it, and why (the consequences). As with all strategies, the teacher also must consider what other environmental changes might increase the student's probability of success. The teacher might want to consider various seating arrangements, maintaining a clear and consistent schedule, or moving into close proximity before delivering the prompt. Of course, our rule of thumb is that we should use the least amount of prompts necessary to facilitate student success. When using verbal prompts, format the prompt as a statement rather than a question (e.g., say "The bell has rung, so it is time to sit down" rather than "Can everyone please sit down?"). Make your voice loud enough to be heard, but do not yell. Also, avoid inappropriate gestures, faces, and an exasperated tone of voice. Make eye contact with students as you are giving the verbal prompt. Table 11.7 presents general guidelines for considering and delivering verbal prompts to guide student success.

GROUP ATTENTION GETTERS AND VISUAL CUES.   Verbal prompts can be used with multiple students as well as with individuals. In fact, most teachers regularly use certain words or phrases to prompt group behavior (e.g., "Cleanup time!", "Line up!", etc.); however, verbal prompts used with larger groups often require a volume that is close to yelling, which creates a poor model for

TABLE 11.7   General Guidelines for Verbal Prompts

1. Provide verbal prompts immediately before the context in which they are necessary and make sure that the student is aware and able to hear the prompt.
2. Be as brief as possible with a verbal prompt. For example, after asking students to line up for lunch, simply say "Quick and quiet."
3. Break complex behaviors down into smaller components and provide prompts for each component step.
4. Pair verbal prompts with naturally occurring environmental cues and call the student's attention to both.
5. Be consistent with the verbal prompt until data indicate sufficient success to fade to a less-intrusive one.

students and wears down the teacher's vocal chords. In these cases, more efficient and effective group attention getters are useful. Group attention getters basically are very obvious prompts that are easily recognized within a crowd and across a room. Group attention getters require instruction on how to recognize the prompt and what the expected behavior is. For example, when attempting to get an active classroom to stop and listen to directions, many teachers teach a rhythmic set of three or four hand claps to which all the students respond with a set of hand claps indicating their acknowledgement of the prompt. For students who may have missed the teacher's prompt, the responding students' claps provide a second and more obvious prompt. The students are taught to make the responding claps and then to quietly look to the teacher for direction. Should the prompt not capture the attention of all the students, it may be repeated. This same basic format may be employed with a flash of the classroom lights and the teacher's choice of student response. A similar but less intrusive example involves the teacher simply raising a hand in front of the students. The students are taught to stop and raise their hands while looking quietly at the teacher when they see the teacher with a hand raised. Generally, a few students will respond to the prompt immediately, and the other students will gradually become aware of the raised hands around them and comply. If a couple of students still do not notice, a quiet verbal prompt may then be used. Again, it is the teaching, consistent use, and consistent reinforcement of the appropriate behaviors that will make group attention getters at all grade levels truly successful.

Because verbal prompts and attention getters are useful only when the teacher is available to deliver them, visual cues are also used for prompting. Visual cues can be used in two ways. First, visual cues can be employed in general visual stimuli, such as posters or other displays, placed in areas around the school building and grounds. For example, a stop sign at the end of a busy hall is a large visual cue that, when taught, reminds students to stop and look before crossing a hall intersection. Likewise, posters in the cafeteria that show students engaging in various positive behaviors (e.g., putting trays away appropriately, using manners, etc.) and a straight line drawn near the doorway to prompt students to line up are visual reminders of expected behavior.

TABLE 11.8	**General Guidelines for Group Attention Getters and Visual Cues**

1. Teach students the routine and expected behavior for any group attention or visual cue strategies.
2. Use the strategies consistently and do not change course until data indicate sufficient success to begin fading.
3. Involve students in the development of visual cues. Have them create posters, signs, and other cues and use what they develop.
4. Use verbal prompts to help make students aware of more visual or kinesthetic cues.
5. Try to use natural cues from the environment as much as possible and call attention to them to facilitate fading later.

Visual cues also can take the form of more individualized visuals or pictures to prompt student behavior. For students with autism and other developmental delays, pictures are often used to communicate schedules and activities (Son, Sigafoos, O'Reilly, & Lancioni, 2006; Long, 2000, p. 210). For example, a student may have several pictures of different activities arranged on a picture board or in a picture book at his or her desk. When it is time to transition, the teacher points to the picture that cues the student on the behavior expected at that time. Each picture cue should be paired with a verbal cue to help the student associate a more natural prompt with the appropriate behavior. Early elementary school teachers also use picture cues to help students learn the new language associated with expected behavior (Ganz & Flores, 2010, p. 83). Table 11.8 presents general guidelines for delivery group attention getters and visual cues in classroom settings.

PRECORRECTION.   Precorrection involves using a verbal prompt delivered prior to behavior and requiring a response from the student. Precorrection originally was used to make adjustments in academic instruction before students had an opportunity to make errors (Colvin, Sugai, & Patching, 1993; Kame'enui & Simmons, 1990; Oswald, Safran, & Johanson, 2005). The most appropriate focus for precorrection is an instructional area in which the teacher anticipates that the student will make errors. Using precorrection involves thinking ahead to the problems or contexts in which stimulus control is not yet firmly established, providing a prompting question to the student, and providing feedback to the student based on the response. As with academics, applying this strategy to prevent student social failure requires teaching the rules and routines that students are to follow, usually during times or routines that typically are less highly structured than academic lessons, such as transitions between lessons or classes.

The most direct strategy is simply to provide a verbal reminder of the stimulus-response relationship (e.g., "If someone calls you a name during this activity, what would be a good thing to do?"). If the student answers correctly, the teacher provides a verbal reinforcer for that response, and another natural reinforcer once the prompted behavior occurs correctly. For example, the teacher may begin the sequence by saying, "Tammy, how fast should we move in the hall?". Tammy then answers, "Walking," to which the teacher responds, "Exactly; very good thinking, Tammy." Once Tammy is walking in the hall, the teacher needs to take the opportunity to acknowledge this success in a more naturalistic manner: "Wow, look at all the responsible students walking in the hall. This means we don't have to go back, so everyone gets a longer lunch. Great job!" If, on the other hand, Tammy was unable to successfully answer the precorrection (e.g., "I don't know" or "run"), the teacher would immediately state the correct answer and then ask the question again: "When we're in the hall, we always walk. So how should you go down the hall to lunch today?" Like most strategies, precorrection does not guarantee student success; it only increases the probability of success. Its purpose is to create the likelihood that the student will succeed so that the teacher will have the opportunity to provide more natural reinforcement.

The most effective way to use precorrection is as an antecedent prompt; however, like all prompting and cuing strategies, it also can be used as part of a corrective sequence. When a student fails, the teacher may elect to ask a precorrective question. Of course, this strategy will be effective only if the student in fact knows what to do. Put another way, the precorrective question will simply be a setup for a second failure if the student genuinely does not know what he or she should have done. Thus, instruction prior to the use of precorrection is essential. In addition, precorrection is most effective when delivered just before the context in which failure is most probable. Table 11.9 presents general guidelines for developing and delivering precorrection as a strategy for increasing student success.

Antecedent Compliance Strategies

Antecedent compliance strategies are defined here as those that focus mainly on student compliance. There is a difference between the student who simply forgets and the student who recalls the expectations but chooses to do otherwise. The strategies presented in this section are antecedent in nature but still focus on compliance. That is, their focus is not on reminding students so much as on encouraging behaviors that they probably are aware of but are not likely to perform.

PROVIDING CHOICE.   Providing student choices is a simple strategy to increase student participation during ongoing classroom routines and instructional tasks

---

TABLE 11.9   General Guidelines for Precorrection

1. Teach the precorrective sequence and ensure that the student understands what is expected.
2. Deliver the precorrective prompt immediately before conditions in which the target behavior is desired.
3. Use question prompts that are clear and unambiguous, requiring a concrete response from the student.
4. When using precorrection for an individual student, use the strategy with other students at the same time to allow the student to hear the correct answer and to avoid singling out the student in front of the class.
5. Reinforce both the correct answer to the prompt question and the appropriate behavior that occurs as a result.

or to increase completion of specific behaviors or activities (Jolivette, Stichter, & McCormick, 2002). There are two basic types of choices. The first type is for beginning a large task. This involves breaking the task into smaller pieces and providing a choice on the order in which the smaller tasks are to be completed. The second type, which involves presenting a choice between two or more specific alternative tasks, is most appropriate when there are multiple task requirements. For example, Edward has a large project that he has barely begun, and frequent reminders have been unsuccessful because the task has become overwhelming. This scenario would dictate that the teacher break the project into smaller tasks and provide Edward with a choice as to which of the smaller tasks he'd like to undertake. Success with each smaller task will create a greater probability of compliance with the next. Fred, however, has two different projects that are coming due. Whenever either of them is mentioned, he immediately comes up with excuses and competing activities that interfere with his ability to complete it. In this case, the teacher creates two concrete expectations and offers Fred the opportunity to choose which one he is most willing to complete. The teacher makes it clear to Fred that he is the sole decision maker—but there are only two choices, and he must pick one or the other.

Choice making requires some skill on the student's part, and implementing the strategy should start with basic and concrete choices. With success, the teacher gradually begins introducing opportunities to make choices during difficult subject areas in which tasks or the order of tasks can be varied. When preparing to implement choice, the teacher must consider whether the student is able to choose one of the options provided and follow through with it. If the student cannot decide on an option or complete the chosen option, simple choice-making skills can be taught, and teacher assistance likely will be required to both initiate and complete any chosen task. In fact, part of the instruction involves teaching the student to choose one option and follow through on it. The teacher also must be certain that, once the student has made a choice, the chosen activities and expectations are consistent and predictable; that is, the choice must be laid out in a very concrete form, almost in the manner of a contract.

Choice opportunities are best provided immediately before the contexts in which the problem is most likely to occur. In addition, consider whether the choice can be delivered privately to the student or must be done as part of the group routine. The strategy of permitting students to choose tasks and curricula has shown promise with students exhibiting behavior problems. Although extensive research has been conducted on allowing students with cognitive disabilities to make choices, this research is only beginning to be done for students with behavioral problems. Research (Dunlap et al., 1994; Jolivette, Wehby, & Canale, 2001) has shown that allowing students with EBD to choose tasks and instructional materials results in increased academic engagement and reduced disruptive behavior. Table 11.10 presents general guidelines for considering and providing choices as an instructional strategy.

BEHAVIORAL MOMENTUM.   Behavioral momentum is an antecedent-based, non-aversive strategy for developing behavioral compliance. In its simplest sense, behavioral momentum involves getting the student to comply with very simple

---

TABLE 11.10   General Guidelines for Providing Choices

1. Identify times of the day in which students can easily make choices and the teacher can provide access to choice options. (Start with convenient times that the teacher can easily manage.)

2. Review existing student data (e.g., running records, anecdotal records) to introduce opportunities for students to make choices within curricular or social areas in which they can experience more success.

3. Present choice opportunities consistently as part of task directions.

4. Choice opportunities should be matched to the function of student behavior by adding predictability to problem situations in which the student chooses the event that will occur after appropriate behavior.

5. Fade individual choice opportunities by providing whole-class opportunities during ongoing academic activities. For example, let students choose where to sit in the room, choose one explorer from a list of explorers to do a report, choose the order of language arts activities, or choose methods to complete a task.

6. Assist students in making positive choices that will result in predictable and desirable outcomes.

7. Combine choice-making opportunities within existing environmental conditions and natural consequences. Students can choose between two options, choose the order of tasks, and choose where in the classroom to complete work.

---

and benign tasks and then providing contingent reinforcement to build momentum toward eventual compliance with a more difficult task (Davis & Brady, 1993; Burns et al., 2009; Lee & Laspe, 2003). For example, the teacher issues a sequence of two or three simple requests that have a high probability of student compliance. Upon completion of each request in the sequence, the teacher provides reinforcement (e.g., verbal praise) and then introduces a request with a lower probability of student compliance. The "momentum" developed by responding appropriately to high-probability requests increases the probability of compliance with the low-probability request. For example, Marla has had difficulty getting started on her spelling work. Just before spelling, the teacher delivers several requests that have been predictive of compliance, asking Marla for help with passing out books, taking roll, and moving a table. (Early childhood examples might include "Show me your finger," "Point to your nose," or "Tell me your name.") The teacher thanks Marla for her assistance and praises her responsibility upon compliance with each request. Then the teacher says, "Marla, thanks so much for all your help this morning. Now let's see if you can get going on the spelling and finish that too." Behavioral momentum as a strategy is simply a manner of raising the probability of successful compliance.

Behavioral momentum is most effective with students who are willing and able to respond to most requests but have difficulty complying with specific tasks. If the student refuses to comply with any directions, there will be no opportunity to establish the necessary momentum. Further, it should again be noted that compliance strategies such as behavioral momentum are effective only with behaviors that the student is capable of completing. Therefore, instruction

TABLE 11.11   General Guidelines for Behavioral Momentum

1. Be certain that the student is capable of performing the desired behavior.
2. Initial requests should be age-appropriate tasks that have a high likelihood of compliance.
3. Provide strong verbal praise using words like "responsibility" and "respectful" in response to compliance with initial requests.
4. Use the relevant words (e.g., "responsibility", "respectful") when delivering the low-probability request. For example, "You've been so responsible this morning. I'm very impressed. Can you get some of your project done now too?"
5. Vary the high-probability requests with each use of the strategy so as not to become too transparent in the building of momentum.
6. Provide reinforcement upon completion of the low-probability task. Because many compliance problems tend to function as an escape from work, free time or other breaks from work provide a functional reinforcer.

in how to complete the task and assessment of the student's capabilities must precede the use of compliance strategies. Table 11.11 presents general guidelines for considering and implementing behavioral momentum as a managerial strategy.

Maintenance and Generalization

The strategies presented in this chapter are designed to help students succeed so that teachers have opportunities to reinforce their success. But however easy these strategies may be to implement, they cannot be used forever because students continually grow, develop, and matriculate while in school. Therefore, we are concerned with facilitating not only that initial success, but also a sustained success that can persist beyond and in the absence of our antecedent strategies. Several of the components built into each of these strategies are specifically designed to encourage maintenance of behavior and generalization to other settings and conditions. First, there is a focus on the use of naturally occurring environmental cues paired with more obvious and intrusive prompts. The more naturalistic the cues are, the easier it will be to fade artificial prompts. Second, the behaviors that are taught must be relevant; that is, they must look like what the typical student might do. Teaching students to engage in bizarre topographies or developmentally inappropriate behaviors will make them unlikely to continue performing the behavior when a particular teacher is absent. This strategy requires some assessment, generally formulated as "What do successful students do under these circumstances?" Thus, behaviors are judged appropriately not by the teacher alone, but by both the teacher and the larger context.

The third consistent strategy used to promote maintenance and generalization is a focus on natural reinforcers and functional outcomes. Clearly, behaviors that result in reinforcement in the natural world are behaviors that are likely to be sustained across settings. As we previously asked about the behavior of successful students, we now must ask, "Why do successful students do that under these circumstances?" This line of thinking helps us to develop responses that are natural, allowing the student to continue responding in the absence of the teacher and artificial consequences. Still, there are students for whom the function of their behavior is unique. These students will require a functional assessment to determine the most appropriate functional consequence for behavior. Sometimes the connections between these individual functions and more naturalistic responses are easy to make—and at other times they are not. The teacher's job will be to pair whatever reinforcers facilitate success in the present with those that may help it to be more generalized later.

Chapter Review

- The general guidelines for using group antecedent strategies include operationally defining behaviors to be changed, determining their functions, teaching new replacement behaviors, and using verbal prompts and praise to increase occurrences of the replacement behavior.
- Some guidelines for facilitating positive teacher-student relationships include establishing eye contact, greeting students, relating to their interests, and being genuine with communications, including admitting when you have made a mistake.

- In order to effectively use routines and physical arrangements in the classroom it is necessary to establish a schedule for the day or period, monitor the intervals for each activity, and then post the schedule as a visual prompt for students.
- Other antecedent strategies include teacher proximity, the application of verbal prompts, and the use of group attention getters and other types of visual prompts.
- Strategies to increase the probability of student compliance include behavioral momentum and the use of choice when presenting requests to students.

Application

1. It is the week before the first day of school. What antecedent strategies could be put in place before the first child even sets foot in the classroom?
2. What is the value of using antecedent strategies in classroom settings to prevent challenging behavior?

3. How can these antecedent strategies be combined to be more effective in preventing challenging behavior and increasing prosocial behaviors?

References

Allday, R. A., & Pakurar, K. (2007). Effects of teacher greetings on student on-task behavior. *Journal of Applied Behavior Analysis, 40*(2), 317–320.

Burns, M. K., Ardoin, S. P., Parker, D. C., Hodgson, J., Klingbeil, D. A., & Scholin, S. E. (2009). Interspersal technique and behavioral momentum for reading word lists. *School Psychology Review, 38*(3), 428–434.

Colvin, G., Sugai, G., & Patching, B. (1993). Precorrection: An instructional approach for managing predictable problem behaviors. *Intervention in School and Clinic, 28*(3), 143–150.

Conroy, M. A., Asmus, J. M., Ladwig, C. N., Sellers, J. A., & Valcante, G. (2004). The effects of proximity on the classroom behaviors of students with autism in general education settings. *Behavioral Disorders, 29*(2), 119–129.

Davis, C. A., & Brady, M. P. (1993). Expanding the utility of behavioral momentum with young children. *Journal of Early Intervention, 17*, 211–223.

Everett, G. E., Olmi, D. J., Edwards, R. P., & Tingstrom, D. H. (2005). The contributions of eye contact and contingent praise to effective instruction delivery in compliance training. *Education and Treatment of Children, 28*(1), 48–62.

Ganz, J. B., & Flores, M. M. (2010). Visual cues for young children with autism spectrum disorders and their classmates. *Young Children, 65*(3), 78–83.

Grossman, H. (2004). *Classroom management for diverse and inclusive schools*. Lanham, MD: Rowman & Littlefield.

Gunter, P. L., & Shores, R. E. (1995). On the move: Using teacher/student proximity to improve students' behavior. *Teaching Exceptional Children, 28*, 12–15.

Hamre, B. K., & Pianta, R. C. (2001). Early teacher-child relationships and the trajectory of children's school outcomes through eighth grade. *Child Development, 72*, 625–638.

Hastings, N. (1995). Tasks and tables: The effects of seating arrangements on task engagement in primary classrooms. *Educational Research, 37*(3), 279–292.

Hodges, R. (2001). Encouraging high-risk student participation in tutoring and supplemental instruction. *Journal of Developmental Education, 24*(3), 2–8.

Jolivette, K., Stichter, J. P., & McCormick, K. M. (2002). Making choices—Improving behavior—Engaging in learning. *Teaching Exceptional Children, 34*, 24–30.

Jolivette, K., Wehby, J. H., & Canale, J. (2001). Effects of choice-making opportunities on the behavior of students with emotional and behavioral disorders. *Behavioral Disorders, 26*(2), 131–145.

Kame'enui, E. J., & Simmons, D. C. (1990). *Designing instructional strategies: The prevention of academic learning problems*. Upper Saddle River, NJ: Merrill/Pearson.

Lee, D., & Laspe, A. K. (2003). Using high-probability request sequences to increase journal writing. *Journal of Behavioral Education, 12*(4), 261–273.

Long, M. (2000). *The psychology of education*. New York: Routledge Falmer.

Oswald, K., Safran, S., & Johanson, G. (2005). Preventing trouble: Making schools safer places using positive behavioral supports. *Education and Treatment of Children, 28*(3), 265–278.

Pianta, R. C. (1996). *High-risk children in schools: Constructing sustaining relationships*. New York, NY: Routledge.

Son, S., Sigafoos, J., O'Reilly, M., & Lancioni, G. E. (2006). Comparing two types of augmentative and alternative communication systems for children with autism. *Pediatric Rehabilitation, 9*(4), 389–395.

Wannarka, R., & Ruhl, K. (2008). Seating arrangements that promote positive academic and behavioural outcomes: A review of empirical research. *Support for Learning, 23*(2), 89–93.

Werts, M. G., Caldwell, N. K., & Wolery, M. (2003). Instructive feedback: Effects of a presentation variable. *The Journal of Special Education, 37*, 124–133.

Wheldall, K., & Lam, Y. Y. (1987). Rows versus tables II: The effects of two classroom seating arrangements on classroom disruption rate, on-task behavior and teacher behavior in three special school classes. *Educational Psychology, 7*, 303–312.

12

Strategies for Responding to Individual Success: Reinforcement

CHAPTER OBJECTIVES

After reading this chapter, you should be able to describe the following concepts:

- Selecting student behaviors to target for reinforcement
- Identifying effective reinforcers for different students and different target behaviors
- Components necessary to implement reinforcers effectively
- Different schedules of reinforcement
- Effective ways to track the progress of students receiving reinforcement

Sean is a new seventh grader at Deane Middle School and he loves to make people laugh. On the bus rides to and from school he entertains his peers by reciting long profanity-laced jokes from his favorite stand-up comedians. His friends howl, laugh, and shout out requests for jokes Sean has recited on previous bus rides. Numerous verbal redirections from the bus driver have not stopped Sean's rants. During the first couple of weeks of school, she used to give Sean bus referrals, but these always elicited protracted arguments with Sean and, if anything, his behavior would be worse on the next bus ride. Sean carries this level of disruption into all of his classes. In first period, every time Mrs. Streeto turns to write on the chalkboard, Sean jumps out of his seat and dances in the aisle. Seemingly every question Mrs. Streeto asks receives a wisecrack response from Sean and peals of laughter from the other students. Sean is never mean-spirited with his disruptive behaviors and, when asked, he said that he likes all of his teachers; it's just that making people laugh is really fun. At the same time, not surprisingly, Sean is earning failing grades in all of his classes. He rarely turns in his homework, never completes in-class assignments, and has failed most of the tests and quizzes in every class. This is despite IQ and achievement test scores that indicate that Sean is very bright and capable of doing excellent schoolwork.

Initially Sean's teachers used standard school disciplinary protocol. They would give him verbal redirections, write referrals, and assign detentions, and eventually Sean spent two days in the in-school suspension room. None of these seemed to stop (or even slow down) Sean's disruptive behaviors. After a few more weeks of these behavior patterns, the seventh-grade team consulted Mrs. Farrelly, the school counselor. To address these issues, Mrs. Farrelly started by talking to Sean's teachers, his grandmother, who is his primary caregiver, and Sean himself. Mrs. Farrelly begins to see what the problem is.

The vignette for this chapter begins with a description of a student engaging in a large number of behaviors that his teachers want to stop, which may seem like a strange beginning for a chapter on reinforcement. In fact, it may seem counterintuitive that when facing students who demonstrate challenging behaviors that we want them to STOP, we instead focus on behaviors that we want them to START. However, research and the prevailing school model for the past 100 years have continually shown us that the head-on approach of trying to stop students' challenging behaviors through punishment is (a) ineffective for many students and (b) creates a number of unwanted side effects (Vargas, 2009). Further, reinforcing desired behaviors is integral in preventing challenging behaviors because when no behaviors are reinforced, many students will use challenging behaviors to fill the void. Because the foundational basis for teaching is to elicit certain desired behaviors, both academic and social (e.g., subtraction with borrowing, turn-taking, conflict resolution), we create environments that make those behaviors occur more often. To do this we need sound, effective reinforcement procedures for individual students.

The steps to taking control of the classroom environment through reinforcement procedures include:

1. Identify social and academic behaviors that would benefit the student if they happened more often.
2. Identify the reinforcers that will make students more likely to engage in these behaviors in the future. (What?)
3. Identify how and by whom these reinforcers will be delivered to students. (How?)
4. Identify an appropriate schedule of reinforcement. (When?)
5. Monitor for behavior change as a result of reinforcement procedures. (For how long?)

In light of Sean's behaviors, Mrs. Farrelly calls a Student Study Team meeting with all of Sean's teachers. No sooner does everyone sit down than the teachers complain about Sean and commiserate with each other about the disruptions he creates in their classes.

"We just need to find something to get his attention. What if we suspend him for 15 days?" offers Mr. Zito. Mrs. Streeto nods her head in agreement.

"Well, what I think we need to discuss is not what Sean is doing wrong. We are all pretty well aware of that. I think we need to focus on what Sean does well," Mrs. Farrelly interjects. A couple of teachers roll their eyes or make faces, but Mr. Parker finally says,

"Well, when he wants to, he buckles down and works some of the time. But then he goes back off-task and starts making jokes again."

"Ok, but wait, I think we're on to something. When Sean buckles down and works, what do you do?" asks Mrs. Farrelly.

"Well, nothing, I mean he's supposed to do his work, right?"

"True, and eventually we'll get him to do his work on his own. But first I think we need to decide what we want him to do, then we can talk about getting him to do it. So what do we want him to do?"

"Buckle down and do his work," says Mr. Parker. "I guess that means looking at his paper or me if I'm talking, making progress in his class assignments, and discussing only the topic that we are covering in class."

"Yes, but he isn't going to just sit down and start doing all of those things all day," Mrs. Streeto interjected.

"Right. And while it is great that everyone agrees with that definition of 'on-task behavior,' we need to break that behavioral definition down into smaller steps and reinforce those more frequently, especially at the beginning," said Mrs Farrelly. The teachers around the table nod their heads. "Now we know what we are looking for Sean to do."

CHOOSING BEHAVIORS TO REINFORCE

The decision to deliberately and intentionally use reinforcement begins with choosing the behaviors that teachers want to happen more often. In fact, throughout the school day, teachers can constantly confront themselves with this strategy for student behaviors: *"This behavior just happened. Do I want that to happen more often or less often in the future?"* For the behaviors that teachers want to happen more often, teachers must be able to define and describe them in a manner similar to the process described in Chapter 4 where we discussed defining and describing challenging behavior. In the vignette, Mr. Parker wanted Sean to "buckle down and do his work" more often, but then he had to define and describe what that would look like. By using criteria like eyes focused on his work, making progress in assignments, and only making comments relevant to the subject, the components of the desired behavior—in this case "on-task"—became clear. This sort of definition allows other adults, such as the other teachers on the Student Study Team, to ensure that they are reinforcing the same behavior consistently. This consistency is key to long-term acquisition of desired behaviors.

As noted in Mrs. Streeto's interjection, the behaviors that we sometimes expect from students may be complex or require considerable effort, or both. In these situations we need to put two reinforcement strategies into place. First, we need either to break the expected behavior down into steps using task analysis (previously described in Chapter 5) or to reinforce behaviors close to the desired behavior that we are looking for (successive approximations). When using successive approximations, reinforcement is provided until the student ultimately ends up demonstrating the exact behavior. With Sean, the teachers might consider sitting at his desk, looking at his work, or raising his hand and waiting to be called on as smaller parts of the global goal of increasing on-task behavior. They would then want to provide smaller-magnitude, but more frequent reinforcers for these behaviors.

When selecting appropriate behaviors to reinforce, we assume that the desired behavior and its demonstration are already in the student's repertoire (e.g., the student knows what to do and how and when to do it). Clearly, deciding to reinforce students only when they demonstrate behaviors that are not in their repertoire is unfair and sets them up to fail. This would be akin to telling a first-grade class that they will get recess when they finish their calculus; no amount of reinforcement will increase their calculus-completing behavior. Teaching or reteaching is often an important first step to perform before beginning a reinforcement plan.

One final note on addressing skill deficits in relation to reinforcement: It is sometimes necessary to teach students to *recruit reinforcement*. Sometimes students, especially younger students or those with impaired cognitive abilities, desire teacher attention and praise but lack the skills to access it appropriately (Craft, Alber, & Heward, 1998; Wallace, Cox, & Skinner, 2003). By equipping them with a series of steps to access teacher attention, students can gain the attention and praise they desire and improve their behavior and classroom success. To teach students to recruit reinforcement the teacher must first determine the ways in which the student may appropriately recruit teacher attention (e.g., raising his hand, walking to the teacher's desk, asking specific questions). Then training can consist of think-aloud strategies (e.g., "I want the teacher to see that I finished this assignment. How can I get his or her attention?"), modeling, role playing, error correction, and praise. This training in attention recruitment is low-cost and requires minimal time, showing students how to recruit attention and praise that can dramatically improve the student's performance. After deciding what behavior to reinforce, and determining that it is in the student's repertoire (or teaching it if it is not), the next step in the process is deciding what type of reinforcers to use.

Mrs. Farrelly made careful notes of the definition of the behavior that they wanted to increase. "Ok, so now that we have decided what we want Sean to do—'be on task'—we need to figure out some ways to get him to do it. Does anyone have any thoughts?"

"Well, obviously Sean likes attention," Mrs. Streeto interjected.

"Ok, but what usually gets him attention from all of us?" probed Mrs. Farrelly.

"Well, when he acts up. . ." answered Mr. Zito.

"Now, how could we use our attention to get him to be on-task more often?"

"When we see him doing a good job, we could tell him how he was doing a good job. But won't that embarrass him and make him less likely to be on-task?"

"Well, if we all do it subtly, you know, a quick wink or a thumbs-up; or even a nod in his direction may be something we could try. I know that's what I do with other students," offered Mr. Parker.

"Ok, that may work for the classes where Sean demonstrates some on-task behavior, but he is basically out of control in my classroom," complained Mrs. Streeto.

"Well, in addition to teacher attention let's think about some activities we could set up that Sean could earn as rewards for being on-task in your class. If those don't work, then we may have to consider some tangible rewards that Sean could earn."

"Well he likes to entertain everyone. What if I let him tell some jokes, CLEAN jokes, at the end of class as long as he stays on-task during lecture and independent work?" Mrs. Streeto suggested.

Identifying the Reinforcers (What?)

Recall that in behavioral terms, reinforcement is separated into positive reinforcement and negative reinforcement. *Positive reinforcement* means *adding* something to the environment to increase future occurrences of the behavior, and *negative reinforcement* means *removing* something from the environment to increase future occurrences of a specific behavior. Because positive reinforcement has several advantages over negative reinforcement including avoiding the use of aversives and allowing teachers to accentuate the enjoyable aspects of their classroom, the next section will first focus mostly on positive reinforcement and then discuss negative reinforcement as another reinforcement option.

In addition to the three categories of direct reinforcers there are systems that function much as money works in our modern society. In these systems, called *token economies*, reinforcers like preferred activities or tangibles are not provided directly. Rather, tokens that give the student access to the three categories of reinforcers referred to as *backup reinforcers* are provided contingent on the student's displaying behaviors that we want to increase in frequency. The tokens themselves, which initially have no intrinsic value, gain reinforcing strength as they are paired with the backup reinforcers (attention, activities, and/or tangibles) and so they become *conditioned reinforcers*. These are neutral stimuli that gain reinforcing strength by being systematically paired with reinforcing stimuli. Token economies will be described in greater depth in the next section because they relate more to how to give reinforcement rather than what reinforcers to use.

Assembling effective combinations of reinforcers and implementing them effectively can be difficult, so teachers should view selecting and using different reinforcers as a dynamic process. The most essential guide to selection and implementation is the use of ongoing data collection to determine whether behaviors are increasing or decreasing based on what the teacher is putting into the environment. Also, it is critical to view both the consequence that the challenging behavior accesses and the one that the new desired behavior should access from a functional perspective. In the vignette, attention is recognized as a primary reinforcer for Sean, so the teachers discuss various ways to ensure that his on-task behavior gets him access to attention. But, as stated, without this data collection teachers may unintentionally reinforce behaviors they are trying to punish and punish behaviors they are trying to reinforce. In the section on how to provide reinforcement effectively we will discuss other environmental conditions that seem to modify the reinforcing strength of the three main categories of reinforcement: attention, activities, and tangible reinforcers.

At the next Student Study Team Meeting, the same group of teachers gathers in the school conference room.

Mrs. Farrelly begins the meeting. "After talking with everyone and looking at some preliminary data, I think the contingent attention we are using is helping. But I also think we need some type of portable system for Sean to earn reinforcement across all of our classes. I want him to see that we are staying consistent across his classes and that we are all looking for the same on-task behavior. What about using a token economy across classes?"

"Oh, no. Those never work. I have a friend who teaches at Highcrest Elementary School and she had a system where she would put marbles in a jar on every kid's desk when they were doing a good job. But kids were always knocking over their jars or stealing each others' marbles. It was way more trouble than it was worth."

"Right, and I tried a system where I gave out Fun Friday poker chips to students when they were doing what they were supposed to. But by the end of the first week, half the kids were smuggling in their own poker chips and the others were playing poker!"

"Well, ok, but what if we tried this? I went to the craft store and bought these different-shaped hole punchers. I have a diamond, a heart, a clover, and a spade shape. And I have this pack of index cards. What if we make Sean a daily point card, then watch for him to be on-task and punch the card when he is doing what he is supposed to be doing? We don't even have to make a big deal out of it. Just punch his card subtly as you walk by his desk—that way, he won't be embarrassed. Then at the end of the day, or maybe a couple of times during the day, he can spend his points on activities he likes—maybe talking to friends or doing some of his stand-up comedy (as long as it is clean) for his classmates."

The point card used in the version of the token economy that Mrs. Farrelly is describing typically looks like the one shown in Figure 12.1.

To implement this type of token economy, the steps are straightforward:

- Get a stamp made just like the one described earlier (typically at an office supply store).
- Get a series of different colored index cards to represent different levels (white–Level 1, blue–Level 2, gold–Level 3, no card–Level 4)
- As students move up in levels they earn fewer points (fading), but privileges cost less, and students have access to additional activities and privileges.
- Make goals specific and positive for each child (e.g., "Follow Directions," "Act Friendly," "Pay Attention").
- Put the student's name and the date on the back of each card.

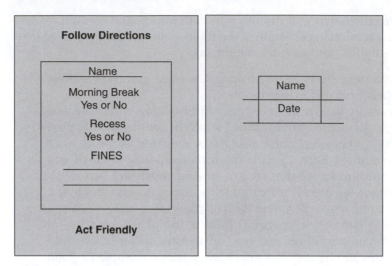

FIGURE 12.1

- Watch carefully for compliant behavior (sitting calmly, working quietly, standing in line), following directions, paying attention, doing something friendly, etc.
- Award points by punching holes in a card using a hole puncher. (Use different hole punch shapes to decrease the probability of counterfeiting.) Points are spent throughout the day for privileges. A point is spent when the teacher circles it in ink. There is no total amount of points for a child to earn. Pair token reinforcement (points) with verbal reinforcement (leads to fading).

  The use of fines, or response cost, will be discussed in Chapter 13 on punishment.

Using Reinforcers (How?)

As an example of how to provide reinforcement, the vignette described the use of a token economy, a highly effective way to provide reinforcement in schools and classrooms. There are several broad principles, however, that will determine how to effectively apply reinforcement for desired behaviors. These other important factors are

- immediacy
- novelty
- consistency
- combining reinforcers with choice

The first factor is the immediacy with which the reinforcer follows the behavior. The longer the time between the behavior and the reinforcer, the weaker the reinforcer is. For example, if Rocco completes his math worksheet but is not praised for completing it until several hours afterward, the praise will be a relatively weak reinforcement for this behavior and relatively unlikely to increase Rocco's future work completion behavior. It also does not create the behavior-response pairing that teachers try to achieve when they reinforce a target behavior.

The second factor that impacts reinforcing strength is the novelty of the reinforcer. Reinforcers that are new, different, or unexpected are stronger than those that have been used for a long period of time. By constantly changing reinforcement options, teachers maintain the novelty of the reinforcer and guard against satiation. As anyone who has ever eaten one too many donuts can tell you, the first one is delicious (and even the second or third one), but donuts eight, nine, and ten are not nearly as enjoyable. A similar effect can occur with students who receive too much of a reinforcer, a condition often referred to as satiation. *Satiation* is when an individual receives a reinforcer too much or too often, causing it to lose its previous reinforcing strength. Using surprise with novel or even some not-so-novel reinforcers can maintain reinforcing strength (e.g., getting a reinforcer that you didn't expect or finding out what it is only when it is awarded can make it more reinforcing). Consider the example of the mystery motivator: By not telling students what they were going to win, desired behaviors increase as the students earn chances to "look inside the envelope" and see what the prize is (Murphy et al., 2007). The act of "finding out" adds to the reinforcing strength of whatever the student wins. One teacher effectively combined a token economy system with the mystery motivators; at the end of every day, students would use leftover points to bid auction-style on a chance to pull from the prize envelope. In the prize envelope were various laminated cards that gave them access to different activity reinforcers for the next day (e.g., 1 hour sitting at the teacher's desk, lunch with the teacher, 15 extra minutes of computer time). Finally, the sheer act of choice (e.g., using a menu to select a tangible or an activity) can impact the reinforcing strength of those stimuli. In fact, being able to choose the order of even typically aversive things (e.g., a math worksheet, a language arts worksheet, and a social studies worksheet) may make them, if not reinforcing, at least less aversive.

The third consideration is consistency. It is vital to be consistent with the behaviors that are reinforced because learning is taking place for students. In other words, students are making connections between behavior and reinforcing consequences (i.e., "When I do this. . . . this reinforcer is added to my environment."). These connections are strengthened through consistency. As mentioned earlier, reinforcement should be faded, but that process should be data-based and done systematically over time. Finally, the use of choice presentation for tasks and reinforcers will strengthen the learning connections between behaviors and reinforcers. In other words, allowing students to decide the tasks they want to complete first, second, or third as well as to choose from a menu of reinforcers make students more likely to complete the tasks and less likely to satiate on identified reinforcers. Everyone likes to feel a sense of control over what happens to them, and it is particularly valuable for students to develop an internal locus of control. This means that students recognize that their choices and their behaviors are what will lead to desired outcomes (or not). Students who demonstrate chronic challenging behavior often truly believe that everything is out of their control and that things happen for various external reasons but never because of what they themselves do. Embedding choices throughout the day helps to reduce this feeling of powerlessness.

Token Economies

While discussed briefly earlier in this chapter, token economies are elaborated on here so that they can be implemented more intensively for individual systems. Systems such as token economies assist in the delivery of frequent reinforcement. Until now, we have noted that the three categories of classroom reinforcers are direct reinforcers; however, another option is the provision of indirect or secondary reinforcers. A token economy is defined as a system in which students earn symbolic reinforcers (tokens) in exchange for demonstrating specific, appropriate behaviors. These tokens can then be exchanged (or spent) on preferred tangible objects or on time doing preferred activities. These tokens may be items that are not easily stolen or counterfeited and can be awarded efficiently and effectively in quantities. A token economy provides a convenient way for teachers to systematically provide reinforcement without interrupting teaching. Like a monetary system, a token economy compensates students for appropriate behavior by providing access to preferred activities. This strategy can be implemented with single students or with smaller groups across the entire school day. One ancillary benefit of the token economy is the impact that it has on the teacher's behavior. A token economy requires that teachers constantly monitor for appropriate and desired behavior rather than inappropriate behaviors and makes it convenient and easy to reinforce desired behaviors when they occur.

Behavior Contracts

A behavior contract is another way to systematically deliver reinforcement. A behavior contract is a formal written agreement between the teacher and student of behavior expectations that specifies (1) clear behavior objectives, (2) the reinforcement that the student will receive when they meet these objectives, (3) a short-term goal statement, and (4) review dates to evaluate performance. The teacher and the student review the contract and sign it, and then each receives a copy. It is important to clearly identify the behavior to be increased or decreased in observable and measurable terms and to select as reinforcers the items and activities that the student finds motivating. There are two other guidelines to ensure eventual success with behavior contracts. First, with younger students the time interval of the contract should be fairly short, usually the end of a day or even the end of a half day; longer intervals of time can be used with older students. Second, regardless of the student's age, it is critically important that students experience success and see the teacher living up to their end of the contract with the first behavior contract that is set up. In other words, let the students succeed with the first contract, then increase the behavioral demands and the time interval over which the expected behavior must be demonstrated.

> "Okay. I like the idea of giving Sean attention when he is on-task with some subtle gestures and some specific praise statements. But do I have to do this all of the time?" asked Mrs. Streeto.
>
> "Right. I mean, I do have other students to teach, content to cover, and student work to grade," added Mr. Parker.

"I hear what you all are saying and I appreciate the demands you have on your time, but don't forget how much of your time Sean takes when he is acting out," answered Mrs. Farrelly. The teachers nod their heads in agreement. "The key to using reinforcement is not that we reinforce every single behavior every time, although we may have to do that for the first few days while Sean acquires the skill to remain on-task for longer periods of time. Rather, we provide reinforcement systematically on a schedule where we gradually reduce the frequency or fade the reinforcement."

"So what you are saying is that at first we give Sean attention every time that he is on-task but then reinforce it every three minutes he is on-task or every third assignment that he completes? And then we go even longer or have him do even more work before we provide reinforcement?" Mr. Zito asked.

"Exactly. By gradually reducing the amount of reinforcement we provide for his behaviors, he won't depend on us so much to tell him he is doing a good job. And if we see that he is starting to slip back into his old ways we can regroup and provide reinforcement more frequently," answered Mrs. Farrelly.

Schedules of Reinforcement (When?)

The question of *when* to provide reinforcement is an important one. There are multiple effects a teacher can have by strategically planning when to reinforce to a desired behavior. First, they can ensure that the reinforcer remains effective. When students are learning new skills (the acquisition phase), reinforcement typically is provided every time the student demonstrates the desired behavior. This schedule of reinforcement, referred to as continuous reinforcement (CRF) or providing reinforcement on a 1:1 basis, is important to strengthen these new skills. During the initial phases of learning, however, reinforcement must be both immediate and consistent. When natural reinforcers are not reliable, the teacher must ensure that desired behaviors are met with reinforcement when displayed in natural environments. If the schedule of reinforcement remains this dense, however, it is likely that the student will become satiated. A second effect of providing reinforcement every time is that the student will come to expect the reinforcement every time they engage in the behavior and may cease demonstrating the behavior as soon as the reinforcement is not presented. Therefore, it is important that the teacher identify the reinforcement schedule that she or he will use purposefully; that is, teachers should be systematic with how frequently they reinforce desired behaviors. In order for this to happen, students must perform the appropriate behaviors at the appropriate times and be prepared for reinforcement schedules under which some, but not all, demonstrations of the desired behavior are reinforced.

Reinforcement schedules are typically divided up by amounts of time (interval) or number of behaviors emitted (ratio). In other words, a teacher can reinforce a student for every three minutes that a student is on-task (intervals) or for every two times the student complies with the teacher's directions (ratio).

TABLE 12.1

	Fixed	Variable
Interval	**Fixed Interval**—Reinforcement is provided based on the emission of a behavior after a fixed amount of time. Real-World Example: An employee receives a paycheck every fourteen days. Abbreviation—FI: 14 days	**Variable Interval**—Reinforcement is provided based on the emission of a behavior after an average amount of time. Real-World Example: At a stoplight, the light turns from green to red every 90 seconds, on average. (The interval may be longer or shorter based on pedestrians and time of day.) Abbreviation—VI: 90 second
Ratio	**Fixed Ratio**—Reinforcement is provided after a behavior is emitted a specific number of times. Real-World Example: A gumball is dispensed after two quarters are put into the machine. Abbreviation—FR: 2 quarters	**Variable Ratio**—Reinforcement is provided after a behavior is emitted a number of times, on average. Real-World Example: A slot machine pays off, on average, after $120 dollars have been deposited into it. VR: $120 dollars

Reinforcement schedules are also divided up by fixed schedules (every 5 minutes or every 5 behaviors) and variable schedules (every 4 minutes or every 4 behaviors, on average). Therefore schedules of reinforcement can be summarized as shown in Table 12.1.

As you think about these reinforcement schedules, remember that we want to use the least amount of reinforcement necessary. This means that we want to fade reinforcement, or systematically reduce the amount of reinforcement provided without reducing occurrences of the desired behavior. Therefore, if we have a behavior on a dense schedule of reinforcement, we want to gradually increase the number of demonstrations required or the intervals of time between reinforcers. Continuous reinforcement should be used only during the acquisition of the skill; then, as the learner becomes more fluent, the reinforcement schedule should be thinned. The topic of making decisions about when and how quickly to fade reinforcers leads to another reinforcement rule.

Reinforcement rule: Collect data continuously to determine what, how, and when to provide reinforcement and to ensure that the contingencies put in place truly reinforce the desired behaviors, removing them as soon as possible without decreasing occurrences of the desired behavior.

These different schedules of reinforcement provide different levels of reinforcing strength. In general, variable schedules have greater reinforcing strength than do fixed schedules because the individual does not know exactly when the reinforcement is coming; therefore, the student will keep emitting the behavior because the next reinforcer may come after the very next behavior or in the very next minute. For example, suppose that someone is playing a slot machine in a casino; they would tell you that they believe the payoff is coming with the next pull of the slot-machine arm—the next reinforcer is always just around the corner. No one inserts money into a slot machine unless they believe that payment is imminent. This logic explains why using fixed versus variable schedules of reinforcement can have highly practical implications for the classroom.

When considering fixed versus variable schedules of reinforcement, two frequently used token economies are point sheets and punch cards. For a point sheet, points are awarded on a fixed interval (e.g., every 30 minutes the student earns a prespecified number of points contingent on their behavior over the previous interval). For a punch card, the teacher monitors student behavior and provides reinforcement on a variable ratio contingent on average numbers of behaviors emitted (e.g., "I just saw you hold the door open for a peer and then say 'You're welcome' when they thanked you; so I am going to give you points (punches) on your card"). With the point sheet approach, desired behaviors increase toward the end of the interval (e.g., 30 minutes) and immediately after the points are dispensed. But toward the middle of the interval (e.g., at the 15-minute mark), students' behavior may deteriorate because they begin to recognize, consciously or unconsciously, that the reinforcement is temporally farther away. Note that other factors, such as the need to collect data on when students do and do not earn their points, may require using a point sheet rather than a point card. This issue of data collection introduces the final section of progress monitoring.

A few weeks later, the Student Study Team has a final follow-up meeting about Sean. Everyone agrees that the reinforcements put in place not only dramatically increased the desired on-task behaviors but also decreased Sean's undesired behaviors. Mrs. Farrelly affirmed their conclusions by presenting the data that she had collected using a momentary time-sampling strategy in several of his classes.

"So obviously we are making tremendous progress with Sean. I think we can now use a strategy that will have Sean chart his own behavior on a daily basis. That way, he can determine whether or not he is improving or slipping back into his old ways."

"I think that's a great idea," interrupted Mr. Parker "Not only will this give us data to help monitor his behavior but it will also let Sean be more self-directed and be reinforced by his own good choices."

"Exactly. I want Sean to feel good about his choices, not just because we tell him he's doing a good job, but because he recognizes it himself," said Mrs. Farrelly.

"Could we use a computer spreadsheet to show Sean a graph of his behavior?" asked Mrs. Streeto.

"Exactly. Here's what I think we can do. At three or four random times during each class we have Sean mark down whether he is on-task or off-task. Teachers can just set a kitchen timer or look up at the clock and cue Sean to mark a '+' or a '−' on a sheet depending on whether he is on-task or off-task. Then, at the end of the day, he can divide how many times he was on-task by how many times he was on-task plus how many times he was off-task and that will give him a percentage that he can enter into a spreadsheet every day. I'll even sit down with him once a week to set a goal for his average percentage on-task every week. Then if he meets his goal, we can celebrate his success. Maybe we all could have lunch with Sean as our guest of honor."

"That sounds great, especially if you're buying lunch," Mr. Parker joked.

Tracking Progress (Is the Reinforcement Working?)

As we have said throughout this chapter, reinforcement works only if it increases future occurrences of a behavior. To determine whether the stimuli that we put into a classroom environment are truly reinforcing, we must monitor student behavior. In previous chapters we have covered viable strategies for collecting data on occurrences of both desired and undesired behavior in the classroom. All of these strategies, however, involved another individual collecting the data. Because the ability to manage one's own behavior is one of the ultimate goals of education, self-monitoring and charting is another viable strategy to determine the effects of reinforcers. It also is an activity that in itself can be a reinforcer. Given instructional tools and support, students manage their behavior and therefore contribute to the development of a personal behavior-change program. Self-monitoring is an effective method for teaching students to record their own behavior, evaluate specific goals to increase academic engagement, and maintain productivity. Specifically, students are taught to monitor their attention to tasks or their rate of task completion, accuracy, or productivity and to evaluate themselves in comparison to a predetermined objective. Self-monitoring teaches students to be more consistent with behaviors already in their repertoire. Changes in student performance can be displayed in charts, visual pictures of past and current responses. Simple and time-efficient, charting is a low-cost method that allows students to track progress, make predictions, and set goals. It is also a versatile instructional intervention, providing students an easy way to get involved in setting academic and behavioral goals through an interactive approach.

The easiest way to set up a charting or self-monitoring program is to begin with some type of worksheet. This sheet will provide the structure for the self-monitoring system. Consider the example of Mary. Mary uses a worksheet to mark each time she is provoked by a peer and how she responds. Ms. Smith furnishes her with a new self-monitoring sheet every day and reminds her how to use it. Then Ms. Smith awards Mary points for each occasion on which she used her replacement behavior. Because the frequency of provocations may decrease as Mary develops the habit of walking away, a sufficient number of points is awarded to make this effort worthwhile. Later in the day (and, as walking away from provocations becomes more typical, perhaps once a week), Ms. Smith allows Mary to trade in her points for things Mary has selected from her own

NAME	DATE		GOAL	
	In Seat	**Raise Hand**		**Complete Work**
Math	0 1 2	0 1 2		0 1 2
Reading	0 1 2	0 1 2		0 1 2
Health	0 1 2	0 1 2		0 1 2
Geography	0 1 2	0 1 2		0 1 2
Humanities	0 1 2	0 1 2		0 1 2
TOTAL	/10	/10		/10
DAILY TOTAL		/30 = %		

FIGURE 12.2   Self-Monitoring Sheet

reinforcement menu (free time, a "get out of one homework assignment card," a pass to the library). Ms. Smith also observes Mary closely in the initial stages of this program to ensure that she is monitoring her own behavior.

These types of sheets can be applied even more broadly to encompass multiple behaviors. Figure 12.2 shows a self-monitoring sheet that allows a student to monitor three behaviors (In Seat, Raise Hand, and Complete Work) across all of the different classes that the student attends. This not only provides a way to access reinforcement but also allows both adults and the student to see the progress being made and whether there are predictable times during which the student struggles with a particular behavior.

Setting this strategy up generally involves discussing the procedure with the student and encouraging the monitoring of socially valid target behaviors that can be easily monitored. Then the student and teacher together set criterion levels of performance that provide attainable goals for the student and agree on a desirable consequence for meeting the goal. Some appropriate behaviors for self-monitoring include engagement with or attention to tasks, in-seat behavior, or hand-raising as a replacement for calling out. It is important to operationally define the target behavior to be monitored and recorded and have the student practice identifying appropriate and inappropriate demonstrations (e.g., the student may practice hand-raising and monitoring behavior). In the beginning especially it will be important to monitor student self-recording by checking the student's data for accuracy versus the teacher's data. Build in periodic accountability checks and reinforcers when data match up and provide structured evaluative feedback regarding the accuracy of the student's monitoring.

This information can also be recorded and tracked on charts that are simply visual displays of student performance that provide concrete feedback regarding behavior. To chart behavior, identify the student, the goal, and the context in which the charting will be used. (Charting in difficult subject areas may motivate the student to increase performance for academic or behavior goals.) Teach students how to collect or record data based on the measure of the target behavior (e.g., have students self-grade assignments, monitor on-task behavior, and record reading fluency data). It will be necessary to determine the most convenient way to display data. Consider the age and ability of the students, the length of time it will take students to record data, the routines within instruction, and the accessibility of materials—visual displays can include anything from simple stickers on a chart to computer-assisted programs. Analyze data with the student to interpret progress, and have the student identify a goal and show the distance between current and future performance. Highlight or mark a line to emphasize the goal. Charting can be used with the whole class on one goal or with multiple students and goals. Charting is an especially efficient data collection system for documenting progress on Individualized Education Programs (IEPs) for students with disabilities.

SUMMARY

Because one of the primary goals within a classroom is the teaching and supporting of new behaviors, reinforcement plays a vital role. Any behavior that teachers want to occur more often in the future must be reinforced. Identifying what behaviors to reinforce is the first critical step in this process, so teachers should constantly be confronting themselves with the questions "What do I want my students to do?", "What would that look like?", and "How would I define these desired behaviors so that others can see and reinforce them also?" By answering these initial questions teachers can then organize the environment to elicit and support these behaviors more frequently using attention, preferred activities, and then tangible reinforcers. Teachers can decide what to use to reinforce their students and then monitor the different effects that these reinforcers have on the desired behaviors. Manipulating the timing and the schedule of reinforcement will then make the desired behaviors more persistent and more likely to occur naturally without teacher interference. Finally, data collection, whether it is teacher-conducted as described in previous chapters or done through the student's own self-monitoring and graphing, enables students to monitor their own progress and earn various reinforcers as they meet set goals and criteria for acceptable performance of desired behaviors.

Chapter Review

- Behaviors identified for reinforcement should be in the students' repertoire and should be relevant and generalizable to multiple contexts. They also should be used to replace maladaptive behaviors.
- Various reinforcers are available that can easily and effectively reinforce target behaviors. A token economy also can be used to create a system of reinforcement.

- Schedules of reinforcement can use either time or events (e.g., interval or ratio) to schedule the provision of reinforcement. These can be either fixed or variable.
- It is critical to evaluate the effect that different reinforcers have on targeted behaviors. If the desired behaviors are not increasing, the reinforcers have to be re-evaluated.

Application

1. How can reinforcement be used to address challenging behavior?

2. What schedules of reinforcement are most likely to be used in general education classroom settings?

References

Craft, M. A., Alber, S. R., & Heward, W. L. (1998). Teaching elementary students with developmental disabilities to recruit teacher attention in a general education classroom: Effects on teacher praise and academic productivity. *Journal of Applied Behavior Analysis, 31*(3), 399–415.

Murphy, K. A., Theodore, L. A., Aloiso, D., Alric-Edwards, J. M., & Hughes, T. L. (2007). Interdependent group contingency and mystery motivators to reduce preschool disruptive behavior. *Psychology in the Schools, 44*(1), 53–63.

Vargas, J. S. (2009). *Behavior analysis for effective teaching.* New York: Routledge.

Wallace, M. A., Cox, E. A., & Skinner, C. H. (2003). Increasing independent seatwork: Breaking large assignments into smaller assignments and teaching a student with retardation to recruit reinforcement. *School Psychology Review, 32*(1), 132–142.

13

Strategies for Responding to Individual Misbehavior: Punishment Issues

CHAPTER OBJECTIVES

After reading this chapter, you should be able to describe the following concepts:

- General considerations in the use of punishment in schools and classrooms
- The use of effective verbal and nonverbal reprimands along a continuum of invasiveness
- The use of negative punishment including planned ignoring, time out, and response cost
- The use of differential reinforcement to decrease challenging behaviors including differential reinforcement of alternative/incompatible behaviors (DRA/DRI), low rates of behavior (DRL), and other behaviors (DRO)
- The use of positive punishment including restitutional or positive practice overcorrection

The murmur of the conversations at the faculty meeting slowly quieted down to silence as Mr. Paolino, the principal, stood to address the teachers. "We have seen an increase in a lot of the challenging behaviors that we want to eliminate from our classrooms and common areas. Believe me, the number of students sitting outside my office every day certainly backs that up."

"Mr. Paolino, we just need some harsher consequences to get their attention," Mrs. Varney interrupts.

"Right; with these parents who refuse to get involved and don't care about their children's education, it is no wonder we are having these kinds of problems. I always say that desperate times call for desperate measures," Mr. Casey chimes in. There is some general murmur as teachers affirm what Mr. Casey is saying.

"Wait a minute. You all are wrong. Kids will be kids, and if we try to punish every little thing they do, they just wind up hating us and school. Kids need to be free to express themselves," said Mrs. Mirizzi.

Mr. Paolino raised his hands to quiet everyone down. "OK, I know that in the past we have ramped up our punishments to deal with challenging behaviors. But I think there is a better way to go about this. I mean, you mentioned their parents—we can't use the level of punishments that some of the parents use, so I think we need to think about punishment procedures in a different way. The first thing I want to do is to stop using the word punishment. From now on, I want us to think about behavior reduction techniques. Changing our language will change how we think about addressing these issues. And from now on I want us to think of anything we do to stop or reduce a behavior, or what we have been calling punishment, as a behavior reduction technique."

PUNISHMENT ISSUES

The use of punishment by either presenting aversive stimuli in the environment (e.g., corporal punishment, writing lines on the chalkboard, etc.) or removing desirable stimuli from the environment (e.g., taking away recess time, loss of privileges, etc.) has a long history within the education system. The traditional use of punishment is ingrained by previous experience and tradition. So for many, thinking about punishment in a different way is a dramatic departure from their previous approaches especially because it differs from the traditional school model of punishment procedures and school exclusion to address challenging behaviors (Kerr & Nelson, 2006). It is true that despite the best efforts toward prevention, teaching, and effective reinforcement, students will engage in behaviors that school personnel need to stop or at least decrease. And it certainly is true that time spent engaging in challenging behaviors or being off-task is time spent not learning; in fact, improving overall classroom management is the best way to improve student achievement (Wang, Haertel, & Walberg, 1993/1994; Murphy & Korinek, 2009; Freiberg, Huzinec, & Templeton, 2009).

Many schools have overused many punishment procedures that lack empirical support. In fact, in a survey 10% of teachers still report using corporal punishment in schools and classrooms (Little & Akin-Little, 2008). Side effects of punishment have been widely reported and include increased aggression, vandalism, truancy, and dropping out (Coon, Mitterer, Brown, Malik, & McKenzie, 2009). So what are teachers and schools to do? There are three guiding principles that serve to direct the use of punishments, or behavior reduction techniques. First, as always, we use the simplest, least invasive, lowest intensity interventions first and use the data to guide a progression to more complex, invasive, and intensive procedures. Second, it is critical to remember that punishment procedures *do not teach*. Getting rid of behaviors is not the same as providing instruction, although with some techniques, unwanted behaviors can be eliminated or replaced with new behaviors. In this chapter, strategies that pair teach or encourage new behaviors while eliminating old behaviors are highlighted.

Third, punishment procedures should always have functional considerations. Consider two widely used and universally applied school punishment procedures, detention and suspension. Suspension, or excluding a student from school, often backfires as a punishment procedure because often the function of students' challenging behavior is to escape or avoid school and school activities. By suspending a student, the school actually makes the challenging behavior functional. Unless the school uses suspension as a time to reset procedures and establish a different plan of action for a student who is experiencing school failure (i.e., engaging in chronic challenging behavior), suspension makes very little sense. Similarly, detention, or having to stay after school, is functional in that it denies the student access to free time; but it is logical as a consequence only if a student has other places and activities that are preferable to being in school. Students who are in abusive home settings, or charged with the responsibility of younger siblings, might prefer being at school rather than the alternative, and this would make their challenging behaviors more functional than engaging in desired or prosocial behaviors. Finally, what if the function of behavior is to escape a required activity? This presents a difficulty for teachers because providing a functional replacement means teaching a behavior that allows escape from that requirement. For example, Shawn is purposefully noisy during math so that the teacher will kick him out and he won't have to do his math work. If the teacher were to dictate that quiet completion of a few problems would equal time away from math, Shawn might logically say, "I already get no math at all by doing no math. Why would I do some to get out of some?" We not only have to make appropriate behavior result in reinforcement, but also to make sure that negative behavior does not. If simply doing nothing is, by itself, reinforcing, then we will have to change the environment so that it is no longer reinforcing. This may involve adding larger punitive procedures. We will use the term "punishment" synonymously with the phrase "behavior reductive technique" simply as a reminder that punishment is the presence or absence of any environmental stimulus that reduces or eliminates a target behavior. As previously stated, whether or not a stimulus is a punishment is based on future occurrences of the target behavior.

As indicated in the opening vignette and as seen in schools across the country, teachers have many opinions on the use of punishment. Consider the next two case examples:

> Mrs. Mirizzi is in her third year of teaching third grade. She has just put the finishing touches on the butterfly garden outside her classroom, and now she is creating paper mâché planets to hang from the ceiling of her classroom as students begin their solar system unit. In her university training, Mrs. Mirizzi learned that children learn best when they have the freedom and flexibility to explore their environment; that is, structure limits a child's learning and imagination. Her room reflects her creativity and free thinking. She encourages her students to work wherever they are most comfortable. The desks are not in any particular order, and she has a section of the room filled with beanbag chairs and overstuffed pillows. She teaches subjects haphazardly (e.g., sometimes they have math, sometimes they don't). When her students go from place to place, they walk as a large group (or herd) because she feels that correcting students or making them walk in line is militaristic and fascist. If students engage in misbehavior, Mrs. Mirizzi ignores it to avoid suffocating their creativity, and she ignores all bus referrals and bad reports that she gets from the resource (art, music, etc.) teachers. The cafeteria monitors, resource teachers, and adjacent classroom teachers have begun to complain about her students' conduct. Her students earn more bus referrals and cafeteria

referrals than any other class. (The principal has started collecting data on such things.)

Mr. Casey, on the other hand, does not take any "nonsense" from his students. He is in his twenty-seventh year teaching ninth- and tenth-grade English, and the kids in his view "just aren't like they used to be." He views the day the school outlawed paddling and corporal punishment as the beginning of the end. When students get out of line, he is quick to deal with it, usually at a voice volume just below a jet engine's roar. Instruction in Mr. Casey's class consists of students getting out their textbooks, taking turns reading aloud from the chapter, and then answering the questions at the end of the chapter (silently). Unfortunately, students are skipping his class at double the rate of any other teacher's class (according to the principal's data collection system), and yesterday, when he reprimanded a student for wearing a baseball cap in his class, the student just sneered at him and looked bored. When Mr. Casey mentioned getting in touch with this student's parents, the student actually laughed out loud. These types of interactions with students are occurring more frequently.

In these two examples, teachers with similar preparation have vastly different perspectives on the use of punishment in school. Is one right and the other wrong? Or, is it possible that both of them have the wrong perspective on punishment? Based on information related to the three key principles outlined and other information already discussed, how would you, as a colleague of either Mrs. Mirizzi or Mr. Casey, discuss their divergent and, perhaps, erroneous views on punishment?

PUNISHMENT STRATEGIES

This chapter will present punishment strategies based on the guiding principle of using the simplest, least invasive procedures first and then moving to more invasive procedures. Therefore, we begin by looking at nonverbal and verbal reprimands, brief teacher-student interactions intended to eliminate or at least reduce challenging behaviors. The next section outlines so-called negative punishment, or the removal of desirable activities, objects, and so forth, to decrease future occurrences of the targeted behavior. Finally, we will briefly outline some strategies that put aversive stimuli in place to decrease future occurrences of the challenging behavior. This final section identifies only two strategies (positive practice overcorrection and restitutional overcorrection) because the current research base has not identified any other strategies in the category of positive punishment that are both ethical and effective.

Verbal and Nonverbal Reprimands

Reprimands, or brief teacher reproaches to discourage behaviors, represent one of the least intensive, least effortful forms of punishments that a teacher can use. Using verbal reprimands such as "Stop it" or "No talking" is typically not a skill

Continuum of Nonverbal and Verbal Reprimands (Van Nagel, 1991)	
Nonverbal Reprimands	
Proximity Control	• Teacher puts their hand on an off-task student's desk
Hand Gestures	• Finger to lips means "Shh . . . Be quiet" • Hand up means "Stop"
Facial Expressions	• The 'evil eye' • Shaking head "No"
Group Verbal Reprimands	
ID–Describe the behavior	"I see people talking."
2D–Describe the behavior. Describe the rule being broken.	"I see people talking. Directions are no talking."
3D–Describe the behavior. Describe the rule being broken. Describe the consequence	"I see people talking. Directions are no talking. If people continue to talk time will be taken off recess."
Boomerang Praise	Erin and Betsy sit in close proximity to Greta, who is off-task "Erin, thank you for getting started right away on the assignment. Betsy, great job getting busy on your work."
Redirection Statements	For a student who is refusing to get in line for recess- "Hold on to my clipboard while we line up and make sure we have every one by putting a checkmark by each student's name."
Individual Student Reprimand	
Use the 3D strategy–Describe the behavior. Describe the rule being broken. Describe the consequence	"You were pushing other students in line. The rule is to keep your hands and feet to yourself. Because you were pushing others you will have to miss recess."
Use a broken record technique	"You were pushing other students." Student tries to argue. "You were pushing other students."

Least Invasive ➞ Most Invasive

FIGURE 13.1 Verbal and Nonverbal Reprimands

that needs to be taught even to rookie teachers. In fact, it is usually the first impulsive response that adults have when they encounter students' challenging or unwanted behaviors. Regrettably, this leads to the first two reasons that this strategy can be ineffective—overuse and repetition. Verbal reprimands lose their effectiveness when they are used repeatedly and are not paired with a more serious consequence, so students tend to disregard them. So while reprimands are a very valuable strategy, there are some important considerations for the teacher who chooses to use them.

As previously stated, reprimands are a low-intensity intervention, which makes them very useful as a behavior reduction technique. They are also efficient and can be effectively paired with other more intensive strategies. As we suggested with the principle on reinforcement discussed earlier, which dictates that we should use the least amount of a reinforcer necessary to effect behavioral change, so we here suggest a similar minimalist approach to behavior reduction procedures. But even within the category of nonverbal and verbal reprimands there is a continuum of strategies that moves from the least invasive and effortful to more invasive and effortful ones. By varying the type of reprimand used, teachers can combat the effects of their overuse and keep this strategy from going stale. The use of nonverbal reprimands represents the least invasive strategy on this continuum. Raising a hand to indicate "Stop" and pressing a finger to the lips to ask for quiet are examples of nonverbal reprimands. Some teachers even teach their students some signs from American Sign Language (ASL). Proximity control or moving toward students to decrease behaviors is also effective. Just putting your hand on an off-task student's desk lets the student know that it is time to get back to work. Nonverbal reprimands have three additional advantages. First, they allow the teacher to reduce a behavior without interrupting instructional momentum. In other words, the teacher can continue teaching while giving a nonverbal reprimand to disruptive students. Second, nonverbal reprimands draw little attention to the student from peers. Because function ("Why does the student engage in the behavior?" or "What do they get out of it?") is always a consideration and because peer attention is often the function of challenging behaviors, using strategies that do not draw undue attention from peers helps to keep the student's challenging behavior from becoming functional. Further, many students will engage in higher-magnitude behaviors if they are embarrassed or challenged by a teacher's reprimand; nonverbal reprimands are a more subtle way to correct and reduce students' challenging behavior without drawing peer attention. Third, folk wisdom says that the more a teacher talks, the less the students listen. By reserving verbal strategies for more severe behaviors teachers can make their words more meaningful and effective. When nonverbal strategies have proven ineffective or when more intensive responses are needed for higher-magnitude behaviors, the next level on the continuum is group verbal reprimands.

The identification of group verbal reprimands as the next level of intervention may be puzzling because it is typically not (or at least we hope not) an entire group of students that engages in challenging behavior. But teachers can use group correction strategies to address challenging behavior even by a small group or an individual student, minimizing the attention given to the students' challenging behavior while gaining the same benefits as with the nonverbal reprimands. Using group verbal correction strategies effectively involves employing specific types of group verbal reprimands as well as some general tips that will improve their effectiveness. One basic group correction strategy that can be used is for the teacher to state exactly what she or he is observing, something that could be called "just the facts." In other words, the teacher does not attach emotionality, judgment, or even consequences to the behavior if it persists (although the teacher may want to add these later if the first statement is not effective). This strategy is as simple as saying, "I see people talking." If this statement is ineffective alone, then the teacher can build on it by also describing the rule that is being broken (e.g., "I see people talking. Directions are no talking."). Finally, if this also is ineffective, then the teacher can also add the consequence that will be enforced if the behavior persists (e.g., "I see people talking. Directions are no talking. If people continue to talk, then time will be taken off recess."). In Figure 13.1 this is referred to as *1D–Describe the behavior, 2D–Describe the behavior* and *Describe the rule being broken,* and *3D–Describe the behavior, Describe the rule being broken,* and *Describe the consequence* that will be enforced (Van Nagel, 1991). Another option in terms of group verbal reprimands is Boomerang praise. This refers to the practice of praising students near the offending student(s) for displaying desired behaviors. By praising on-task students who are to the right or left of an off-task student, the teacher can provide a gentle prompt for the desired behavior.

Another category of verbal behavior reduction strategies fits between group verbal reprimands and individual verbal reprimands in that it can be used either with groups of students or with individual students. This category is described as redirection statements. Redirection is defined as a short, quick statement or action made by the adult to interrupt a challenging behavior by shifting the student's attention from the undesired behavior to a more appropriate behavior or focus. For example, suppose that the students are supposed to be working on a task and a couple of students get off-task and start talking about an unrelated topic. The direct approach of pointing out their off-task behavior only serves to distract other students and can also set the occasion for an escalating power struggle. But by asking the students something like "What did you get on number 4?" or "Would you write number 12 on the board for the class?" teachers can use a more gentle, less invasive approach before going to something more severe and invasive. This indirect approach is a gentler way of decreasing unwanted behaviors because it does not overtly tell the student to "Stop," but rather directs their attention elsewhere. This makes it nonconfrontational and highly effective because it does not draw attention to the undesired behavior (and attention is often the function of the undesired behavior). This strategy is used very frequently with young children, but it is usually effective up and down the age continuum.

The most intensive strategy is individual verbal reprimands for students who continue with challenging behaviors after less intensive reprimands or for students engaging in seriously challenging behavior that warrants a more intensive reprimand. For example, a teacher should immediately use an individual verbal reprimand when a student physically endangers self or others through physical aggression or reckless behavior. When using an individual reprimand, make the reprimand as private as possible. This will make it more effective for a number of reasons. First, it removes other peers from this interaction, which keeps the student from feeling embarrassed or "losing face" in front of his peers. Minimizing the audience also reduces the student's opportunity to put a show on for friends and peers. For individual reprimands, the 3D strategy (*Describe the behavior, Describe the rule being broken,* and *Describe the consequence*) also can be applied. The other strategy to use in the individual reprimand is the broken-record technique. If a teacher has gotten to the point of using an individual reprimand, the student will very likely try to argue. Rather than arguing with a potentially escalating student, the broken-record technique simply has the teacher restate the 3D strategy in spite of the student's protests.

Some students are masterful at baiting teachers into arguments, so there are some other general tips besides using a broken-record technique that will make verbal reprimands more effective and keep students' behavior from escalating or devolving into verbal sparring matches. Using a quiet tone of voice when reprimanding a student can increase the student's attention to the reprimand, increase the student's compliance, and avoid disturbing the rest of the class. Teachers who raise their voice decrease their overall effectiveness in the classroom. No one likes to be shouted at, and a shouting teacher creates an unpleasant environment not only for the target student but for all peers. Using a quiet voice communicates authority and control to students. Furthermore this strategy is minimally invasive, easy to use, and quickly applied. It allows the teacher to model how an adult effectively handles emotions in a potentially frustrating situation. This can be a particularly challenging obstacle with many students, which makes modeling more important.

Other general tips for verbal redirections are to be explicit, use words that students understand, and stay close to the student that you are redirecting without being threatening. Keeping the distance between yourself and students nonconfrontational is also effective because it does not draw peer attention to the undesired behavior. It is also especially vital for teachers of young children and children who have been the victims of abuse. After verbal and nonverbal reprimands comes the next category of negative punishment: the withholding of reinforcers to decrease unwanted behaviors.

Negative Punishment

Extinction, or the withholding of reinforcement contingent on the display of undesired behaviors, is the first strategy in the continuum of behavior reduction techniques. This first strategy usually refers to the withholding of attention in an effort to reduce a behavior, a technique sometimes called planned ignoring. Using planned ignoring as a consequence strategy to reduce minor misbehaviors is an invaluable part of a teacher's repertoire. Many teachers pay attention to students who engage in inappropriate behaviors, and inadvertently reinforce these inappropriate behaviors. Simply choosing to ignore certain misbehaviors allows teachers to continue their delivery of instruction without being disrupted by these misbehaviors.

However, some questions should be asked before this first strategy is employed. First, is teacher attention the function of this challenging behavior? Matching strategies to behavioral functions has been identified as a key component of effective management throughout this book. The decision to withhold attention should be made with the realization that the goal of the inappropriate behavior is to access the teacher's attention. Observe the student to determine whether it is actually being reinforced by *teacher* attention. Consider also whether peer attention reinforces the behavior in a similar manner. In this situation, planned ignoring is unlikely to be effective because the student continues to get attention for the behavior from other students, unless attention from other students can also be stopped (by changing the seating, etc.).

Second, teachers must be consistent with the decision to ignore certain, specific misbehaviors. Inconsistent use of planned ignoring actually strengthens the reinforcing attention on occasions when the behavior is not ignored, making the behavior even harder to decrease. A teacher who ignores a behavior like calling out sometimes but then pays attention to it at other times is actually setting up a variable ration schedule of reinforcement—the most powerful reinforcement schedule for creating a durable behavior. Consider this example: In the checkout aisle of the grocery store, a young child begins to ask for candy and the mother decides to try to use planned ignoring. After the sixteenth request of candy, however, the mother finally says "Fine, here's some candy." In this situation, the child has now learned that reinforcement can be accessed on a schedule of about 16 requests (variable ratio, VR: 16). Without a doubt, the next time they go to the grocery store the child will ask for candy 16, 17, or even 18 times. So if there is a behavior that the teacher plans to ignore, it must be ignored every single time it occurs.

The third consideration, especially notable in a classroom setting, is the issue of an extinction burst. This is defined as the tendency for behaviors placed on extinction to escalate in frequency, duration, and intensity before they begin to decrease. Therefore, be aware that the behavior will become much worse before it begins to decrease, and ensure that this behavior is not so dangerous or disruptive that ignoring it would be unethical. Also, teachers should guard against the contagious transfer of this behavior to peers who may be tempted to engage in it when they see it being ignored. This process can be helped with a strategy referred to as the "Ignoring Game." In the Ignoring Game, the peers who do not attend the misbehavior of a student who is engaging in challenging behavior receive a prespecified reinforcer. Depending on the age of the students, we could say that we are playing a game to see who can do the "best job" ignoring inappropriate behaviors. One example of a reinforcer to use in this situation is to add a minute to free time or to recess for every minute that students ignore a challenging behavior that is intended to access peer attention. Some teachers have demonstrated this strategy to be particularly effective when the students know beforehand that when the teacher writes "1 minute" (then "2 minutes," then "3 minutes," etc.) on the chalkboard, he or she is aware of their ignoring challenging behaviors and is adding minutes of free time or recess. This is one way to further combat the sometimes contagious nature of students' challenging behavior and can be used effectively in combination with a teacher's use of planned ignoring.

To determine the effectiveness of planned ignoring, continually monitor the effect that planned ignoring is having on the target behavior through data collection strategies. Although occurrences of the behavior may increase initially, if they do not begin to decrease after 8 days they probably are being reinforced in another way, such as by peer attention. Because planned ignoring places minimal demands on teacher time and energy, it should be an initial strategy for decreasing challenging behaviors. If planned ignoring is used too frequently, however, it will become ineffective and should be replaced with more intensive measures.

Fourth, for a teacher who plans to ignore a specific behavior a good rule of thumb is to perform other activities. This avoids a situation in which the teacher practically tells the student, "I'm not looking at you. I am not going to give you attention for that behavior," which is precisely what the teacher is doing by saying that they are doing the opposite. Planned ignoring is effective when used simultaneously with other strategies that reinforce appropriate behaviors (e.g., differential reinforcement). Therefore, while withholding attention for undesired behaviors, the teacher should also provide attention when the student engages in an appropriate behavior. Consider the following example:

> Kevin begins tapping his pencil. The teacher uses planned ignoring and helps other students with their work. Kevin continues tapping his pencil, and the teacher continues using planned ignoring and helping other students. Kevin stops tapping his pencil and resumes independent work. After ensuring that the behavior has stopped, the teacher comes over to Kevin and says, "Wow, you are doing a great job on your work. Keep it up."

This approach is referred to as differential reinforcement of an incompatible behavior (DRI). DRI is a procedure that replaces an inappropriate or challenging behavior by reinforcing an incompatible response and ignoring the inappropriate behavior. So the undesired behavior is put on extinction, while any behavior that the student cannot do at the same time, and hence is incompatible, is reinforced through teacher attention. There are several variations on the use of differential reinforcement. All differential reinforcement is grounded in the idea that we use the least aversive, least intensive intervention available. This can be done by providing positive alternatives to aversive consequences or punishment when trying to reduce the occurrence of the problem behavior. Differential reinforcement works by reinforcing behaviors that make problem behaviors impossible or irrelevant for the student by increasing the efficiency or effectiveness of the new incompatible behavior to make it more relevant for the student. In other words, it is like a see-saw on which the teacher drives up the rate of the desired behavior on one end of the see-saw, while the other end with the challenging behavior is driven down. For example, teachers reinforce students for sitting as an incompatible response to out-of-seat behavior or for writing with a pencil as opposed to tapping it, which means that an incompatible behavior is reinforced to decrease a specific challenging behavior.

Teachers can also reinforce using a fork as an alternative response to using fingers to eat, or raising a hand as opposed to calling out. But because students can eat with a fork and with fingers at the same time, or call out and raise their hand at the same time, the behaviors reinforced are not incompatible behaviors but rather alternative ones, so this strategy is referred to as differential reinforcement of alternative behaviors (DRA). The combination of the two differential strategies, called DRA/DRI, focuses on reinforcing behaviors that are either alternative or incompatible to problem behaviors while at the same time simply withholding reinforcement in the absence of those positive behaviors.

Other versions of differential reinforcement focus on reducing, but not eliminating the occurrence of specific behaviors. The next type of differential reinforcement strategy that is available is differential reinforcement of low rates of behavior (DRL). This is the strategy of "A little is ok, but too much is not." Consider the following example:

> Josh loved to ask questions. When Mr. Wilhoit would begin a discussion in social studies, Josh's hand would be up in the air immediately,

and every question that Josh asked and Mr. Wilhoit answered led to another question. Mr. Wilhoit did not want to eliminate Josh's questioning behavior completely, but it was impossible for him to cover the material he needed to cover in the allotted time. Plus, Josh's questioning behavior was really starting to annoy the other students. For Josh's own protection, Mr. Wilhoit needed to reduce, but not eliminate Josh's questioning behavior. So he spent a couple of days counting the number of questions Josh asked in a single 20-minute class discussion. He also evaluated the function of Josh's behavior—Josh asked questions to get attention, not necessarily to get information. Based on these considerations, Mr. Wilhoit limited the number of questions Josh could ask during a 20-minute discussion. If Josh asked less than five questions, then Mr. Wilhoit would talk with him for the last five minutes of social studies about anything Josh wanted to discuss; but if Josh went over his five-question limit, then he simply had to complete his work independently. To help Josh, Mr. Wilhoit created a check sheet that had sets of five boxes in a row. This allowed Josh to monitor how many questions he had asked and provided data to determine whether or not he had earned reinforcement.

For behaviors that teachers want to reduce but not eliminate, a strategy to consider is the differential reinforcement of low rates of behavior. DRL reinforces a small number of occurrences of the behavior using a set criterion that the student must stay under (e.g., less than five questions), and exceeding the criterion number results in withholding of reinforcement or an extinction procedure. The criterion number typically is established by observing the behavior before the intervention, often referred to as a baseline phase. The teacher then can gradually reduce the number of times the behavior is emitted and reinforced until a socially appropriate level is reached. A similar procedure, referred to as differential reinforcement of high rates of behavior (DRH), is used in the same way except that a criterion number is set for a behavior (e.g., saying "Please") to increase, and the behavior is reinforced only after the criterion is exceeded.

The final differential reinforcement strategy is the differential reinforcement of other behaviors (DRO). Reserved for the most severe behaviors, this strategy is the "anything but that (behavior)" strategy in which any other behavior earns reinforcement as long as the student does not demonstrate the identified target behavior.

Mark was transitioning into Mr. Barry's fifth-grade class from a long-term residential facility, and while Mark demonstrated a wide array of maladaptive behaviors, the most problematic was spitting at other people. Outraged parents of peers who had been targets of Mark's spitting had already called to complain, and Mr. Barry knew he had very little time to make progress before Mark was returned to a locked residential facility. To target Mark's spitting behavior that was both aggressive and presented a severe health risk, Mr. Barry set up a very simple schedule for Mark. For every thirty minutes that Mark did not spit on anyone, he received 10 minutes of computer time,

Mark's favorite activity reinforcer. At times, this could be tough for Mr. Barry, because Mark was engaging in a lot of other problem behaviors. Mr. Barry did not always want Mark to get access to the computer, but because the spitting was so problematic, he stuck with this strategy. Gradually he increased the intervals of time that Mark had to go without engaging in his spitting behavior to earn computer time until this behavior was extinguished and he could begin targeting Mark's other problematic behaviors.

As is apparent from the vignette, DRO procedures should definitely be reserved for the most extreme challenging behaviors that school personnel are trying to eliminate. The reason for the limited application of this strategy is that reinforcement is provided contingent solely on the nonoccurrence of a specific behavior. In other words, as long as the student does not do "blank" (whatever challenging behavior is to be eliminated), then he gains access to reinforcement. This may not seem so bad until you consider the wide repertoire of challenging behaviors that many of these students have at their disposal. So, in this type of system, Mark would gain access to reinforcement as long as he does not spit, but Mr. Barry cannot withhold reinforcement if Mark is disruptive in other ways or even physically aggressive. Nothing erodes trust in a teacher-student relationship faster than a teacher who changes the parameters of arrangements that they make with their students.

Time Out

Up to this point we have discussed negative punishment in terms of withholding attention from the teacher (and peers) to decrease a behavior; but if that is ineffective, the next level of negative punishment procedures is time out. This is the next level because, in addition to withholding teacher attention, time out withholds all forms of reinforcement to decrease a behavior for a brief prespecified

TABLE 13.1

Differential Reinforcement Strategy	Also known as . . .	Example of a behavior to be reduced or eliminated	Example of a replacement behavior to be reinforced
Differential Reinforcement of Alternative Behavior (DRA)	"This, not that"	Calling out	Raising your hand
Differential Reinforcement of Incompatible Behavior	"This, not that" (when you cannot do this and that at the same time)	Out of seat	Bottom in seat, touching chair
Differential Reinforcement of Low Rates of Behavior	"A little of this is ok, but too much is not."	More than five questions during a 20-minute discussion	Five or fewer questions during a 20-minute class discussion
Differential Reinforcement of Other Behaviors (DRO)	"Anything but that"	Spitting at others	All behaviors except for spitting at others

period of time. In fact, the full, and far more descriptive, name for time out is "time out from reinforcement." This includes limiting peer attention, activities, and any tangible reinforcement (but not primary reinforcers such as food, air, water, or access to a bathroom). Time out has certainly received considerable attention over the past 30 years from both proponents and opponents of the strategy. One of the reasons it has garnered this attention is that while it can be effective, time out needs certain basic environmental elements in place. Absent these essential elements, time out is wholly ineffective or becomes the impetus for more severe behaviors. This has prompted the publishing of popular articles like "Family feuds: How to make 'timeouts' less like bar fights" (Kazdin, 2008). Clearly, time out from reinforcement, if not used effectively, can escalate and increase challenging behavior.

Time out is defined as a procedure that reduces or eliminates challenging behavior by removing access to reinforcement contingent upon demonstration of the problem behavior. First, as with all strategies, the function of the behavior must be determined because, in order for time out to be effective, the student *must want to participate* and not escape from the activity or the people within the activity. Clearly, removing a student from a task that they do not like anyway just makes them more likely to engage in the same challenging behavior in order to escape from the same aversive situation. But what if academic work can become a situation in which the student will not actively try to escape the classroom and the work? As discussed in previous chapters, this is where effective instruction really makes a difference. Instruction that helps students actively engage in their learning, succeed with their efforts, and see their own progress produces students who will want to stay in that environment. After determining that the classroom environment *from* which students are being removed sufficiently reinforces the removal as a punishment, the teacher must decide the environment *to* which students should be removed. Typical time out levels, as they escalate in severity, become increasingly exclusionary and more restrictive of access to any types of reinforcers. They can be thought of as inclusionary (in-classroom time out), exclusionary (out-of-classroom time out), and seclusionary (a separate room).

In-classroom time outs can take a number of different forms, but they are predicated on the idea that access to reinforcement can be withheld even while the student is in the room. This can be a particularly challenging strategy, especially when trying to withhold peer attention. Some teachers use a separate desk facing away from other students to decrease proximity and access to attention from peers and other adults. For younger students, time out ribbons have been employed with empirical success (Fee, Matson, & Manikam, 1990). The time out ribbon is a ribbon (or some other object like a point card, a sticker, etc.) that is removed for a short period of time in order to punish a student's challenging behavior. Removing the ribbon indicates that the student cannot access teacher or peer attention or participate in activities for a specific amount of time. There are two ancillary benefits to the use of the time out ribbon. First, it communicates to other adults who may enter the room not to provide attention to a student who has engaged in some type of challenging behavior. Nothing sabotages a time out procedure more quickly than the student's accessing attention from another unknowing adult. Second, as with the use of effective nonverbal prompts and cues, the very presence of the ribbon on the student's desk or its visibility to the student can remind the student to refrain from challenging behavior.

The next level of time out is the exclusionary time out where the student is actually removed from the classroom environment. This strategy relies first and foremost on the teamwork of school personnel. Obviously, a teacher cannot be in multiple places at once, and leaving a classroom unattended is never recommended; therefore, exclusionary time out relies on another teacher or other school personnel to supervise the student in time out. Too many teachers have learned the hard way not to seat students who are already demonstrating challenging behavior unattended outside the classroom, and many districts prohibit this practice today. Similarly, sending a student to sit in the front office, where numerous adults walk by and attend the student, is equally ineffective. One of the authors of this text even witnessed a school secretary who kept candy out that students could access when they were sent to the office. (Talk about reinforcement to get into trouble!) The ideal scenario for an exclusionary time out is a separate classroom supervised by a teacher with study carrels spaced apart far enough that multiple students can be in the room, but away from each other. Otherwise, the room should be sparsely furnished and decorated and should not have the warm, inviting environment recommended for classrooms. Also, students must understand that return to the classroom (and a more reinforcing environment) is contingent on compliant behavior in this separate room. Students spending long periods of time in a separate time out classroom are an indication that the alternative environment (the exclusionary room) is a more reinforcing environment than the classroom. The reassessing and strengthening of reinforcement contingencies in the classroom often are neglected when students make frequent trips to exclusionary time out settings. In other words, focusing on what the student could and would be doing rather than what is currently going on is an important element in reducing unwanted behaviors. At the very end of the continuum, seclusionary time out is the most severe form of time out and perhaps the most severe form of punishment other than corporal punishment. The separate room used in seclusionary time out typically is secured in some way, and the following key procedures that treat the safety of all individuals involved as paramount are performed. First, the student's behavior is constantly supervised and documented. Teachers and other school personnel should keep annotated documents recording all school behaviors so that the notes can be used in legal proceedings (although we hope that will never happen). Second, planning is critical before seclusionary time out is ever used. This includes outlining exactly what behaviors justify the use of seclusionary time out, what personnel are involved in its use, and what the process is for returning students to the classroom as quickly and systematically as possible. Third, and most important, all applicable laws and regulations should be understood by all personnel and followed precisely; the use and procedures of seclusionary time out are highly specific to individual districts and states.

Response Cost

Response cost is the next most intensive and severe behavior reduction strategy in the continuum of negative punishment strategies. Because it removes something

✓ −10 points Lying, Stealing, Destroying Property
✓ −10 points Physical Aggression
✓ −5 points Lost Card
✓ −5 Buy Back (for confiscated toys and other items brought to school)

FIGURE 13.2

that a student has earned, it should be used carefully and only for severe behaviors because it can elicit more intense and aggressive behaviors. Response cost is a punishment procedure in which a student loses a specific amount of earned reinforcing stimuli, such as an object (e.g., a sticker or points from a token economy) or activity (e.g., minutes of recess), as a consequence for behavior that is targeted for reduction. The first key principle in this strategy is that it is set up in advance. From the beginning of the year, students should be taught what the response cost penalties are for specific behaviors. This avoids the impression that teachers are "making it up as they go along," and also avoids the power struggle that ensues from inflicting punishments on students that they are not expecting. One strategy that works well when these strategies are set up in advance is to attribute it to "the system." In other words, the teacher presents the response cost to the student as a penalty that has to be enforced because of "the system" (even though it was the teacher who set up the system) rather than as a decision made by the teacher; for example, "I'm sorry that you didn't turn in your math homework and will have to miss the first ten minutes of recess; but that's the system." Because the teacher appears to be bound to enforce these penalties, the "us versus them" mentality is neutralized, which gives teachers the opportunity to reassert the fact that they want all of their students to succeed. Response cost works particularly well when it accompanies a token economy. (See Chapter 12 for a discussion of token economies and see Figure 13.2 for a list of fines to accompany the sample token economy.)

There are three other key features for using response cost effectively. First, students should never feel like they no longer have anything to lose (i.e., have a negative total for a token economy). A student who feels like they cannot access any reinforcement will no longer try to engage in any desired prosocial behaviors. In fact, teachers should always try to emphasize the idea that reinforcement is just around the corner if students engage in the appropriate behaviors. Second, response cost must be set up and explained in advance and applied equally for all students at all times. Any variations can be perceived as unfair treatment and will distract the student from connecting the behavior to the consequence. Third, data and documentation of all response cost procedures should be kept and carefully maintained. Continued or increasing the use of the same punishment procedure across time indicates that the procedure is not effective. For example, if a student continues to engage in behaviors that cost him minutes out of recess, at some point it should be concluded that this student is trying to escape recess. Monitoring and data collection will assist in revealing these behavior patterns.

Positive Punishment

There is limited documentation on the value of adding aversives to the environment to decrease behaviors. In fact, the prevailing school model has shown that adding aversives such as corporal punishment, writing lines on a chalkboard, and extra school work has little desired effect on student behavior. That is why this text identifies very few strategies in terms of positive punishment. Therefore, this section includes the two types of overcorrection, positive practice overcorrection and restitutional overcorrection, and concludes with a discussion on the impact of positive punishment in educational settings.

Overcorrection can be helpful because it teaches appropriate behaviors while trying to decrease inappropriate behaviors. Overcorrection is defined as the repetitive practice of desired behaviors in an effort to extinguish the undesired behaviors. It differs from differential reinforcement strategies because students are required to engage in the desired behavior(s) multiple times. For positive practice overcorrection, this may be a single incompatible behavior that is repeated a number of times (e.g., practicing walking instead of running in the hall five times). For restitutional overcorrection, offenders are required not only to correct the results of their inappropriate behavior (e.g., leaving trash at the lunch table), but also to leave the environment in a better condition than they found it (e.g., cleaning up the rest of the cafeteria).

There are four key features to using overcorrection effectively. First, it is critical to connect the behavior to be reduced with the behavior that is being taught through overcorrection. For example, connecting the a student's cleaning the rest of the cafeteria with the mess he or she left at the table ensures that this consequence will diminish the future occurrence of the undesired behavior. Second, there must be as little time as possible between the targeted challenging behavior and the overcorrection behavior (consequence) that is to replace it. Third, when the student displays the appropriate behavior in the overcorrection phase, this behavior must be reinforced, often through verbal praise; for example, "Thank you for showing me that you can walk rather than run in the halls." Finally, the student may need to be taught the correct behavior with systematic verbal directions, so the teacher must teach the right behavior rather than just expect it. This teaching and then repeated rehearsal of the desired behavior can be time-consuming, so anyone choosing to use overcorrection should acknowledge that this strategy is time-intensive not only for the student but also for the supervising teacher. Consider this and other limitations illustrated in the following vignette:

> Mrs. Braxton, the principal, buzzed down to Mr. Ladd's room, "Mr. Ladd, may I speak with you for a minute?" Mr. Ladd was puzzled about what this could be about because, as the Behavior Resource Teacher, he was often called on to address many different tasks, and not all of them were pleasant. When he arrived at the office, Mrs. Braxton was speaking to a third-grade boy named Michael. "Michael, since you stomped on all of the flower beds out front, we have to do some restitutional overcorrection. Because you messed them up, you now have to clean them up. You will weed all of the flowerbeds around the school and Mr. Ladd will supervise." "Ok, Mrs. Braxton,"

Mike said. Mr. Ladd groaned inwardly—the temperature was almost 90 degrees with 95% humidity. Mr. Ladd was in a tie and long sleeves, while Mike had on shorts and a t-shirt.

As he began weeding the flowerbeds Mike was whistling to himself, while Mr. Ladd tried to find a shady spot to sit and do paperwork while supervising Mike. Mr. Ladd was already sweating through his shirt. After about 30 minutes, Mike asked Mr. Ladd what time it was.

"It's 11:30, Mike."

"Oh, man, all the kids in my class are doing math right now, ha-ha. In a few minutes they'll have to start writing in their composition books. I hate writing."

"Mike, just get back to work."

"Ok, Mr. Ladd." After 2 more hours and five more flowerbeds, Mike looked at Mr. Ladd, who was still sweating, red-faced, and drinking water. "Hey, Mr. Ladd, do you think Mrs. Braxton will let me out of work to do this again?"

SUMMARY

Behavior reduction or punishment procedures are a necessary part of school and classroom discipline plans; however, they should be used with care and constant monitoring. Data collection is vital because any punishment procedure that has to be used repeatedly for the same behavior is not a punishment at all because it is not decreasing the behavior. The wide range of views about punishment procedures indicates both their importance and their potential for misuse. Teaching and reinforcing new behaviors to replace any behavior targeted for reduction or elimination is the single most important final consideration for any punishment procedure.

Chapter Review

- Schools continue to use punishment procedures, often in spite of prevailing research suggesting their deleterious effects. Punishment needs to be considered functionally and paired with instruction and reinforcement.
- Verbal and nonverbal reprimands can be used along a continuum of invasiveness where teachers focus on avoiding power struggles and guiding students to make appropriate choices.
- Withholding access to reinforcers to decrease behaviors, or negative punishment, can be implemented in many ways including planned ignoring, time out, and response cost.
- Differential reinforcement refers to putting undesired behaviors on extinction while reinforcing appropriate behaviors. This includes decreasing challenging behaviors through the differential reinforcement of alternative/incompatible behaviors (DRA/DRI), low rates of behavior (DRL), and other behaviors (DRO).
- Overcorrection, including positive practice overcorrection and restitutional overcorrection, can be used to reduce challenging behaviors.

Application

1. What are some punishment procedures that you have seen implemented in schools? Were they effective?
2. Besides tradition, are there other reasons teachers might be more likely to implement punishment procedures as opposed to reinforcement procedures?
3. What are some logical arguments you could make to the contrary when other teachers advocate for harsher punishments in response to challenging behavior?

References

Coon, D., Mitterer, J., Brown, P., Malik, R., & McKenzie, S. (2009). *Psychology: A journey.* Independence, KY: Cengage Learning.

Fee, V. E., Matson, J. L., & Manikam, R. (1990). A control group outcome study of a nonexclusionary time-out package to improve social skills with preschoolers. *Exceptionality, 1*(2), 107–122.

Freiberg, H., Huzinec, C. A., & Templeton, S. M. (2009). Classroom management—a pathway to student achievement: A study of fourteen inner-city elementary schools. *The Elementary School Journal, 110*(1), 63–80.

Kerr, M. M., & Nelson, C. M. (2006). *Strategies for addressing behavior problems in the classroom.* Upper Saddle River, NJ: Merrill/Pearson.

Little, S. G., & Akin-Little, A. (2008). Psychology's contributions to classroom management. *Psychology in the Schools, 45*(3), 227–234.

Murphy, S. A., & Korinek, L. (2009). It's in the cards: A classwide management system to promote student success. *Intervention in School and Clinic, 44*(5), 300–306.

Van Nagel, C. (1991). *How to organize and manage your classroom to keep from going crazy: The PADD System: Positive Approach for Developmental Discipline.* Santa Fe, NM: Synergetic Psychology.

Wang, M. C., Haertel, G. D., & Walberg, H. J. (1993/1994). What helps students learn? *Educational Leadership, 51*(4), 74–80.

14

Behavior Support Plans

CHAPTER OBJECTIVES

After reading this chapter, you should be able to describe the following concepts:

- A rationale for the use of Behavior Support Plans (BSPs) based on the results of a Functional Behavior Assessment (FBA)

- The key components of a Behavior Support Plan

- The critical features to move effectively from FBA results to a technically adequate BSP

- How to collect and use data to guide decision making throughout the process

- Characteristics of behavioral goals and methods for writing behavioral goals

- Who are the critical team members for a behavior support team

As described in previous chapters, an FBA is used to guide development of an intervention to increase prosocial behavior and decrease problem behavior. This is accomplished via a multicomponent intervention consisting of strategies for (a) preventing the problem behavior (antecedent interventions), (b) teaching the desired behavior (skill building interventions), (c) increasing the desired behavior (reinforcement components), and (d) minimizing reinforcement for the problem behavior. In this chapter we describe how a comprehensive behavior support plan can be developed and implemented. The focus here is less on the technical components of the support plan (the specific intervention features) and more on how a support plan is developed, formatted, and implemented. We begin with a rationale for documenting behavior support plans. Then, we describe key components of behavior support plans. Finally, we delineate the process of moving from a functional behavior assessment to a support plan.

RATIONALE FOR BEHAVIOR SUPPORT PLANS

Mr. Jentzen, a school psychologist, had conducted an FBA and worked with teachers to develop intervention ideas for a seventh-grade student, Elmer. Elmer had long-standing behavioral difficulties including defiance, lying, and disruptive behavior, so, understandably, everyone was eager for an effective intervention because previous efforts had failed to produce significant improvement. Mr. Jentzen held a team meeting attended by Elmer's teachers, his parents, and the principal. At the meeting he reviewed results of the FBA that suggested that Elmer's problematic behavior was maintained by task avoidance and usually happened whenever Elmer didn't understand an assignment. Led by Mr. Jentzen, the team developed several intervention ideas, all linked to the FBA. Many good ideas were developed, and at the end of the meeting, Mr. Jentzen summarized the team's decisions on how to prevent problems in the first place (review assignment details with Elmer and check for understanding), teach appropriate behavior (teach Elmer, who was unwilling to raise his hand, how to ask for help without letting other peers know), ensure that these appropriate behaviors were reinforced (respond immediately to Elmer's requests for assistance), and minimize reinforcement for problem behavior (require Elmer to finish uncompleted assignments during his study hall at the end of the day). Everyone left the meeting very excited, but no one recorded any details of the intervention—Mr. Jentzen had a full caseload and figured that everyone would "just remember what to do." A few days later, Mr. Jentzen stopped by Elmer's 4th-period class. To his surprise, Elmer was sitting in the back of the room looking at a book unrelated to the subject of the class. When Mr. Jentzen asked the teacher why, he learned that Elmer had teased a peer and was sent to the back of the room as punishment. When Mr. Jentzen reminded the teacher of the plan, the teacher confessed that he simply had forgotten what he was supposed to do about Elmer's problem behavior. After a few more weeks, the team met again because Elmer was not making satisfactory progress. Mr. Jentzen quickly realized that all the teachers were doing something different and that this inconsistency was likely contributing to Elmer's problems. Mr. Jentzen realized that, had he given a written summary of the intervention, the teachers probably would have been more consistent in implementation.

As this example illustrates, conducting an FBA and identifying intervention strategies is not enough: Effective interventions are documented. Documenting the FBA and the support plan is important for several reasons. First, as illustrated by Mr. Jentzen's experience, documentation provides a cue for implementers; teachers and others can review the document to ensure that they are implementing the intervention as planned. This is especially important when interventions are modified or carried out over extended periods of time. Putting the initial intervention and subsequent modifications into writing will help all parties involved remember what has been tried as well as what was (and was not) effective. Second, documentation facilitates accountability—written documents show exactly what was implemented and why. Third, written support plans can follow students if they move to a new teacher or a new school, allowing new educators to see what has been tried thus far and what was (and was not) successful.

Many behavior support plans focus exclusively on intervention specifics, that is, what will be done to prevent problem behavior and teach prosocial behavior. This information indeed is critical, but effective behavior support plans also specify what needs to be in place to ensure implementation (systems features) and on how the intervention will be monitored.

KEY COMPONENTS OF BEHAVIOR SUPPORT PLANS

Behavior support plans are written documents that describe the intervention (i.e., what specifically will be done to decrease the problem behavior and increase the likelihood of prosocial behavior). Sugai and Horner (2002) noted that if our goal is achieving desired outcomes, then evidence-based practices are necessary, but not sufficient. We also must have systems in place to implement those practices efficiently and with fidelity and use data to guide decision making. Thus, a behavior support plan should have the following features: intervention measures linked to the results of a functional behavior assessment (FBA), systems to ensure that the intervention will be *implemented* with fidelity and sustained over time, and a plan for data collection to monitor outcomes and guide decision making. A behavior support plan template that includes all these features is in the Appendix at the end of this chapter.

PRACTICES: KEY FEATURES OF THE INTERVENTION

As stressed throughout this book, effective interventions are linked to the results of an FBA; that is, they address features in the environment that are related to the occurrence of the problem behavior. Behavior support plans generally consist of antecedent interventions, skill building interventions, and consequences to decrease problem behavior and enhance prosocial behavior. When needed, a safety plan is included as well. When determining the specific interventions components to include in a support plan, ask the following questions:

1. *Antecedent Interventions:* Can we take steps to *prevent* the problem behavior from occurring or *increase* the likelihood that the student will do the right thing?
2. *Target Desired Behaviors:* What do we want the student to do and are there acceptable alternative behaviors?
3. *Skill Building:* What *skills* does the student need to learn and what behaviors need to occur more often?
4. *Reinforcement:* How can we make sure that appropriate behavior pays off (i.e., is reinforced)?

5. *Minimizing Reinforcement:* What can we do to minimize reinforcement for problem behavior?

6. *Safety Plan:* Is this student's behavior ever dangerous to self or others?

Antecedent Interventions

Taking steps to prevent problem behaviors or to increase appropriate behavior is referred to as an antecedent intervention. Implementing an antecedent strategy requires planning; however, it is always easier to prevent a problem than to respond to one. Antecedent interventions might include modifying the setting event or the discriminative stimuli. Antecedent interventions in a support plan are documented by noting precisely what will be done, when, and by whom. Consider the following example:

> One of the authors once worked with a child ("Suneeta") who was experiencing a great deal of parental conflict at home. Several days per week she would come to school with her hood over her head and her eyes red and swollen from crying. Sadly, Suneeta's teachers could do nothing to help her parents get along better, so they had to instead help Suneeta succeed at school. Suneeta's teachers had learned that on days when she came in with her hood up and eyes red, it was futile to engage Suneeta in academics: She ignored teacher directives and simply stared into space. If a teacher approached her directly and requested that she begin a task, Suneeta often would begin to sob hysterically or run out of the room. A neutralizing routine was implemented to diminish effects of problems at home and to help Suneeta succeed. On days when Suneeta reported "feeling sad" she was given the choice of beginning the day as usual, spending 15 minutes with the school counselor, or going to the library for 15 minutes. After the intervention, Suneeta rarely refused to engage in academic tasks and almost never cried at school. At first she frequently chose to either visit the counselor or go to the library; but over time (after about 4 weeks) she often chose to just begin the day as usual, only without crying or disengagement.

The neutralizing routine component of Suneeta's support plan is depicted in Figure 14.1. The plan identified who was responsible for implementing the intervention, when it would be implemented, and precisely what would occur. These details clearly inform all the involved parties exactly what the intervention consists of and what their role in it is.

Desired Behaviors

It is usually very easy to identify what a student should be doing instead of performing the problem behavior. For example, "Jasmine should be sitting in her seat doing her geometry, not talking to her peers or doodling." Sometimes, however, the distance between what the student is doing now (e.g., constantly doodling and whispering to peers) and where we want the student to be (e.g., working quietly for 50 minutes) is very large, and it can be difficult to develop a

7. What will be done to prevent problem behavior?

a. Modifications to setting event

When Suneeta comes to school with her hood up or eyes swollen or simply tells Ms. James (or another adult) that she had a rough night or morning, she will be asked if she would like to visit with Ms. Marcolm, go to the library, or just start the day. She will have 15 minutes with the counselor (more if Ms. Marcolm determines more time is needed) or in the library. She will go to the library by herself and let Mr. James know she is there. Suneeta will watch the clock and return to class (with a book if she desires) after 15 minutes. If she loses track of time, Mr. James will remind her when time is up. If Suneeta needs more time, she can let Mr. James know and then she may remain in the library for a longer time.

FIGURE 14.1 Setting Event Portion of Suneeta's Support Plan

feasible plan to move directly from what is going on right now to where we all want to be. In this case, we suggest following the recommendation of O'Neill et al. (1997) and using alternative (i.e., replacement) behaviors (Gable, Hendrickson, & Van Acker, 2001, p. 250). Alternative behaviors serve the same function as the problem behavior but are more acceptable than the problem behavior. Let's continue with Jasmine. Jasmine's teacher obviously would like her to work quietly the whole class period; but it is unlikely that an intervention can be developed that could get Jasmine to work quietly for 50 minutes when currently she often works for less than 2 minutes at a time.

The FBA conducted by the school's counselor suggested that although Jasmine's behaviors were maintained by task avoidance, Jasmine indeed could do the work—her geometry work, although challenging and not Jasmine's favorite task, was at her ability level. Thus, Jasmine's teacher was asked to think about how Jasmine could unobtrusively indicate that she needed a break. Her teacher decided to allow Jasmine to put her head down on her desk or doodle quietly for 2 minutes when she raised her hand and asked for a break. Although her teacher would have preferred Jasmine to work the entire time, this certainly was preferable to distracting others or to the teacher's constantly nagging Jasmine to work. Jasmine indicated that this was her preference as well, saying that she didn't like the entire class noticing that she was frustrated and needed a break. Jasmine's teacher decided to begin by allowing her three breaks per class period, with the number to be gradually reduced as she learned to work through her frustration. She also told Jasmine that she was more than happy to help Jasmine at any time and that they could work together in the back of the room to prevent anyone else from knowing that she was struggling.

Skill Building

Skill building interventions help students learn new skills or learn to more fluently exhibit skills already in their repertoire. This part of the support plan focuses on identifying supports needed to help the student exhibit the alternative and desired behaviors fluently. There are two different approaches. First, the plan could include a new behavior that the student currently does not know how

1. **What is the desired behavior and are there any acceptable alternative behaviors?**

Jasmine will work on geometry the entire class period without doodling or distracting other students. She will ask for help when needed. An acceptable alternative is requesting a break. Jasmine can raise her hand (two fingers in the air) to indicate she wants to take a break.

2. **What new responses will you teach or arrange the environment to increase and how?**

   a. **Desired behaviors**

   If Jasmine wants help with the work, she can ask Ms. Thompson to work with her either at her desk, at Ms. Thompson's desk, or in the back of the room.

   b. **Alternative behaviors**

   Her teacher will nod her head to indicate this is okay. After two minutes (Jasmine can doodle or put her head down), she will get back to work. Jasmine can take up to three breaks per class period; she will track her breaks by making an "X" on her paper.

FIGURE 14.2

to do. Second, the plan might include a behavior that the student can do, but doesn't do well. In either case, steps are taken to teach the student how to engage in the desired behavior as well as when it is appropriate (and sometimes not appropriate) to exhibit the behavior. Steps also are taken to provide the student sufficient opportunities to practice using these skills. The behavior support plan must document exactly what behaviors will be taught and how they will be taught. For Jasmine (see Figure 14.2), no new behaviors were taught; instead, the plan was designed to help Jasmine learn to exhibit behaviors she already knew how to do, at the appropriate time (e.g., raising her hand to ask for a break).

Sometimes an intervention requires teaching new skills. Functional communication training is an example of such an intervention, in which an individual is taught a communication response that serves the same function as the problem behavior. Social skills training also could meet this goal. Whenever a new skill is taught, the support plan must document precisely what will be taught and how it will be taught. Examples of this type of plan are depicted in Figures 14.3 (for functional communication training) and 14.4 (for a social skills program). The functional communication training program was implemented with Dartez, a nonverbal 14-year-old boy diagnosed with severe mental retardation. Dartez frequently raised his hand when he needed help but did not possess the knowledge of how to ask his teacher to come and talk to him—Dartez wanted more interaction with his teacher; thus, this skill deficit resulted in significant disruptive behavior. The social skills program was implemented with Teri, an adolescent who frequently got into arguments with her peers, which occasionally turned into physical fights. Teri reported to adults that it was not "her fault" and that everyone was against her. She didn't seem to know how to resolve disputes, so conflict training was implemented. As illustrated in Figure 14.4, any time a packaged intervention, or a group program as part of an intervention, is used, it is important to specify the logistics and the desired outcomes. In addition, be sure to describe how the newly acquired behaviors will be reinforced, because simply teaching a new skill generally does not result in the use of that

1. **What is the desired behavior and are there any acceptable alternative behaviors?**

   Getting along with peers is the desired behavior, learning to resolve conflicts. An acceptable alternative is that Teri walk away from the situation and tell a teacher what happened.

2. **What is the desired behavior and are there any acceptable alternative behaviors?**

   Dartez will work quietly for up to 15 minutes. If Dartez wants teacher feedback, he will raise his hand and give his teacher the "How am I doing?" card.

3. **What new responses will you teach or arrange the environment to increase and how?**

   a. Desired behaviors

   Working quietly, continuing to raise his hand for help.

   b. Alternative behaviors

   Dartez will hand Mr. Brown his card to request feedback/attention. Mr. Brown will teach Dartez to use the card via errorless learning during 5-min practice sessions conducted every day until Dartez is using the card independently. During these practice sessions, Mr. Brown will tell Dartez that if he wants to check in, he needs to hand Mr. Brown the card. Initially Mr. Brown will then physically guide Dartez to hand him the card. After 5 trials, Mr. Brown will pause for 5 seconds before guiding Dartez to hand him the card. When Dartez hands Mr. Brown the card, Mr. Brown will talk to Dartez about the good work he is doing for about a minute. Once Dartez is handing Mr. Brown the card independently for 95% of opportunities during the practice sessions Mr. Brown will begin implementing the card during class.

   During implementation, Mr. Brown will verbally prompt Dartez to use the card at the beginning of class and when Dartez exhibits any precursor behaviors (e.g., fidgeting, whispering).

FIGURE 14.3   Support Plan for Functional Communication Training

1. **What new responses will you teach or arrange the environment to increase and how?**

   a. Desired behaviors

   Teri will participate in a conflict resolution group taught by Ms. Whitcomb. The group is a standard curriculum package *(Solving Problems with Positive Teen Power)* and lasts 6 weeks. Groups will run during Teri's study hall period. She will learn to identify private feelings of stress and to count to ten when she feels angry or stressed. In addition, she will learn specific communicative skills to use to resolve conflicts with peers—these are delineated in the SPPT program. All of Teri's teachers will receive a copy of the target behaviors and will provide Teri with verbal acknowledgements and Star Points [the school-wide acknowledgement system] when they see her use any of these target behaviors.

   b. Alternative behaviors

   If Teri is in a situation with a peer whom she perceives as negative or if she thinks someone has "wronged" her, she may talk to a teacher about it. The teacher will not deliver consequences to the other students but will allow Teri to vent. In addition, the teacher may ask Teri if she wants to go and talk with Ms. Whitcomb about how to handle the situation or may review the conflict resolution skills Teri has learned thus far and talk about how Teri might choose to handle something like this next time. This interaction will remain positive (do not criticize Teri for not using her new skills—praise her for not fighting) but will also not focus on her perceptions of what the other students did—the goal is to re-teach new skills. If Teri comes to an adult instead of engaging in an altercation with another student she may earn a Star Point.

FIGURE 14.4   Support Plan for Social Skills Training

skill. For Teri, all teachers were given a copy of the target behaviors Teri learned each week and were asked to praise Teri when she used them. They also could give her a schoolwide acknowledgement when she engaged in these desired behaviors.

Reinforcement

Throughout this text we have stressed the fact that behaviors persist only when reinforced. Consequently, a critical part of any support plan is documenting how desired and alternative behaviors will be reinforced. Reinforcement needed during initial acquisition is often much more intense than that needed to maintain the behavior. Thus, a support plan should describe not only the plans for reinforcing desired behaviors early on but also how reinforcement will be reduced over time. When the plan is first implemented, reinforcement for the desired behavior must be more powerful than any reinforcement that follows problem behavior. Consider, for example, a student, Satish, whose disruptive behavior is maintained by peer attention. Satish starts a behavior support plan in which sitting quietly for an entire class period for two days results in 10 minutes of free time at the start of school the next day. How effective would this plan be if disruptive behavior typically occurred only a couple of times per week? How effective would it be if disruptive behavior occurred—and was followed by peer attention—10 or 11 times per class period? You probably can see that while the plan might work in the first case, it may not be effective in the second scenario because here the student receives *more* reinforcement for disruptive behavior than he would for working quietly. The teacher might want eventually to reinforce only every few days; however, this is unlikely to work initially. She will have to implement a denser schedule of reinforcement early on, and then gradually shift to a leaner schedule. The support plan implemented for Satish is shown in Figure 14.5.

Minimizing Reinforcement

Because reinforced behavior will continue, reinforcement for problem behavior should be minimized. Of course, it is not always possible to simply terminate the consequences that were maintaining a behavior; for example, it may be difficult to stop peers from giggling when a student makes inappropriate body noises. As another example, self-injury that is maintained by teacher attention may be impossible to ignore; students must be kept safe. Thus, the goal is not always to totally halt reinforcement. Rather, it should be minimized so that the reinforcement for desired and alternative behaviors is better (e.g., occurs for more time, is qualitatively more preferred, is more readily available) than whatever follows the problem behavior. As you might imagine, minimizing reinforcement for problem behavior usually involves careful planning the consequences for appropriate behavior; the goal is to make sure that the student prefers those consequences to those of the problem behavior. A sample BSP is shown in Figure 14.6 for Jake, an eighth-grade student who often got out of his seat, a behavior that was maintained by teacher attention. You can see that Ms. Blackwell minimized this attention by ensuring that she had a consistent way to respond. Ms. Blackwell would prompt Jake back to his seat because she had learned that he typically would wander around the room and get

1. **What is the desired behavior and are there any acceptable alternative behaviors?**

   Getting along with peers is the desired behavior, learning to resolve conflicts. An acceptable alternative is that Teri walk away from the situation and tell a teacher what happened.

2. **What new responses will you teach or arrange the environment to increase and how?**

   a. **Desired behaviors**

   Work quietly without disrupting peers. Each morning, Satish's teacher will check in with him and remind him of what he has to do to earn stars and what happens with the stars.

   b. **Alternative behaviors**

3. **How will desired and alternative behaviors be reinforced?**

   a. **What will you do initially to make sure these behaviors occur frequently?**

   Satish will earn a star at the end of each 45 minute activity. If he earns five or more stars (out of 7 possible activities) during the day he will earn computer time for the class and will get to choose a friend to buddy with during computer time. If he doesn't earn five or more stars, there will not be computer time at the end of class.

   b. **What changes will you make over time to enhance maintenance?**

   Fades based on Satish's behavior: (a) increase the stars across two days—computer time every other day, (b) keep the stars and let him choose a buddy but return to the old schedule of computer activities two to three times per week, (c) fade out the stars but continue to let Satish choose a buddy when he has had a good day.

FIGURE 14.5   Support Plan Illustrating Reinforcement Schedule

into things until she "had to say something." She hoped that a consistent response, paired with increased attention for working appropriately, would succeed given that he was now getting only minimum attention for wandering around. In addition, she ensured that Jake did not disrupt others and still finished his work by sending him to the office and having him work alone in a small room if he was disruptive—something that Jake did not enjoy.

8. **How will desired and alternative behaviors be reinforced?**

   a. **What will you do initially to make sure these behaviors occur frequently?**

   b. **What changes will you make over time to enhance maintenance?**

9. **What will be done to minimize reinforcement of problem behavior?**

When Jake is out of his seat, Ms. Blackwell will remind him to sit down (e.g., "Where are you supposed to be?") If Jake does not sit down she will say, "Jake you can sit down or you will owe me 5 minutes of your lunch time so you can finish the work you are missing." If Jake does not sit down OR if he is argumentative, Ms. Blackwell will ignore Jake unless he is disruptive to others. He will be required to remain after class (missing 5 min of lunch) to finish his work. If Jake disrupts others, he will be sent to the office; he will remain there, in the "cool down" room until his work is done. If Jake sits down at any time, Ms. Blackwell will look for an opportunity to call on him or praise him for working very shortly thereafter.

FIGURE 14.6   Sample Support Plan for Jake

Safety Plan

Interventions linked to the function of the problem behavior generally are effective for reducing the problem behavior and increasing desired behaviors. These plans, however, rarely stop the behavior immediately. Students usually have learned problem behaviors over a fairly long period, so time will be needed to help them "unlearn" these behaviors. For students whose behavior is dangerous to themselves or others, a safety plan should be implemented. A safety plan is (a) designed only after antecedent, skill building, and reinforcement strategies have been designed (based on an FBA) and (b) implemented at a predetermined time to ensure consistency. The goal of the safety plan is to keep everyone safe, not necessarily to reduce future occurrences of the student's problem behavior and enhance skills. This is why the safety plan is only part of an intervention, not the entire intervention.

The specific components of a safety plan will vary depending on the severity of the student's behavior, the setting, and who is around. The plan should delineate precisely who will do what and when each step will occur. First, note exactly which student behavior will put the safety plan into action; this will help to ensure consistent use of the plan. As in all behavior support planning, the specific behavior should be operationally defined using observable terms. First, instead of stating, "Use the safety plan when Jan is out of control," state exactly what Jan must do and say for the safety plan to be used; for example, "If Jan hits or attempts to hit another student or the teacher, the safety plan will be implemented." Next, delineate each step of the safety plan, being sure to indicate the consequences at each step if the student does not comply or escalates. Third, indicate who will be involved and notified, specifying backup individuals in case someone is not available.

SYSTEMS FOR IMPLEMENTATION

Interventions are unlikely to be implemented properly or sustained over time if systems features are not included. Important systems features include the date that implementation will begin, needed resources, a plan for informing key stakeholders, and a plan for working with substitutes. The behavior support plan template in the appendix at the end of the chapter provides a space for documenting these decisions in the section entitled "Practices for Implementation."

When a new intervention plan is developed, the temptation often is to begin implementing it immediately. But there are several good reasons to delay implementation for at least two to three days. First, delaying implementation provides time to ensure that all stakeholders are informed, that needed materials are gathered, and that everyone involved is familiar with their role and willing to implement the intervention. Second, the delay allows all involved to review the plan carefully to uncover any inconsistencies or strategies that might be difficult to implement. Third, delaying implementation provides time for training implementers in the support plan. The final reason to delay implementation is to allow the collection of baseline data, if this has not begun already. As discussed in the next section, you will collect data to monitor the intervention; this is easier to do if you know how often the target behaviors occurred before the intervention was implemented. One way to facilitate this baseline evaluation is to use the same data collection forms both before and during the intervention. The strategy for data collection will be developed when the support plan is written (see the next section), and thus collecting the baseline data will involve simply using those data collection tools a few days in advance of the intervention.

Attention should also be given to the resources required for implementation. These resources could include items to use as rewards or acknowledgements, data collection forms, and actual space to implement parts of the intervention (e.g., a quiet room). Resources also include the people needed to implement all parts of the intervention. It is important that resources be available upon initial implementation and that there be a plan to ensure that these resources are available over time. For example, for a student who will self-monitor his or her behavior on point cards, a person to collect the cards and a place to store them should be arranged. Next, key stakeholders who are to be informed of the plan should be noted. Note who will discuss the plan with them as well. This obviously includes parents or guardians, if they were not present at the meeting, as well as the student. The student should be told the purpose of the plan in age-appropriate and positive terms. For example, instead of saying, "This will make you behave" say, "We are going to help you learn to get along better in school." All students should be given an opportunity to provide input on the intervention plan. Many of them may have valuable information on items that might serve as incentives or ways to decrease the likelihood that problem behavior will occur.

Beyond the family and the student, other people at the school might need to be informed of the plan. For example, if a student is on a point card throughout the entire day, including recess, then the recess aides need to know about the plan and how to implement it. When discussing the plan with stakeholders, all must have the opportunity to share their opinions on the plan and to make modifications if they desire. This often results in a delicate balance between the technical precision of the plan (the extent to which it aligns with the results of the FBA) and the needs and desires of stakeholders. Benazzi, Horner, and Good (2006) documented this balance in a study of support plans developed by twelve different school-based teams. They asked behavior analysts to assess support plans developed by (a) teams without guidance from a behavior specialist, (b) behavior specialists without input from team members, and (c) teams that included a behavior specialist. Benazzi et al. found that although teams without a specialist developed plans that the team members approved of, the plans tended not to have what Benazzi et al. termed "technical adequacy." In other words, the plans did not match the function of the behavior and thus probably would not be effective. In contrast, although behavior specialists developed plans with high technical adequacy, team members rated these plans as unlikely to be implemented; the plans did not have what Benazzi et al. called "contextual fit." Teams that included a behavior specialist, however, developed plans with both high technical adequacy *and* good contextual fit. We return to this issue when we discuss support teams in a later section.

DATA TO GUIDE DECISION MAKING

Once a plan has been developed, progress monitoring is critical to determine whether the plan is having the desired effect and to help guide any needed modifications. Although we may cringe at the idea of collecting data on a child's behavior in addition to teaching a roomful of students, in fact, data collection can be done both efficiently and effectively. Developing a data collection system that both provides useful information *and* is feasible requires planning prior to implementation. During the support planning process, decisions should be made on the following questions: (a) In what settings should data collection occur? (b) What behaviors are most important to monitor? (c) How often should data be collected? and (d) How will data be analyzed and used to guide decision making? Each of these decisions should be documented in the support plan (see the end-of-chapter appendix).

Note that the first decision to be made is not what behaviors should be monitored, but rather in what settings data collection should occur. This is because a student might exhibit different behaviors in different settings, or the intensity of the behavior might vary sufficiently to warrant collecting data differently. For example, for a student who was out of his seat an average of 30 times during history but only once or twice during art, data might be collected only during history or, if data is collected in both classes, less frequently during art. Data should be collected in the setting(s) in which problems most often occur. If the target behavior occurs throughout a class period or in a specific setting (e.g., recess), then data might be collected across that time period. But if the target behavior occurs only during a specific routine (e.g., independent reading, tasks involving writing), then data might be collected only during that routine. The goal is to collect the data during the problematic times because this will allow for better evaluation of the intervention. The problematic settings or routines were identified during the FBA, so this information can be used to guide this step of developing the data collection system. Once the settings are identified, be sure that the persons in those settings are willing and able to collect data and that they understand the data collection system.

After the settings are identified, the next questions to answer are (a) on what behaviors will data be collected and (b) how will this occur. Determining the target problem behavior should be easy because the behavior of interest was defined operationally during the FBA. Teams should also consider collecting data on behaviors that they hope to increase. Remember Ms. Blackwell, who was concerned about Jake's out-of-seat behavior? The team decided to target out-of-seat behavior as well as to measure hand-raising because the results of the FBA suggested that Jake was frequently out of seat to get her attention and Ms. Blackwell indicated that she would prefer hand-raising as a method of obtaining her attention. The metric used to measure target behaviors should be considered. One rule of thumb is to use a numeric metric because this will allow the data to be graphed. Many schools collect data by asking teachers to describe how an activity went; but such anecdotal summaries, although interesting, do not allow for monitoring over time. A sample data collection tool for a student who touches peers without permission and is frequently out of seat is shown in Figure 14.7. A team that desires more specific data might assign a range to each numerical rating. For example, "1" might indicate that the behavior occurred 0–1 times and a "4" would indicate that the behavior occurred 9 or more times.

Data should be collected frequently enough to allow for adequate monitoring of progress. For students with significant behavioral challenges, data typically are collected at least once a day. Remember, the more often data are

Date: _____		Setting: <u>Circle time</u>		
Out of Seat	1 Did not occur	2 Occurred rarely	3 Occurred several times	4 Occurred often
Touching Others	1 Did not occur	2 Occurred rarely	3 Occurred several times	4 Occurred often
Raises Hand	1 Did not occur	2 Occurred rarely	3 Occurred several times	4 Occurred often

FIGURE 14.7 Sample Progress Monitoring Form for Aliza

collected, the more likely it is that the data will reflect what actually is occurring. To illustrate this point, let's try a little exercise. Think about the last five days, from when you got up until you went to sleep. Make a list of everything that you did and everyone you saw. Pretty difficult, isn't it? Now, think about the last hour and make the same list. You will find that it is much easier to remember recent events. Thus, we recommend collecting data daily in all problematic settings.

Last but not least, determine how the data will be analyzed and used to guide decision making. First, the team should set an intervention goal to assist in monitoring progress. Teams often set short-term goals and long-term goals. The long-term goals are what will be achieved if the intervention is successful, whereas the short-term goals are intermediary steps. Short-term goals are updated by teams periodically. Table 14.1 shows sample long-term and short-term goals. These are not meant to be used as they are; rather, they are examples of goals that might be set. The first example shows goals for Jackson, a seventh

TABLE 14.1   Sample Behavior Goals

Date Plan Began	Short-Term Goal 1	Target Date	Short-Term Goal 2	Target Date	Long-Term Goal	Target Date
10/2/08	Jackson will leave class only after using his "Office" pass and will complete at least one assignment each math period	12/1/08	Jackson will request to leave class one time or less and will complete 60% of assignments within time-frame allotted.	2/15/09	Jackson will remain in class throughout the entire math period and will complete 90% of assignments within time-frame allotted.	4/4/09
10/2/08	Destiny will complete 50% of all art projects without aggressive or destructive behavior.	11/22/08	Destiny will complete 80% of all art projects without aggressive or destructive behavior.	1/4/09	Destiny will complete group art projects with no aggressive or destructive behavior.	2/11/09

grader who often left math class without permission when his teacher tried to get him to complete assignments. Because Jackson often became quite disruptive when leaving the room, a major intervention goal was to help him learn to request breaks in a more appropriate manner. Thus, the intervention consisted of allowing Jackson to sit in the office for brief periods whenever he asked to do so. A contingency was set up such that if Jackson asked to go to the office fewer times than a set number (which changed as the intervention was in place), he could earn preferred activities. The initial goal was simply that he would use the pass instead of leaving without permission and would complete one assignment.

Once goals are defined, the logistics of the data collection are set. Logistical steps include identifying who will (a) gather the data from the various individuals completing the data collection process and (b) graph the data. Graphing should occur at least once per week so that the data can be evaluated frequently. Graphs should be evaluated at least weekly to assess progress and to determine whether modifications are necessary. Graphs should be examined by someone familiar with the intervention who understands how to assess trends.

PUTTING IT ALL IN PLACE: THE PROCESS OF SUPPORT PLANNING

Too often, training on FBA and behavior support plans focuses exclusively on the "how to," paying little if any attention to critical process variables—key steps necessary to ensure that a good plan is written and actually implemented. Earlier we discussed process variables needed for implementing a plan, including gathering needed resources, providing training, and determining how data will be collected and analyzed for progress monitoring. Attention to the process of actually developing the support plan is key as well, however. In this section we describe how support teams are developed, including who should be involved in those teams and their roles. We also discuss how to facilitate team meetings so as to increase the likelihood of positive outcomes.

BEHAVIOR SUPPORT TEAMS: WHO IS INVOLVED?

Comprehensive behavior support in a school means that all students who need interventions receive them in an efficient manner and that interventions effectively meet the needs of most students. In addition, interventions are monitored to assess the extent to which intervention goals are met. Schools will be better able to meet these goals if they use team-based planning (Anderson & Scott, 2009).

Historically, behavior support planning has occurred in schools somewhat haphazardly. Often only one person has expertise in behavior supports and makes most intervention decisions, usually in conjunction with an administrator. In such a model, a small team (e.g., a Teaching Assistance Team) meets weekly or less often. Teachers who have concerns regarding a student come to the meeting to discuss the student. After the problem is discussed, decisions may be made regarding the intervention. Often, once an intervention has begun, follow-up is somewhat sporadic. There are several limitations to this approach. First, an FBA often is not part of the process because the team typically does not do an assessment before the meeting, and so the meeting often focuses on brainstorming interventions. As a result, the interventions may not be effective. Second, there is often little or no follow-up with the teacher(s) to determine whether the intervention has been or can be implemented and whether further assistance is needed. Third, because interventions are developed only for students whose teacher requests assistance, some students who might benefit from intervention do not receive support. This could occur, for example, with a student who is exhibiting behavior problems across multiple classes, but the teachers are not overly concerned because each teacher sees the student for only 45 minutes. If the student was with only one teacher, however, the behavior problems would be more likely to be noted.

In an attempt to more comprehensively and effectively meet the needs of all their students, some schools are adapting a tiered system of behavior support and team-based planning. The number of teams varies from school to school; however, the roles played by these teams remain consistent. These roles include selecting students who may need interventions, matching student needs to available interventions, conducting FBAs and other assessments, building support plans, and monitoring interventions for progress. These roles may be accomplished by the School Behavior Team.

The *School Behavior Team* has a stable membership and meets regularly (e.g., every other week). Members include an administrator responsible for student discipline decisions; the behavior specialist, who conducts FBAs and builds support plans (discussed further below); and at least one teacher. Selection of teaching representation varies from school to school. Enough teachers should be selected to ensure that all are represented as well as to facilitate communication between the team and teachers without the team becoming too large. In elementary schools, the team usually has one or two teachers (e.g., one teacher from regular education and one from special education), whereas middle schools often have grade-level representation and high schools have representation across departments or divisions. The School Behavior Team oversees support planning in the school, which includes (a) selecting students who may benefit from intervention, (b) matching students to intervention, and (c) progress monitoring.

Students who may benefit from intervention can be selected via teacher-generated requests for assistance and by reviewing office discipline referral patterns. Schools also may embark on formative evaluation—periodic screenings of all students to select those who may benefit from further intervention. Once students who may need additional support are selected, the team makes a determination regarding interventions. Recommendations could include not to intervene at this time but to continue monitoring, to begin an existing group intervention such as check-in/check-out (Horner et al., 2005; Campbell & Anderson, 2008) or social skills training, to conduct an FBA, or to refer to an outside community agency. (An in-depth discussion of these selection procedures is beyond the scope of this text, but see Anderson and Scott (2009) for recommendations on building systems for selecting students who need interventions.)

A second function of the School Behavior Team is matching students to available interventions. First, it is determined whether the student might be a good candidate for a group (secondary, Tier II) intervention such as check-in/check-out (cf. Campbell & Anderson, 2008) or social skills training. If a student requires function-based support, then the behavior specialist is responsible for conducting an FBA and building and implementing a support plan. At this point, you may be wondering who fills the behavior specialist role. Schools increasingly are organizing to provide behavior and academic supports to students in an efficient and effective manner. As a result, they are working to build within-school capacity around functional behavior assessment. Schools with this capacity have a minimum of three (or more) individuals trained in FBA and behavior support planning. The rationale for having three people with this skill set within a school is that (a) the school may be without this needed resource if the only individual who can conduct FBAs leaves the school or takes on new responsibilities and (b) the school may have more children than can be served by one person. Of these three individuals, at least one should be dedicated to FBA and support planning to meet the school's needs. This means that this person cannot be a full-time teacher because support planning requires multiple hours for each student in need of this level of support. In many schools, a counselor or a part-time teacher fulfills this role. In other schools the behavior specialist might be a school psychologist, and in still others a general education teacher with significant release time.

A third role for the School Behavior Team is progress monitoring. Once an intervention is in progress, this support team meets regularly to review progress. As described earlier, part of intervention planning for each student is determining how data will be collected and setting intervention goals, so the team simply reviews data for all students receiving intervention to assess the extent to which students are meeting behavioral goals and to determine next steps. For example, if a student on a behavior support plan is not meeting her goals, the team might meet with the teacher to discuss fidelity or to conduct a more in-depth FBA. A student who has been successful for 10 weeks, however, might be ready to have the intervention faded out. The School Behavior Team does progress monitoring because this reduces the work load for teachers involved with the student, who otherwise would have to schedule weekly meetings to assess progress. (Additional meetings are required only when the data suggest an intervention change is needed.) In addition, because one group is responsible for progress monitoring all the students receiving behavior support, students are less likely to fall through the proverbial cracks.

Facilitating Support Planning

For students who require function-based support, the assessment and intervention development are guided by the school behavior specialist and those who know the student best. Thus, student-specific teams are formed because the membership varies for each student. At minimum, team members include the behavior specialist and concerned teachers. An administrator also usually is either part of the team or is informed of all decisions. In addition, parents and the student are involved in the assessment and intervention planning process. Although students rarely attend intervention planning meetings—it is not very fun to have a group discuss your "problems"—students should be included in the FBA, and their opinions regarding intervention strategies should be obtained and used when possible.

Because school days are very full and it can be difficult to schedule meetings with multiple teachers and administrators, we recommend scheduling meetings associated with behavior support planning in advance. When a student needs more intensive support, several steps are taken before completing the FBA. First, previously attempted interventions are documented to determine whether a less intensive intervention has been attempted. Because function-based support is resource-intensive and time-intensive, teams should consider implementing a group (targeted) intervention prior to function-based support. Next, the following meetings are scheduled: a meeting to complete the FBA (which might be an informal chat if only one teacher is involved), a meeting to build the support plan, and—if there is no School Behavior Team—a follow-up meeting. The intervention should be in place within three weeks of the FBA, so scheduling should take this into account.

After the FBA is completed, the support plan meeting occurs. To facilitate this meeting, a hypothesis statement should be developed. In addition, the person coordinating the FBA should develop ideas for intervention strategies. At the support plan meeting, the first step is to ensure that there is consensus among all involved about the hypothesis statement. If there is disagreement, the findings of the FBA should be reviewed to resolve any disputes. If resolution cannot be reached, more FBA data should be collected. Once consensus is reached on the hypothesis statement, the team develops a comprehensive intervention consisting of antecedent, skill building, reinforcement, and consequence strategies. The team should agree on all intervention components. Once agreement is reached, the team defines the systems and progress monitoring components of the intervention.

Chapter Review

- The chapter described why it is necessary to connect the results of an FBA with the Behavior Support Plan (BSP). Strong connections between the FBA and the BSP make it more likely that the student will succeed and ensures that school personnel are not using procedures that actually elicit more challenging behaviors.
- The key components of a Behavior Support Plan are antecedent interventions, skill building interventions, and consequences to decrease problem behavior and enhance prosocial behavior. Sometimes a safety plan is included as well.
- The critical features to move effectively from FBA results to a technically adequate BSP include antecedent interventions, targeting desired behaviors, skill building, minimizing reinforcement, and a safety plan.
- This chapter described how to collect and use data to guide decision making as well as characteristics of behavioral goals and methods for writing behavioral goals.

Application

1. What are some of the roadblocks that school personnel may encounter when planning to implement a Behavior Support Plan? What are some solutions to these hurdles?
2. Who are some other individuals that may be important team members at particular schools?
3. In what instances would it be difficult to connect the function of certain behaviors with an effective BSP?

References

Anderson, C. M., & Scott, T. (2009). Function-based support: A systems-change model (pp. 705–728). In W. Sailor, G. Dunlap, G. Sugai, & R. Horner (Eds.), *Handbook of positive behavior support*. New York: Springer.

Benazzi, L., Horner, R., & Good, R. (2006). Effects of behavior support team composition on the technical adequacy and contextual fit of behavior support plans. *The Journal of Special Education, 40*(3), 160–170.

Campbell, A., & Anderson, C. M. (2008). Enhancing effects of check-in/check-out with function-based support. *Behavioral Disorders, 33*(4), 233–245.

Gable, R. A., Hendrickson, J. M., & Van Acker, R. (2001). Maintaining the integrity of FBA-based interventions in schools. *Education and Treatment of Children, 24*(3), 248–260.

Horner, R. H., Sugai, G., Todd, A. W., & Lewis-Palmer, T. (2005). School-wide positive behavior support. In *Individualized supports for students with problem behaviors: Designing positive behavior support plans* (pp. 359–390). New York: Guilford Press.

O'Neill, R. H., Horner, R. H., Albin, R. W., Sprague, J. R., Storey, K., & Newton, J. S. (1997). *Functional assessment and program development for problem behavior: A practical handbook* (2nd ed.). Boston: Brooks/Cole.

Sugai, G., & Horner, R. (2002). The evolution of discipline practices: School-wide positive behavior supports. *Child & Family Behavior Therapy, 24*, 23–50.

Behavior Support Plan

Student: <u>Last Name</u>   <u>First Name</u>   Referred by: <u>Name</u>   Date: _____

        1. Student ID #   DOB: _____   Grade: _____
        IEP: Y ☐ N ☐

1. What will be done to prevent problem behavior?
   a. Modifications to setting event

   b. Modifications to trigger/discriminative stimulus

2. What is the desired behavior and are there any acceptable alternative behaviors?

3. What new responses will you teach or arrange the environment to increase and how?
   a. Desired behaviors

   b. Alternative behaviors

4. How will desired and alternative behaviors be reinforced?
   a. What will you do initially to make sure these behaviors occur frequently?

   b. What changes will you make over time to enhance maintenance?

5. What will be done to minimize reinforcement of problem behavior?

6. What will be done if the safety of the student or others is at risk?

Practices for Implementation

1. Target date to begin implementation:

2. Getting the support plan started: (what materials/resources are needed? what training is needed?)

3. Process for informing parents and student (who, what, when)

4. Others who need to be informed (Who else might intervention impact?)

5. Plan for notifying substitutes of intervention

Evaluation, Review, and Adaptation

1. How will we know if the plan is being implemented? (What information will be collected, by whom, how summarized, and when reviewed?)

2. How will we know if the plan is being successful? (What student outcomes will be monitored, by whom, how summarized, and when reviewed?)

NAME INDEX

SUBJECT INDEX

Page numbers followed by *f* and *t* indicate figure and table respectively.